METROPOLITAN ART AND LITERATURE, 1810–1840

Gregory Dart expands upon existing notions of Cockneys and the 'Cockney School' in the late Romantic period by exploring some of the broader ramifications of the phenomenon in art and periodical literature. He argues that the term was not confined to discussion of the Leigh Hunt circle, but was fast becoming a way of gesturing towards everything in modern metropolitan life that seemed discrepant and disturbing. Covering the ground between Romanticism and Victorianism, Dart presents Cockneyism as a powerful critical currency in this period, which helps provide a link between the works of Leigh Hunt and Keats in the 1810s and the early works of Charles Dickens in the 1830s. Through an examination of literary history, art history, urban history and social history, this book identifies the early-nineteenth-century figure of the Cockney as the true ancestor of modernity.

GREGORY DART is a senior lecturer in the English Department of University College London. His research, both current and prospective, is centrally concerned with the modern city, as a cultural and material phenomenon. His first monograph, *Rousseau, Robespierre and English Romanticism* (Cambridge University Press, 1999), examined the influence of the French Revolution on English Romantic writers. Since then he has published widely on Romantics and the city, edited two selections of Hazlitt's writings and co-edited a collection of essays called *Restless Cities* with Matthew Beaumont.

CAMBRIDGE STUDIES IN ROMANTICISM

This series aims to foster the best new work in one of the most challenging fields within English literary studies. From the early 1780s to the early 1830s a formidable array of talented men and women took to literary composition, not just in poetry, which some of them famously transformed, but in many modes of writing. The expansion of publishing created new opportunities for writers, and the political stakes of what they wrote were raised again by what Wordsworth called those 'great national events' that were 'almost daily taking place': the French Revolution, the Napoleonic and American wars, urbanization, industrialization, religious revival, an expanded empire abroad and the reform movement at home. This was an enormous ambition, even when it pretended otherwise. The relations between science, philosophy, religion and literature were reworked in texts such as *Frankenstein* and *Biographia Literaria*; gender relations in *A Vindication of the Rights of Woman* and *Don Juan*; journalism by Cobbett and Hazlitt; poetic form, content and style by the Lake School and the Cockney School. Outside Shakespeare studies, probably no body of writing has produced such a wealth of comment or done so much to shape the responses of modern criticism. This indeed is the period that saw the emergence of those notions of 'literature' and of literary history, especially national literary history, on which modern scholarship in English has been founded.

The categories produced by Romanticism have also been challenged by recent historicist arguments. The task of the series is to engage both with a challenging corpus of Romantic writings and with the changing field of criticism they have helped to shape. As with other literary series published by Cambridge, this one will represent the work of both younger and more established scholars, on either side of the Atlantic and elsewhere.

For a complete list of titles published see end of book.

METROPOLITAN ART AND LITERATURE, 1810–1840

Cockney Adventures

GREGORY DART

CAMBRIDGE
UNIVERSITY PRESS

CAMBRIDGE
UNIVERSITY PRESS

University Printing House, Cambridge CB2 8BS, United Kingdom

Cambridge University Press is part of the University of Cambridge.

It furthers the University's mission by disseminating knowledge in the pursuit of education, learning and research at the highest international levels of excellence.

www.cambridge.org
Information on this title: www.cambridge.org/9781107507746

First published 2012
First paperback edition 2015

A catalogue record for this publication is available from the British Library

Library of Congress Cataloguing in Publication data
Dart, Gregory.
Metropolitan art and literature, 1810–1840 : Cockney adventures / Gregory Dart.
p. cm. – (Cambridge studies in romanticism ; 94)
Includes bibliographical references and index.
ISBN 978-1-107-02492-2 (hardback)
1. English literature–19th century–History and criticism. 2. Art and literature–England–History–19th century. 3. Romanticism–England. I. Title.
PR468.A76D37 2012
820.9′357–dc23
2012014574

ISBN 978-1-107-02492-2 Hardback
ISBN 978-1-107-50774-6 Paperback

To my father and mother

Contents

Figures

Acknowledgements

Special thanks go to Richard Cronin and Nicholas Roe, whose work provided me with the initial inspiration to write on Cockney-related themes. Heartfelt gratitude also to those who have invited me to contribute essays, give seminar papers or offer plenaries over the years, and whose own work has been a consistent source of instruction and pleasure. These include John Barrell, Andrew Bennett, Alison O'Byrne, Gavin Budge, Stephen Cheeke, Phil Connell, Vivien Dietz, David Duff, Lindsay Duguid, Markman Ellis, Tim Fulford, Kevin Gilmartin, James Grande, Harriet Guest, Paul Hamilton, David Higgins, Simon Hull, Felicity James, Juliet John, Ludmilla Jordanova, Cora Kaplan, Lawrence Klein, Nigel Leask, Sara Lodge, Robert Morrison, Uttara Natarajan, Fred Parker, Tom Paulin, Daniel Roberts, John Snelson, John Strachan, Barbara Taylor, David Trotter, James Watt, John Whale, Timothy Webb and Duncan Wu. Thanks also to Stevie Edge at the Dulwich Picture Gallery and Owen Hopkins at the Royal Academy of Arts in London for inviting me to give Cockney-related talks at these venues. I first conceived of this project when I was still at the University of York, and would very much like to thank some of my former colleagues there, especially Jack Donovan, Mark Hallett, Hugh Haughton and David Peters-Corbett. I also owe a deep debt of gratitude to my colleagues at UCL for their very considerable patience and kindness over the last twelve years. Of those who have had a direct impact on my work I would particularly like to thank Rosemary Ashton, Matthew Beaumont, Kasia Boddy, Rachel Bowlby, Ardis Butterfield, Paul Davis, Mark Ford, Helen Hackett, Philip Horne, Susan Irvine, Leya Landau, Charlotte Mitchell, John Mullan, Neil Rennie, Michael Sayeau, Hugh Stevens, Peter Swaab and Henry Woudhuysen. Valuable advice and support has also been offered by Rebecca Beasley, Kiera Chapman, Norma Clarke, Richard Hamblyn, Judith Hawley, Henri Justin, Alison Light, Rebecca Newman and Michael Newton. Practically speaking, this project could not have been completed without the kind help of staff from the British Library, the Newspaper Library at Colindale, the Guildhall Library, the Brotherton Library at Leeds and the University of London Library at Senate House. Regarding the production of the book itself, I am particularly grateful to Linda Bree, Jim Chandler, Josephine Lane and the anonymous readers for Cambridge University Press, who have all done their bit to lick this particular urban miscreant into shape. Thanks also to *Romanticism*, the *Charles Lamb Bulletin*, *History Workshop Journal* and Carcanet Press, who have given homes to earlier, shorter versions of several of these chapters. Last but not least I would like to thank my parents for all their boundless love, my family generally, and especially my wife Vibeche Standal Dart, and our two Cockneys Teddy and Clara.

Introduction

THE COCKNEY MOMENT

The Cockney Moment begins in January 1813 with the sentencing of the poet and radical journalist Leigh Hunt to two years in prison for libelling the Prince Regent. Politically, Hunt's imprisonment in the Horsemonger Lane Gaol in Southwark, South London was part of that long struggle for constitutional reform that dominated British politics in the early 1800s. But there was a cultural aspect to it as well, which had to do with the very flamboyant way in which this particular martyr for liberty strove to reconcile himself to his condition. Given two rooms of the prison infirmary by special dispensation of the jailer, the controversial editor of *The Examiner* set to work in unprecedented fashion:

> I papered the walls with a trellis of roses; I had the ceiling coloured with clouds and sky; the barred windows I screened with Venetian blinds; and when my book-cases were set up with their busts, and flowers and a pianoforte made their appearance, perhaps there was not a handsomer room on that side the water. I took a pleasure, when a stranger knocked at the door, to see him come in and stare about him. The surprise on issuing from the Borough, and passing through the avenues of a jail, was dramatic. Charles Lamb declared there was no other such room, except in a fairy tale.[1]

Horsemonger Lane, Surrey's County Gaol, was a hanging prison, and one that lumped men and women, rich and poor, criminals and debtors together. Given the harshness of the sentence, and the fact that, according to its jailer, the Lane was 'not fit for a gentleman', it is impossible not to see something heroic in Hunt's suburban makeover, as he strove to put art and nature in the service of liberal optimism.[2] With characteristic spirit, he set to work refashioning his surroundings, brightening the shades of his prison-house in a way that had clear parallels with his notion of social reform as a natural process:

> But I possessed another surprise; which was a garden. There was a little yard outside the room, railed off from another belonging to the neighbouring ward.

> This yard I shut in with green palings, adorned it with a trellis, bordered it with a thick bed of earth from a nursery, and even contrived to have a grass-plot. The earth I filled with flowers and young trees. There was an apple tree from which we managed to get a pudding the second year. As to my flowers, they were allowed to be perfect. Thomas Moore, who came to see me with Lord Byron, told me he had seen no such heart's-ease … Here I wrote and read in fine weather, sometimes under an awning. In autumn, my trellises were hung with scarlet runners, which added to the flowery investment. I used to shut my eyes in my arm-chair, and affect to think myself hundreds of miles off. (I, p. 293)

One feature of the little bower Hunt built for himself was the conscious collapsing of conventional distinctions between city and country, interior and exterior, English and Italian. Another equally deliberate element was the elaborate screening of his prison surroundings. By continuing to edit *The Examiner* from prison Hunt showed that he had not been cowed by government repression; but by transforming a place of punishment into a dream-space he had gone one step further, papering over the bare walls of political opposition with an aspirational poetic vision.

Hunt's quarters must have had a striking effect upon his visitors, which included leading liberals such as Henry Brougham and Jeremy Bentham, and fellow writers such as Lamb, Byron, Tom Moore, the historical painter Benjamin Robert Haydon and an important new friend, the radical journalist William Hazlitt. But however inspirational his rooms must have been to some, they must also have seemed a little incongruous, and even disconcerting, to others, openly flaunting, as they did, the complete lack of fit between the imaginative 'nest' Mr Examiner Hunt had built for himself and the objective reality of his condition. Lamb's comment, that he had seen 'no other such, except in a fairy tale', was clearly meant as a compliment, but to those of a more sober disposition it must have seemed that Leigh Hunt had simply been too much of a milksop to live in a prison *as a* prison.[3]

This was by no means Hunt's first foray into imaginative nest-feathering; only the previous year he had written a long essay entitled 'A Day by the Fire' for his short-lived periodical *The Reflector* (1811–12). Coterminous with the Prince Regent libel, this piece has a great claim to inaugurate the Romantic familiar essay as a genre, pre-dating, as it does, most of Hazlitt, Lamb and De Quincey.[4] The essay begins in mock-heroic manner with the narrator extolling the pleasures of the domestic fireside, berating the cat for his lack of 'sociality' and trying to convince himself he did the right thing in swapping his tea-kettle for a tea-urn: 'I say to myself every now and then during the tea', Hunt writes, '"A pretty look with it – that urn" or "It's wonderful what a taste the Greeks had".'[5] He then goes on to paint a vivid picture of a cosy fire on a winter's day, prefiguring, by some ten years, the vivid fireside tableau that prefaced De Quincey's 'Pleasures of Opium'.[6]

As the essay develops, the epicurean narrator's thoughts meander, modulate and intertwine, drawing heavily on the rich associations that surround the domestic fireside, while also, like Coleridge's 'Frost at Midnight' (1798), transforming it into an image of the mind in a state of poetic association. The argument is made that English liberty, like English comfort, is something that has had to be cultivated against the hard season. A strong link is asserted between 'our blazing fire' and 'our freedom of speech', the former being at once the spiritual symbol and practical breeding-ground of the latter. So too, the narrator goes on to suggest, the cold, wet climate of Britain has proved an unfailing inspiration to its poets, with their imaginative flights having had to be all the more resourceful because of it. Quoting Cowper, Dryden and Milton, Hunt then embarks upon a little history of hearthside conviviality, making repeated reference to the sheer universality of the experience: 'It is thus [with one's feet on the fender] that the greatest and wisest of mankind have sat and meditated; a homely truism perhaps, but such a one as we are apt enough to forget' (II, p. 410). The moon that we see out of our window, he reminds us, is the same moon that enchanted Homer and Virgil; our fire is the same fire that inspired Milton and Horace. The aim here is to turn one of the commonest and most ubiquitous of household spots into a little link with past greatness, with the daring suggestion being that merely to sit by one's fire, whether one is aware of it or not, is to take part in a rich cultural history. Gradually, as teatime approaches, and the essayist is briefly left alone with his thoughts, the hearth is turned into a symbol for the deepest yearnings of the private imagination. But he is then called back to himself, and to social reality, as his wife and children gather for tea: 'Alas, that flights so lofty should ever be connected with earth by threads as slender as they are long, and that the least twitch of the most common-place hand should be able to snatch down the viewless wanderer to existing comforts!' (II, 412). Here as elsewhere, Hunt seems to have had a gift for turning even the most apparently impertinent and anodyne of subjects to account. Everyone drinks tea, he says, but 'if there is any one station in which it is enjoyed to most advantage, it is that of mediocrity, – that in which all comfort is reckoned to be best appreciated, because while there is taste to enjoy, there is necessity to earn the enjoyment' (II, p. 414). In the final section of the essay the narrator reflects on the moment when all the meals of the day are over and the last visitor has gone home. 'Then, for imagination's sake, not for superstition's', he adds, 'are recalled the stories of the Secret World and the midnight pranks of Fairyism … idle fancies these, and incomprehensible to minds clogged with everyday earthliness, – but not useless, either as an exercise in invention, or even as adding consciousness to the range and destiny of the soul' (II, p. 418).

'A Day by the Fire' is a seminal Hunt text, both in tone and in subject matter. Almost of all his key traits as a writer are present in it. Most notably, the way that it relates many of the most apparently inconsequential details of common, domestic life to larger questions of literary history, politics and culture is highly characteristic. It is a rhetorically inclusive essay, but it does make a point of favouring those readers of a 'mediocre' station, for whom the simple pleasures of the fireside might be deemed especially valuable. So too it insists on the value of fancy – what we might think of as the idle or recreational imagination – as a kind of healthful exercise, an important stopgap between social aspiration and fulfilment. Rather subtly, Hunt manages to serve up patient reformist optimism in the guise of domestic complacency, supplying us with a kind of key, if one were needed, for interpreting his subsequent aesthetic experiments in the infirmary of the Surrey County Gaol.

THE BARD OF HORSEMONGER LANE

It must have been clear to Hunt's conservative critics relatively early in 1813 that his opposition to imprisonment had taken on an aesthetic as well as a political dimension, but it wasn't until the autumn of that year that the battle was fully joined. On 29 August Hunt had taken his imaginative yearning to a new level, publishing a 'Sonnet to Hampstead' under the signature 'L.H.' sign in *The Examiner*:

> Sweet upland! to whose walks with fond repair,
> Out of thy western slope, I took my rise,
> Day after day, and on these feverish eyes
> Met the moist fingers of the bathing air,
> If health unearn'd of thee I may not share;
> Keep it, I pray thee, where my memory lies,
> In thy green lanes, brown dells, and breezy skies,
> Till I return, and find thee doubly fair.
> Wait then my coming on that lightsome land,
> Health and the joy that out of nature springs,
> And freedom's air-blown locks:– but stay with me,
> Friendship, frank entering with the cordial hand,

> And Honour and the Muse with growing wings;
> And Love Domestic smiling equably.[7]

Only one month after the appearance of this sonnet, there appeared a long article in *The Satirist* lampooning Hunt as 'The Bard of Horsemonger Lane'.[8] This piece was, in effect, a line-by-line critique of Hunt's poem, and it was prefaced by the ironic announcement that, it being natural for poets to 'love to confer immortality on those places which have been honoured with their presence', the *Satirist*'s readers would be 'delighted to find' that 'the Muse of Mr Examiner Hunt has been called from the depths of Horsemonger Lane jail, to save Hampstead from oblivion – Yes, Mr Editor, this mighty task has been happily performed by Mr Leigh Hunt; and cockney apprehensions on this head are now set at rest for ever by the following delicious *morçeau*'. The *Satirist* then proceeded to play merry havoc with Hunt's loose-limbed versification, pretending not to understand 'took my rise' or 'fond repair', and worrying at great length over the meaning of such phrases as 'if health unearn'd of thee I may not share' and 'keep it … where my memory lies'. It also made fun of (what it considered to be) the flat stupidity of Hunt's imagery ('green lanes, brown dells, and breezy skies') before concluding with some sly insinuations about the upstart arrogance of the whole.

Ostensibly *The Satirist's* reference to 'cockneyism' could not have been more casual, but in fact the entire article drew heavily on a long tradition of Cockney satire. The Cockney had been a figure of fun in English culture for well over four hundred years. In Chaucer's time the word had been a synonym for a stupid milksop or cissy, and by Shakespeare's it had developed strong links with town-dwellers, especially Londoners.[9] The etymology of the term was always a matter of debate, not least in the early nineteenth century, with some commentators considering it to derive from *Cocagne*, a mythical land of peace and plenty, some from *coken-ey*, a misshapen or 'cock's' egg, and some from the old French word *coqueline*, an effeminate or pampered child.[10] But even though nobody was sure of its provenance, everyone knew what it meant: a Cockney was a living paradox, a metropolitan provincial, the stunted offspring of a big city. In the literature of the early modern period the Cockney was invariably a comic type. In his *Anecdotes of the English Language* (1803), the antiquarian Samuel Pegge had located a typical example of this kind of humour in the second act of *King Lear* (1603):

LEAR O me! my heart, my rising heart! but, down!
FOOL Cry to it nuncle, as the cockney did to the eels when she put 'em i'th' paste alive; she knapp'd 'em o'th'coxcombs with a stick, and cried, 'Down,

> wantons, down!' 'Twas her brother that, in pure kindness to his horses, buttered his hay. (II. iv. 119–23)

Here, as elsewhere in early modern literature, the Cockney is characteristically pert but clueless, especially when it comes to practical or 'country' matters. There was something very traditional and reassuring about this stereotype, and this in spite or perhaps even because of the fact that it was often the Cockney's very modernity that was the object of satire. Cockneys, it was suggested, were curious hothouse flowers, early casualties, as it were, of the modern division of labour. Puffed up by the important role they see themselves as playing in a highly specialized urban environment, they come a cropper as soon as they stray beyond the narrow confines of their place and profession. 'Of all the fools I e'er knew', opined the *New London Magazine* in 1788, 'Cockneys, I'm sure, the world out-do.'[11] Typically, both on the stage and on the page, they are completely lacking in any awareness of the way in which the city has misshapen them, hence their characteristic combination of ignorance and self-conceit. 'There is no popular subject of satire, on which the modern common-places of wit and ridicule have been exhausted with more success', wrote the *London Magazine* in 1761, 'than on that of a mere cockney affecting the pleasures of the country.'[12]

'The Bard of Horsemonger Lane' is very much part of this tradition, for the overarching joke about Leigh Hunt in this piece is not just that he is a Cockney jailbird dreaming of the countryside, but that the only countryside he can conjure up for himself is the already suburban and semi-domesticated landscape of Hampstead. There is something astonishingly blinkered and self-deceiving about this, or so the *Satirist* suggests, but what really rounds off Hunt's Cockney character, in its eyes, are his extraordinary delusions of grandeur:

> '*Freedom's air-blown locks*' is what every poet must feel, who has had the opportunities afforded to Mr. Hunt of contemplating *locks* of a different description. His kind invitation to *Honour, Friendship, the Muse with growing wings* and *Love domestic smiling equably*, to stay with him, is not less beautiful, and will doubtless be eagerly accepted by those gentry. *The Muse* in particular will feel overwhelmed with gratitude for the honour, and perhaps want words to express it.[13]

Unobtrusive though it might seem on first reading, the idea of Leigh Hunt as a Cockney is in fact the controlling idea of 'The Bard of Horsemonger Lane'; not only that, it is an idea pursued with some persistence and rigour, a little reminder, if reminder were needed, of the political animus that Hunt unfailingly provoked.

The irony is that the cue for this use of Cockneyism as a term of contemporary satire may have come from *The Examiner* itself. Early in 1813, in the first few months of Hunt's incarceration, the task of writing the paper's theatrical reviews had been taken up by Thomas Barnes, the future editor of *The Times* and a former schoolfellow of Hunt's at Christ's Hospital. On 14 March 1813 a review had been published in the 'Theatrical Examiner', probably by Barnes, in which significant praise had been given to James Kenney's new farce, *Love, Law and Physic*, which had recently opened at Covent Garden. The highlight of the piece was John Liston's performance as Lubin Log, an ignorant Cockney shopman from Southwark. This character was by no means the first comic Cockney on the London stage; and on paper at least he was not markedly different from his predecessors. But to Barnes there was clearly something new about Liston's performance – something genuinely cutting and contemporary. 'In the present little piece', he says,

> there is an able delineation of a *Cockney*, being, as far as we recollect, the first, and certainly the best description of that facetious animal on the stage. It is a most amusing exhibition: the invulnerable self-complacency, the prim conceit arising not more from the contemplation of his own qualities, than from the circumstance of his being a citizen of no mean city, the unaccommodating selfishness, and the illiterate vulgarity of manner and of idiom which distinguish the native London shopman, render him one of the fittest subjects in the whole range of character, for the lash of comic satire. Mr Kenney's picture is to the life; the phraseology at once dull and vivacious, while its pert *slang* and ungrammatical idiomacy is rendered with an accuracy which makes one half-suspect that the author has more than a geographical knowledge of Tooley-street. The diction of a Cockney is fairer game for ridicule than that of a rustic or provincialist. The most uncouth dialects have the authority of antiquity on their side, and are indeed but remnants of separate languages now obsolete: but the dialect of a cockney is mere barbarous inaccuracy, and false pronunciation.[14]

Barnes was not alone in seeing something special in Lubin Log, for he went on to become one of the characters that really made Liston's name.[15] With only the playtext to hand, and without the benefit of the original performance, it is not at all easy to tell why Log was so popular, but I think that the *Examiner* review does furnish up a few interesting suggestions. Clearly, one of Kenney and Liston's achievements was to make Barnes think not of a theatrical but of a real social type. There seems to have been a startling sociological accuracy about the depiction, both in language and in attitude, and this seems to have helped generate a genuinely satirical effect. Inspired by this, Barnes was evidently encouraged to think of Cockneyism as a new phenomenon that had not yet been properly represented, and to locate it not, as most of his predecessors would have done, in a few verbal tics or in a particular mental perspective, but in a specific social niche.

In the seventeenth and early eighteenth centuries the term 'Cockney' was always more or less a term of derogation, but it had no special class character.[16] It still hadn't attained that low dignity with which it was imbued in the late Victorian period, when, as Gareth Stedman Jones has shown, it became an affectionate, and even a sentimental term for the East End working classes.[17] On the stage, a Cockney might be the equivalent of the old-style 'cit' of seventeenth-century comedy, but he might equally be a London apprentice or artisan. He could be a rich grocer like the aptly named Cockney in Charles Dibdin's comic opera *Love in the City* (1767), or a stock-broker, like Cosey the reluctant country-dweller in Thomas Morton's *Town and Country* (1807). Sometimes Cockneys spoke dialect, as was the case with Tom Tug in Dibdin's 1774 ballad opera *The Waterman*, sometimes they were more faux-genteel and country-loving, like Mrs Bundle in the same play.[18] Cockneyism, in short, *could* be about speech, and *was always* about attitude, but it was *never* the preserve of a specific rank or class.[19]

In Barnes's review, however, the shop-keeping class has been singled out – as if for the first time – as the real home of the Cockney character, the place where its peculiar mixture of pertness and illiteracy, dullness and vivacity, was most fully expressed. This is not mere idiosyncracy on his part, I would argue: it is a sign of the times. Whether he was fully aware of it or not, Barnes's new vision of Cockneyism was simultaneously a social narrowing, and a geographical expansion, of earlier versions of the type. In eighteenth-century literature the Cockney was generally a child of the City, that is, the old medieval city at the eastern end of the metropolis. Sometimes, indeed, it was precisely his status as the product of a curious, neo-medieval polity that was held up for mockery.[20] But what happens in the early nineteenth century, as we shall see, is that the Cockney starts to lose that exclusive connection with the City proper, and begins, with increasing regularity, to be associated with its environs – old suburbs such as Southwark and Clerkenwell, but also newer ones such as Islington, Pentonville, Dulwich and Camden Town.

The reason is not hard to find. Between 1810 and 1815, with the dust finally settling on twenty years of European conflict, and attention slowly turning to social changes at home, the rapid dilation and transformation of one particular stratum of British society was gradually becoming more visible, not least in London where its growth had been most marked. Clerkenwell, Islington, Pentonville and Camden Town were suburbs now swollen with clerks and attorney's apprentices who commuted to the City every day. In a seminal article on the subject, Geoffrey Crossick has argued that the term 'lower middle class' can be used to designate the conflation of two broad occupational groups in the early 1800s: the old petite bourgeoisie of shopkeepers and small businessmen and the new and burgeoning army of urban white-collar workers who manned the expanding service sector.[21] But such labels as 'lower middle class' and 'petite bourgeoisie' did not exist in the early 1800s. In the eyes of many, the phenomenon could only be thought of as a worrying expansion of that unfortunate no man's land between the polite and the plebeian. In 1833 Edward Gibbon Wakefield sought to sum it up in terms of the growth of an 'uneasy' class.[22] In Barnes's review, however, a more evocative name was being hazarded – and that name was 'Cockney'.

That the growth of this milieu was by no means a matter for celebration, even for a liberal such as Barnes, can be seen from his withering critique of Cockney dialect. Ten years earlier Samuel Pegge had striven hard to defend the London vernacular in his *Anecdotes of the English Language*, arguing that 'what is called *vulgarity* is barely a residuum of what was antiently the established national dialect, at different time periods, from time immemorial'.[23] Cockney, he insisted, was 'for the most part, composed of *Saxonisms*' with the odd little bit of Latin or Old French thrown in. Committed to a notion of the Cockney as a traditional, even reassuring figure, Pegge tried to represent him as a much-maligned custodian of the most important Old English dialect. Barnes's view, however, which was also that of many of his polite contemporaries, was that Cockney language had no authenticity at all. 'Barbarous', 'false', 'ungrammatical' and full of 'pert slang', it was all about the shock of the new, not the secret survival of the old. Of course, it is very difficult to tell how far the author of *The Satirist*'s 'The Bard of Horsemonger Lane' might have been inspired by Kenney's *Love, Law and Physic*, or by Barnes's *Examiner* review of it. But what one can say, I think, is that these two instances are highly representative (if not constitutive) of a subtle but important shift in social attitudes, as the figure of the Cockney begins to accrue new freight and meaning in the 1810s. Growing as never before in pertness and ambition, the old milksop was fast becoming a symbol for all that was wrong with modern life, not least in his promiscuous straddling of city and suburb, old and new, vulgar and genteel.

THE POLITICS OF FAMILIARITY

Within a year of being released from the Surrey County Gaol in January 1815, Hunt moved with his wife and children to the Vale of Health near Hampstead Heath, where he lost no time in embellishing his cottage with classical busts, books and bowers. Before long, many of London's artistic and journalistic avant-garde had tasted his Hampstead hospitality, including figures as diverse as the Novellos, Shelley, Byron, Keats, Hazlitt and B. R. Haydon. Hunt's Cockney aesthetic, which had been incubated (and consolidated) in Horsemonger Lane, was now ready to start a revolution in the suburbs.[24] Politically, Hunt remained as engaged as ever, continuing to write regular editorials for *The Examiner* as the national situation worsened; but he was also to become remarkably active in the field of poetry and belles-lettres. This was the period in which he did more than anyone else to found second-generation Romanticism. In his prose writings he wrote manifestos for a New School of writing, championed Keats and Shelley in *The Examiner* and collaborated on a collection of reflective essays, *The Round Table* (1817), with the radical journalist Hazlitt. In his poetic productions he continued to pursue his own particular brand of suburban pastoral: retelling Dante's tragic tale of Paolo and Francesca in the *Story of Rimini* (1816), doing an English version of Greek myth in his 1818 poem *The Nymphs* and writing more sonnets in praise of Hampstead.

Like 'A Day by the Fire', many of the literary works that Hunt wrote in this period are explicitly recreational in nature. But even his most apparently frivolous pieces had a serious message. What unites them all is what one might call an aesthetics of familiarity. Familiarity was a key concept for Hunt; indeed it had something of the same status in his work as the idea of sympathy had in Hazlitt. Primarily, it was a way of thinking about the ideal writer–reader relationship – a relationship of warmth and candour and shared common feelings. 'I look upon a periodical essayist, as a writer who claims a peculiar intimacy with the public', he had written, in an early essay on this subject, in January 1808.[25] But it was also a way of positioning oneself in relation to politics and high culture. 'It is a curious and pleasant thing to consider', he wrote in an essay on 'Social Genealogy' for *The Indicator*, 'that a link of personal acquaintance can be traced up from the authors of our own times to those of Shakespeare, and to Shakespeare himself'.[26]

Perhaps the best example of Hunt's habit of familiarizing the classics is in the sonnet 'To Robert Batty, M.D., on His Giving Me a Lock of Milton's Hair', which was first collected in *Foliage* in 1818. In this poem, the poet's own breath stirs the thin outer strands of the dead poet's hair, as though he were standing next to him talking, and his thoughts run on to the possibility of Milton himself perhaps having pressed this self-same lock while composing his poetry.[27] 'There seems a love in hair', he muses, 'though it be dead'. It is not simply that the poet feels closer to Milton after having touched his hair, it also that, for a moment at least, the great English poetic tradition itself can be grasped as a family relationship. Hunt's sonnet concludes with a most unusual but stately pentameter: 'Behold affectionate eternity.'[28]

Hunt's aim in this poem is to try to domesticate such things as art, genius and national identity without, somehow, diminishing them; it is entirely consistent, in this respect, with his hearthside sentiments in 'A Day by the Fire'. A large number of Hunt's essays turn on the notion that, whether one is aware of it or not, to indulge in common activities and common pleasures is to place oneself in a long line of historical inheritance and in direct proximity to the classics. The *Indicator* essays 'On Hats', 'On Sticks' and 'On Tea-Drinking' are all of this type, as is the piece from the same periodical 'On Sleep' (this last being a particular favourite of Hazlitt's on account of its gloriously levelling portrait of a tyrant stupefied by slumber). Hunt's interest in classical paganism as a libertarian, erotic discourse has been brilliantly explored by Marilyn Butler and Nicholas Roe.[29] But it did also appeal to him as a religion of the local and the seasonal, the personal and the private. In 'Household Gods of the Ancients' (1819), he wrote enthusiastically about how the ancients loved to domesticate their deities and give them a special place within the home: 'The Penates', he wrote, 'were chosen at will out of the number of the gods, as the Roman in modern times chose his favourite saint. In fact they were only the higher gods themselves, descending into a kind of household familiarity.'[30]

Familiarity was a technique for coming to terms with past high culture; it was also a means of surviving the political iniquities of the present. To the third issue of *The Indicator* (27 October 1819), which was published shortly after the Peterloo Massacre, Hunt contributed an essay on 'Pleasant Recollections Connected with Various Parts of the Metropolis' that showed how literary kinship across the centuries could help bind oneself to the built environment and screen out some of its more unpleasant political realities.[31] Throughout his essayistic career, Hunt remained committed to the simple poetry of everyday life, which means that even his most original pronouncements are often accompanied by the apparently unselfconscious pitter-patter of tiny platitudes. His essays on weather are a particularly good example of this, ranging as they do from 'A Rainy Day', 'Mists and Fogs' and 'Getting Up on Cold Mornings' to 'Fine Days in January and February' and the well-known Hot and Cold 'Nows', co-written with Keats. In the fifth *Indicator*, which was published on 10 November 1819, Hunt opened with an essay addressed 'To Any One Whom Bad Weather Depresses', urging them simply to get out and get some exercise. In 'Mists and Fogs', which appeared in *The Indicator* No. 8 (1 December 1819), Hunt wrote that 'the poets, who are the common friends that keep up the intercourse between nature and humanity, have in numberless passages done justice to these our melancholy visitors, and shown us what grand personages they are'.[32] The great lesson of bad weather, as Hunt was to argue some years later in *The Companion*, was that 'there is always something to enjoy':

> It is not by grumbling against the elements, that evil is to be done away; but by keeping one's self in good heart with one's fellow creatures, and remembering that they are all capable of partaking our pleasures. The contemplation of pain, acting upon a splenetic temperament, produces a stirring reformer here and there, who does good rather out of spite against wrong, than sympathy with pleasure, and becomes a sort of disagreeable angel.[33]

Finding the good in things – bad weather, or an imperfect social order – did not necessarily imply quietism, in Hunt's opinion; it was, on the contrary, precisely the kind of optimism that was required to ensure improvement. This was one of the ways in which Hunt strove to justify projects such as *The Indicator* to the radical liberal in himself – that they were morale-boosting as well as culturally educative, and that they had the effect of preparing a fast-growing reading public for the long haul of reform.

Hunt's work was regularly sprinkled with gentle political allegories of this kind, allegories which often had a self-reflexive element to them. One of the best examples of this is the essay on 'Godiva' that appeared in *The Indicator* No. 3. This took as its subject the true story of Leofric, Earl of Leicester's challenge to his wife, the philanthropic Lady Godiva, that he would only give up his oppressive tax on the people of Coventry if she rode through the city *nuda*. What follows, in Hunt's rendering, is, as he himself describes it, a beautiful story of 'principled excess'. Heroically, Godiva set off on her ride, and all the people of Coventry were ordered to keep within doors and not give a glance into the streets 'on pain of death'. 'What scene can be more touching to the imagination', Hunt writes, 'beauty, modesty, feminine softness, a daring sympathy; an extravagance producing by the nobleness of its object and the strange gentleness of its means, the grave and profound effect of the most reverend custom.' 'The whole story', he concludes, 'is as unvulgar and as sweetly serious, as can be conceived.'[34] 'Unvulgar' is a curious word to use in this context, calling the very possibility of vulgarity to mind even as it hopes to dismiss it, and the same might be said of many of Hunt's literary productions. Hunt was himself, in many ways, something of a Lady Godiva in his writings, a man who put a principled, even slightly puritanical spirit of exhibitionism in the service of social improvement, with even his most barefaced revelations of the commonplace often containing a coquettish element.

'THE IDEAL OF A COCKNEY POET'

A political hero to many, Leigh Hunt was also an inspirational companion to the many budding writers that he sponsored in this period – men such as Keats, Shelley, John Hamilton Reynolds, Lamb, Haydon and Hazlitt. But even his closest allies were sometimes put off by his exhibitionist tendencies. After visiting Hunt in prison, Lord Byron noted in his journal that Hunt was 'an extraordinary man' and 'a man worth knowing', but also 'a bigot of virtue'.[35] In *The Spirit of the Age* (1826), his great friend Hazlitt couldn't help remarking that 'from great sanguineness of temper, from great quickness and unsuspecting simplicity, he runs on to the public as he does at his own fireside, and talks about himself, forgetting that he is not always among friends'. Qualities that softened his egotism when you met him in person were not always present on the page: 'His look, his tone are required to point many things that he says: his frank, cordial manner reconciles you instantly to a little overbearing, over-weening self-complacency.'[36] The editor of *The Examiner* was a man of taste, especially in literature, music and the theatre, as his friends were only too willing to admit, but the manner of his recommendations did also, as Keats noted, have an unfortunate habit of 'making fine things petty and beautiful things hateful'. 'He understands many a beautiful thing', the young poet wrote, 'but then, instead of giving other minds credit for the same degree of perception as he himself possesses – he begins an explanation in such a curious manner that our taste and self-love is offended continually.'[37] What Hazlitt and Keats objected to most in Hunt, it seems, was a self-centred, somewhat pedagogic habit of conversation, which was saved only, and only sometimes, by a habitually friendly manner. Even in the presence of his equals he could often be patronizing, as if at some level he felt he was always addressing a culture-hungry but naive public.

These were the misgivings of his friends. His political enemies, of course, went a good deal further. When in late 1817 and 1818 *Blackwood's Edinburgh Magazine* finally began its sequence on the 'Cockney School of Poetry' – a series of vicious satirical attacks on Hunt and his circle – memories of *The Examiner* editor holding court in his makeshift bower in Southwark inevitably fed into a vivid portrait of him as a kind of latter-day Lord of Misrule:

> Your vulgar vanity, your audacious arrogance, your conceited coxcombery, your ignorant pedantry, – all the manifold sins and iniquities of Cockneyism lie spread before me as in a map; and I will not part with your Majesty till I have shown your crown, which you imagine is formed of diamonds and pearls, to be wholly composed of paste and parchment, and glass-beads; your robes to be worthless as old rags from St. Giles'; your sceptre to be a hollow-hearted broom-stick, which no hawker could vend without dishonesty; and your throne itself, though glittering with gew-gaws, to be no better than a broken-armed kitchen chair.[38]

The satire in this 'Letter from Z. to Leigh Hunt, King of the Cockneys', which came between the second and third of the 'Cockney School' attacks, shows the humour of 'Z.' (alias J. G. Lockhart) at its most hyperbolic. Hunt might have thought he was setting up a kind of 'counter-court of sociality and wit', to borrow a phrase from Greg Kucich.[39] But Z. insists on presenting it as a holiday Feast of Fools. This carnivalesque idea was linked with another element in the *Blackwood's* critique, which drew on the incest plot at the centre of *The Story of Rimini* and Hunt's much-publicized distaste for the institution of marriage, to mount a serious charge of immorality against him and his circle. It was not merely that its author had a 'polluted muse', Z. argued, his private life was similarly infected. Coded insinuations were made about an incestuous relationship between Hunt and his wife's sister, Elizabeth Kent, who had stayed behind to look after him in prison.[40]

This is *Blackwood's Magazine's* Cockney criticism at its most fanciful and vituperative, but it is one of the most interesting things about this series of articles, and one of the main reasons why scholars of Romanticism keep returning to them is that they are, on the whole, much more suggestive and sociologically nuanced than this. Indeed it is one of the enduring fascinations of these attacks that, spiteful and sectarian as they undoubtedly were, they did also have a deep purchase on their subject. Despite being Scots writing out of Edinburgh, Lockhart, Wilson and their collaborators had very good contacts in London and a very close knowledge of the metropolitan milieu. Hence in large part the 'Cockney School' series presents a picture of Cockneyism, and of Hunt's place within it, that is remarkably acute and pertinent.

Hunt's books, Z. said, were not known in the country – his fame was 'entirely confined to the young attorneys and embryo-barristers about town'. The disgust that one felt on reading *The Story of Rimini*, he continued, is like that of 'a man of fashion, when he is invited to enter, for a second time, the gilded drawing room of a little mincing boarding school mistress, who would fain have an *At Home* in her house':

> Everything is pretence, affectation, finery, and gaudiness. The beaux are attorneys' apprentices, with chapeau bras and Limerick gloves – fiddlers, harp teachers, and clerks of genius: the belles are faded fan-twinkling spinsters, prurient vulgar misses from school, and enormous citizens' wives. The company are entertained with lukewarm negus, and the sounds of a paltry piano-forte.[41]

Attorneys' apprentices, embryo-barristers, school-mistresses, clerks: these were among the expanding professions in early-nineteenth-century London (factory workers being, for a variety of reasons, far less in evidence in the capital).[42] This stratum was also roughly commensurate with that broad band of people swelling the ranks of the new reading public: working people but not labourers, aspirant but not affluent, imperfectly educated but hungry for culture. As Richard Altick wrote in *The English Common Reader* in 1957: 'It was principally from among skilled workers, small shopkeepers, clerks and the better grade of domestic servants that the new mass audience for printed matter was recruited during the first half of the nineteenth century.'[43] In the eyes of *Blackwood's* it was this constituency, above all, that Hunt was addressing in his works of recreation: a class of limited education but high aspirations that had come to a new and worrying prominence in contemporary urban society.

In using the word Cockney to refer to this realm, Z. was clearly drawing on, and indeed consolidating, that new sense of the term that had been expressed in Barnes's review. In his famous attack on Keats, for example, which was contained in the fourth of the 'Cockney School' articles (August 1818), he began by lamenting the contemporary mania for writing poetry, complaining that 'our very footmen compose tragedies and there is scarcely a superannuated governess in the island that does not leave a roll of lyrics behind her in her band-box'.[44] Like clerks and shopkeeper's apprentices, footmen and governesses were perfect examples of Cockney incongruity in this period, being social and cultural amphibians, neither one thing nor the other. Z. also harked back to Keats's former status as an apprentice to Thomas Hammond, a London surgeon and apothecary, mainly in order to position him as firmly as possible within that realm of shopkeepers, apprentices and lawyer's clerks which was now being seen as Cockneyism's heartland. About Hunt the 'Blackwoodsmen' were, if anything, even more outspoken, Z. declaring that everything the *Examiner* editor did betrayed 'low birth and low habits' and that he was 'the ideal of a Cockney poet'.[45] In this way *Blackwood's* explicitly linked the rise of Hunt and Keats as writers with the growth of a specific sector within early industrial society, what we would now call the lower middle classes. As Lockhart wrote in 'Extracts from Mrs. Wastle's Diary' in *Blackwood's* in March 1820: 'Their sphere lies entirely among a set of half-educated, would-be elegant clerks, and apprentices, and superfine shopkeepers and shopkeepers' ladies – all of whom are creatures of the present age, and totally unlike anything that ever London harboured till now.'[46] Modern critics have agreed, arguing moreover that this connection was a feature not solely of Hunt's recreational writings but of his political journalism as well. Referring to a series of four memorandums on constitutional reform that Hunt had written for *The Examiner* in 1818, Kevin Gilmartin has usefully pointed out that 'it was to the hegemony of the petty bourgeoisie as much as to "leading spirits" like Shelley and Keats, that Hunt's four "memorandums" pointed'.[47]

Both Keats and Hunt had impeccable Cockney credentials. Keats was born the son of an ostler at a coaching inn in the City, and was extremely sensitive about his humble origins. Hunt, by contrast, was by nature far more insouciant, and seems to have had considerable difficulty grasping even the first principles of class shame. The son of a clergyman, he had been brought up in Southgate, North London, and had gone to school at Christ's Hospital in the City, an august charity school hidden away in the medieval labyrinth of streets between St Bartholomew's Hospital, St Sepulchre's Church and Newgate Prison. At school he was a promising scholar but also (like Charles Lamb, his near contemporary at Christ's) a stammerer, and because at that time the school only awarded scholarships to those intended for the priesthood, this impediment effectively barred him from going up to Oxford or Cambridge.[48] Not that this seems to have held Hunt back in any way. A published poet in his teens and a crusading radical journalist in his twenties (he founded *The Examiner* newspaper, with his brother John, in 1808), he lost no time in making his mark upon the new reading public. So much so, indeed, that between 1808 and 1822 he emerged as one of the most important political journalists in the British Isles, even if his real passion, as he kept insisting, was for poetry and belles-lettres.[49]

The *Blackwood's* 'Cockney School' articles always strove to make the most of what they perceived to be Hunt's highly circumscribed background. The notion of Mr Examiner as a pert but blinkered city-dweller, whose literary efforts only exposed his limited experience, was continually being rehearsed in this brilliant, biting series. Of Hunt's muse, Z. commented that 'she talks indelicately like a tea-sipping milliner girl'.[50] Of the marriage ceremony in *Rimini* he argued that '[Hunt] draws his ideas of courtly splendour from the Lord Mayor's coach, and he dreams of tournaments after having seen the aldermen on horseback, with their furred gowns and silk stockings'.[51] And after quoting a line from the same poem that referred to 'the thick reckoning' of hooves, he made a point of commenting, 'was it really so, that Mr Hunt could find no nobler image to represent the quick yet regular motion of horses than that of an apprentice counting bank notes on his fingers' ends'.[52] The secret of the *Blackwood's* critique, like that of *The Satirist* before it, lay in its insistence that far from the poetic imagination being free, as Hunt himself was always trying to argue, in his case it was always retracing the bounds of his prison. Their critique of Hunt was thus based on a relentless *repositioning* of his productions within a specific geographical and social milieu. He doesn't know nature apart from Highgate Hill and the Serpentine, Z. argued, bringing a nice degree of geographical specificity to his sniping.[53] Hunt's enemies invariably acted like the most reductive kind of historicist critics in this respect – always trying to reduce his work to its context. Where the author of *Rimini* was writing from, and whom he was writing for – these were the insights that they kept pressing upon their readers: 'He raves perpetually about "green fields", "jaunty streams", and "o'erarching leafiness"', Z. opined, 'exactly as a Cheapside shop-keeper does about the beauties of his box on the Camberwell Road.'[54]

The King of the Cockneys wrote about nature, in other words, like a man who had always been deprived of it, and gathered all his ideas of it from books. As a judgement on Hunt himself this was no doubt hugely unfair, but it did identify something – what shall we say – artificial, consumerist, fetishistic, in short *modern*, in his writing about the rural. In his 1818 collection *Foliage*, for example, Hunt had included a sonnet to his friend Horace Smith in which he openly celebrated those little touches of Nature that 'manage to oppose the town's encroachments':

> Vulgar he, who goes
> By suburb gardens which she deigns to dress,
> And does not recognise her green caress
> Reaching back to us in those genial shows

> Of box-encircled flowers and poplar rows,
> Or other nests for evening weariness.[55]

To modern eyes this is completely uncontroversial, but to many nineteenth-century readers it would have seemed the very height of vulgarity, not least in this particular instance, because the 'suburb gardens' mentioned here are only too easily recognizable as the commercial tea-gardens of Islington and Clerkenwell. Of course, some polite Londoners did frequent tea-gardens, and even more would have taken pleasure in urban greenery, but it took a Leigh Hunt to celebrate such things in so shamelessly provoking a fashion. The objection was not simply social, it was also generic, for what Hunt was doing, in effect, was celebrating the breakdown of aesthetic distinctions – between town and country, but also between nature and culture – and transforming all leafiness into a kind of visual commodity. 'There is a great deal about "Hampstead's" whole merits', the *Eclectic Review* said of *Foliage*, 'but the worst is, we never get out of the reach of the smoke. A most distressing *cockneyism* pervades Mr. Hunt's ideas of the beautiful in scenery, which, in the sonnet to Horatio Smith is more than half-avowed.'[56]

THE COCKNEY PHENOMENON ON THE STAGE AND ON THE PAGE

Not unreasonably, in the past, critical discussion of the 'Cockney School' debate has tended to concentrate on it as a political battle between emergent periodicals competing for sales and influence in the literary marketplace. Seen in these terms, it is a polemical storm cooked up by *Blackwood's* and later taken up by the *Quarterly* and the ultra-Tory *John Bull* to tackle the two most eminent liberal-leaning, London-based publications of the day, Leigh Hunt's *Examiner* and John Scott's *London Magazine*. But what has not perhaps been sufficiently attended to is the extent to which these exchanges, although clearly central to an understanding of the period, were only part of a larger cultural conversation, in which Cockneyism was fast becoming *the* new way of addressing (and often deploring) some of the more dramatic changes in contemporary society. A brief glance at the plays and periodicals of the period can help show how widespread the Cockney phenomenon really was. In 1821 W. T. Moncrieff put on a two-act farce that was clearly inspired by the recent 'Cockney School' controversy. There were a number of Cockney characters in *Lost Life* but Natty Daffodil, a young Cockney perfumier, was immediately recognized by the reviewers of the day as a broad satire on the Hunt coterie. 'This character', said the *Literary Chronicle*, 'who writes verses, celebrates the birthdays of all the poets … and wears his hair divided on the forehead, and falling on his shoulders à la Petrarque … is a smart satire on the Cockney School of Poetry, and one of its leaders in particular.'[57] Instances such as this provide further evidence, if evidence were needed, of the sweeping influence the *Blackwood's* attacks were to have within the culture. But, equally, the other interesting thing to note, from our point of view, is that the fashion for Cockney characters on stage had actually begun somewhat earlier, and was already, by the 1820s, turning into something of a cliché.

Kenney's *Love, Law and Physic* had appeared in 1813, and in the years that followed, Robert Jameson was to produce a number of successful farces for the Haymarket Theatre, almost all of which were centred on comic Cockney characters. In his *Exit by Mistake* (1816) there was a character called Crockery, a foolish fat servant, who, as the *Examiner* pointed out, behaved exactly like a Cockney version of Edmund Burke, endlessly crying over improvements.[58] Many reviewers were struck by Crockery's timeliness and originality: 'This character', said *The British Stage*, 'we look upon as perfectly original; that it is perfectly natural we ourselves can testify, having repeatedly met with its prototype in real life.'[59] But Jameson's greatest success was to come in the following year with a farce called *Teasing Made Easy*. This play had a smash-hit character by the name of Peter Pastoral, an attorney's clerk, 'a chubby, vulgar Cockney, deeply enamoured of rural life, and the society of Damon and Phillis',[60] who was played with extraordinary panache by a portly young actor called James Tokely. Tokely had played Crockery too, and was clearly, like Lamb's beloved Liston, a dab hand at the Cockneys.[61]

It is interesting to reflect, therefore, that in the couple of months immediately preceding *Blackwood's Magazine's* very first 'Cockney School' article of October 1817, *Teasing Made Easy* had been the major hit of the London summer season, closely followed by *Exit by Mistake*, which had been revived from the previous year. There had also been a revival of Dibdin's *The Waterman* of 1774, probably in order to cash in on the current craze. In September 1817 the *British Stage* ran a special feature on Tokely, which began with an illustration of him in his current role as Peter Pastoral. But this is only the tip of the iceberg: Cockneys were littering the stage in this period, so much so, indeed, that by 1820 a number of critics were growing heartily sick of them. In October 1820 Theodore Hook, the future editor of *John Bull*, had put on a piece called *Over the Water* for the Haymarket, and the butt of this farce was one Mr Daddikey, a rich Cockney. But for once nobody seems to have been laughing. 'The frequency of Mr. Hook's intrusions begins to render them intolerable', wrote the *Theatrical Inquisitor*, 'particularly when we find that the oftener his appeals are made, the more destitute they become of every claim to success.'[62] *The Examiner* even wondered whether Jameson's recent successes might not have 'exhausted the subject of Cocknies'.[63] In the event, however, the appetite of the public seems to have remained as capacious as ever, and writers continued to serve up new versions of the type. Moncrieff produced *Lost Life* in 1821, and in the following year *Tom and Jerry*, a quickfire adaptation of Pierce Egan's *Life in London*, which opened a whole new chapter in the Cockney story.

With all this in mind we must conclude that, brilliant as the Blackwoodsmen had been in their *politicization* of the Cockney phenomenon, they were clearly building on currents of amusement and anxiety that were already at large within the culture. The 'Cockney School' debate that they initiated was not, as it can sometimes seem, an isolated piece of literary infighting; it was actually at the core of something broader, a veritable sea of public representation and discussion. The burgeoning life of the comic Cockney in the theatrical farces of the period is one part of this larger conversation, but so too is the sustained interest of the minor periodicals, not only in London but throughout the country.[64] It is the suppleness of the term that I want to emphasize here. Some representations of Cockneys and Cockneyism were clearly inspired by the attacks in *Blackwood's*, and were directed at the same figures for the same ends.[65] Parodies of Hunt's Hampstead manner continued well into the 1820s. ''Tis well I see the beautiful of things', began the *Literary Journal*'s 'Pleasant Walks: A Cockney Pastoral' of March 1819, 'Else, K[eats], there thousands are that wouldn't see | Scarce anything in this most stupid age | Worth calling poetry'.[66] Other magazines, however, preferred to take a less personal line on the phenomenon. Cockney sporting satires of the kind that had been current since the eighteenth century still continued to be very popular, some of them looking forward to the later successes of Robert Surtees.[67] In September 1826 the *Mirror of Literature* introduced one such sporting sketch with the title 'The First of September, or the Confessions of a Cockney', and began by asking: 'Gentle reader, is not this an alluring announcement? … "There's magic in the name"'.[68] But, on the whole, the preoccupation of Cockney contributions was with more contemporary issues, most notably the rapid transformation of the city and its suburbs. Some Cockney contributions of the period contained Crockery-style laments about the pace of 'improvement'.[69] Others, of a more obviously comic nature, concentrated on the increasing exodus of Cockneys into the new London suburbs.[70] Often it was clear that Cockney ambition was being targeted even though it had not been explicitly named. In 1822, for example, the *New Monthly Magazine* produced an article on 'The London 'Prentices', in response to the latest Waverley novel, *The Fortunes of Nigel*, in which it pointed out that in medieval times apprentices had been 'very different persons from the essenced *petits-maitres*, who in our times value themselves not on their play at bucklers or broad-sword, but on the glories of ambitious Dandyism'.[71]

Nor was Cockneyism solely an obsession of the Tory magazines. The *New Monthly* is an interesting case in this respect: having been virulently conservative in the 1810s, when it regularly published parodies and critiques of Hunt and Hazlitt, it rapidly became a much more literary and liberal concern from 1821 onwards, under the editorship of Thomas Campbell and Cyrus Redding. But it still retained a healthy interest in Cockneys. In 1824 it published Horace Smith's comic sketch, 'The Dinner in the Steam-Boat', which showed a group of Londoners laughing and joking as they enjoyed a slap-up lunch on a Thames pleasure boat, lurching between pretentiousness and vulgarity as their boat bumps and rolls. Significantly for us, their defining characteristic, the thing that really identifies these people as Cockneys in the 1820s sense, is not their dialect but their word play, for they all engage in a constant patter of little skits, jokes and puns.

> 'Shall I give you a little salad? La, it isn't dressed; what a shame!'
> 'Not at all,' cried Smart, 'None of us dressed for dinner, so that we can hardly expect it to be dressed for us. He he he!'[72]

There is a little sprinkle of Cockney dialect in the story, which is spoken by the hostess's son, but it only seems to be present to remind us of what lies beneath the apparently respectable veneer of the other characters. Essentially the piece is a satire on lower-middle-class manners, with the Cockneyism of the group residing precisely in the slipping, sliding familiarity of its discourse – a kind of bumptious, presumptuous promiscuity of manner.

But it is the right-wing press proper that shows us how truly powerful and influential Cockney criticism could be in the political culture of the time. Only a few short months after this *New Monthly* sketch, Hook's *John Bull* began a series of diatribes on the plans for a London University, the brainchild of a number of leading liberals including the *New Monthly*'s own editor,

Thomas Campbell. Hook was profoundly opposed to the idea of a 'Cockney College', which seemed to him, as to many conservatives of the day, a sort of flagrant category mistake. He was also opposed to the designedly secular foundation of the new institution, and what he saw as its politically irresponsible ambition to 'to instruct butchers in geometry, and tallow-chandlers in Hebrew'.[73] As Hook's attacks became more insistent, so it became necessary for Hunt's *Examiner* to oppose them. 'The miserable toad-eater qualifies everything permanently connected with this great metropolis', the editor wrote, 'however enlarged and intellectual its object, as *cockneyish*.'

After his attempt to sneer, with marvellous consistency he denounces the new University as the result of a deep design to overturn the religion and government of the country! Hear how he sounds the tocsin for all loyal and pious people:–

> It is madness for people to blind themselves to the consequences of such an Institution – let them look at the Continent, let them see that Universities in cities are the places in which all political tumults originate – let them consider the results of an education which is to expand and excite the minds of an underbred cockney population, unrestrained by religious instruction.

'We are quite at a loss', *The Examiner* went on, 'how the danger will be increased because the education is to be bestowed on an "*underbred cockney population*"':

[Fine word, that '*underbred!*' especially as applied by a profligate vulgar jester to the numerous and intelligent class occupying the middle rank in this vast metropolis. And what does it mean, beyond a stupid slang of contempt? Would not 'under-crust' be as much to the purpose?] An essential part of 'cockneyism' is ignorance, and the self-conceit consequent upon narrow views, both moral and physical. Education will necessarily correct these defects: our ultra-genteel sneerer is therefore decrying the very means that will remove the danger and capacity which he attaches to an 'underbred cockney population'.[74]

So powerful had this nickname become, it seems, that even the 'Political Examiner' was to find itself forced into close analysis, like a literary bomb-disposal expert trying to defuse destructive potential. 'A nickname', as Hazlitt had written in 1818, almost certainly with this particular one in mind, 'is a bugbear to the imagination, and though we do not believe in it, it still haunts our apprehensions.'[75] But of course the really interesting thing about the passage quoted above is that, notwithstanding its spirited opposition to Hook, *The Examiner does* actually seem to believe in the nickname, tacitly acknowledging not only the existence of a Cockney class (which it insists is 'numerous and intelligent'), but also (and somewhat self-contradictorily) 'Cockneyism', a moral and cultural malaise within that class, which improved education will hope to cure.

By the mid 1820s, then, we can see that, for liberals and Tories alike, the word Cockney might still denote a Londoner of any low or middle rank, but it was especially coming to refer to a particular sector of metropolitan society, that ambitious, amphibious stratum just above the traditional labouring classes. But what did it mean to posit a Cockney class, a lower middle class in all but name, in an age when even the concept of a middle class was still only a work-in-progress? One answer is to see a dialectical relationship between the two. Between 1815 and 1832, as Dror Wahrman has argued, the British middle class finally came of age, attaining a new level of self-consciousness, and successfully naturalizing its particular claims to power.[76] One of the ways in which it defined itself was by differentiating itself from the aristocracy. Another, just as important, was by positing another amorphous, uneasy class lying just below it: a precariously propertied middle class that did not have the education or equipment for full citizenship, and was therefore (as many conservatives thought) to be excluded from it. Something concrete was given to this distinction with the property qualification limiting the 1832 extension of the franchise, but in truth it was always a more subjective judgement than that – as much cultural as economic.

The concept can be seen as especially subjective (and self-regarding) to the degree that many of the commentators who were most interested in lampooning and de-legitimizing the lower middle (or Cockney) class in the 1820s – let us call them periodical journalists – were actually from that class themselves. Not John Wilson or J. G. Lockhart perhaps, who were of thoroughly bourgeois stock, but Thomas Barnes, Cyrus Redding, P. G. Patmore, Theodore Hook, William Hazlitt, Horace and James Smith, Thomas Hood and George Cruikshank were all social amphibians of one kind or another, who knew their subject inside out. Hence the Cockney controversy, as it developed in the 1820s, should not really be considered as a class war between two clearly defined sets of combatants, but more of a debate within the realms of 'mediocrity' about where the dividing line of cultural legitimacy lay.

Blackwood's Magazine addressed itself to an audience that was not wholly different, in social terms, from that of Leigh Hunt, but its class perspective – as well as its perspective on class – could not have been more antagonistic. In *Blackwood's* the ascent to 'middle-classness' was all about quietly and invisibly coming into one's inheritance; and what one inherited was a set of values that were fundamentally gentlemanly and polite.[77] Any discrepancies between those values and one's actual social condition, either as a writer or a reader, were for the most part silently fudged, so that the actual was never permitted to undermine the ideal. What inflamed the Blackwoodsmen about Hunt, however, and this was above and beyond his political opinions, was the extraordinary manner in which he was continually revealing, sometimes unconsciously, sometimes with great deliberation, the clear discrepancy between his aspirations and his real conditions, both cultural and material. Lockhart and Wilson always took great delight in exposing Hunt's performances, but in truth they were only extending a tendency that was already at work in his own writings, for whether as an *Indicator* or an *Examiner*, he was always exposing himself.

In the second issue of *The Indicator*, which was first published in October 1819, Hunt had taken advantage of the dateline to write an essay on the 'Autumnal Commencement of Fires – Mantel-Pieces – Apartments for Study', enthusiastically revisiting the 'Day by the Fire' topos from seven years before. Shorter than the *Reflector* essay, the 'Autumnal Commencement of Fires' did nevertheless go over some of the same ground, the main difference being that, with the passage of time, and in spite of the repeated attacks upon him, the element of Cockney fantasy had become, if anything, even more shameless. 'We like to have any little curiosity of the mantel-piece kind within our reach and inspection', the essayist wrote, '[and] for the same reason, we like a small study, where we are almost in contact with our books.'[78] Having stated his preference for the kind of study one might find in a petit-bourgeois villa, Hunt then went on to cite Montaigne, the lord of a great chateau, as a man of his own mettle, the comfortable 'smallness' of his library being held up as a model. But the most deliciously Cockney move of all was in the final paragraph, where Hunt did a wonderful job of reconciling himself, and many of his readers, to the city's circumscribed conditions: 'A great prospect we hold to be a very disputable advantage, upon the same reasoning as before; but we like to have some green boughs about our windows, and to fancy ourselves as much as possible in the country when we are not there' (p. 11). This is Hunt the Cockney jailbird still in love with his prison, his main requirement of a dwelling being that it shouldn't prevent him from dreaming of other places and other times. In formulations such as this, the suburban study is presented as a kind of halfway house of the fancy – a place whose very insufficiency is turned into an imaginative fetish. Leigh Hunt's Cockneyism was always, to this degree, a form of confessionalism, but the truths that it confessed were never wholly confined to him or, indeed, to the lower middle class. For as we shall see in the next chapter, what his recreational works seemed most interested in exploring, whether he knew it or not, were the actual conditions of contemporary life, that experience of dichotomy and disproportion that was being seen and felt everywhere, but which modern metropolitan living was now bringing into new relief.

THE COCKNEY MOMENT 1810–1840

There has been some exceptional scholarly work done on the Cockney School over the last twenty years. The foundations for a culturally and historically informed reading of the Keats and Hunt circle were laid by Nicholas Roe's *John Keats and the Culture of Dissent* (1997) and Jeffrey Cox's *Poetry and Politics in the Cockney School* (1998). Since then there has been a constant stream of always stimulating, sometimes masterful work on the subject, with some of the most notable contributions coming from Richard Cronin, Elizabeth Jones, Jane Stabler, Greg Kucich and Kim Wheatley.[79] This book is deeply indebted to this body of work. The whole nexus of concerns surrounding class and the city have also been very well served in recent years, not least by two superb collections of essays, *Romantic Metropolis*, edited by James Chandler and Kevin Gilmartin (2005), and *Romanticism and Popular Culture* edited by Philip Connell and Nigel Leask (2009). In this study I want to build on this rich legacy, while also seeking to extend its scope. Cockneyism, I want to argue, need not simply be a concern of Romanticists investigating the politics and culture of the Peterloo period. It could also serve as a more general, guiding principle to help us to navigate through one of the most interesting transitional periods of English literature, as the periodical revolution of the Romantic period gives birth to a truly metropolitan culture, and prepares the ground for the Victorians. One way of thinking about Cockneyism, indeed, is to see it as the misshapen 'foster-child' of Romanticism and Social Realism, the crucial missing link between Keats and Dickens.

Recent investigations of the Cockney phenomenon have been right to focus on Hunt, Keats and Hazlitt, for it was in the contemporary responses to their work that the debate really came into being. But Cockneyism, it is important to recognize, did not begin and end with the Cockney School. Other people and things were frequently brought into the arena; figures who, in some instances at least, had little or no connection with the *Examiner* coterie. The conflict between *Blackwood's* and the *London Magazine* over Cockneyism is already well known, not least because it led to the death of John Scott, the *London*'s editor, in a bungled suburban duel.[80] But there were other victims too. The painter

Haydon was a target, in spite of his Toryism; and so too was the hugely popular apocalyptic artist John Martin. In fact, the question of who is and who is not convicted of Cockneyism in this period is a matter of considerable interest. Time and again, figures such as Pierce Egan, Charles Lamb, Thomas Hood and George Cruikshank are all brought to the bar, examined closely and then acquitted. 'But what a bitter disappointment!' *Blackwood's* said of Hood's *Whims and Oddities* in 1827, 'Thomas Hood, so far from deserving to be knouted to death, or sent with his stripes into Siberian silence, turns out to be a most admirable fellow.'[81] Hood had strong connections with the *London Magazine*, Hazlitt and Lamb, but such was his political tact, and his growing popularity with the reading public, that they were not deemed sufficient to sink him. Nor was Cockneyism all about one's proximity to Leigh Hunt, for even as writers such as Lamb and Hood were being let off the hook by the Tories, the Royal Academician John Soane, a man with no obvious connection to the *Examiner*, was being lambasted in Cockney terms.

What this Introduction has shown, I hope, is that while the concept of Cockneyism is by no means a difficult one, its ramifications are, or were, remarkably diverse. It is this diversity, I want to suggest, that makes it such a suggestive, if occasionally somewhat slippery, object of study. It was primarily, as we have seen, a way of thinking about an interstitial class, a class that was, or seemed to be, on the rise during the Regency, but which was later to find itself in a kind of political no man's land after the Great Reform Act of 1832.[82] (The transition from Cockney potential to Cockney impotence is thus one of this book's underlying themes.) But it was also a way of thinking about suburbanization, and the increasingly blurred boundary between city and country, with all of the moral and generic confusion which that entailed. On a slightly different level, Cockneyism also developed into an aesthetic term, a means of referring to anything that seemed out of scale, significance or perspective; anything, that is, that seemed to have been disfigured by modern metropolitan conditions. When John Soane's House Museum was first opened to the public in 1836, a wag at *Fraser's Magazine* took it apart in these terms: 'There is hardly a closet, a cupboard, or a corner in the whole house', the reviewer commented, 'that is not distinguished by some fanciful, fine-sounding and truly imposing appellation. Thus we have the "Parloir of Padre Giovanni", the "Corinthian Colonnade", with columns almost as high as those of a shop front.' 'It's not for us to say', he concluded, 'that this is all in singularly bad taste, – in the style of a Cockney tea-garden, or the bills of a puppet show.'[83] Lastly, and in a related spirit, Cockneyism was also a means of addressing that new desire for independence that we find in many writers and artists of the period, as they turn their noses up at the artistic establishment and strive to make it on their own. This is one reason, I think, why embattled egotists such as Hazlitt, Soane, Haydon and Martin were to find themselves on the receiving end so often, for what Cockney criticism often tried to register, in these cases, was a terrible disjunction between ambition and actuality, form and subject matter, the artist's own perception of himself and his real position in the world. For in conservative eyes these Cockney artists were all, to borrow the subtitle of one of Moncrieff's theatrical extravaganzas of the 1830s, 'Napoleons of Humble Life'.[84]

The ramifications of Cockneyism, then, were at once social and spatial, formal and professional, and it is for this reason, I think, that it can serve as a powerful tool for exploring the dynamic relationship between early-nineteenth-century notions of class, the city, artistic identity and aesthetic form. This book is not a social history of Cockneyism, or a cultural history of the representation of Cockneys in literature. Rather it seeks to use the Cockney debate as a starting-point for a series of explorations into metropolitan art and life in the 1820s and 1830s. To the cultural conservatives of the day, Cockneyism was all about fanciful imaginings in restricted settings; to many twenty-first-century readers, however, its milieu will seem very close to our own conditions of living. With this in mind, the following chapters will be interested in exploring the conflict between imagination and actuality in relationship to a number of archetypally urban spaces – suburban tea-gardens, lodging houses, offices, house museums and debtors' prisons. It will look at the Cockney as the ancestor of the modern. But, in tandem with this, the other leading interest of the book will be to explore the responses of the Cockneys themselves to the Cockney phenomenon. How writers such as Hunt, Hazlitt and Haydon chose to respond to their Tory critics is one thing, but what I am more engaged by here is the larger question of how they themselves dealt with issues of urban discrepancy and disproportion in their own work. To this end, the first three chapters will deal with the three main victims of the *Blackwood's* attacks – Hunt, Keats and Hazlitt. Chapter 1 explores the dialogue between Hunt and Keats on the nature of the suburban imagination, and on what it might mean to be a Cockney poet. Chapter 2 looks at Hazlitt's thoughts on the Cockney as a cultural and political phenomenon in his 1823 essay 'On Londoners and Country People', and the following chapter explores his even more complicated and self-thwarting views on the Cockneyesses. Chapters 4 and 5 are both on writers who were thoroughly soaked in the Cockney milieu but who nevertheless managed to avoid being put in the pillory. The chapter on Pierce Egan looks at *Life in London* as a Tory Cockney fantasy significantly enabled by the sporting culture of the Regency. The next chapter, on the metropolitan picturesque, is about Charles Lamb's consummately metropolitan take on the contemporary issue of urban beggars, a perspective that was deeply influenced by his own experience as a full-time clerk at the East India House in the City. Chapters 6 and 7 are on art and architecture. The first shows how the Cockneyfication of form and genre in the work of John Martin and John Soane sparked criticism from some members of the Cockney School themselves. The second looks at Cockney space and Cockney genre in Haydon's debtors' prison picture *The Mock Election* (1828). Chapter 8, which attempts to bring all of these various strands together, is on the greatest Cockney writer of them all (but again, one who cleverly managed to sidestep Tory criticism), the novelist and sketch-writer Charles Dickens. One way of reading Dickens is to see his work as synthesizing the subjective Cockneyism of Keats, Hunt and Hazlitt with the critical tradition that had been pitted against it; a highly distinctive, one might almost say unique fusion of sympathy and satire.

One further thing to be stressed is that this Cockney debate, if debate is the right word for it, was of relatively limited duration, at least in its most intense form. So much so, indeed, that it seems appropriate to think of the period 1810–40 as being, in effect, a 'Cockney moment', that is, a brief window of time in which a particular set of interests and concerns were addressed (by artists and critics alike) in a particular set of ways. This period was a kind of golden era for the new periodical press; it was also (especially before the crash of 1826) a period of great 'metropolitan improvement', with huge changes taking place in London's social and material infrastructure. In keeping with the expansive spirit of the times, there was a certain kind of openness in the treatment of the city. The relationship between 'the metropolis and mental life' had never been more freely discussed. By the mid 1840s, however, attitudes had hardened: with crime and sanitation at the top of the agenda, the Victorians saw the big city as, first and foremost, a problem to be solved. Bourgeois anxieties about the working class proper had become, if anything, even more acute in the interim, but the lower middle class, though still seen as ridiculous, was no longer an object of the same concern. It is interesting to note, therefore, that it is precisely in the mid-Victorian period that the word 'Cockney' gradually starts to slip down the social scale, moving down into the London working class, and also to change its valency in the process.[85] No longer a term of abuse, it became more and more a term of affection; no longer a synonym for social ambition, it referred increasingly to those who, like Sam Weller in Dickens's *Pickwick Papers* (1837), seemed strangely content to remain low. The word changed, in short, from being a way of worrying about the petite bourgeoisie to being a way of reassuring oneself about the urban proletariat. Cockneyism had finally found a home.

CHAPTER I

Leigh Hunt, John Keats and the suburbs

By 1819 England was a country in political turmoil, and as editor of *The Examiner* newspaper Leigh Hunt found himself in the thick of every controversy. All the more astonishing, then, that it was in the autumn of that very year – and only a few short weeks after the Peterloo Massacre – that he decided to launch a weekly periodical that was explicitly intended as a retreat from politics: 'The Indicator', he announced,

> will attend to no subject whatsoever of immediate or temporary interest. His business is with the honey in the old woods. The Editor has enough to agitate his spirits during the present eventful times, in another periodical work; and he is willing to be so agitated; but as he is accustomed to use his pen, as habitually as a bird his pinion, and to betake himself with it into the nests and bowers of more lasting speculations, when he has done with public ones, he is determined to keep those haunts of his recreations free from all noise and wrangling, both for his own pleasure, and for those who may choose to accompany him.[1]

Here, in the very first issue of 13 October 1819, we can see a close relationship being set up between spaces or 'haunts' of recreation, natural spaces such as nests and bowers, and the space of belles-lettres itself, as embodied by this new periodical. This triangulation already looks forward, in its coy way, to the later Victorian idea of the aesthetic as a timeless, disinterested place, removed from everyday controversies. Hunt's counterparts on the other side of the political spectrum, J. G. Lockhart and John Wilson, the young editors of *Blackwood's Edinburgh Magazine*, were no less interested, as it turns out, in this potential of the aesthetic to function as a faction-free realm. But what was distinctive, and especially vexing to the Blackwoodsmen, was the explicitly feminized and privatized quality of Hunt's vision, and its pointed identification of the 'space' of culture with the cosy little interiors and exteriors of the new London suburbs.

The early nineteenth century saw the first flowering of the suburban ideal. The notion of making a clear separation between work and home, and of home itself as a private, leisured, semi-rural realm – both of these grew considerably in influence and attractiveness during this period, and were tied to actual suburban development. As F. M. L. Thompson writes,

> while the idea of the residential suburb as an attractive emblem of material and social success and not as evidence of failure and rejection was in circulation before 1815, and its realization on the ground was already sprouting particularly in South London, it was not until the years after Waterloo that modern suburban development got properly under way on a significant scale.[2]

John Nash's Regent's Park, which was planned and built in the 1810s, was the aristocratic version of this dream-space; places such as Hampstead, Denmark Hill, Camberwell and Dulwich were the bourgeois equivalent. Escapism was a crucial element in the suburban ideal from the beginning, for, as Ann Bermingham has very aptly expressed it, 'in its purest form the suburb was an abstraction of the rustic tradition, a utopian ideological construction that provided a refuge from the disappointing realities of both urban and rural life'.[3] As it turned out, the fantastical aura that surrounded Regency suburbanism was only enhanced by the speed of its progress. Witness this *Literary Magnet* article from 1824, evocatively titled 'The Last of the Cockneys':

> Henceforth, villas began to rise, in all directions, as though the ground had been touched with Harlequin's wand, or had been sprinkled with some of the oil from Aladdin's lamp. The Cockney was no longer a Cockney! He had his country house, his garden, and his grounds – he kept his poultry, his pigs, and his cow – he brewed his own ale, and made his own butter – or Dorothy did it for him, which amounts to the same thing.[4]

In retrospect, the really surprising thing about suburbanism was that a movement which had been imagined in the late eighteenth century as a form of polite retreat from the city could expand so quickly in scope and character. By the early nineteenth century the lower middle classes had joined the exodus, and the London suburbs were becoming ever more mixed in consequence. This democratization was so rapid that by 1820 some of the more established of the 'new' suburbs – places such as Camden Town, Somers Town and Pentonville – had become increasingly associated with the lower middle (or Cockney) classes, heavily populated, as they now were, by milliners, seamstresses, lawyer's clerks and shopkeeper's apprentices who commuted every morning to the Inns of Court and the City. To cultural conservatives this was a worrying development in the suburban story, since it appeared to undermine all proper distinctions between city and country, nature and culture, polite and plebeian.

But to other, more liberal commentators like Leigh Hunt it was a sign of 'improvement'.

Inevitably, as the suburbs grew, social perspectives and social realities fluctuated, shifted and changed. The view of the country altered, with nature coming increasingly to be seen as a kind of resort. The cultivation of little garden plots led to a new miniaturism and pragmatism in the practice of horticulture, with Repton's picturesque aesthetic gradually giving way to J. C. Loudon's gardenesque.[5] In Elizabeth Jones's view, Hunt and Keats played no insignificant part in this taste revolution, being 'partially responsible for "inventing" a poetic of suburbia that … came to exert a powerful influence over Victorian literary culture'.[6] Characteristically, Hunt's suburban idealism was of the most accommodating and inclusive kind: his aim was to encourage private cultivation in everyone, Camden Town clerks as well as Camberwell stockbrokers. 'I need not inform any reader acquainted with real poetry', he wrote in the Preface to *Foliage* (1818)

> that a delight in rural luxury has ever been a constituent part of the very business of poets as well as being one of the very best things which they have recommended, as counteractions to the more sordid tendencies of cities. But I may as well insinuate, that the luxuries which poets recommend, and which are thought to be beautiful on paper, are much more within the reach of everyone, and much more beautiful in reality, than people's fondness for considering all poetry as fiction would imply.[7]

For Elizabeth Jones it was Hunt's suburbanism, as the expression of a broader Cockney confidence and ambition, which really threatened J. G. Lockhart, and not poetic impropriety as such.[8]

There are regular celebrations of suburban vistas and suburban bowers in Hunt's poetry of the post-Waterloo period, but the most controversial example is probably the little pavilion where Paolo and Francesco finally succumb to their incestuous passion in Canto III of *The Story of Rimini* (1816): 'Never, be sure, before or since was seen | A summer house so fine in such a nest of green.'[9] Hunt, like Keats, specialized in 'sensually charged lyrical bowers and blushful dalliance', as Jones has so aptly described it, but to Lockhart such scenes only revealed the true nature of 'Cockney' suburbanism – at once coyly vulgar and sexually licentious.[10] They reminded him of the atmosphere of the suburban pleasure gardens with their unpleasant combination of pasteboard and promiscuity. Lockhart patented this idea when he linked Keats and Hunt with the 'fanciful dreaming tea-drinkers' at Vauxhall in the fourth of the

'Cockney School' articles.[11] But later commentators were to put more flesh on these bones. Byron, though a political ally, couldn't help thinking of the Hunt circle as 'Sunday Bloods', Cockney upstarts of the kind that would dress up at weekends to haunt the public gardens. 'It is in their *finery*', he wrote, 'that the new under-school are *most* vulgar.'[12] In 1819 the *New Monthly Magazine* pretended to have spotted Leigh Hunt in a Hampstead tea-bower, and made fun of the natural scenery on offer: 'Or with a glass we peep at Leigh, | Whilst sipping up gossiping tea. | Thy little hill is sure a mountain! – | Each turbid pond a crystal fountain!'[13] In 1823 *Blackwood's* staged another fake sighting of Hunt as the new proprietor of the White Conduit Tea Gardens, a Cockney pleasure resort in the North London suburbs: 'I saw him in the bar … in a straw hat, and a foreign air, quite smirking and genteel-like.'[14] In this chapter I want to explore the relationship between Hunt, Keats and the suburban pleasure gardens not least because, once again, I feel that the connection that the conservative magazines were making was not merely spiteful. There is a deep affinity, I would suggest, between this kind of space and the social and cultural outlook of both of these poets, and to explore this affinity is not only to develop a greater understanding of their common characteristics as writers, but also to gain a clearer sense of the differences between them.

THE COCKNEY TEA-GARDEN

The vast majority of London's suburban tea-gardens had been laid out in the early to mid eighteenth century, and were most thickly congregated in a green belt immediately north of the City. As James Stevens Curl has said in his recent history of the subject, 'in that part of London lying between Clerkenwell and Islington, where the New River Head lay in the centre of a series of open fields, many Springs and Wells abounded, and several sites were exploited by entrepreneurs for the alleged medicinal qualities of the waters'.[15] Of these, Sadler's Wells, the Islington Spa, the English Grotto, Bagnigge Wells, White Conduit House and Merlin's Cave were the most popular. Structurally, these places were often very mixed in style, with disparate elements casually interposed. Some consisted of formal alcoves and gardens; some (like White Conduit House) had sports fields adjoining them; and most contained a bewildering variety of diminutive decorative elements, classical statuary, ornamental fishponds, little summer-houses and gothic follies. In many ways the layout of the tea-garden that Cyrus Redding described for the *London Magazine* in August 1822 was quite typical of its kind:

We now entered the garden, surrounded by boxes, in which people of every age, and both sexes, were regaling themselves. Every spot was occupied with a table or form, save where the green sward extended itself, and a number of children were gambolling. We entered the tavern, and while sipping our port, amused ourselves with contemplating the company outside.[16]

Often these gardens were lined with boxes, alcoves or arbours. The latter were especially popular, as W. S. Scott tells us in his *Bygone Pleasures of London* (1948):

They were separated, one from another, each one containing a small table and sufficient seating-room for a family, since it was the custom for father, mother, and a host of children to arrive *en famille* to spend the day in the gardens. The arbours were usually backed by shrubs, and were earwiggy to a degree, the taste of the day demanding 'shady boscage', even if it also meant that a certain element of insect life attended the feast uninvited.[17]

Whether it was the walks or the arbours, the sports grounds or the formal gardens, North London resorts such as the White Conduit House and Bagnigge Wells were highly popular, and decidedly fashionable, in the mid 1700s. It was only in the early nineteenth century that their respectable appeal started to dwindle. The semi-plebeian order had always provided a proportion of the clientele, as we can tell from a satirical squib, *Bagnigge Wells*, which was first published in 1779:

Thy arbours, Bagnigge, and the gay alcove,
Where the frail Nymphs in am'rous dalliance rove;
Where prentic'd Youths enjoy the Sunday feast,
And City Matrons boast their Sabbath's rest.[18]

By the 1820s, however, the tea-gardens of this district had begun to take on a more plebeian character, as Warwick Wroth, in his late-Victorian history of London's pleasure gardens, acknowledged:

Bagnigge Wells and White Conduit House, the classic tea gardens of London, were prettily laid out and pleasantly situated, but in their later days became decidedly cockneyfied. The great day at these gardens was Sunday, especially between five and nine o'clock. The amusements were of a simple kind – a game of bowls or skittles, a ramble in the maze, and a more or less hilarious tea-drinking in the bowers and alcoves which every garden provided.[19]

Two things contributed to this 'cockneyfication'. One was the rapid encroachment of bricks and mortar. Between 1800 and 1820 what had once been a sizeable swath of green between Clerkenwell in the south and Islington and the new suburbs of Pentonville and Somers Town in the north was completely swallowed up by urban development.[20] The other was the equally rapid invasion of the lower middle and working classes, which forced the bourgeoisie proper to move even further afield. In 1822 the *Literary Gazette* noted that 'many of us can recollect Bagnigge Wells, Chad's Wells, Acton Wells, and Islington Spa, but fashion has deprived these of their virtue, and substituted Cheltenham, or Bath, or Tunbridge, or Leamington'.[21] Ten years later the *New Monthly Magazine* remarked of the Pentonville region, which was only a little further to the north, that

> The march of town-innovation upon the suburbs has driven before it all that was green, silent and fitted for meditation. Here, too, is that Paradise of apprentice boys, White *Cundick Couse*, as it is cacophoniously pronounced by its visitors, which has done much to expel the decencies of the district. Thirty years ago this place was better frequented'.[22]

Topographical overviews of the old tea-gardens are not easy to come by, but one beautiful watercolour has survived, which gives a view of White Conduit Gardens from the balcony of the house in 1848 (see Figure 1). This paints a good picture of the site in its declining years, more confined than it would have been in the 1700s, but still full of fanciful charm. More importantly, it does also give some sense of the kind of space that the early-nineteenth-century periodicals were talking about, with its lawns and gazebos, recreation grounds and private arcades.

One result of this social descent in the Islington and Clerkenwell tea-gardens was that the references to them in the polite periodicals of the day did tend to be either supercilious or ironic. Here are the terms, for example, in which one reviewer of 1823 attacked the contemporary taste for make-believe in domestic garden design:

> With respect to such frigid conceits and barbarous masquerade, as barns masked under the disguise of churches and castles, and dairies bearing the semblance of ruins, we enter our most vehement protest against them. Such fantastical apery serves to remind us of the ass accoutred in the lion's skin. – In point of taste, indeed, conceits of this nature are utterly unworthy of any place superior to a cockney tea-garden.[23]

The running joke in many of these articles was that the tea-garden was the only form in which many Cockneys encountered, or knew how to encounter, nature, and this was a joke precisely because the gardens themselves had come to seem so artificial and incongruous. In 1822 the *Literary Speculum* published a superb skit called 'The Rural Recollections of Christopher Cockney, Gentleman'. This told the story of a nature-loving Cockney apprentice, a writer for the periodical magazines and, as he himself boasts, 'supreme monarch of Cockney bardlings', who used

Figure 1. Frederick Crace, *Bird's Eye View Looking over the Gardens of the White Conduit House in Islington*. Watercolour. 1848. The ornamental walks, arcades, alcoves and skittles grounds are all clearly visible in this picture.

to spend his Sunday afternoons sampling 'the rural delights of Bagnigge Wells, White Conduit House or Highbury Barn!' The punch-line of the piece was that despite having been 'partial to a rural life' from his early childhood, the Cockney's one serious attempt to rusticate himself (in the suburban paradise of Walworth) turns out to be a complete disaster. Realizing his mistake, he promptly returns to the City, where he spends most of his time reading Wordsworth with a Cockney friend of his, and railing bitterly against urban development: 'London, with its overweening rapacity, is gorging up the gay fields in its capacious maw, and spreading, like a cancer, its *brachia* of bricks and mortar, in all directions, over the "green bosom" of our parent earth. It will soon be a day's journey to a corn field, and a smart five hours' walk to a tea-garden!'[24]

Not all of the references to tea-gardens in the polite periodicals were scornful, however, and indeed it is but one short step from the last example, with its mock-tragic regret at the pace of change, to a performance like 'Crockery's New Lamentations', which appeared in the *Literary Chronicle* in March 1823. Though borrowing its narrative persona from a character in a stage farce by Robert Jameson (*Exit by Mistake*, which was discussed in the Introduction), this article was in fact a serious complaint about the city's encroachment upon White Conduit House in Islington, offering a detailed, affectionate register of its imperilled charms: 'And is all this to be lost? Is it to be buried amid bricks and smoke? Is London thus to advance, and throw her murky and horrid arms around such delicious places? Forbid it, all ye Sylvan deities! Forbid it, Love!'[25] A few months later, however, the same magazine was to strike a much more sarcastic note on the subject, as 'Crockery Junior' expressed a mock-Burkean regret at the choking of Clerkenwell. 'No more', he said, 'can the cockneys' radical appetite be whetted by the stimulating speeches of the champion of universal suffrage and annual parliaments, from the windows of Merlin's Cave; and the once famed well, where erst was enacted the sacred mystery of the "Creation", is buried in oblivion for ever.'[26] The second reference is to the ancient well of Clerkenwell itself, where mystery plays had been performed in the Middle Ages. The first is to a series of speeches given by Henry 'Orator' Hunt in the winter of 1816–17 at Merlin's Cave, a converted tavern near the New River Head, which had been attended by vast crowds of radical sympathizers. Of this run of speeches, it was the second, which was given on 2 December 1816, that sparked the infamous Spa Fields riot, an event that effectively brought an end to mass assembly in this period. Facetious though Crockery Junior's article was, it was also remarkably accurate. Clerkenwell was an overwhelmingly Cockney realm at this time, heavily populated by craftsmen and artisans, lawyer's clerks and City apprentices, and, as he suggested, it was a region with a strong historical and political identity. The 'sacred wells' and tea-gardens were very numerous, and stretched all the way up into Islington. But interspersed among them were spaces such as Clerkenwell Green, Coldbath Fields and the aforementioned Merlin's Cave, which had hosted a large number of radical meetings in the crisis years after Waterloo.

Political anxiety may have played some part in the distaste that the polite periodicals felt for the old pleasure gardens, but the primary cause was aesthetic. Not only, it was argued, were these spaces fanciful and flimsy in their décor, they also looked increasingly out-of-place as the city extended around them. In 1827 William Clarke glossed the old line about cits repairing to Bagnigge Wells 'to swallow dust and call it air', by suggesting that the resort had now 'changed its character, being the evening resort of the half-and-half people in the vicinity'.[27] At first Hunt seems to have resisted this viewpoint, championing the notion of the suburb as a kind of mixed space that could combine politics and pleasure. In *The Descent of Liberty* (1815), the political masque that he wrote in prison, the pageant of Liberty is represented as taking place in 'A PLEASURE GROUND in the suburbs of a great city laid out in a natural stile with wood and turf, the spires and domes appearing over the trees toward the side'.[28] But by 1819, when he launched his recreational paper *The Indicator*, such spaces seem to have lost their virtue.

Perhaps it was the rapid expansion of the city that had made Hunt rethink the old suburbs; perhaps it was Henry 'Orator' Hunt haranguing the crowds from the window of Merlin's Cave. Certainly he had been very keen to distance himself from his namesake at the time, declaring that he was 'heartily sorry to see the cause of Reform injured by the interference of such men, – men, whom all its advocates, but one, of any taste or reputation, avoid, and from even the leaders most acceptable to the people at large evidently shrink with disgust'.[29] But whatever the reason, and notwithstanding the fact that Clerkenwell's curious patchwork was in many ways a perfect mirror for the mixed nature of Hunt's own output in this period, from the autumn of Peterloo onwards he was continually directing himself – and his Cockney readership – to some of North London's more outlying 'nests and bowers'.

In the very first issue of *The Indicator* Hunt had included an article on 'Country Houses Near Town', in which he argued that when citizens went out of the city, they did not make nearly enough of the out-of-town estates (Caen Wood Park in Hampstead would have been foremost in his mind here, it being a favourite haunt of his and Keats's). 'Their pleasure', he wrote, 'is rather of a negative than positive kind; rather a fidgeting respite from smoke and noise, than a sense of the beauties of the scenery or of the solitude. When the citizen gets out of the town he contrives to be almost as much confined as when he is in it.'[30] The allusion, of course, was to the suburban tea-garden, whose cosy arbour could be seen as a mere reproduction, in a faux-rural setting, of the interior of a London tavern or coffee-house.

> This, and a confinement all the rest of the week to close and noisy streets, – the transition from dark rooms with windows half dust and half board, to the bargaining uproar of an Exchange, – the total ignorance of all intellectual pleasures, an utter deadness to what is called sentiment – a person which has no graces in consequence, – a face, sometimes jovial but not happy, generally care-worn, and always vulgar, – an enjoyment, such as it is, allied to gambling, and cut with a thousand anxieties, – an unhealthy temperament, always contradicting his comfort also, though he may not know as much, – toil, toil, toil, every morning, – indigestion, indigestion, every evening, – a gout in his old age, and a bad conscience all his life; – such is the picture of a complete, successful, flourishing, sophisticated, money-getting animal; who is called a 'good man' because his knaveries enable him to pay; and a knowing one, because he has found out with infinite labour and pains how to make himself forty times as uncomfortable as other people. (p. 7)

This might seem like a strange outburst to come from the so-called 'King of the Cockneys' but it is, of course, quite different from the line followed by *Blackwood's*. What they wanted to do was put Cockneys back in their place, to get them to accept their social and cultural limits. What Hunt wanted them to do was discover a new health and freedom in nature. One of the most interesting things about Hunt's critique of Londoners, I think, is that it actually reverts to the old seventeenth-century idea of the Cockney or 'cit' as a creature who does not belong to any one class or station, but is the warped product of a particular, highly specialized urban environment. Significantly, it is impossible to tell whether he has rich bankers in mind or counting-house clerks. Everyone seems implicated. That is the egalitarian aspect of this critique. But its negative corollary is that he cannot help suggesting, almost in proto-Victorian fashion, that the city is a place that will inevitably corrupt everybody.

There was a political aspect to this, as has been mentioned. Whether he was fully aware of it or not, in *The Indicator* Hunt was always attempting to pull his readers away from the busy, smoky, intensely public spaces of the City and its old suburbs and out towards the open fields. This sweeping gesture is suggestive on a number of levels. Not only does it anticipate

Hunt's own gradual move away from politics into recreational literature during the course of the 1820s, it also helps sum up his view of politics itself. For him, as for many of the middle and lower middle classes at this time, it was at bottom a matter of independent conscience, a private feeling for the public; hence he was always troubled by the mass manifestations of popular radicalism, which recalled to him the mob rule of the French Revolution. If there was a secret agenda behind Hunt's championing of the outer suburbs it was not to shoo Cockneys away from politics per se, but rather to encourage them to privatize it, to start behaving, in other words, like armchair *Examiner* readers, and not like the rowdy audiences of 'Orator' Hunt.

SUBURB WONDERS

Heartfelt as Hunt's recommendation of Hampstead was, the issue for him was never really about the quality of a particular urban space in and of itself, but rather its ability to foster the private imagination. This was a feature of all his recreational writing. 'Far Countries', a piece for the ninth *Indicator*, was one of his fullest explorations of this idea (and an early essay on a theme that was later taken up by William Hazlitt in 'Why Distant Objects Please'):

> In childhood, the total ignorance of the world, especially when we are brought up in some confined spot, renders everything beyond the bounds of our dwelling a distance and a romance. Mr Lamb, in his Recollection of Christ's Hospital, says that he remembers when some half-dozen of his schoolfellows set off, 'without map, card, or compass, on a serious expedition to find out *Phillip Quarl's Island'*. We once encountered a set of boys as romantic. It was at no greater distance than at the foot of a hill near Hampstead; yet the spot was so perfectly Cisalpine to them, that two of them came up to us with looks of hushing eagerness, and asked, 'whether, on the other side of that hill there were not robbers:' to which, the minor adventurer of the two added, 'And some say, serpents'. They had all got bows and arrows, and were evidently hovering about the place, betwixt daring and apprehension, as on the borders of some wild region. We smiled to think which it was that husbanded their suburb wonders to more advantage, they or we: for while they peopled the place with robbers and serpents, we were peopling it with sylvans and fairies.[31]

The most telling thing about this, I think, is its confessional insouciance; Hunt makes use of a Cockney anecdote from one of the more acceptable London writers of the period – Charles Lamb – and adds one of his own for equal measure. Clearly, from the *Indicator*'s point of view, there is no difference between the 'suburb wonders' of young boys and those of Cockney poets, for both can be seen as the healthy flexings of private fancy.

Of all the leading Romantics, nobody seems to have been less worried about the epistemological status of the imagination than Leigh Hunt. In an essay for the twenty-fourth issue of *The Indicator*, 'On the Realities of the Imagination', he rather baldly insisted that 'there is nothing imaginary in the common acceptation of the word', and that the habitual distinction between the imaginative and the real was, if it really came down to it, a false one. 'If a passage in King Lear brings the tear into our eyes', he argued, in a line of reasoning that recalls his sonnet on Milton's hair, 'it is as real as the touch of a sorrowful hand'.[32] To his mind, troubling over whether our imaginings were philosophically true (as Wordsworth and Coleridge had done) was far less profitable than trying to ensure that they were sunny: 'The ground-work of all happiness is health. Take care of this ground, and the doleful imaginations that come to warn us against its abuse, will avoid it. Take care of this ground, and let as many glad imaginations throng to it as possible. Read the magical works of the poets, and they will come' (p. 187). Where the Lake Poets' notion of the imagination was (in the end) religious, Hunt's was recreational, with him seeing it, above all, as a form of healthful exercise. Hence the striking equivalence, in his mind, between weekend walks and imaginative fictions; hence also his sense that one did not need to own a particular plot of land to creatively colonize it. 'It is not mere words', he wrote, in 'On the Realities of the Imagination', 'to say that he who goes through a rich man's park, and sees things in it which never bless the mental eyesight of the possessor, is richer than he' (p. 187).

A decade-and-a-half later, in the pages of another short-lived periodical, Hunt was still making the connection between the recreational imagination and the suburbs, only this time the emphasis was less on the 'nests and bowers' that had seemed so attractive in 1820 and more on the open ground of the suburban country houses. 'The *London Journal*', he announced, 'is a sort of park for rich and poor; for the reflecting and the well intentioned of all sorts; where every one can be alone, or in company, as he thinks fit, and see, with his mind's eye, a succession of Elysian sights.'[33] Not that he had completely forgotten the old tea-gardens; indeed he was to return to them, most memorably, in an article for the *Journal* called 'Sunday in the Suburbs', which was first published in March 1835. What is most fascinating about this vignette, I think, is the way in which Hunt tries to represent this space sympathetically, as a sort of contingent landing-stage of the cultural imagination, a stepping-stone on the road to something better:

> Meanwhile, we who are old enough to consult our inclination in preference to our grandeur, turn into the tea-gardens, where there is no tea going forward, and not much garden, but worlds of beer, and tobacco-pipes, and alcoves; and in a corner behind some palings there is (we fear) a sound of skittles. May no clergyman hear it, who is twisting his thumbs, or listening to the ring of his wine glasses. How hot the people look! How unpinned the goodly old dames! How tired, yet untired, the children! And how each alcove opens upon you as you pass, with its talk, smoke, beer and bad paint! Then what a feast to their eyes is the grass-plat! Truly, without well knowing it, do they sit down almost as much to the enjoyment of that green table of Nature's in the midst of them, as to their tobacco and 'half-and-half'. It is something which they do not see all the rest of the week; the first bit of grass, of any size, which they come to from home; and here they stop and are content. For our parts, we wish they would go further … and get fairly out in the fields; but they will do that, as they get freer, and wiser, and more comfortable, and learn to know and love what the wild-flowers have to say to them. At present how should they be able to hear those small angelic voices, when their ears are ringing with stocking-frames and crying children, and they are but too happy in their tired-heartedness to get to the first bit of holiday ground they can reach?[34]

The narrator's class status – his 'grandeur' – would seem to argue against him entering the tea-garden, but it is his 'inclination' (which is also perhaps a leaning towards his own Cockney roots) that wins the day. What follows is highly characteristic. Other periodical writers visiting the tea-gardens tended to express a kind of consternation at what they saw before them. In his 1822 essay on the subject, Cyrus Redding observed that 'English people, of a certain class in particular, have a strange method of pleasure taking. Nothing could be more extraordinary than their sullenness and stiff unbending manner on such occasions'.[35] But Hunt made a point of empathizing with these hard-working Londoners flopping down at 'the first bit of holiday ground they can reach'. He also expressed a blithe confidence in their status as incipient adventurers, fellow travellers, people on the move. And if there is something undeniably patronizing about the tone in which his final prediction is couched, there is also something rather patient and optimistic too, as he imagines social and cultural improvement in terms of a slow voyage out.

When Hunt embarked upon the *London Journal*, he had moved away from political journalism; 'recreational writing' (as I have dubbed it) now occupied most of his time. Nor, he insisted, was this a species of backsliding on his part; it was simply that, with the constitutional reforms of the late 1820s and early 1830s – the Great Reform Act, Catholic Emancipation, the repeal of the Test and Corporation Acts – he felt that all the really big battles had been won. Sentiments such as these, in the very decade that saw the rise of Chartism, reveal the limits of Hunt's middle-class liberalism. Where his progressive tendencies did continue, however, was in his continuing aspiration to educate and elevate the Cockney classes. Some members of this stratum had been given the vote in the Reform Act of 1832, some had not, but the crucial consideration from our point of view is that, as before, it was still a class hovering on the edge of legitimacy, placed in that ambiguous realm between the middle and working ranks. What this meant in practice was that at the very moment when the proletariat proper was beginning to develop a sense of itself as a corporate constituency, the lower middle class, as a class, was still only a collection of individuals. It was a stratum, moreover, that always seemed to be looking beyond itself for aspiration and inspiration; its attentions invariably fixed either above or below. It is for this reason, I think, that Hunt's 'inclination' took him back to the old suburban tea-gardens – not because they were solely populated by the lower middle class, but because they offered such a vivid and concrete embodiment of that class's condition. To him it seemed the most natural thing in the world that the Cockney would want to escape this realm, and its cramped community, in favour of the open fields of the private imagination, where one could 'learn to know and love what the wild-flowers have to say'. It was the *London Journal*'s task, therefore, to offer a kind of brochure for this realm of immortality, by allowing its readers to sample some of the 'Elysian sights' on offer. There is, of course, a double sense at work here. On a literal level, the journey that Hunt is offering his Cockney readership is one of pure imaginative self-fulfilment, but what was already clear enough, even from an 1830s perspective, was that this could also be seen as an allegory for social ascent.

RECREATIONAL FANCY

The most notable peopling of a suburban landscape with sylvans and fairies in Hunt's early career had been in a poem called 'The Nymphs', which first appeared in *Foliage* in 1818. This piece was, in effect, an inventory of the various orders of nymphs that its narrator was fortunate enough to come across while wandering in a non-specific (but recognizably Hampstead-like) setting:

> Arrived! Arrived! O shady spots of ground,
> What calmness ye strike round

...
O ye whom ancient wisdom, in its graces,
Made guardians of these places;
Etherial human shapes, perhaps the souls
Of poets and poetic women, staying
To have their fill of pipes and leafy playing.[36]

The poet lists his nymphs, some of whom have a distinctly erotic charge, in terms of where they live and what they represent; he even invents a new set – the Nepheliads – whose purpose it is to protect the rain clouds. In the conclusion to the poem, this 'fair blooming throng' enlist the poet to 'go tell our song | To such as hang their pale home-withered heads | For winter-time, and do our kindness wrong' (p. xxxvi).

Appearing at the height of the 'Cockney School' controversy, 'The Nymphs' was widely reviewed in the periodicals of the day. A number of critics commented on the peculiar fluency and effervescence of Hunt's verse, and the emphasis on health and pleasure was also remarked upon. But because Hunt had used the collection's Preface to extol paganism at the expense of that 'unnattractive creed', Christianity, many of the critics of the day felt obliged to tackle the poem's use of mythology. As might have been expected, the *Quarterly Review* devoted most of its review to defending the faith, while the *New Monthly* baulked instead at Hunt's imitation of the classics: 'Mr. Hunt is in a state of miserable delusion', it spluttered, 'if he conceives he bears any resemblance to those lofty spirits of the "olden time," who were the demigods of poetry.'[37] The most suggestive response, however, was in the *Eclectic Review*. 'The Nymphs', it decided, was an 'elegant mistake', because the mind rejects the absurdity of 'second hand legends' being passed off for 'grave matters of fact'. The reviewer then went on to quote a long section of Wordsworth's *Excursion* in order to show what a properly historicized attitude to classical paganism would look like, and argued that while 'no one can doubt that the author of these lines feels and appreciates all the beauties of classical fable', he still approaches them as the 'fictions of a remote superstition'. In Hunt's case, however, such was the earnestness with which he had thrown himself into his supernatural encounters that the final effect was as degrading as it was absurd: 'Those beautiful mythological personages, dissociated from the circumstances which lent them a sort of credibility, and brought out of their obscurity into broad day, suffer much the same degrading violence as the marble majesties of Greece, when torn from their climate and their pedestals, to form the unimpressive ranks of a museum.'[38] Not for the first time, Hunt is seen as an emblem for all that is most pretentious and hollow about modern metropolitan culture, with the *Eclectic*'s reviewer seeing an unfortunate kinship between Hunt's nymphs and the deracinated statues in the new British Museum. It is significant too that, reading between the lines, these statues show every sign of being placed in a fundamentally lower-middle-class predicament, doomed as they are to hover in 'unimpressive ranks', together and yet apart, in a kind of abstraction that is at once vulgar and improbable. And this class element to the *Eclectic*'s critique is further reinforced a few sentences later when the reviewer makes one further, pointed attempt to resituate Hunt's mythological reveries in a particular social setting. Noticing a 'distressing cockneyism in the poet's ideas of the beautiful in scenery', he insists that the 'Tea-Gardens' are the true origin of his '"fair-limbed nymphs" and deities', noting their generous provision of such figures 'in marble, wood, and lead' (p. 493).

What this criticism taps into, of course, is a growing set of polite prejudices surrounding Cockney tea-gardens, their thin fictiveness, their sexual licentiousness and their absurd semi-genteel ambitions. 'The Nymphs', it was suggested, was a product of exactly the same atmosphere: it was a pretentious daydream, a sly romp, a little five-finger exercise in mythological make-believe. The truth was, however, that Hunt was actually rather serious about ancient mythology; it wasn't, for him (as some critics have tended to assume), merely a masquerade to enable him to write more freely about nature and sexuality.

Two years after *Foliage*, Hunt wrote a piece for *The Indicator* on the 'Spirit of the Ancient Mythology', in which he questioned the modern presumption that the ancients had regarded their fables 'in the same poetical light as ourselves'. The greater likelihood, he said, was that 'the people in general were strong upon points of faith'.[39] 'The ordinary run of pagans', he continued, 'were perhaps more impressed with a sense of the invisible world, in consequence of the very visions presented to their imagination, than the same description of men under a more shadowy system' (by which he meant Christianity).

> There is the same difference between the two things, as between a populace believing in fairies, and a populace not believing. The latter is in the high road to something better, if not drawn aside into new terrors on the one hand, or mere worldliness on the other. But the former is led to look out of the mere worldly common-places about it, twenty times to the other's once. (p. 115)

Several of Hunt's contemporaries had become fascinated by the duality at the heart of classical paganism, the fact that it could simultaneously permit the development of a kind of forward-looking rational religion in the social elite while also continuing to permit all kinds of old-style animism in the populace. In his *Essay on the Mysteries of Eleusis*, which had been translated into English in 1817, Sergei Ouvaroff had presented the famous Eleusinian shows as the primary manifestations of this double doctrine. The main purpose of these shows, he suggested, had been to reveal to the chosen few the hidden truths of nature (which had probably been the fundamental unity of God and the immortality of the soul). But by cloaking these revelations in ritual secrecy the mysteries had also succeeded in protecting the beliefs of the unenlightened masses. There was a certain liberalism, as well as pragmatism, in this rationing of the truth, and the shows were, to this degree, entirely representative of the broader faith they served. For 'the grand principle on which polytheism rested', as James Christie reiterated in his 'Observations' on Ouvaroff's *Essay*, 'was the admission of all religious ideas'.[40]

It was the proto-Christian element in classical paganism that was the main preoccupation for many mythographers and freemasons of the period – the hidden seed of modern-day monotheism that was being secretly nurtured at Eleusis. But Hunt was as interested in the popular, benighted side of pagan belief as he was in its more forward-looking elements. 'The greatest pleasure arising to a modern imagination from the ancient mythology', he wrote, 'is in a mingled sense of the old popular belief and of the philosophical refinements upon it' (p. 114–5). However progressive it was, in the long run, not to believe in fairies, in the short term, he was convinced, it must have been much more interesting to do so, because such belief was committed to seeking the invisible through the visible, and the ideal through the real. 'Every forest, to the mind's eye of a Greek, was haunted with superior intelligences', he wrote, 'every stream had its presiding nymph, who was thanked for the draught of water' (p. 114). Purely as an imaginative habit, this all-embracing faith seemed far preferable to the 'over-refining followers of Plato' on the one hand, and the slaves of materialism on the other, 'who measured everything according to their own vain and petty standard'.

Untroubled by paganism's status as a historical dead-end, what Hunt saw in it was a glorious sceptical pluralism that tolerated all things. In 1817, the year before *Foliage* was published, S. T. Coleridge had made a distinction in his *Biographia Literaria* between the Imagination, which was the truly divine and creative faculty within man, and the Fancy, which was 'no other than a mode of memory emancipated from the order of time and space'. The Imagination, Coleridge argued, 'dissolves, diffuses, dissipates, in order to re-create; or where this is impossible, yet still, at all events, it struggles to idealize and unify'. 'Fancy', on the other hand, 'has no other counters to play with but fixities and definites.'[41] What Coleridge kept proposing at various points in this book was, in effect, a class distinction within the creative faculty, with the Imagination being accorded a spiritual and moral seriousness that was far beyond the reach of the cribb'd and confin'd Fancy. For the Fancy, in his formulation, was forever hamstrung by 'as ifness', a faculty seemingly given over to artificiality and bad faith. Such demarcations made no sense to the imaginative pagan in Hunt. Recognizing that the imagination might have different modes of operation, he was nevertheless uninterested in Coleridge's philosophical and moral distinctions, and unwilling to condemn the fancy for its self-consciously make-believe character. 'The essence of poetical enjoyment', he wrote in a review of Keats in 1820, 'does not consist in belief, but in a voluntary power to imagine.'[42] It was creative exercise, and not epistemology, that was the crucial concern. It is for this reason, I think, that the conservative critics were right to think of Hunt as the Cockney poet par excellence, for what was evident from his critical pronouncements was that in his theory of the relationship between nature and the imagination, there was no such thing as false consciousness.

KEATS'S SUBURBAN YEARNINGS

In the fourth of *Blackwood's Magazine's* 'Cockney School' articles, dated August 1818, satirical attention had been switched from Hunt to Keats, one of the former's young protégés, much trumpeted in *The Examiner* a couple of years before.[43] The attack by 'Z.' delved deep into the early modern stereotype of the Cockney as a cock's egg, a mother's darling, a sickly and pampered child. He represented Keats as a victim, both of the current mania for writing poetry ('metromanie', as he called it) and, more specifically, of the deleterious influence of Leigh Hunt. 'Mr Keats has adopted the loose, nerveless versification, and Cockney rhymes of the poet of Rimini', Z. pointed out, 'but in fairness to that gentleman, we must confess that the defects of the system are tenfold more conspicuous in his disciple's work than in his own'.[44] Keats was, it seems, a living symbol of Cockneyism as a disease of incongruous, absurd ambition; he was the epitome of the metropolitan miscreant. He should have been satisfied with his condition as a 'bound apprentice to a worthy apothecary in town', the inference was, but dreams of classical antiquity and poetic immortality had turned his head disastrously. 'The phrenzy of the "Poems" was bad enough in its way', Z. opined, with mock concern, 'but it did not alarm us half so seriously as the calm, settled, imperturbable drivelling idiocy of "Endymion" ' (p. 519).

Hunt had always professed to be unconcerned about the 'Cockney School' attacks, in spite of the fact that, as he himself admitted, they did indeed 'frighten the booksellers' in 1817–18 and wrought considerable damage on his subsequent career. Notwithstanding all this, he was to insist in his *Autobiography* of 1850 that 'the jests about Londoners and cockneys did not affect me in the least … They might as well have said that Hampstead was not beautiful, or Richmond lovely; or that Chaucer and Milton were cockneys when they went out of London to lie on the grass and look at the daisies'.[45] In his 'Literary Reminiscences' of 1839, Thomas Hood had taken a similarly robust line on the matter, arguing that

> a literary man should exult rather than otherwise that he first saw the light – or perhaps the fog – in the same metropolis as Milton, Gray, De Foe, Pope, Byron, Lamb, and other town-born authors, whose fame has nevertheless triumphed over the Bills of Mortality. In such a goodly company I cheerfully take up my livery; and especially as Cockneyism, properly so called, appears to be confined to no particular locality or station in life.[46]

There was no metropolitan monopoly on cocky provincialism, Hood argued, it was a feature of everyone from London to Orkney.

Hood and Hunt could be playful and combative on the Cockney issue. But in Keats's case the issue was more sensitive. Of all the liberal writers on the receiving end of class criticism in this period, he was the one who most resembled the twentieth-century idea of a Cockney. The son of a stable-keeper at a coaching inn on the edge of the City, Keats lived on Cheapside and in the Borough in the 1810s before moving out to be near Hunt in Hampstead. He felt his social origins acutely, in a way that his mentor, who was the son of a clergyman, did not. Where Hunt was blithe and insouciant about class, Keats was proud and defensive; it is therefore hardly surprising that he took the Cockney attacks to heart. So much so, indeed, that when he died of tuberculosis in Rome in 1821, a tradition quickly grew up among his friends that it was the bad reviews that had killed him. Hazlitt was to rehearse this line in a number of his *Table-Talks* of the 1820s,[47] as too, to a lesser extent, did Shelley and Hunt.

Z. saw many of the same attitudes to nature and to classical culture in Keats as in Hunt, but with the former he was, if anything, even more withering. Reflecting on Hunt's praise of his young charges at the expense of some of the established poets of the eighteenth century, Lockhart was to rail against those 'fanciful dreaming tea-drinkers' whose poetry was full of 'descriptions of flowers seen in window-pots, or cascades heard at Vauxhall'.[48] Z. was right to point out that much of Keats's poetry, whether contemporary or classical in setting, did always seem to be set in some form of suburban retreat, garden or bower. In 'Sleep and Poetry' (1816), the young man's first great statement of poetic faith, he had written of 'bowery nooks' and 'my fire-side' as the two great training-grounds of his creativity, spaces from which he would eventually grow 'wings to find out an immortality'. Bowers are here imagined as a kind of provisional platform of the imagination, and that is indeed the way in which they tend to function in his work. So too pleasure-grounds, as we can see from *Endymion*, whose epic story of ardent aspirations and immortal longings begins at an outdoor festival. The spectacle at the centre of Book I is of young people, playing, singing and dancing; the setting is classical antiquity, though with some suspiciously Cockney touches:

> High genitors, unconscious did they cull
> Time's sweet first-fruits – they danced to weariness,
> And then in quiet circles did they press
> The hillock turf, and caught the latter end
> Of some strange history, potent to send
> A young mind from its bodily tenement.
> Or they might watch the quoit-pitchers, intent
> On either side; pitying the sad death
> Of Hyacinthus, when the sacred breath
> Of Zephyr slew him, – Zephyr penitent,
> Who now, ere Phoebus mounts the firmament,
> Fondles the flower amid the sobbing rain.[49]

Just as Leigh Hunt, in his 1819 poem 'Hero and Leander', had made a point of reminding his readers that 'Sweet Hero's eyes, three thousand years ago, | Were made precisely like the best we know',[50] so too Keats, in his first classical narrative, does all he can to establish a sense of 'social genealogy'. The young people dancing on the lawns of Latmos are 'high genitors' in that they are a great race 'whose children's children bred | Thermopylae its heroes', but also in the more general sense of being a historically distant generation that nevertheless displays a striking family relationship to the present. There is a semi-deliberate blend, here, of sameness with difference, which generates an unusual, incongruous effect. The key detail, the Cockney detail, if you like, is the reference to quoit-pitching, which whisks us immediately away from the plains of antiquity and into the pleasure-gardens of Clerkenwell. In his *Bygone Pleasures of*

London, W. S. Scott has written of how in the suburban tea-gardens, of a Sunday, 'skittles and quoits, accompanied, of course, with pipes and tobacco, offered their fascinations to the male customers; while the ladies and juveniles were beguiled with cakes and ale, tea and shrimps, strawberries and cream, syllabubs and junkets, swings and mazes, lovers's walks and woodbine bowers'.[51]

On further reflection, however, it is not perhaps the quoit-playing per se that creates the Cockney effect, but rather its sudden, curious juxtaposition with the tragic story of Hyacinthus, who had died after being hit by a discus, which even in the poem's own terms seems strikingly juvenile and jarring (although a certain callowness may be exactly the effect Keats is seeking here, given the nature of the subject matter). Whether one likes it or not, what this technique does achieve is a kind of historical double vision, as we flicker uncertainly between the ancient and the modern. Disconcerting as this can be, it is also thrillingly immediate; it makes us feel the past as a fleetingly familiar presence. Conservative critics were not impressed, however, and indeed all that *Blackwood's* could see in the poem was bad costume and vulgar feeling:

> His Endymion is not a Greek shepherd, loved by a Greek goddess; he is merely a young Cockney rhymester, dreaming a fantastic dream at the full of the moon. Costume, were it worth while to notice such a trifle, is violated in every page of this goodly octavo. From his prototype Hunt, John Keats has acquired a sort of vague idea, that the Greeks were a most tasteful people, and that no mythology can be so finely adapted for the purposes of poetry as theirs.[52]

Critics are always discovering new niceties in the Hunt–Keats relationship, and it remains, to that extent, a very rich subject, but the broad truth remains that Keats *does* write like Hunt's disciple. Though a far greater poet than his mentor, Keats did owe a lot to his example, most notably in terms of the freedom and suppleness of his tone, his versification, and his handling of classical subjects. What is more, Keats also inherited from Hunt a deep interest in themes of self-education and escape, and like his mentor could not help thinking of the voyage out into the suburbs as the imagination's *Gradus ad Parnassum*. But where Hunt, for the most part, will simply pontificate on this subject (as in his article for the *London Journal*), Keats habitually writes like an ardent and anxious inquirer.

Keats's fixation is on immortality, whether conceived in personal, poetic terms, or in the terms of classical mythology. *Endymion*, *Hyperion* and *The Fall of Hyperion* are all about mortals ascending to the realm of godhood; 'Ode to a Nightingale', 'Ode to Psyche' and 'Ode on a Grecian

Urn' all describe the poet's own yearnings for a realm of timeless, deathless, eternal beauty. 'Immortality' is a multivalent term in these poems. It is a way of thinking about life and death, art and posterity, romantic longing and its fulfilment; but it is also, because of the way in which the poetry situates itself, an issue of social and geographical mobility. Keats's poems are often prompted by settings that serve to encourage pleasure, ambition and imaginative longing while also tending to defer it, distance it, and throw it off into the future. They do take place, to that extent, in the equivalent of a Cockney tea-garden: a space of precarious promise that is always understood to be a kind of halfway house to somewhere else. In *Endymion*, the poem begins on the open lawns of a popular festival before moving on, in Book II, to a secluded, enchanted bower, the place where Endymion's journey towards immortality will begin in earnest. In the opening stanza of the 'Ode to a Nightingale', the poet describes how the sound of distant birdsong has aroused a peculiar kind of drowsy numbness and heartache within him, while insisting at the same time that this feeling is about satiety, not envy:

> 'Tis not through envy of thy happy lot,
> But being too happy in thine happiness, -
> That thou, light-winged Dryad of the trees,
> In some melodious plot
> Of beechen green and shadows numberless,
> Singest of summer in full-throated ease.[53]

Hunt must have had this stanza in mind when in his 1835 article, 'Sunday in the Suburbs', he said of the vast army of tea-garden Cockneys that they were 'but too happy in their tired-heartedness to get to the first bit of holiday ground they can reach'. Try as he might, however, the poet of the 'Ode' cannot help aspiring further, pulled on by, and towards, the nightingale's 'melodious plot'. Quite soon, too, this desire becomes identified with a powerful wish to escape from the everyday sites of human misery 'Where youth grows pale, and spectre-thin, and dies; | Where but to think is to be full of sorrow | And leaden-eyed despairs'. Eschewing the lures of wine, the poet finally chooses poetry as his transport – and within an instant begins to feel himself in fancy's own true bower:

> Already with thee! tender is the night,
> And haply the Queen-Moon is on her throne,
> Cluster'd around by all her starry Fays;
> But here there is no light,

> Save what from heaven is with the breezes blown
> Through verdurous glooms and winding mossy ways.

'Arrived! Arrived!' the poet narrator of 'The Nymphs' had blurted out, after a similar transport, at the very beginning of Hunt's poem of the previous year, 'Nymphs of all names, and woodland Geniuses, | I see you, here and there, among the trees'.[54] But what differentiates Keats from Hunt at such moments is how hard the former presses his escapist fantasies, and how bravely he faces their inevitable disappointment. In the case of the 'Ode to a Nightingale', it is not merely that the vision is a transitory one, with the last stanza famously lamenting that 'The fancy cannot cheat so well | As she is famed to do, deceiving elf'. It is also that the final destination of the imagination, in its very desperation to go through and beyond death, turns out to be a landscape markedly inhuman and agoraphobic. It is a vision of 'magic casements, opening on the foam | Of perilous seas, in faery lands forlorn'. In Virgil's *Aeneid*, Book VI, immortality was represented by the warm, open fields of Elysium; but in the 'Ode to a Nightingale', as in the 'Ode on a Grecian Urn', it is a very cold realm in comparison, however much the poet still seems hooked on reaching it.

Keats puts extraordinary pressure on the idea, familiar in Hunt already, of poetry itself functioning as a kind of 'melodious plot' or space of recreation in its own right. In the 'Ode to a Nightingale', for instance, 'poesy' can readily be interpreted as a synonym for the Imagination in its most general terms – the High Romantic meaning it carries in both Hazlitt's 'On Poetry in General' (1818) and Shelley's *Defence of Poetry* (1819). But 'poesy' can also refer to the simple printed product – the words on the page. One of the things that makes the imaginative journey in the 'Ode to a Nightingale' so vivid and so involving is that it takes place in real time, while we are reading the poem, so that it feels like a dramatic soliloquy. Any reader encountering the poem for the first time in the first edition of 1820 would follow the poet to the Nightingale's realm of song on page 109 and then, on turning the leaf, stumble suddenly upon the lines, 'I cannot see what flowers are at my feet | Nor what soft incense hangs upon the boughs'. There is a powerful, double sense at work in moments such as this. In one way, of course, the flowers cannot be seen simply because the imagined landscape is so dark ('But here there is no light', etc.). But the other, more potent reason why they cannot be seen is because their only real existence is on the white sheet before us. That is their strength, that is their weakness; and to this degree the power of the poem as a whole comes directly from its identification of the half-formed, intermediate landscape of the suburban garden with the heavily fetishized, infinitely deferred promise of poetic language itself.

There is a line of criticism, begun by Byron in the 1820s and then developed with considerable theoretical sophistication by Marjorie Levinson in the late 1980s, which sees Keats's poetry as being essentially masturbatory in nature, the product of an imagination that is in some fatal sense self-pleasuring and self-cancelling, unconsciously committed to delay and deferral. In Levison's view:

> Keats's poetry was at once a tactical activity, or an escape route from an actual life, and a final construction: the concrete imaginary to that apparitional actual. What was, initially, a substitute *for* a grim life became for Keats a substitute life: a real life of substitute things – simulacra – which, though they do not nourish, neither do they waste.[55]

There is clearly a good deal in this, although the terms in which these observations have been couched may want breadth and understanding. One way of interpreting the agoraphobia at the end of the 'Ode to a Nightingale', for example, would be to see it as reflecting some of the great fears Keats seems to have had about 'coming out into the open', either as a lover or as a poet. David Trotter has written brilliantly about paranoia and agoraphobia as conditions endemic to the modern freelance writer as he or she tries to forge a career outside of conventional institutions or professional markers.[56] Seen from this perspective, 'immortality' in Keats might be seen as a figure for that kind of public life which is simultaneously a consummation devoutly to be wished (the Elysian fields of eternal fame) and a cold, dead, all-too-exposed realm ultimately to be shied away from (the barren hillside of personal and professional disappointment).

One of the strengths of Levinson's line is that it finds a link between the rich but often inconclusive manner of Keats's poetry and his all-too-evident class anxieties. What it doesn't do is generalize them. To a greater extent than even Levinson is willing to recognize, Hunt and Keats's vision is a vision of the future of modern culture, is our vision. This is not merely because so many of us, nowadays, have either chosen, or been forced, to live in suburbs. It is also true in a more general sense as well. What Hunt and Keats do is reveal a socio-geographical context to Romantic longing, they give it a setting, and this setting is, pre-eminently, that of the metropolitan miscreant who hovers perpetually between freedom and bondage, work and home, country and city. There is an important sense in which we cannot diagnose Hunt and Keats without also diagnosing ourselves, for nowadays we are all Cockneys.

'THE NURTURE OF TRIPTOLEMUS'

In *The Indicator* No. 9, 'More News of Ulysses', Hunt had argued that it was the privilege of great poets to supplement ancient myths: 'Talking the other day with a friend [which he later identified as Keats] about Dante, he observed, that whenever so great a poet told us anything in addition or continuation of an ancient story, he had a right to be regarded as a classical authority.'[57] In the fiftieth issue of *The Indicator*, which came out on 20 September 1820, Hunt was to accord himself the same privilege, freely translating a particularly intriguing classical narrative. The story was entitled 'The Nurture of Triptolemus' and was based on a few highly diverting but also divergent scraps in Pseudo-Apollodorus, Hyginus and Ovid. It tells of how the goddess Ceres, while wandering in search of Proserpina, is welcomed and taken in by the citizens of Eleusis, a suburb of Athens, and how they seek to console her for the loss of her daughter. The son of the king of Eleusis is a youth named Triptolemus, a great spirit trapped in an ailing body, who has come to be regarded with great envy by those 'who were interested in being thought wiser'.[58] Triptolemus greets Ceres's arrival 'with a pleasure that overcame him like pain', feeling that 'some extraordinary good' was now approaching; but inwardly he cannot help grieving that he will probably not live to see it (pp. 393–5).[59]

When Ceres is informed of Triptolemus's sickness, she immediately takes him under her wing, nursing him privately in the temple attached to the palace. The young boy goes from strength to strength, and starts accruing some of the attributes of a demi-god, but one night a servant hears terrifying screams coming from the temple. Overheard exchanges between Ceres and Triptolemus make clear that the goddess is slowly initiating the boy into immortality, with his body being put through the most terrible ordeals while his spirit closes in on godhead. Finally, his mother can endure it no longer and rushes into the temple, only to be confronted by the spectacle of her son, prostrate on a bed of burning coals 'with a face of bright agony' (p. 397). The effect is instantaneous: Ceres calls off the trial immediately, and the shock proves too much for the king and queen, who die shortly afterwards. Immortality is no longer open to Triptolemus – at least not in his present form – his mother's mortal timidity has ruined that opportunity. '"Oh Fear! what does thou not do! Oh my all but divine boy," continued [Ceres], "now plunged again into physical darkness, thou canst not do good so long as thou wouldst have done, but thou shalt have a life almost as long as the commonest sons of men, and a thousand times more useful and glorious"' (p. 397).

Triptolemus's consolation is to be the man who introduces agriculture to mankind: 'Ceres gave him the first seeds of the corn that makes bread', Hunt writes, 'and sent him in her chariot round the world to teach men how to use it. "I am not immortal myself," said he, "but let the good I do be so, and I shall yet die happy"' (p. 397).

Allegorically, the story of Triptolemus was closely related to the larger message of the Ceres–Proserpina myth, to which it functioned as a kind of supplement. The reason that Proserpina is lost to Ceres is because she has been abducted by Pluto, the king of the underworld, but in the conclusion to the story an agreement is struck between Ceres and Pluto that they will each have her for six months of the year; hence the spring, which is the goddess's celebration of the return of her daughter, hence also the cycle of death and rebirth at the heart of the seasons. The compromise between Ceres and Triptolemus runs on similar lines: the immortal realm is barred to him, but he is allowed to become mankind's immortal benefactor, the seeds he spreads being subject to death and yet also the source of perpetual renewal. In Hunt's rendering, the young boy cannot help retaining 'a certain melancholy' from his near-divine recollections, but we are also told that 'it did not hinder him from sowing joy wherever he went' (p. 397). Both stories are thus, in a sense, 'paradise lost' narratives, two different but related versions of the fortunate fall.

There is a seasonal element to 'The Nurture of Triptolemus', as there was to many of Hunt's *Indicator* essays. The Ceres and Proserpina story was the core myth upon which the Eleusinian mysteries had been based, and there was a strong connection between these mysteries and the autumnal equinox, which was when they had traditionally been performed. For James Christie, author of the *Disquisition upon Etruscan Vases Displaying Their Probable Connection With the Shows at Eleusis* of 1806, their main function had been to teach the immortality of the soul, 'though imperfectly, by analogous reasoning from observations upon the vicissitudes of nature'. Comparing them to the Hindu festival of Diwali, which also took place in the autumn, Christie argued that 'the object of these nightly shows, was chiefly to display nature resuscitated, generally by means of some vivifying gift'.[60] One of the most influential commentators on the story was the English Platonist Thomas Taylor, who had written of Ceres's attempts to recover Proserpina as an allegory for the strivings of the intellect to rescue the soul from the corruptions of the body (for him, the underworld always represented the corporeal life). The related story of Ceres giving the gift of agriculture to the Eleusinians was a further elaboration of this same idea: 'As the art of tillage, therefore, and particularly the plantation of corn, becomes the greatest possible benefit to our sensible life, no symbol can more aptly represent the unparalleled advantages arising from the evolution and procession of intellect with its divine nature into a corporeal life.'[61] In theory, Hunt was in favour of such formulations, and of any model that saw proofs of the immortality of the soul amid nature's seasonal changes. This can be seen from 'November', one of a series of little essays on the months that he produced in 1819 for *The Examiner* (and which was later reproduced en masse in his popular *Literary Pocket-Book* of 1819. 'In no system', Hunt asserted boldly, 'is there really any such thing as death. All is but change and vitality. We become either spiritual essences, or new physical beings, or rather both; and, with November's leave, if Pythagoras did not shrink from the idea of becoming a bird, we do not see why Tomkins should be so fastidious.'[62] This last touch, it hardly needs saying, is characteristically facetious and jarring. Diminutive surnames like Tomkins, Larkins and Pipkins were often used to refer to stereotypical Cockneys in this period, placing a more or less conscious emphasis on the unfledg'd nature of the lower middle class.[63] But the first part of the quotation betrays a neo-Shelleyan intensity.

A similarly earnest tone is adopted in 'The Nurture of Triptolemus' when Ceres starts teaching the boy how to see nature through the eyes of an immortal. But in this case I think we can feel the presence of an intriguing Romantic irony, as Hunt's inner resistance to philosophical over-refinement (expressed earlier in the 'Spirit of the Ancient Mythology' essay) is gradually brought to bear upon the narrative. What Ceres has to say to Triptolemus is not relayed to us directly, but emerges as mere scraps of dialogue overheard at the temple door by his anxious parents. 'Thou dost know', the goddess says, 'and thou knowest in the very heart of thy knowledge, which is in the sympathy of it and the love. Thou seest that difference is not difference, and yet is so; that the same is not the same, and yet must be; that what is, is but what we see, and as we see it; and yet that which we see, is' (p. 396). This is deliberately mysterious, as befits an immortal truth half-overheard by mere mortals. Of course, if we were forced to speculate, we might suggest that Ceres seems to be trying to teach her disciple something about the unity of God and nature and of subject and object, and certainly this does broadly tally with what Hunt himself had to say about the secrets of Eleusis when, in a brief reference to the matter in the fifteenth *Indicator*, he wrote that 'a system of refined theism is understood to have been taught to the initiated in the celebrated Mysteries'.[64] But I think the main point of this passage is that we are not supposed to be able to grasp its meaning, because such knowledge is, by definition, beyond our ken. There is something similarly vague about Triptolemus's final vision in the temple. On being confronted by it he immediately names it, with horror, as 'utmost deformity', only for Ceres to urge him 'in a soothing and earnest manner' to 'look again'. 'Oh my heart', he says, in sudden astonishment, 'they are perfect beauty and humanity'. 'They are only two of the same', the goddess replies, 'each going out of itself' (p. 397). To see what a goddess knows and feels, it is implied, is to glimpse the single soul animating and unifying nature, all deformity being nothing but an external imposition by the eye of cold 'analysis'; but once again this message is couched in a language so elusive and elliptical that it is anything but revelatory.

In 'Spirit of the Ancient Mythology', Hunt had written of the modern enjoyment of Greek myth being based on 'a mingled sense of the old popular belief and of the philosophical refinements upon it'. But what the dialogue of 'The Nurture of Triptolemus' really shows is that Hunt was actually much more interested in communicating the fixed fancies of paganism – the stories themselves – than he was in refining on them philosophically. Far from this being a weakness of the story, however, it actually feeds into its message. So cold and abstract does Ceres's immortal vision seem, in Hunt's rendering, that it cannot help strike us as no great loss when Triptolemus is deprived of it, which only goes to reinforce that reading of the story as an instructive, and in a sense fortunate, fall. Close as Triptolemus was to becoming a Coleridgean visionary, in the end this chilly realm is denied him, and what he becomes instead is that much more useful, if also more fragile thing, a popular disseminator, or spreader of seeds.

In the autumn of 1819 Hunt had used the launch of *The Indicator* and the 'Autumnal Commencement of Fires' as a means of recharging his private and poetic batteries. One year later and the revolution of the seasons had brought about another revolution in politics, with the Queen Caroline affair having replaced Peterloo as the main object of controversy. For Hunt, looking back upon the periodical's first year, it must have been difficult not to think of Shelley's 'Ode to the West Wind' – that revolutionary 'breath of Autumn's being' – and Keats's 'To Autumn', both products of the autumn of 1819 which had finally been harvested into print in August 1820. And with that his thoughts must also have turned to Keats's recent departure for Italy, an event that is commemorated in the short third article that concludes *Indicator* No. 50: 'Ah, dear friend, as valued a one as thou art a Poet, – John Keats, – we cannot, after all, find it in our heart to be glad, now thou art gone away with the swallows to seek a kindlier clime' (p. 399). Keats's health had taken an irrevocable turn for the worse in the spring and summer of 1820. In June he had been a patient of the Hunts in Kentish Town after a particularly nasty convulsion. That summer also saw the publication of the young poet's last collection, *Lamia, Isabella, The Eve of St. Agnes and Other Poems.* Very well received by the critics, on the whole, it was reviewed at length in *The Indicator* that August. In this review Hunt had made a point of introducing the 'Ode to a Nightingale' in particular as the foster-child of illness and the recent 'Cockney School' attacks.[65]

What was clear to Hunt in October 1820 was that the young poet, who had written of 'gathering swallows' the previous autumn, was now departing, like a swallow, perhaps never to return (in fact he was to be dead within four months). In 'To Autumn' Keats had famously refused to think of the songs of spring, 'think not of them, thou hast thy music too', and these melancholy, backward-looking lines may well have been in Hunt's mind when he looked forward to his young friend returning again in the following spring:

> But thou hast 'a mighty soul in a little body;' and the kind cares of the former for all about thee shall no longer subject the latter to the chance of impressions which it scorns, and the soft skies of Italy shall breathe balm upon it; and thou shalt return with thy friend the nightingale, and make all thy other friends as happy with thy voice as they are sorrowful to miss it. (pp. 399–400)

Such are the narrative and linguistic parallels between Keats's predicament, as represented here, and that of Triptolemus set forth a few pages earlier in *Indicator* No. 50, that it is very difficult not to see a Keatsian subtext to Hunt's classical story. Prior to 'To Autumn', Keats's attitude to immortality had been obsessive and agonized: his early *Endymion* had described the successful graduation of its shepherd-hero to becoming one of the gods, and the mature *Hyperion* had been all set to do the same for Apollo – except that the manuscript had broken off just at that excruciating, ecstatic moment when the new sun-god was about to enter into being. It is not easy to tell why Keats discontinued the poem at the very point when its hero was about to ascend from one class of being into another, but it is possible it may have been prompted as much by social as by literary anxiety. Perhaps when the time came to inhabit this butterfly moment, the Cockney caterpillar in him flinched in fear and loathing. Perhaps it is always thus with those who conceive of graduation as a profound and alienating metamorphosis. This episode of the poem was one of the few details in Keats's 1820 volume that Hunt had singled out for criticism, it having struck him 'that there is something too effeminate and human in the way in which Apollo receives the exaltation which his wisdom is giving him. He weeps and wonders somewhat too fondly'.[66]

Like Keats's Apollo, Hunt's Triptolemus is a fretful apprentice whose initiation is arrested at the last minute; and like the knight-at-arms in 'La Belle Dame sans Merci' he has 'a certain melancholy' for the Elysian realm he has left behind. But in the case of Hunt's hero, the fall from godhead does have positive, progressive consequences. The failed candidate becomes the practical benefactor of mankind. Such are the correspondences between Hunt's 'Nurture' and Keats's *Lamia, Isabella &c.* that it is impossible not to see it, on some level, as a message from the older poet to his ailing friend. Triptolemus, like Keats, is subject to widespread critical malignity; ultimately, however, he is the one chosen to be the instrument of Ceres. But if 'The Nurture' is in a sense about Keats it is also a corrective to him, for it is not a narrative of disappointment and detumescence of the kind that the younger man tended to favour. Quite the contrary, in fact: it is an allegory of the writer as failed visionary but successful liberal enabler. It is a blueprint for being a real Cockney author: 'Triptolemus, strong in body, cheerful to all in show, cheerful to himself in many things, retained, nevertheless, a certain melancholy from his recollections, but it did not hinder him from sowing joy wherever he went. It excited him but the more to do so. The success of others stood him instead of his own' (p. 397). That Hunt was more than usually preoccupied by seasonal thoughts when he was composing *Indicator* No. 50 is further suggested by the second of its three articles, a short essay called 'Return of Autumn'. The essayist begins as if writing a private diary entry: 'The autumn is now confirmed. The harvest is over; the summer birds are gone or going; heavy rains have swept the air of its warmth, and prepared the earth for the impressions of winter' (p. 398). He is reminded that he had begun the first volume of *The Indicator* in the same season – September 1819, exactly one year before. The article then takes a deliberately fanciful turn, with Hunt suddenly taking it upon himself to imagine Nature as if he were a waiter at an unnamed holiday resort proudly offering up his seasonal bill of fare: 'Imagine us seated at the bar of a fashionable harbour [Hunt changed this to 'retreat' in *The Seer* of 1840], or boxed in a sylvan scene of considerable resort. Enter, a waiter, the September of Spenser, – that ingenious and … oddly dressed rogue … "Heavy laden with the spoil | Of harvest's riches, which he made his boot."' The charms of autumn are then offered to the reader precisely as if they were the goods and shows on offer at a Cockney tea-garden:

> … Cyder and Perry.
> Arbours of ivy, wild honey-suckle, arbutus, &c. all in flower.
> Other flowers on table.
> The ante-room, with a view into it, immense, with a sky-blue cupola, and hung round with landscapes confessedly inimitable.
> Towards the conclusion, a vocal concert among the trees.
> At night, falling stars, and a striking panoramic view of the heavens; on which occasion, for a few nights only, the same moon will be introduced, that was admired by the 'immortal Shakespeare!!!'
> N.B. It is reported by some malignant persons, that the bird-concert is not artificial: whereas it will be found, upon the smallest inspection, to beat even the most elaborate inventions of the justly admired Signor Mecanical Fello. (p. 399)

The proximity of this piece to 'The Nurture' is very striking and suggestive, for just as in that story Triptolemus was invited by Ceres to throw off the eye of habit and 'look again' at the spectacle before him, so too in 'Return of Autumn' the Cockney consumer is invited to throw off his tea-garden tastes and open up to nature proper. Making fun of Londoners' characteristic preference for the artificial over the natural was very popular in this period. In May 1823 'Crockery Junior' had offered a different version of the same joke in a squib for the *Literary Chronicle* called 'Nature Outdone'. 'Winter has extended his "iron reign"', he said,

> and so prevented Dame Nature (all-bounteous as she is) from sending our buds and blossoms among us. But, really, we cockneys have but little to regret … thanks to the plastic hands of the artificial flower makers, and the unbounded beneficence of our haberdashers, milliners, and other shopkeepers, who make gay *parterres* of their windows, and so take away the necessity of gardens altogether.[67]

It is intriguing to see the King of the Cockneys indulging in this kind of satire, especially when we consider how close the tendencies he ridicules were to his own most notorious practices – his habit of collapsing the difference between interior and exterior, for example, as he had done in the Horsemonger Lane prison, and of using common experiences to bond with the 'immortal Shakespeare'. Perhaps the best way of thinking about 'Return to Autumn' is to consider it as an antidote to the solemn allegory of 'The Nurture of Triptolemus'. For in spite of Hunt's constant urging of his readers out onto 'the high road to something better', the cage of Cockney Fancy was still for him the place from which you started, and the place to which you might always have an 'inclination' to return.

CHAPTER 2

William Hazlitt and the periodical press

> I do not agree with Mr. *Blackwood* in his definition of the word *Cockney*. He means by it a person who has happened at any time to live in London, and who is not a Tory – I mean by it, a person who has never lived out of London, and who has got all his ideas from it.
>
> The true Cockney has never travelled beyond the purlieus of the Metropolis, either in the body or in the spirit. Primrose-hill is the Ultima Thule of his most romantic desires; Greenwich Park stands him in stead of the vales of Arcady. Time and space are lost to him. He is confined to one spot, and to the present moment. He sees everything near, superficial, little, in hasty succession. The world turns round, and his head with it, like a roundabout at a fair, till he becomes stunned and giddy with the motion. Figures glide by as in a *camera obscura*. There is a glare, a perpetual hubbub, a noise, a crowd about him; he sees and hears a vast number of things, and knows nothing. He is pert, raw, ignorant, conceited, ridiculous, shallow, contemptible. His senses keep him alive; and he knows, inquires, and cares for nothing farther. He meets the Lord Mayor's coach, and without ceremony treats himself to an imaginary ride in it … He is, in short, a great man by proxy, and comes so often in contact with fine persons and things, that he rubs off a little of the gilding, and is surcharged with a sort of second-hand, vapid, tingling, troublesome self-importance.[1]

In this extract from William Hazlitt's 'On Londoners and Country People', which was first published under the rubric of 'Table-Talk No. VII' in the *New Monthly Magazine* for August 1823, Cockneyism is defined as the tendency to confuse an acquaintance with London with a knowledge of the world. In Hazlitt's eyes, the Cockney interprets reality solely in terms of his own immediate surroundings; he has no sense either of process or perspective. Life, for him, is a perpetually entrancing, endlessly enveloping panorama of proximate sights and sounds. He is the epitome of all that Hazlitt hated about the Hartleyan philosophy in this respect:

he does not think, but simply picks up ideas by sympathetic vibration, reverberating with associations culled from his environment.[2] His brain contains a microcosm of the world, but one in which all the elements have been arbitrarily juxtaposed, like a wall of advertisements; yet such is the extent of the Cockney's false consciousness that he mistakes superficial acquaintance for proper knowledge. He believes himself the absolute master of his milieu, rather than its bewildered dupe: 'A real Cockney is the poorest creature in the world', Hazlitt writes, 'the most literal, the most mechanical, and yet he too lives in a world of romance – a fairy land of his own' (p. 172). Above all, he is a living embodiment of the principle that familiarity breeds contempt, priding himself on his status as a citizen of London, and yet despising all other distinctions: 'let him be as low as he will, he fancies he is as good as anybody else' (p. 171).

Presently Hazlitt fleshes out his caricature of Cockneyism with a series of concrete personifications:

> He is a shopman, and nailed all day behind the counter: but he sees hundreds and thousands of gay well-dressed people pass – an endless phantasmagoria – and enjoys their liberty and gaudy fluttering pride. He is a footman – but he rides behind beauty, through a crowd of carriages, and visits a thousand shops. Is he a tailor? The stigma on his profession is lost in the elegance of the patterns he provides, and of the persons he adorns; and he is something very different from a mere country botcher. (p. 172)

As this list continues Hazlitt proceeds to cast his net ever wider, bringing in barkers, slop-sellers, beggars and drabs, as if to make clear that there is no class monopoly on Cockney presumption. But the preponderant emphasis of 'On Londoners' is that Cockneyism is a semi-genteel phenomenon. What Hazlitt's foremost examples share, apart from boundless imagination and self-conceit, is a petit-bourgeois milieu. They all occupy that interstitial space between the polite realm of the bourgeoisie and the plebeian world of the urban working classes. In the 1810s and 1820s this space was becoming ever more densely populated by representatives of the new service industries, the scriveners, clerks, apprentices and shopkeepers of early industrial London. It is in this portion of society, Hazlitt suggests, that Cockneyism most regularly resides: it is the one that engages most energetically in fantasies of individual self-betterment; it is also the one that stands in the most tantalizing proximity to polite culture.

When Leigh Hunt had criticized the Londoner as a type, in his early *Indicator* article 'Country Houses Near Town', he had done so by representing him as a slave of Mammon, his confined nature being that of 'a complete, successful, flourishing, sophisticated money-getting animal'.[3]

In his view the only way to counteract this situation was to get out into the country and cultivate one's private imagination: the spirit of fancy was not the disease but the cure. The line that Hazlitt takes on the subject is very different from his friend's in this respect, for in spite of expressing his political opposition to 'Mr Blackwood' at the very beginning of the essay, deep down his conception of the Cockney seems very similar to J. G. Lockhart's own. Cockneyism, in this opening salvo at least, is all about false consciousness, and the terms in which the essayist chooses to describe it – with the true Londoner 'living in a world of romance – a fairy-land of his own' – cannot help but recall the work of Hunt and John Keats, his erstwhile literary allies, and the suburban landscapes they were forever 'peopling with sylvans and fairies'.[4] Admittedly, the tone of Hazlitt's critique was more playful than disdainful, but it was still a curious one to come from a radical liberal, and the question of what he thought he was doing writing an essay on this subject, and in this manner, is made all the more intriguing when we recall how often he himself had been lambasted as a Cockney.

Lockhart had started the 'Cockney School' attacks in 1817 for political reasons, but also to attract publicity for the strategic relaunch of *Blackwood's*, and in the years that followed this noisy controversy had become one of the key elements in the magazine's success, helping establish it as a lively and entertaining agent in the literary marketplace, while also offering an uncompromising statement of its core values. One of the most significant aspects of the series was that, even as he was engaging in a spate of probing and often rather personal diatribes, Lockhart, like many of his fellow *Blackwood's* contributors, insisted on preserving absolute anonymity, presenting himself only as 'Z.'. Maintaining an old-fashioned, gentlemanly mistrust for full-time professional literary journalism, he sought to keep his secret existence as a literary critic quite separate from his public identity as an Edinburgh lawyer, steadfastly refusing to reveal himself to his enemies. Not surprisingly, however, this was a source of great resentment to writers such as Hunt and Hazlitt, who both enjoyed and endured a much more transparent relationship with the reading public, regarding such manipulations of literary anonymity as a perpetuation of 'Old Corruption'. Notionally, the *Table-Talks* that appeared in the *New Monthly Magazine* were anonymous, but in practice there was no mystery at all surrounding their authorship. In the first place, 'Table-Talk' had become a personal trademark of Hazlitt's, especially after the publication of his two-volume collection *Table-Talk: Original Essays on Men and Manners* in 1822. Second, there were countless clues to the identity of their author in the essays themselves. In 'On Londoners', for example, the easayist says that if his readers want to know what he thinks of rural life they should consult *The Round Table*, volume II, page 116 – a publication that had already appeared under Hazlitt's own name. There is a sliding scale of anonymity in the periodical writing of this period: on the one hand, the well-kept secret of Z., on the other the comparative transparency of Hazlitt and Hunt, and even Charles Lamb's 'Elia'.

The purpose of the 'Cockney School' articles was to expose the *Examiner* set as a group of vain, vulgar and badly educated literary upstarts, producing work which was at once aesthetically embarrassing and morally corrupt. Hunt was the main object of Lockhart's scorn, for reasons that are fully explored in the Introduction, but Hazlitt always came a close second. In the review of *Table-Talk* that appeared in *Blackwood's* in August 1822, the way Hazlitt was described by the magazine was remarkably reminiscent of Lockhart's earlier attacks on Hunt. Like the author of *The Story of Rimini*, the 'Cockney Aristotle' was seen as a monster of vanity and vulgarity. The only perceived difference was that, whereas Hunt was a picture of self-complacency, Hazlitt always seemed to be flaunting his status as a professionally disappointed man:

> In other words, his prevailing topics are three; – first the stupidity of the world, in not acknowledging his merits; second, the absurdity of those prejudices, which lead mankind in general to approve of the literary productions of men born gentlemen, and educated like gentlemen, rather than those of people in a different situation, thirdly, the shocking anti-cockneyism of *Blackwood's Magazine* and the *Quarterly Review*.[5]

Given Hazlitt's deep involvement in the Cockneyism debate, it is highly intriguing that in the middle of his next run of 'Table-Talks' (which were undertaken the following year for the *New Monthly Magazine*) he should have accorded the concept such credibility by foregrounding it in 'On Londoners'. Was this an attempt to deflect the *Blackwood's* criticism by broadening it? Or was it an acknowledgement of 'Cockney' roots? The fact that what Hazlitt says of the Cockney tallies so closely with what *Blackwood's* had alleged about Hunt, Keats and himself only enhances the curiousness as well as the courage of his endeavour. It suggests a certain interest, and even engagement, with what the Tories had been saying. In sum, this chapter will argue that the second half of 'On Londoners' *does* represent a full-scale reappraisal of the author's own relation to 'Cockney' culture, understood in both literary and social terms. But before I explore this, it is important to remind ourselves of the condition of periodical essay-writing in the early 1820s, for a grasp of this milieu will be crucial to the kind of argument I want to make about Hazlitt's position.

THE STATUS OF THE PERIODICAL JOURNALIST

In his seminal work *The Making of English Reading Audiences 1789–1832* (1987), Jon Klancher was to interpret the polite periodicals of the 1820s in terms of a broad project to define middle-classness not through the inculcation of a set of core values, but through the dissemination of a cultural practice. What the periodicals taught by example, he argues, was the capacity of the enlightened mind to come to true self-knowledge through self-conscious acts of reading.[6] Bourgeois identity was defined in terms of the ability to abstract oneself from particulars (rigid bodies of knowledge, static categories of experience) and to reflect upon one's own capacity for such acts of abstraction. It was by this means, Klancher suggested, that magazines such as *Blackwood's* sought to reach deep into the growing body of the semi-genteel classes and to offer them the possibility of a new kind of cultural consciousness. As a corollary of this, he argues, a corresponding emphasis was placed upon the ability of the middle-class writer or reader to abstract himself from society and to transform it into an object of knowledge, with the result that the identifying characteristic of bourgeois identity became precisely the capacity to see oneself as being somehow above or outside the social system. In this analysis, the figure of the anonymous essayist as a metropolitan *flâneur* becomes crucial to the construction of middle-classness, principally because of the way in which he combines a certain kind of impersonal representativeness with the ability to move at will through each and every social space.

One of the only shortcomings of Klancher's book is the rather easy equation it makes between those men and women who wrote for the polite periodicals and the middle-class identity they were supposedly promoting, for not only was the socio-cultural identity of the reading public in a state of flux at this time, so too was the status of the professional writer. The virtue of Lee Erickson's work on *The Economy of Literary Form* (1996) is its vivid dramatization of the paradoxical position occupied by the periodical journalist between 1815 and 1835. On the one hand, Erickson suggests, periodical writing was, relatively speaking, a highly fashionable and remunerative activity during this period: 'as the market for the form reflects, essay writers were at the centre of public attention in the 1810s and 1820s in a way they never were before or have been since.'[7] Especially in the period immediately prior to the rise of the great Victorian novel, some of the sums to be earned from regular reviewing and/or essay-writing were (potentially at least) very big, considerably larger than for writing fiction or non-fiction in book form. This meant that almost for the first time in history it was possible to make a living as a freelance essayist. In spite of this, however, there remained a residual scepticism about journalism in many of the periodical writers of the period, partly on account of its obvious insecurity and partly because of lingering doubts about its status and value. So it was that, as Erickson argues, 'despite the advantages in dissemination and remuneration, authors generally felt that writing for periodicals and especially for reviews required them to prostitute their talents' (p. 90). Qualifying Klancher in the light of this, we might have to begin by acknowledging that, on occasion at least, the self-reflexive writing style of the period might have emerged at least as much out of a widespread ambivalence towards periodical journalism *as an activity* as out of a self-conscious project to manufacture the middle-class 'mind'.

The periodical revolution of high culture began with the rise of the Whig *Edinburgh Review* and its Tory counterpart, the *Quarterly Review*, in the first decade of the nineteenth century. In these publications the review-essay was reinstated as a prestigious and influential cultural form. But it was only in the revolution's second phase, which took place in the late 1810s and early 1820s, that the new possibilities – and anxieties – that surrounded periodical culture really began to emerge. With the rise of literary monthlies such as *Blackwood's*, the *New Monthly* (which were both Tory, at least in the 1810s) and the *London Magazine* (solidly Whig), something new was being attempted in the field of the periodical magazine. These publications sought to combine the high cultural habits of the *Edinburgh* and the *Quarterly* with the most compelling features of popular journalism. They contained critical reviews, travel accounts and analytical essays, but they also included gothic tales, city sketches, crime stories and satirical squibs – thematic material which, superficially at least, was not far removed from some of the cheap, popular 'flash' literature of the day. Writers who had been educated to aspire to the restricted field of high literature were thus encouraged – or forced – into occupying a new literary register, somewhere between the formal, lofty idiom of the two elite reviews and the unashamedly sensationalist tone of mass magazines (such as *The Hive*) and street broadsides. They were also caught uneasily between two different journalistic models: there was the dignified anonymity and reserve cultivated by Francis Jeffrey and his fellow *Edinburgh* reviewers, and then there was the easy, familiar idiom of popular journalists such as William Cobbett, the author of the *Political Register*, or

Pierce Egan, the celebrated sports writer of the *Weekly Despatch*. Nor was the problem simply one of style. In a very material sense, there was a deep contradiction in the status of the new periodical essayists. In print they liked to cut a figure for themselves as leisured gentlemen; in reality they were often all too conscious of being little better than hired hacks, intermittently condemned to living from hand to mouth.[8] Seen from this perspective, the self-reflexivity of the periodical essay begins to take on a more uncertain nature. If at times it still looks like a vaunting of the capacities of the mind in accordance with Klancher's powerful model, at others it is more like an expression of profound discomfort, in which not only the social status of the professional writer but also the literary identity of the polite periodical are called into question.

LONDON COCKNEYS AND EDINBURGH MOHOCKS

In the immediate aftermath of the 'Cockney School' articles, what had begun as a specific attack on Hunt, Hazlitt and Keats gradually developed, in the hands of *Blackwood's*, into a general tendency to foist 'Cockneyism' upon a broader range of London writers, some of whom had little or no connection with the *Examiner* group. In some respects this debate was politically driven, with the Whig *London Magazine* providing a natural target for the Tories of *Blackwood's*. In some respects it was commercially driven: the result of an ever-increasing number of periodicals fighting for public attention. But it was also generated by a growing anxiety within the field of periodical journalism about the nature and value of periodicals. What one finds in the pages of *Blackwood's* is a whole series of misgivings about modern urban culture (and the journalism that was concomitant with it) being displaced onto a variety of London writers and publications. In an article called 'The General Question', which was published in September 1823 (one month after the first appearance of Hazlitt's 'On Londoners'), *Blackwood's* crowed heartily over the demise of Byron and Hunt's *Liberal* before offering an extraordinary group portrait of the contributors to the *London Magazine*:

> There seems to be a quorum of Cockneys among them, and that leavens the whole mass. They know little, and care less, about what is going on in the world, and keep chattering away fluently enough about various small matters, 'great to little men' and sometimes in no disagreeable vein. The criticism of this Magazine is not below contempt, but exactly on a level with it; and its attempts to delineate manners, and so forth, most abortive.[9]

Reminiscent of the portrait of George Cruikshank that *Blackwood's* had produced a few months earlier, this picture can be seen to draw on eighteenth-century Grub Street traditions, while also looking forward to later nineteenth-century representations of literary Bohemia. The *London*'s Cockney writers don't belong in the 'flash' ranks of popular journalism, the reviewer argues, nor yet are they on a par with university men on the other; instead they seem to float in a kind of strange, semi-amphibious realm, 'low-born, underbred radicals, who feel awkward at the existence of a gentleman, persons of any condition, lords, ladies, and so forth' (p. 339). Nor was this mere speculation, *Blackwood's* insisted, for such was the confessional spirit within Cockneyism that the *London*'s writers were always confessing their humble backgrounds: 'the contributors being, as they inform us, young attorneys, solicitors, half-pay officers, quondam pedagogues, young men of genius of no profession, and anonymous correspondents in county-towns' (p. 338).

When reflecting on the vulgarity of modern periodical culture, then, the characteristic manoeuvre of Lockhart, Wilson, Maginn and their *Blackwood's* colleagues was generally one of projection, in which all blame was put upon the 'profligacy' of the London press.[10] But for their metropolitan counterparts the more frequent response was one of self-reflection and self-analysis. In the writings of P. G. Patmore, John Scott, Hazlitt and Lamb, for example, there is a soul-searching attitude to the periodical essay as a genre, not least because of its rapid ascendancy to the very height of fashion. In July 1822 the *London Magazine* published an article titled 'On Magazine Writers', in which an anonymous Patmore launched a measured critique of the periodical press. He considered that, with the expansion of the cultural field, and the growing appetite for current and accessible reading matter among the public, the literary profession had been transformed out of recognition. Most periodical writers were now nothing but magpies and chameleons, forever chopping and changing their opinions to suit their editors and stealing shamelessly from all comers in order to provide quick copy. That rich blend of philosophical inquiry and conversational ease, the historical legacy of the essay form as it had been handed down by Joseph Addison and Richard Steele, had been unceremoniously laid aside in favour of a highly tendentious street-currency, an increasingly specious 'flash' style. From being active and reflective, essay-writing had become passive and thoughtless, the literary equivalent of a reflex action: 'I have heard, that a patent has been, or is about to be taken out for an automaton writer', Patmore wrote, 'the principle of which is, that after being wound up it is only necessary to fling into it a certain number of pages of Johnson, or any other vocabulary, and they come out completely formed in the shape of an article.'[11] His grudge against the periodical essay was that it was simply writing that grew out of writing: it did not strive to convey information or to expand the field of knowledge. The sole ambition of the modern writer, it seemed, was simply to sustain a literary texture, to elaborate, for the duration of an essay's length, a kind of meaningless play on words. He had no philosophical method to build upon, but constructed his essay haphazardly, as it were by casual association.

> He ransacks his brains in the first place, for images and illustrations; for by a singular inversion of the old method of writing, his illustrations suggest the ideas, and not the ideas illustrations. This, it must be admitted, is a much more compendious and expeditious way of writing. There is no necessity that there should be any connexion or congruity between the opinions. The law of succession is shamefully disregarded, and *each second*, does not, *as in the old gradation*, stand heir to the first. (p. 23)

This is an interesting gloss on Klancher's notion of the middle-class periodicals' project to construct a readership by dramatizing the self-conscious abstraction of the mind from matter, principally because the process *it* describes has much stronger links with the mental habits of Hazlitt's Cockney. Far from effectively demonstrating the capacity of the cultivated mind to comprehend the whole, the modern periodical essayist is, according to Patmore at least, nothing but an abject slave to particulars – he moves not from point to point, but from phrase to phrase:

> There is yet another *style*, which though limited in its circulation, is still pretty often before the public. It may be called the confectionary style of writing. It is full of … 'intense and genial dallyings,' – 'delicate crispnesses,' and 'jagged venerablenesses;' it finds 'a sense of deep and mysterious antiquity in everything,' – and 'everything is imbued with sympathy and imagination'. (p. 25)

The specific (although unnamed) target in this extract is Thomas Noon Talfourd, whose *New Monthly* review of B. W. Proctor's *Mirandola* is later quoted from at length. But much of what is said about these affected compound phrases is also highly reminiscent of what Lockhart had argued about Hunt's essays and *The Story of Rimini* a few years before. 'The confectionary style of writing', Patmore suggests, is a very modern form of composition in which language has become obsessed with its own surface novelty, luxuriating in its status as a commodity. 'It ensures a never failing variety, inasmuch as recognising no necessary connection between words and things, and no relations between words themselves, the consequence is, that one epithet is as fit and becoming as another, and whether we say *venerable jaggedness* or *jagged venerableness*, it is equally intelligible and correct' (p. 25).

In the work of the editor of the *London Magazine*, John Scott, there was a similar anxiety about the condition of modern journalism. Scott had grown tired of seeing his contributors being stigmatized as 'Cockney authors', not least because the stigma was showing the potential to affect sales. In 1818 Hazlitt's publishers had told him that they were no longer willing to purchase his *Lectures on the English Comic Writers* for £200 because the *Blackwood's* articles had lessened the value of his work.[12] Hunt suffered too, noting many years later in his *Autobiography* how the term 'Cockney' had frightened the booksellers, hampering his publishing options for many years to come. Scott, for his part, chose the autumn of 1820 as the moment to strike back, spicing up the November issue of the *London* with a particularly heated diatribe on the anonymous assassins from the North. Flinging the charge of urban vulgarity back upon Z. and his cronies, he likened their critical practices to the most nefarious crimes of city life. In a series of elaborate metaphors, he compared their prying into the private lives of innocent individuals to a species of urban scavenging, their oscillation between violent criticism and hypocritical remorse to the ruses of street pickpockets, and their hiding of themselves behind a mask of anonymity to contemporary commercial fraud. In sum, the clear imputation of Scott's article was that *Blackwood's Magazine*, far from being a steadfast champion of traditional values, was actually thoroughly 'modern' in the worst and most corrupting sense. It was the source of all the leading literary contagions of the day, not the cure:

> It has never contained a severe article, that has not, at the same time, been a dirty one; the pungency has never been of the fair sterling quality, like that of the real cognac, but of a filthy, and cheating nature, like that of the trash they sell in the common liquor-shops under the name of brandy – which is seasoned with burning poison to recommend it to the diseased tastes of drabs and dustmen.[13]

In January 1821, that is, only a month before his tragic death in a duel with the *Blackwood's* representative Jonathan Christie, the *London*'s editor had gone even further, tackling the 'Edinburgh Mohocks' head on. The context was a subsection of that month's 'Town Conversation' labelled 'On Cockney Writers'. That there was such a thing as literary Cockneyism Scott was willing to concede, but he denied that it had anything to do with the *London Magazine. Blackwood's*, he insisted, had been making use of a *word* without having a clear *idea* behind it, and had started bandying it around in the most indiscriminate manner. The concept did have some substance to it, he agreed, but it required a far stricter definition:

> Cockneys, in general, are little men; but they are smart, clever and active; quick observers and wonderfully occupied with whatever is going on about them. They observe everything, however, with an immediate and exclusive reference to themselves: being born and bred up in the metropolis renders each, in his own estimation, a member of a privileged class, and all novelties and varieties from their habits, are set down by them as singular exceptions, remarkable occurrences, things to be entered in their journals ... Cockneys are thus unpleasantly pert in their manner, without meaning to be offensive: they are prone, too, to make mountains out of mole-hills, and this is apt to turn the laugh against them, and cause them to be considered as more ignorant than they are ... A Cockney author is likely to be found clever, but with his talent will almost constantly go a certain air of *smallness* belonging to his character generally. He will seem to want actual experience, and be inclined to make up the deficiency by egotism. His good manners will be pert; his observations too minute and particular; he will make too much use of all he knows, and too little of what other people, who are not of his set, tell him.[14]

We have already acknowledged what Hazlitt's 'On Londoners' might have owed to *Blackwood's*, but here I think we can see how it might have drawn on Scott's conception as well. (Indeed, such comparisons do reveal something of the magpie quality of contemporary periodical writing, with authors continually borrowing and stealing from one another, as Patmore had suggested.) What Scott does, in this mini-essay, is make the connection between a particular kind of metropolitan psychology – the mental habits of the true Cockney – and a particular kind of authorship. He also makes a telling point about the Cockney's large sense of himself and his actual limitations, both of knowledge and experience. What he doesn't do, however – and this is in stark contrast both to *Blackwood's* and to Hazlitt – is try to link these traits to a particular class. 'Cockneys, in general, are little men', he says, and a Cockney author, clever as he may be, 'will also have a certain air of *smallness* belonging to his character.' They can be 'pert', he suggests, and often 'think themselves a member of a privileged class' (p. 70). One can read further into these hints if one wishes, of course, but the official emphasis harks back to the old seventeenth-century definition of the Cockney as a psychological rather than a social type, an example of a particular type of *character*.

Gradually, however, Scott's portrait of the Cockney becomes ever more individualized, until we realize that he must have a particular author in mind. 'Should he have chance to "have stout notions on the marrying score"', he quips,

> we are likely to have him telling us that Shakespeare was an enemy to marriage, not because he has any reason to say so, or because there are not innumerable reasons to say the reverse – but because a Cockney author is always eager to associate himself with Shakespeare, and, out of tenderness to the 'bard's' reputation, will not suppose it possible a difference of opinion could exist between them. (p.70)

Scott does then confess that he has 'one of our popular writers in our eye at present' and it is for this reason that he wishes his charges against the 'Mohocks' to be rightly understood. The 'Blackwoodsmen' may have written many abominable and unfounded scandals against this author, he continues, 'but that his style and sentiments are not provocative of severity we would be the last persons to deny' (p. 71). The most interesting thing about this, I think, is that it shows Leigh Hunt being made a scapegoat by the Left as well as the Right, serving as a lightning rod for all the literary anxieties of the day. To a large extent, the sins that Hunt was accused of having committed were really those of the familiar essay form itself – its fatal facility, its 'confectionary' quality and also what Theodor Adorno later considered to be its unearned authority – the fact that it was always beginning *in medias res*, off the top of its head, without having properly laid out its professional or philosophical credentials.[15]

What *Blackwood's* had said of Hunt's work was fair comment, Scott implied, but they shouldn't seek to tar the writers of the *London* with the same brush. Within its pages, he insisted, the reader would encounter works that were thoroughly urbane without being vulgar, and he cited the essays of Elia and the *Table-Talks* as two cases in point. Of the Elia essays, he was especially proud, largely because he felt that they were of such a tone and quality as to transcend their milieu:

> Our ELIA, too – the pride of *our* Magazine, and *the object of the praise of their's under his real name* – he is set down as a 'Cockney scribbler!' This gentleman, in his capacity of acknowledged author, they have never mentioned but to eulogize; as, indeed, who does not eulogize his writings for displaying a spirit of deep and warm humanity, enlivened by a vein of poignant wit, – not caustic, yet searching, – and recommending a shrewdness of judgment on men, books, and things, which seems to revive the old times when magazines were not, and literature and knowledge were the better for it. (p. 69)

Lamb had started his 'Elia' series in the *London* in the preceding autumn, and had fallen head first into the Cockney controversy as a result. In November 1820 *Blackwood's* had accused Elia of being a 'Cockney scribbler', finding 'impertinencies' in his third contribution 'On Christ's Hospital Five and Thirty Years Ago'.[16] But Scott was right to suggest that Lamb had rarely attracted this kind of criticism when publishing under his own name, and nor was he to prove a real target for the Tories in the long term. On their first publication in 1818, his *Works* had received a rather warm reception from 'Maga'. Lamb 'never has been, and … never will be a popular writer', the reviewer remarked, but 'he is without doubt a man of genius … there is in him a rare union of originality of mind with delicacy of feeling'. Popular as he was with the Cockney School (whose leading members were always praising him), he was not one of their ranks: 'Mr Lamb's Parnassus', it was concluded, 'is not in the kingdom of Cockaigne'.[17] With the benefit of historical distance, it is actually relatively easy to see why Lamb's essays, irredeemably Cockney though they were in terms of their social milieu and subject matter, should have proved more broadly acceptable to contemporaries than those of Hunt or even Hazlitt. Though known to be the friend of many in the *Examiner* circle, the fact that Lamb was neither associated with, nor given to indulge in, radical politics did undoubtedly contribute to his essays' broad appeal. But the characteristic mode and manner of the 'Elia' series was also very important. The language of the essays was designedly old-fashioned. Lamb's literary models were the great essayists of the seventeenth and eighteenth centuries: Thomas Browne, Jeremy Taylor, Sir Richard Steele. This lent them an air of whimsical gentility; so much so, indeed, that they often seemed delightfully, even poignantly out-of-touch. Steele was an important touchstone for Hunt too, but the lessons he drew from him were rather different. He too strove to emulate the ease and elegance of *The Tatler*, but he also wanted to dress his prose up in the fashions and familiar references of his own day. This is what both tickled and provoked his readers, and gave them a thrilling sense of the old mingling with the new. Often, Hunt self-consciously reworked traditional topoi from an identifiably modern perspective. In his two *Indicator* essays 'On the Sight of Shops', he combined many of the features of the traditional literary stroll through the city with a kind of aesthetic attention to detail normally reserved for reviews of the Royal Academy exhibition. He viewed the various shop windows of the metropolis as if they were large painted canvases, regarding them with the eye of a connoisseur.[18] Not only would this have represented a pernicious confusion of high and low culture in the eyes of many contemporaries, it would also have been seen as rather vulgar, deconstructing, as it does, the high-minded concept of the aesthetic back into the grubby, tactile language of consumer desire.

Lamb's descriptions of London, by contrast, though often shot through with the same kind of enjoyments, were always mediated by Elia's self-deprecatory humour, with the result that the essays' 'Cockney' flights of fancy were always tempered by their fundamentally unassuming character. The fact that Elia works as a London clerk was used to explain the narrowness of his knowledge and experience, its fragmentary nature, its inescapably urban bias; and his status as an amateur antiquarian also helped supply him with a certain kind of fusty respectability. Most importantly of all, perhaps, Lamb's Elia knows his place. He has a deferential air towards the authors and institutions that he comes into contact with, as the early essay 'Oxford in the Vacation' makes only too clear. He does not try to pass himself off as an independent gentleman of letters, nor does he have a fantasy of himself as Sir Richard Steele. 'There is a sort of timidity about him that chains his wings', *Blackwood's* had said in 1818, not entirely disapprovingly, 'He seems to want ambition'.[19] In Leigh Hunt, by contrast, there was no such mock-modesty. His essays regularly assumed an easy familiarity with their eighteenth-century forebears, while sporting an unashamedly modern dress. It was this lack of respect for differences, both historical and social, that appalled both Lockhart and Scott. But at the bottom of Scott's mind there was not merely an aversion to Hunt's familiarity, there was also a more general anxiety about the form of the modern essay itself, based as it was on a kind of unearned intimacy with the classics. How interesting, then, that Scott should attribute at least some of Lamb's popularity to the fact that he did *not* write like a contemporary periodical essayist, as if he had been successful precisely insofar as he had transcended the 'Cockney' traits of the form.

HAZLITT ON THE PERIODICAL PRESS

That Hazlitt himself was preoccupied with the status and value of modern periodical journalism when he came to write 'On Londoners and Country People' is all the more evident if one looks at other pieces he was working on at the same time: the large article 'The Periodical Press', published in the May 1823 edition of the *Edinburgh Review*, and the essay entitled 'Arguing in a Circle' that was published a couple of months later in *The Liberal*. In the first of these, Hazlitt asked himself '*Whether Periodical Criticism is, upon the whole, beneficial to the cause of literature?*', to which he then hazarded the equivocal reply '*That periodical criticism is favourable – to periodical criticism*'.[20] In order to explain his position, he then embarked upon an extended survey of the contemporary state of letters, beginning with generalities, and then moving down to an assessment of individual newspapers and magazines. To begin with, he agreed with a number of his fellow commentators that, in a general sense at least, the great golden age of poetry and drama in English literature had come to an end. Writers of the present age, whatever their personal abilities, would never be able to write in the same vein again: 'thus genius, like the sun, seems not to rise higher and higher, but from its first dawn to ascend to its meridian, and then decline; and art, like life, may be said to have its stated periods of infancy, manhood, and old age' (p. 353). Partly this was an effect of social and political change; partly it was a result of what we would now call 'the burden of the past' – the idea that the ancients had left the moderns with comparatively little left to do. Hence, it was quite wrong, Hazlitt argued, to blame the periodicals of the present day for any falling-off in the higher genres, as there was nothing they could do to offset this decline. His second point was that, given the fact that periodical criticism had come to represent *the* new literary form of the nineteenth century, writers and readers effectively had no choice but to embrace it in spite of its faults: 'We are nothing if not critical', he quipped, before adding, 'be it so: but then let us be critical, or we shall be nothing' (p. 351). He admitted that modern periodical journalism was more self-conscious, superficial and politically partisan than the traditional genres of the past, but it was also more critically sophisticated, civilized and democratic: 'Knowledge is no longer confined to the few', he pointed out, 'the object therefore is to make it accessible and attractive to the many. The *Monarchism* of Literature is at an end; the cells of learning are thrown open, and let in the light of universal day' (p. 358). Broadly speaking, in this essay Hazlitt tries to balance a respect for the educational potential of periodical writing with an acknowledgement of its artistic drawbacks. He does not think of it as a genre in which great writing is going to be possible ('literary immortality is now let on short leases' (p. 358)), but nor does he think, as Wordsworth and Coleridge did, that it should be treated with disdain: 'If we are superficial', he urges, 'let us be brilliant. If we cannot be profound, let us at least be popular' (p. 357).

On the whole, 'The Periodical Press' is written in Hazlitt's best *Edinburgh Review* manner, that is, in a tone more lofty and 'objective' than he tended to use elsewhere (although how much of this was due to him being edited by Jeffrey must still be a matter of conjecture). Still, his partisan feelings continued to shine through. The article was, for example, extremely warm in its praise of Hunt's *Examiner* newspaper, insisting that 'with the exception of a little egotism, and *twaddle*, and flippancy, and dogmatism about religion or morals, and mawkishness about firesides, and furious Bonapartism, and a vein of sickly sonnet-writing, we suspect that *The Examiner* must be allowed … to be the ablest and most respectable of the publications that issue from the weekly press' (p. 368). It also devoted considerable space to the ill-treatment of Keats and Hunt at the hands of *Blackwood's* and the *Quarterly Review*.

The response from *Blackwood's* was powerful and direct, fuelled as it was by a recent revival of anti-Cockney animosities. The publication, in April 1823, of *Liber Amoris, or the New Pygmalion*, Hazlitt's ill-advised (and ill-disguised) memoir about a doomed infatuation with his landlord's daughter, had provoked instant and widespread ridicule in the Tory reviews, and prompted Hazlitt to sue Thomas Cadell, the *Blackwood's* agent in London, for damages. But the Mohocks were in no mood to back down, with William Maginn, their new recruit, having a particular appetite for conflict. One result of this was the resumption of the *Blackwood's* 'Timothy Tickler' series, which saw two new instalments in the summer of 1823. In August, Tickler, who was presented as a kind of gentleman amateur, took it upon himself to review the May issue of the *Edinburgh Review* in its entirety, with Maginn contributing a brilliant, extended review of Hazlitt's 'Periodical Press'.

Tickler's letter was presented to the reader as a feat of unmasking. Not only was the 'Periodical Press' article revealed as the work of 'the gallant of Southampton Row, Holborn – the "modern Pygmalion" himself … Mr William Hazlitt', a fact that ought to have been embarrassing enough for Jeffrey, in Tickler's view.[21] Even more scandalous, however, was the little local evidence in the text that Jeffrey had actually edited Hazlitt's copy, getting down and dirty, as it were, with the Cockneys. Low as Tickler's opinion of Jeffrey was, he said, he never would have imagined that such a 'sharp and petulant, if not a deep critic' would 'sit down in company with such a literary flunkey' (p. 221). Part of the accusation here is that Jeffrey has allowed his *Review* to be contaminated by Cockney principles – with the praise by 'Periodical Press' of *The Examiner* coming to represent a new low. But the other part relates to Hazlitt's precarious status as a professional writer, a status that he had repeatedly made into an object of public lament. 'He told us already, in his Table-Talk, that all of the people of London will not look upon his books, for fear of being thought Cockneys', Maginn writes, 'and by this account [in *Liber Amoris*] it would seem that his person gets little better treatment among them' (p. 222). So desperate was Hazlitt for a decent review, he continued, that he might have to buy a few drinks for his old newspaper cronies in order to obtain one.

'On Londoners and Country People' appeared in the same month as this article, and so, given the highly topical nature of these journalistic inquiries, it seems appropriate to return to it with these questions in mind: what was the relation between Hazlitt's caricature of Cockneyism and his sentiments on the periodical press? How was it that he should appear to be liberal and democratic in his attitude to modern urban culture in the *Edinburgh Review* article, and yet brimming over with supercilious snobbery in a contemporaneous article for the *New Monthly Magazine*? The only way to answer this question is to follow the argument of Hazlitt's essay through all its various twists and turns, for it is only after a couple of telling shifts that it finally succeeds in articulating its position. And even then, one might argue, the meaning of the essay is to be found less in its final resting place than in the sum of the various positions it has seen fit to adopt.

'A GROUND OF NATIVE SHALLOWNESS MOUNTED WITH PERTNESS AND CONCEIT'

A few pages ago, in 'On Londoners and Country People', we left Hazlitt's Cockney in the full pomp and circumstance of his metropolitan condition. There then follows a comic section in which the author seeks to explode his subject's self-complacency, by taking him out of London, and exposing him to the elements:

> The *Cockney* lives in a go-cart of local prejudices and positive illusions; and when he is turned out of it, he hardly knows how to stand or move. He ventures through Hyde Park Corner, as a cat crosses a gutter. The trees pass by the coach very oddly. The country has a strange blank appearance. It is not lined with houses all the way, like London. (p. 173)

Outside London, the Cockney loses all sense of his own consequence. The limited nature of his experience is brought home to him. The country people are not impressed by his airs and graces, nor are they as ignorant and unfashionable as he assumed. Understandably, therefore, he prefers a suburban tea-garden, or a Cider-Cellar in winter, 'where he sweetens the air with the fumes of tobacco, and makes it echo to the sound of his own voice'. There is something self-enclosing and narcissistic about the suburban escapism depicted here, and one wonders whether Hazlitt's mind hadn't started wandering in Leigh Hunt's direction. 'The imagination', he writes, 'long pent up behind a counter or between brick walls, with noisome smells, and dingy objects cannot bear at once to launch into the boundless expanse of the country, but "shorter excursions tries", coveting something between the two, and finding it at White Conduit House, or the Rosemary Branch, or Bagnigge Wells' (pp. 173–4). Whatever the buried associations, it is at the mention of the suburbs that 'On Londoners' suddenly starts to shift focus, with the critique of Cockneyism becoming (all of a sudden) more detailed and 'familiar'. 'The landlady is seen at a bow-window in near perspective', Hazlitt continues, 'with punch-bowls and lemons disposed orderly around – the lime-trees or poplars wave overhead to "catch the breezy air"'. 'Hampstead and Highgate are seen in the back-ground, and contain the imagination within gentle limits – here the holiday people are playing ball; here they are playing bowls – here they are quaffing ale, there sipping tea – here the loud wager is heard, there the political debate' (p.174). The essayist then sets about exemplifying some of the central traits of Cockneyism by referring us to some of his own acquaintances. He introduces us to Dr Goodman, who is a type of the Cockney critic 'curious in opinion, obstinate in the wrong, great in little things, and inveterate in petty warfare' (p. 174). In his repeated attacks on the aesthetic deficiencies of Richard Pinch, a noted fives-player and would-be professional singer, Goodman exhibits all of the 'imperturbable vanity' of the Cockney character, Hazlitt says, as well as its characteristic volubility. Then there is Richard Pinch himself, who is a perfect specimen of the *knowingness* of Cockneyism: 'he never has anything to say', says the essayist, 'and yet is never at a loss for an answer' (p. 175). Pinch's response to a cutting remark, whatever its nature, is always '*The same to you, sir*'. Finally, there is Mr Dunster, the fishmonger from the Poultry, who is forever rhapsodizing about his schooldays in Clapham, endlessly wearying his interlocutors with his inconsequential song of himself: 'The same idle vein might be found in the country', Hazlitt writes, 'but I doubt it would find a tongue to give it utterance. Cockneyism is a ground of native shallowness mounted with pertness and conceit' (p. 177). At first sight, the satirical tone of this section seems like a continuation of the essay's opening, in which Hazlitt had adopted a recognizably 'middle-class' attitude of superiority towards his petit-bourgeois subject. In his discussion of Dunster's habit of reminiscence, for example, he continues to identify the 'native ground' of Cockneyism with the public and private spaces of the lower-middle class:

> A man shut up all his life in his shop, without any thing to interest him from one year's end to another but the cares and details of business, with scarcely any intercourse with books or opportunities for society, distracted with the buzz and

glare and noise about him, turns for relief to the retrospect of his childish years; and there, through the long vista, at one bright loop-hole, leading out of the thorny mazes of the world into the clear morning light, he sees the idle fancies and gay amusements of his boyhood dancing like motes in the sunshine. Shall we blame or should we laugh at him, if his eye glistens, and his tongue grows wanton in their praise? (p. 177)

This might seem like mere elaboration, but in fact a significant shift has taken place. All of a sudden, Hazlitt collapses the critical distance between himself and his subject. At the beginning of the essay, the picture of the Cockney was highly abstract in nature – it was not so much a portrait as a caricature. In this middle section, however, the satire is based upon the observation of a set of individual types – it is at once more concrete and more humane. There is a sense of Hazlitt warming sympathetically to his subject. Partly this is due to a perceptible lowering of the critical temperature: as the essay digresses into a series of anecdotes, the mood becomes noticeably more tolerant and affectionate. Partly it is a result of Hazlitt's decision to acknowledge his own deep familiarity – and sympathy – with the Cockney milieu he describes. This point is made all the more forcibly when he makes a direct reference to the editors of *Blackwood's Magazine*. 'Forgive me, dear Dunster', he writes, at the end of his brief biographical study, 'if I have drawn a sketch of some of thy venial foibles, and delivered thee into the hands of these Cockneys of the North, who will fall upon thee and devour thee, like so many cannibals, without a grain of salt!' (p. 177). And immediately after apologizing to Dunster for exposing his weaknesses, Hazlitt begins the next section of his essay by affirming that 'familiarity in cities breeds contempt' (p. 177). What is interesting here, I think, is the fact that Hazlitt's displacement of the stigma of Cockneyism away from himself and onto the representatives of a particular social class is never quite accomplished. It is arrested, at the last moment, in favour of a suggestion concerning the intriguing similarity between the contentious debates of Goodman and Pinch on the one hand, and those of *Blackwood's*, the *Edinburgh Review* and the *London Magazine* on the other. Like Scott and Patmore before him, Hazlitt implicitly entertains the possibility that the periodical essay itself might be an irredeemably 'Cockney' form; unlike them, however, he seems to embrace this unpleasant thought rather than displace it. He also dares to suggest that contemporary periodicals are never more 'Cockney' in character than when they are engaging in polemical squabbles – that the 'Cockney School' debate, in other words, might itself be one of the primary examples of literary Cockneyism on offer, with both *Blackwood's* and the *London* being guilty of saying 'And the same to you, sir!'

The notion that 'familiarity in cities breeds contempt' is a belated judgement on the contentiousness of Pinch and Goodman, as well as a following-on from his recent reference to *Blackwood's*. But it is also a form of auto-critique. What Hazlitt is partly acknowledging is the extent to which the opening of 'On Londoners and Country People' was itself a characteristic piece of Cockney contempt – a dismissive summary judgement based on superficial, unearned familiarity. In the middle section of the essay, by contrast, there is not only a softening of the original critique, wherein the author begins to find much that is admirable about Cockney presumption when he gets down to individuals, there is also a self-reflexive turn, in which he calls his own previous critical position into question. In the opening pages Hazlitt had hidden behind the anonymous disguise of the middle-class *flâneur*, but here he emerges in his own person and places himself in social proximity to his subject. As an attack on *Blackwood's* this operates on two levels: it offers a pointed critique of the disengaged prejudice at the heart of the 'Cockney School' series, but it also makes a rather subtle statement about contemporary periodical journalism, suggesting a strong link between literary anonymity and urban contempt.

COCKNEY CITIZENSHIP

But of course the essay does not end there. Implicit in its title was the promise of a critical comparison between town-dwellers and country-dwellers, and that is what follows. The surprising thing, however, is that far from seeing country life as an antidote to urban corruption, as Wordsworth or Cobbett would have done, Hazlitt has no time for the pastoral ideal. Such is his impatience, indeed, that he is not even prepared to engage in a proper analysis: those readers who want to read his critique of rural life are referred instead to his review of *The Excursion* in *The Round Table* (1817). In place of a full-scale comparison, then, we are given only a short paragraph contrasting the levity and indifference of London life with the 'harshness, moroseness and disagreeable restraint' that prevails in the country (p. 178). Hazlitt skips a stage in the argument in order to get to what is, for him, the more pressing question: 'If these then are the faults and vices of the inhabitants of town or of the country, where should a man go to live, so as to escape from them?' According to Hazlitt, he should spend his youth in the city and his retirement in the country. That way he will stand the best chance of preserving his sociable instincts from the destructive influence of excessive familiarity: 'We may find in such a one a social polish, a pastoral simplicity. He rusticates agreeably, and vegetates with a degree of sentiment' (p. 178). In his closing paragraphs, Hazlitt returns to the topic of life in the city, but in a significantly different spirit from before:

> In London there is a *public*; and each man is part of it. We are gregarious, and affect the kind. We have a sort of abstract existence; and a community of ideas and knowledge (rather than local proximity) is the bond of society and good fellowship. This is one great cause of the tone of political feeling in large and populous cities. There is here a visible body-politic, a type and image of that vast Leviathan the State. We comprehend that vast denomination, the *People*, of which we see a tenth part moving daily before us; and by having our imaginations emancipated from petty interests and personal dependence, we learn to venerate ourselves as men, and to respect the rights of human nature. Therefore it is that the citizens and freemen of London and Westminster are patriots by prescription, philosophers and politicians by the right of their birth-place. In the country, men are no better than a herd of cattle or scattered deer. (p. 179)

In the final peroration, of which this is but a small extract, Hazlitt offers a character of the ideal citizen of London to set against the rabid anti-metropolitanism of that born-again Tory William Wordsworth (and also, implicitly, of rural radicals like Cobbett). What is more, he explicitly identifies himself with this new urban type: his writing shifts into the first person plural as a clear statement of his solidarity. What is less explicit, but no less significant, is the extent to which this new stereotype draws on some of the old traits of the 'Cockney' character, while cleverly inverting its terms. Like the Cockney, Hazlitt's urban democrat is defined by habits of imaginative abstraction, political volubility and self-conceit. But in him these traits appear to have changed their nature. They are no longer vices but virtues. The bad abstraction of the Cockney, in which the external world was conceived entirely in terms of a free-floating and arbitrary juxtaposition of objects, is exchanged for the good abstraction of the political citizen, in which a personal experience of the urban crowd forms the ground and seedbed for general ideas like 'liberty' and 'the people'. The passive existence of the Hartleyan associationist has been replaced by the outgoing imaginative life of the benevolent democrat. The Cockney's promiscuous tactility, his unreflective life of the senses, has been replaced by a more detached perspective on the world. So, too, the contentiousness of the Cockney politician is reimagined as the 'gregariousness' of the free-born Briton. The most telling transformation of all, however, pertains to Cockney egotism itself, for this is a shift that the middle section of the essay, detailing the habits of Mr Dunster, had partly served to anticipate.

Whereas the Cockney egotism of the opening was based on an idiotic sympathy with power, Dunster's egotism is a result of his intense immersion in his own history: he is, in this respect, a little Rousseau of the suburbs, a man whose imaginative connection with his own past self has the status of a libertarian principle. This might help explain why Hazlitt is, finally, in spite of all his faults, persuaded to view him as 'a man of spirit' and 'a true Englishman and a loyal subject' (p. 177). Ever since his first reading of Rousseau's *Confessions* Hazlitt had made a strong association between autobiography and liberal politics; indeed in his early *Essay on the Principles of Human Action*, he had argued that the capacity to identify intensely with one's past self was a prerequisite for sympathizing with the present and future concerns of others. In this light, Dunster's 'idle vein' of sentimentalism begins to look like a preparation for the essay's final democratic flourish: it is the prompt, the associative link, that leads Hazlitt back from Cockney false consciousness to civic virtue.

Such tactics were by no means new to Hazlitt. There was a similar move at the end of one of his *Table-Talk* essays from 1822, 'On Coffee-House Politicians'. This highly entertaining piece had begun by railing against the ephemerality and superficiality of London pub conversation, in which 'light and worthless materials float on the surface', and 'the solid and sterling … often sink to the bottom', but then moved slowly, almost involuntarily, into celebrating the sheer friendliness, if not intellectual effervescence, of the essayist's old cronies at the Southampton Tavern.[22] And as with 'On Londoners', when the essayist finally returned to the level of abstract argument at the end of the piece, it was in a very different spirit from its opening, one that had benefited enormously from rubbing shoulders with individuals, and laid itself open to being cheered and consoled. 'I like the country very well', Hazlitt concluded, 'if I want to enjoy my own company: but London is the only place for equal society' (II, p. 89). Structured as they are, these metropolitan sketches do not merely assert the value of dropping one's blasé detachment and rediscovering a common urbanity, they dramatize the process taking place in the mind of the essayist himself. Moreover, they do so in a way that lets the force of the original critique, whether it be of Cockneys or coffee-house politicians, remain as compelling as ever. They are openly dialectical and dialectically open.

The country is ideal but uninhabitable in Hazlitt's writings, the city compromised but convivial. The former is associated with the utopian aspirations of the revolutionary decade, as can be seen in 'On Going a Journey', where Hazlitt remembers his youthful pilgrimage to see

Wordsworth and Coleridge in Somerset in 1798.[23] The latter is connected with professional disappointments and their consolations, a place where 'life is short, but full of mirth and pastime', to borrow a phrase from 'On Coffee-House Politicians'.[24] London is for Hazlitt a milieu where it is almost impossible to hang on to distant dreams, but where the very nearness of others has, paradoxically enough, a reconciling effect. In 'On Why Distant Objects Please', he argued that while places and things have a more romantic effect when viewed from a distance, people gain enormously from being seen close-up. 'Ignorance alone makes monsters and bugbears', he wrote, 'we can scarcely hate any one that we know.'[25] These are the tensions – the forces of attraction and repulsion – that went into the composition of 'On Londoners' and which its final tripartite structure still continues to express.

One of the most striking things about the structure of 'On Londoners' is the way that it bears out John Barrell and John Whale's arguments about the painful tension in Hazlitt's work between the political and the aesthetic.[26] Politically, they argue, Hazlitt was a democrat, but he held fast nevertheless to a rather elitist conception of artistic production and appreciation, believing that there was no universal suffrage in matters of taste. In the first part of 'On Londoners', Hazlitt's aesthetic prejudices are given objective, social form. The Cockney is offered as an exemplum of vulgar taste in its natural habitat – the milieu of the petite bourgeoisie. In the second half of the essay, he is able to redeem this class and this character, but only by shifting the focus from a social to a political perspective, laying aside questions of status and culture in order to address the larger issue of modern citizenship. And as soon as he has done this, all of those qualities that had seemed pernicious from an aesthetic point of view can be reimagined as political virtues. Suddenly, the egotism of the Cockney, his overweening pretension, is precisely what makes him a good citizen, fully conscious of his own rights and privileges. What had been merely an indiscriminate flattening of distinctions at the beginning of the essay ('Your Cockney is your only true Leveller') is transformed into a wholesome egalitarian consciousness by the end. Broadly speaking, this gives a good account of what takes place in the course of the essay. But it is worth emphasizing, I think, just how porous to its neighbours each of its successive positions is. The form of the essay is all-important here. The middle section provides an important bridge between the discussion of Cockneyism and the description of true citizenship; so much so, indeed, that it is finally quite difficult to say on which side Goodman, Dunster and Pinch belong. And this seems an apt emblem of Hazlitt's unwillingness to draw a hard and fast distinction between the two kinds of urban character. Each is quietly present in the other, just as the vices of the periodical press are inextricable from its virtues. Indeed 'On Londoners' might be seen to exemplify a very similar position to that of the article 'The Periodical Press' in this respect: it expresses the same equivocal feelings about modern metropolitan culture, while finally accepting the trade-off between high art and democratic politics.

CHAPTER 3

Liber Amoris and lodging houses

> I cannot describe the weakness of mind to which she has reduced me. This state of suspense is like hanging in the air by a single thread that exhausts all your strength to keep hold of it; and yet if that fails you, you have nothing in the world else left to trust to.
>
> (*Liber Amoris*, Part II, Letter V)[1]

William Hazlitt's *Liber Amoris, or the New Pygmalion* (1823) is the most powerful account of unrequited love in English literature. Exasperating, embarrassing and reprehensible in many of the sentiments it expresses, it is also movingly candid and compelling, an exemplary case study of 'that madness we want'.[2] The book is a paradoxical amalgam of the artful and the abject, of literary sophistication and undigested feeling, and offers itself to us, as it were simultaneously, as a romance and a satire. Never has the sweet sickness of unreflecting passion been better captured, nor the characteristically modern spectacle of high sentiments in a low setting. Based on real events, Hazlitt's book of love 'has all the romance of private life' (as he himself said of Thomas Dekker's Jacobean drama *The Honest Whore*). In August 1820 the writer had taken two second-floor back rooms at No. 9 Southampton Buildings, Holborn, in a house owned by a tailor named Micaiah Walker. He was forty-three at the time, and a radical journalist, critic and essayist of some renown (his *Lectures on the Dramatic Literature of the Age of Elizabeth* had been published six months earlier, and he was publishing regular *Table-Talks* in the *London Magazine*). Sarah Walker, the anti-heroine of *Liber Amoris*, was the second of his landlord's three daughters, the oldest of whom, Martha, had recently made a highly advantageous marriage to a former lodger. Part mistress, part maid, the nineteen-year-old Sarah cut an ambiguous figure in the household, both in terms of status and character. 'Her face', wrote Hazlitt's friend B. W. Proctor, 'was round and small, and her eyes were motionless, glassy, and without any speculation (apparently) in them … she was silent, or uttered monosyllables only, and was very demure.'[3]

Hazlitt's private life was in a disturbed state even before he arrived at Southampton Buildings. His marriage to his first wife Sarah Stoddart had broken down the previous year, and his elderly father, also named William, had died only a few weeks before. He had also fallen out with his closest literary friends, Leigh Hunt and Charles Lamb. Added to this the terrible damage done to his political hopes by the Queen Caroline affair and to his literary reputation by the repeated Tory attacks upon him (in *Blackwood's Edinburgh Magazine* and the *Quarterly Review* especially), and his morale, if not his literary productivity, was at a low ebb. 'My public and private hopes have been left a ruin, or remain only to mock me', he wrote in February 1822, in 'On the Fear of Death', 'I would wish them to be re-edified'.[4] This need for 're-edification' goes some way towards explaining why a shy, suspicious man of books like Hazlitt should have become so quickly besotted with a girl half his age. When Sarah brought up his breakfast tray for the first time on that fateful August morning in 1820, turning 'full round' before leaving (as the writer himself recalled it) and fixing her eyes 'full' upon him 'as much as to say "Is he caught?" ' (p. 23), what he saw before him was not a pretty, diminutive young woman with little or no conversation, but pure 'fullness', complete redemption, the lovely return of all his late departed hopes.

Sarah Walker may well have been in a hurry to secure a good match like her sister's; that is one explanation, at least, for the flirtatious attitude she seems to have adopted with the gentleman lodgers; another, and equally likely, is that, as her parents' eldest unmarried daughter and a domestic servant in all but name, she was actually *obliged* to indulge the residents, as a filial duty. But whatever the nature and motive of Sarah's behaviour (and it has been debated many times, by critics, novelists and biographers),[5] one thing is clear: Hazlitt was immediately thunderstruck by her, and fell passionately in love. Intoxicated by the easy intimacy she so speedily granted him, he took no heed of her early warning that they could never be lovers. Instead, he grew ever more importunate and demanding towards his 'Infelice' and she ever more taciturn, evasive and even fearful towards him.

In the spring of 1822 Hazlitt asked his estranged wife, Sarah Stoddart, for an Edinburgh divorce, an undertaking that was both costly and degrading, as her journal for the period shows.[6] Filing for divorce in Scotland required a forty-day residence qualification, and Hazlitt chose to spend it at Renton, in the Borders, working on the extra essays required to make up a second volume of *Table-Talk*. (It was in this period that he composed pieces such as 'On the Knowledge of Character', 'On the

Fear of Death' and 'On the Disadvantages of Intellectual Superiority'.) With the divorce proceedings dragging on interminably, Hazlitt returned to Southampton Buildings in the second half of May, hoping to prepare Sarah for a proposal of marriage. But the brief meeting between them (which is described in Part III of *Liber Amoris*) was so catastrophic that it only compounded his torment. Two months later, with the divorce finally granted, Hazlitt discovered quite by chance that Sarah had been secretly involved with another lodger for much of the time he and she had been intimate, and that she was still continuing to see this man in his absence. The gentleman in question was one John Tomkins, a young lawyer's clerk, with whom she was eventually to set up home after becoming pregnant in 1824.[7] It was some time prior to this revelation, however, while en route to Scotland in the spring of 1822, that Hazlitt first hit upon the idea of penning a volume on his relationship with Sarah, a *Liber Amoris*, or 'book of love'.

The desire to cure (and also revenge) himself in print must have been irresistible, because even before the spring of 1822 his feelings had begun to obtrude into his writings. In the manuscript draft of his celebrated boxing piece 'The Fight', which dates from late 1821, there were already a number of ardent references to Sarah, and it was only at a very late stage that he decided to remove them. Even in the published version of the essay there are a number of personal allusions. Think of the opening dedication addressed to the 'fairest of the fair [who] kill [more] with poisoned baits than ever fell in the ring'.[8] Think also of the narrator's 'particular satisfaction' at discovering that his friend Pigott (P. G. Patmore) had brought a volume of Jean-Jacques Rousseau's *Nouvelle Heloise* to the ringside, proving that 'a love of the FANCY' was in no way incompatible with 'the cultivation of sentiment' (p. 111). The entire essay, in fact, can be seen as a drastic attempt on Hazlitt's part to cure himself of effeminacy by plunging into the brutal, heroic world of Regency boxing.

No such self-censorship took place, however, in the case of another *New Monthly Magazine* essay titled 'On Great and Little Things', published in the same month, where the writer talks freely of his general weakness for 'humble beauties' and also of one 'fair creature' in particular whose image was 'engraven' on his 'inmost soul'.[9] Sarah Walker was embarrassed and alienated by this declaration, and by the underlying insinuation that she herself was nothing but a servant. But worse was still to come, for it was in some of the essays written in Scotland in February 1822 that his frustration really boiled over. Hazlitt was an outspoken democrat in his politics, and a regular frequenter of the coffee-house and the fives court, but in

'On the Disadvantages of Intellectual Superiority' we find him complaining about the ridicule and suspicion with which he was treated by working men and women. In his memoir *My Friends and Acquaintance* (1854), Patmore ventured the explanation that Hazlitt 'always lived in furnished lodgings … of a very secondary class', fearing that more genteel landlords would object to his strange, solitary habits and irregular hours. 'Now, by keeping himself among a class of persons, to a certain degree removed from the vulgar', Patmore muses, 'his name and pursuits would have secured him from personal disrespect, if they did not procure him the opposite; whereas in descending one or two steps lower in the scale, the effect of his intellectual pretensions was not merely nullified, but turned against him.'[10] The implication is that, while not being a Cockney himself, Hazlitt suffered greatly from choosing to live among Cockneys, and not only at the hands of *Blackwood's Magazine*.

Hazlitt could certainly be satirical about the male Cockney, as we saw in the previous chapter; taking a leaf, as it were, out of the *Blackwood's* book. But female Cockneys were to open up a whole new vein of resentment in him, borne of intense mutual incomprehension and frustrated desire. In 'On the Disadvantages of Intellectual Superiority' (which must be one of the most provoking titles ever given to an essay), we find him railing bitterly at the Sarah Walkers of the world – chamber-maids and wenches at lodging-houses – whom he accuses of being driven by 'trick, ignorance, and cunning'.[11] On the one hand, he says, there is the naive idealism of scholars (himself being a prime example), on the other there is the native chicanery of women and the working classes. 'On the Knowledge of Character' is a broader, more magnanimous treatment of some of the same themes, but once again we can see the image of Sarah Walker hovering ambiguously in the background. 'The greatest hypocrite I ever knew', the essayist confides to us, near the beginning, 'was a little, demure, pretty, modest-looking girl with eyes timidly cast upon the ground, and an air soft as enchantment.'[12] Designedly irascible in places, 'On the Knowledge of Character' is also remarkably detached in others, offering some new perspectives on the *Liber Amoris* experience. The delightful meditation on the mystery of one's own character is one example of this, the little passage on *love at first sight* another: 'We generally make up our minds beforehand to the sort of person we should like', Hazlitt writes, 'grave or gay, black, brown or fair; with golden tresses or with raven locks:– and when we meet with a complete example of the qualities we admire, the bargain is soon struck … it has been present to our waking thoughts, it has haunted us in our dreams, like some fairy vision.'[13]

For months on end Hazlitt seems to have wandered around London like a metropolitan Ancient Mariner, telling 'the whole story' over and over to anybody who would listen. In his diary for 9 August 1822, his friend, the painter Benjamin Robert Haydon, noted that 'Hazlitt called last night in a state of absolute insanity about the girl who has jilted him', before adding that '[his] candour is great and his unaffected frankness is interesting'.[14] Proctor also related that

> Upon one occasion I know that he told the story of his attachment to five different persons in the same day, and at each time entered into minute details of his love story. 'I am a cursed fool,' he said to me. 'I just saw J— going into Wills' Coffee-house yesterday morning; he spoke to me, I followed him into the house; and whilst he lunched, I told him the whole story. Then' (said he) 'I wandered into the Regent's Park, where I met one of M—'s sons. I walked with him some time, and on his using some civil expression, by God! Sir, I told him the whole story … Well, sir, then I went and called on Haydon, but he was out. There was only his man, Salmon, there; but by God! I could not help myself. It all came out; the whole cursed story! Afterwards I went to look at some lodgings in Pimlico. The landlady at one place, after some explanations as to rent, etc., said to me very kindly, "I am afraid you are not well, sir?" – "No, Ma'am," said I, "I am not well"; and on her enquiring further, the devil take me if I did not let out the whole story, from beginning to end!'[15]

The discovery of Sarah's affair with Tomkins had been made in July 1822, but even that didn't seem to bring any closure. Bewitched by an alternating vision of Sarah as an angel or a whore, Hazlitt seemingly couldn't be satisfied until he had revealed her in one guise or the other. He moved out of Southampton Buildings in September of that year, but was back, in spirit if not in body, in March 1823, having commissioned a young friend of his, F., to take up residence there and 'try her'. The unpublished diary that Hazlitt kept during this period, the so-called 'Journal of F', gives further evidence, if evidence were needed, of the snobbish, bullying nature of Hazlitt's sexual obsession, but it also goes to show that, even with *Liber Amoris* on the brink of going to press, he still didn't feel he had plucked out Sarah's mystery.[16] Still the poison of 'contemnèd love' was circulating in his bloodstream, and still he could find no peace. Writing, during this period of Hazlitt's career, becomes the desperate search for an antidote. Whether it is the simple, stoical masculinity celebrated in 'The Fight' or the dry, old-world cynicism of *Characteristics, after La Rochefoucauld* (1823), many of the pieces that he wrote at this time can be seen as extreme attempts at self-therapy, as well as mordantly honest investigations of personal prejudice and class feeling.

ROUSSEAU *REDIVIVUS*

Published anonymously on 9 May 1823, *Liber Amoris* was offered to the public as the memoir of a 'native of North Britain', now dead, it was supposed, 'of disappointment preying on a sickly frame and morbid state of mind'. Apologizing for the presence of many details 'either childish or redundant', the fictional editor explained that it had been the author's last wish that the manuscript should appear without revisions; the text was thus presented to the reader as a raw record of events. Under this thin disguise Hazlitt then proceeded to offer an account of the Sarah Walker affair that was painfully minute in its detail and increasingly obsessive in its force. Part I succeeds in presenting the central relationship with a kind of dramatic impartiality, recording a series of past dialogues between a harrying, love-lorn H. and a cagey, reluctant S. But almost all sense of S.'s voice – and of her side of the story – is lost in Part II, which is based on the letters Hazlitt sent to his friend Patmore while awaiting his divorce. A high proportion of what the essayist actually wrote to Patmore during this period was included in *Liber Amoris*; it was only those letters and parts of letters which betrayed the ferocious extent of his sexual jealousy that were omitted from the text. (These extracts include a number of references to Sarah as a 'bitch' and a 'whore', and a couple of prophetic appeals to Patmore for him to get a friend to 'try her'.)[17] Part III, which brings the unhappy story to an end, is also presented as a series of letters – to 'J. S. K.' (another friend of Hazlitt's, the dramatist James Sheridan Knowles). But in this case the correspondence was entirely fictional, deliberately concocted as a means of relating the dénouement. Hence *Liber Amoris* starts off by trying to maintain a degree of distance from H.'s monomania, yet slowly but surely becomes consumed by it. It moves inexorably from dialogue to monologue, and from trial to conviction:

> One more count finishes the indictment. She not only discovered the most hardened indifference to the feelings of others; she has not shown the least regard to her own character, or shame when she was detected. When found out, she seemed to say, 'Well, what if I am? I have played the game as long as I could; and if I could keep it up no longer, it was not for want of good will!' (p. 190–1)

There were two main factors serving to undermine *Liber Amoris*'s anonymity when it first hit the bookstands in the spring of 1823. The first was that, Hazlitt's confessional tendencies being what they were, it was already quite well known to many that the author of *Table-Talk* had recently been 'jilted' by his landlady's daughter. The second related to the book itself.

Sticking purely to the information contained in the published text, H. was presented to the public as a London-based author, a former supporter of Bonaparte, who had a young son called William and who had recently gone up to Scotland to seek a divorce. With all this information so freely avowed, Hazlitt might as well have put his name on the title page; literary London was still a small place at this time, and the biographical jigsaw puzzle was only too easy. Sure enough, within a week of *Liber Amoris's* publication the *Literary Register* had successfully identified all of the main *dramatis personae*, including Hazlitt and Sarah. On 31 May the *Literary Gazette* twisted the knife in still further:

> This matchless conjunction of vulgar sensuality and Cockney affectation – of the sensibilities of the pot-house and the loves of Fleet-street – has been cruelly ascribed to Mr Hazlitt; and we are only surprised that a writer so prone to resent attack has not leaped forth to disclaim the foul reproach, through all the channels of Cocaigne-periodical literature.[18]

On 22 June the virulently Tory *John Bull* somehow got hold of an unpublished love letter from the essayist, parading it before the public as a risible example of Cockney mawkishness. Conservative critics were appalled by the naked candour of the book; to them it summed up all that was worst about the current craze for autobiography. As one *Blackwood's* contributor had complained only a few months earlier, with Rousseau's notorious *Confessions* (1788), Thomas De Quincey's *Confessions of an English Opium-Eater* (1821) and Lamb's recently republished 'Confessions of a Drunkard' (1822) foremost in mind: 'This is confessedly the age of confession, – the era of individuality – the triumphant reign of the first person singular. Writers no longer talk in generals. All their observations are bounded in the narrow compass of self. They think only of number one.'[19] In one of the few positive reviews of *Liber Amoris*, the *Examiner* defended the book in precisely these terms, that is, by comparing H. to those other great amorous confessors, Goethe's Werther and Rousseau's Saint-Preux.[20] Hazlitt would certainly have approved. In his 1816 *Round Table* essay, 'On the Character of Rousseau', the essayist had highlighted the peculiar paradox of the author of the *Confessions*, which was that a man so egotistically narrow in his sympathies should have evoked such powerfully sympathetic feelings in his readers. He even went on to argue that the two things were connected: '[Rousseau's] interest in his own thoughts and feelings was always wound up to the highest pitch', he wrote, 'and hence the enthusiasm which he excited in others.' 'He owed the power which he exercised over the opinions of all Europe, by which he created numberless disciples, and overturned established systems, to the tyranny which his feelings, in the first instance, exercised over himself.'[21] Represented in these terms, Rousseau steps forth as a revolutionary martyr whose self-immolation at the burning stake of sensibility had helped others to discover a new democracy of feeling. The *Confessions* had undoubtedly been important to the men of 1789; indeed Robespierre had singled it out as Rousseau's most inspirational text on becoming a French deputy. But it was indicative of Hazlitt's rather curmudgeonly post-revolutionary republicanism that, for him, Jacobinism was now *all* about personality. In his eyes, those new 'state-doctors', the utilitarians, had hijacked the French project to regenerate the human race and turned it into 'petty projects, speculative details and dreams of practical matter-of-fact improvement',[22] and so the only possibility for an old-style Jacobin like himself was to incubate idealism within the ego, remain steadfast in defence of the old values, and devote himself to being a 'good hater'.[23] *Liber Amoris* takes this attitude, which is so effective in his political writings, and directs it towards the private. It is a daring if foolhardy experiment in the pursuit of virtue through candour.

LODGING-HOUSE ROMANCES

Tory reviewers disliked *Liber Amoris*'s confessional quality, but it was only in combination with the book's 'Cockney' setting that it became truly contemptible. There was something in the idea of love in a lodging-house that they found both ridiculous and reprehensible. To the *Register* the story was 'unprincipled and indecent trash' and 'the ordure of a filthy mind'.[24] *The Times* considered it 'tawdry', and the *Weekly Review* thought it 'an insult to public decency and public morals'.[25] Abuse was also showered on the character of S., who was pilloried as a 'pert, cunning, coming, good-for-nothing chit', and 'a tradesman's daughter – a common flirt – a common lodging-house servant – nay, a common trader in indecencies with every fellow in the house'.[26] Tellingly, the violently reactionary *Blackwood's Magazine*, which been directing anti-Cockney abuse at Hazlitt and John Keats and Leigh Hunt for years, was (by its standards) fairly restrained. The reviewer simply quoted large chunks of the text – clearly considering that it condemned itself – and kept his own remarks to a minimum: 'What delicacy! What manliness! What a veil is here rent away! What abomination is disclosed! What, after this, is a COCKNEY and a LIBERAL?'[27]

Hostile critics of *Liber Amoris* returned again and again to the lodging-house setting, contrasting the grubby, cramped milieu of the story – the sheer littleness of it – with the soaring, self-important language in which it had been related. Lodging-houses, such as the one kept by the Walker family, were curiously indeterminate in status, hovering in an ambiguous, aspirational realm somewhere between the polite and the plebeian. One of the main aims of *Blackwood's* was to put such Cockney places – and their inhabitants – *in* their place, to insist upon their fundamentally vulgar character. The task was particularly urgent in the case of lodging-houses because of the challenge they seemed to pose to middle-class respectability. The product of a kind of artificial intimacy, the relationship between a lodger and his landlord might pretend to the familial but was always in fact commercial, and the same might often be said, in a more provocative sense, of that between lodgers and their landlord's daughters. It was for this reason that lodging-houses were often seen as a challenge to domestic morals, with the threat being all the more insidious because thinly veiled by gentility.

An amphibious, anticipatory, morally elusive space, the characteristic abode of young doctors, attorneys and clerks, the London lodging-house was also seen by *Blackwood's* as the natural habitat of Cockney writers and artists. In July 1823, in an article on George Cruikshank, the magazine made a playful swipe at the painters of the day, offering a vivid caricature of Regency bohemianism: 'They live among themselves – they marry [most commonly as the modern Pygmalion would fain have married] or they are bachelors – men of the third floor and the mutton chop – cheerful over ale or gin-twist "of an evening" … dry, yellow absurd men with fantastic curls or picturesque baldness.'[28] And two months later, in an article on the 'Cockney' authors of the *London Magazine*, the lodging-house was again invoked as the emblem of all that was loose and vulgar: 'The writers seem all to have lived in lodgings', the reviewer said, 'and to be distinguished rather by the smoothness, than the variety of their wearing apparel.'[29]

In 1816 Hazlitt's friend, the radical writer and editor Leigh Hunt, had preceded a short comic vignette, 'On Washerwomen' ('Now, drat that Betty!'), with a long introduction defending the literary representation of homely subjects. Slight as it was, and notorious as it was to become, the essay was, in its way, a kind of prose *Preface to Lyrical Ballads*, offering a new and more democratic aesthetic for the nineteenth century:

> The fastidious habits of polished life generally incline us to reject, as incapable of interesting us, whatever does not present itself in a graceful shape of its own, and a ready-made suit of ornaments. But some of the plainest weeds become beautiful under the microscope. It is the benevolent provision of Nature, that in

proportion as you feel the necessity of extracting interest from common things, you are enabled to do so.[30]

As with 'On Washerwomen', so too with *Liber Amoris*: it was not the coarseness of the canvas or the pretentiousness of its critical frame that vexed *Blackwood's*, but the embarrassing lack of fit between them. This was that subversive muddying of genres and distinctions that they dubbed 'Cockney'.

Five months after *Liber Amoris*, in October 1823 *Blackwood's* published a 'Letter from a Contributor in Love' in which 'Christopher North', the fictional editor, was regaled with all the latest gossip from the English capital. 'But these last two Numbers of yours',[31] the correspondent declared eagerly, 'have played the very devil in Cockaigne. Poor Hazlitt, I am told, is going absolutely frantic; and all the ale at the Southampton Arms turned sour the moment "The General Question" came out. Tell Tickler this, if you love me.'[32] This is characteristic *Blackwood's* fare: heartily congratulating itself on another successful bout of Cockney-baiting, while giving a vivid (and not entirely inaccurate) picture of some of the London authors 'at home'. (The Southampton Tavern, which was just a few doors down from the Walkers' lodging-house, was indeed Hazlitt's local, featuring prominently in the essay 'On Coffee-House Politicians'.) The contributor then moved on to Leigh Hunt, who had gone to Italy in November 1821 to set up *The Liberal* with Byron and Shelley:

Talking of Hazlitt, I had the strangest dream of King Leigh last night! I thought he was come over from Italy, and had taken the White Conduit House Tea Gardens. It's true, upon my word. I saw him in the bar, as plain as ever I saw him in my life – in a straw hat, and a foreign air – quite smirking and genteel-like. He was 'setting down' the little loaves, and pats of butter, as they went out from the *sanctum*, in a bran new Fairburn's pocket-book, with a red morocco back; while the waiter boys ran about, scalding people with the hot water out of the tea-kettles. Very odd, wasn't it? – You haven't heard anything of the kind? I did understand, certainly, some time back, that Cockaigne was rebellious, about his Majesty's stay abroad, and refused any longer to be governed as a province; but White Conduit House is so near Islington, and that affair of the washerwoman; it can hardly be! (p. 472)

The idea that Hunt, that outspoken hankerer after all things Italian, might actually have been in the process of realizing some of his Mediterranean aspirations was clearly a source of some irritation to *Blackwood's* – and so this dream-fantasy has been concocted to bring him back where he belonged. White Conduit House, the Islington tea-garden, has been chosen because (as we saw in Chapter 1) it sums up all that is 'genteel-like' and fake classical in Cockney culture, while the washerwoman has been mentioned in order to remind us of a recent sequel to Hunt's notorious essay.

Earlier in 1823, and only a few months before *Liber Amoris*, *Blackwood's* had published another anti-Cockney parody, this time a very funny 'Letter from a Washerwoman'. The piece, which was written with great verve by Robert Southey's wife Caroline Bowles, is a wonderful bit of comic satire. The letter is written by a semi-literate Islington washerwoman and lodging-house landlady, Patience Lillywhite, and tells of the abduction of her young daughter, Nance, by two poet lodgers. These two men are bookish, effete, quietly spoken, yellow (exactly in the manner of the 'George Cruikshank' article), and take an unhealthy interest in the young girls of the vicinity. They also share many of the same passions as Hunt, Keats and their circle. Their first thought, for example, is to turn Mrs Lillywhite's little suburban garden into 'a grove', and then they set about erecting what the washerwoman herself refers to as 'a temple to Pollar'. Soon after, a number of the prettier young girls in the neighbourhood are brought in to 'personify the Mooses' at a pagan feast, with Nance herself being cast in the role of 'Hairy Toe'.

> Then the feest was to begin. 'Sich a feest,' i says, an' the Mooses was to sarve em wi necktur, meenin nothing else, your honor, then a power of wishy-washy tea that was made in owr grate hurn; an' when i was a goin to fetch owt the best chany cups an' saasurs wi the goold rims, for i liks to see everything hansom, they axed me if so be i hadn't a got anny antik vessels; an' afor i culd puzzle owt the meenin o that, they goes an' rummages owt sum owld cracked butter-botes, an' squatt bottles, an' empty oil flasks, an' for what wuld yur worshipp think? – why to drink tea owt on, ass i'm a livin woman, an' mi name's Patience; becawse, they sedd, the heethen Turks, that mi best cupps an' saasurs wasn't classycull.[33]

The 'Letter from a Washerwoman' is very funny on the absurd pretensions of these pagan poets, while also managing to suggest that there is something a little sinister about them as well, as shabby creatures with loose manners and loose morals, feckless corrupters of youth. The use of dialect in this piece is highly effective, anticipating Dickens's *Pickwick Papers* (1837), and the comic orthography looks forward to Thackeray's *Yellowplush Correspondence* (1838).

One important thing to note here, especially in the light of subsequent developments, is that there are, in effect, two types of Cockney in this story. There is the working-class washerwoman, who speaks in dialect and is funny. Then there are the lodger poets – who are clearly Cockneys in the usual *Blackwood's* sense of being pretentious impostors, urban miscreants, amphibious creatures of no fixed abode. It is a similar opposition, in fact, to the one at the heart of Charles Dibdin's ballad opera *The Waterman* (1774), which was mentioned briefly in the Introduction. In that piece the hero Tom Tug is a vulgar Cockney, who is unapologetically and charismatically low, and Mrs Bundle, the comic villain of the piece, is a pretentious suburban social climber. In Dibdin's utopian rendering, the main point of the plot is to reward Tug for his unpretentiousness by giving him the hand of Mrs Bundle's daughter Wilhelmina; Mrs Bundle, by contrast, is forced to rein in her social and cultural ambitions. There is a similar social logic to Caroline Bowles's story, where the washerwoman is a creature of good, sensible values, a salt-of-the-earth figure, whose kindness and hospitality is exploited by upstart scoundrels. Ignorant and small-minded she may be, but her great virtue (at least from a contemporary conservative perspective) is that she really does know her place. To 1820s ears, therefore, her dialect speech can be seen to function as a kind of charm against bad Cockneyism, with her unconsciously comic narration helping bring everything – her lodging-house, her garden and especially her fraudulent lodgers – down to size. Oppositions between working-class and lower-middle-class Cockneys are not common in this period, but they are interestingly prophetic when they do occur. What they look forward to, as I hope the final chapter of this book will demonstrate, is a gradual shift in the meaning of the word 'Cockney' over the course of the 1800s, as the working-class version slowly triumphs over the petit-bourgeois version. Concomitant with this is a radical change in the word's moral connotation, as it gradually stops being used to abuse pretentious upstarts and comes increasingly to be a term of affection for those content to remain low.

ON GREAT AND LITTLE THINGS

Shortly before embarking upon the composition of *Liber Amoris*, at a time when he was already seriously infatuated with Sarah Walker, Hazlitt composed an essay titled 'On Great and Little Things', in which he reflected at great length on the tiny and the trivial. One of the most compelling things about this essay is that it feels like it has been written by the unconscious, with the chain of association all the more eloquent for being implicit. The imagination has a peculiar affinity, Hazlitt says, with minor details – so much so, indeed, that it is invariably the little things in life that we become really obsessed by: 'people have been known to pine and fall sick from holding the next number to the twenty thousand pound prize in the lottery. Now this could only arise from their being so near winning in fancy, from there seeming to be so thin a partition between them and success.'[34] Later in the essay, class difference between husband and wife is invoked as another 'little thing' that shouldn't in theory provide an obstacle but in practice does, and this immediately leads the essayist into thoughts of servant girls in general and Sarah Walker – his 'Infelice' – in particular:

> But shouldst thou ever, my Infelice, grace my home with thy loved presence, as thou hast cheered my hopes with thy smile, thou wilt conquer all hearts with thy prevailing gentleness, and I will show the world what Shakespeare's women were! – Some gallants set their hearts on princesses, others descend in imagination to women of quality; others are mad after opera singers … I admire the Clementinas and Clarissas at a distance; the Pamelas and Fannys of Richardson and Fielding make my blood tingle. I have written love-letters to such in my time *d'un pathétique à faire fendre les rochers,* and with about as much effect as if they had been addressed to stone. (p. 134)

'On Great and Little Things' was advertised in the *New Monthly* as 'Table-Talk No. 11', which meant that this reference to servant girls was spectacularly indiscreet. But laying aside, for a moment, the acute pain that it must have caused Sarah Walker, and the powerful ammunition that it gave his political enemies, we can see, in this passage, the imaginative seed of *Liber Amoris.* Cyrus Redding had written fondly of semi-genteel working girls in his 1822 *New Monthly* article 'London and the Country', arguing that 'there is much more of the imaginary character of a nymph, in a pretty London shop-girl, or a neat-footed little milliner than can be found in half-a-dozen country villages among the assembled Blouzelindas'.[35] But these were Cockney sentiments of a comparatively general (and genteel) kind, and could easily come under the rubric of modern 'improvement'. Hazlitt's revelation of a lifelong passion for servants was of quite a different order, erupting, as it does, out of an apparently very unrelated discussion, and yet burning fiercely with a most tortured literary longing.

We know from Sarah Stoddart Hazlitt's journal that Hazlitt made regular use of prostitutes in the early 1820s, indeed that they sometimes came to visit him at Southampton Buildings. The essayist himself seems never to have tried to hide the fact – neither from Sarah Walker nor even from his eleven-year-old son William. But we also know from his fervent reference to Raphael's St Cecilia at the beginning of *Liber Amoris* that his sexual imagination was heavily invested in both sides of the angel/whore dichotomy (p. 3). The servant girl was an interesting figure for Hazlitt to fix upon in this respect not least because the status she occupied in the mind of the middle-class Regency male was somewhere between that of a domestic angel and a 'common trader'. Sometimes considered as only one step up from a prostitute because of her singleness, sexual availability and subservience, the London servant girl could also be seen in Pamela-like terms, as a gentlewoman in embryo, a veritable lady-in-waiting. Reminding ourselves of Hazlitt's uncertain status at this time as an unsociable scholar, a precarious freelance, 'a man of the third floor and the mutton chop', we could well conclude that his focus on servant girls was but a poor attempt to maintain power and superiority in the face of personal disappointment. But in the passage quoted above, what seems equally striking is his conception of the servant as a figure of social possibility, a potent mix of politeness and affability. Shakespeare's heroines, after all, are frequently paragons of womanhood disguised as servants, and here too Sarah Walker is explicitly imagined as a creature of revolutionary potential, promising a new intimacy and transparency between the sexes, a 'plain weed' that could become 'beautiful under the microscope'. The irony of this, of course, in both 'On Great and Little Things' and *Liber Amoris*, is that this promise is not fulfilled. In the essay Hazlitt describes how he has written ardent letters to servant girls in the past and 'the simpletons only laughed' (p. 134). And the experience is even more painful in *Liber Amoris* where S. develops into a figure of extraordinary elusiveness and antipathy. But the book still captures both sides of the stone-splitting joke, functioning simultaneously as an agonized complaint from the pen of a middle-aged, middle-class idealist, and a lacerating critique of that same author's snobbery, sexism and self-delusion.

The reference to stone also has further interest, given that the ironic subtitle of *Liber Amoris* is 'The New Pygmalion' and the book itself is referred to by H. in Part II as 'a record of my conversations with the statue'. The *Literary Register* had picked up on this in its review of the book, nicknaming the protagonist 'Pyg' throughout. Less well known is the fact that only three years previously, in May 1820, Hazlitt's friend Leigh Hunt had devoted half an issue of *The Indicator* to a new translation of Rousseau's one-act studio drama *Pygmalion*, supplying a brief critical preface on the various ways of interpreting the legend. Hunt criticized the way Rousseau had made Pygmalion fall in love with his own work 'almost out of vanity', wishing instead that he had represented him 'fashioning the likeness of a creature after his own heart, lying and looking at it with a yearning wish that he could have met such a living being, and at last, while indulging his imagination with talking to her, making him lay his head upon hers, and finding it warm'.[36] Clearly for Hunt the Pygmalion story should have been about a real romantic connection between two separate beings – about imagination becoming real. What he disliked about Rousseau's rendering was that it was so unapologetically solipsistic; to him it hovered uneasily between romance and satire.

Something of the same claustrophobic air surrounds Hazlitt's 'New Pygmalion', both in the tone of the piece and in its setting, and this lack of distance has sometimes made it difficult for readers to get any perspective on the drama. Rather as if one were trapped in the same small room as the disputants, the urge has always been to take sides, get involved, defend or prosecute S. But what the passage from 'On Great and Little Things' suggests is that we should concentrate less on her character in the book, enigmatic and intriguing though it is, and more on her social and spatial position within it. In Parts II and III especially she is a liminal, shadowy figure, powerful only through her ability to remain elusive, a figure of tantalizing proximity and maddening illegibility for H., the ultimate negation of a great critic's powers of reading.

It was perhaps natural that Hazlitt's first published mention of Sarah Walker should be in an essay on the perplexing nature of little things, because everything about Hazlitt's lodging-house affair was little. There was S. herself, who is described at various points in *Liber Amoris* as 'a sublime little thing', 'my little all', a 'precise little puritanical person' and a 'little dissembler'. There was the room he rented and in which she served him breakfast; the presents he showered her with (including the 'little image' of Bonaparte); the space between them (she always seems to be hovering in H.'s doorway in *Liber Amoris*, taking up the servant's characteristic station). What is more, the conversations H. has with her, or overhears, always seem to turn on little things – set phrases, half-heard innuendoes, indistinct vulgarities. There is the 'below-stairs conversation' darkly referred to in Part I's 'The Quarrel' (p. 27), and more fully exhibited in Hazlitt's original letters. There are also those little remarks of S.'s – 'I despise looks' and 'you are the same to me as ever' – that H. keeps returning to in the course of the narrative.

Littleness – the mind's capacity to linger self-tormentingly over tiny details – is central to Hazlitt's analysis of the role of the imagination in love. But so too is likeness. In the opening section of *Liber Amoris* H. shows S. a picture that he believes bears a great resemblance to her. S. cannot see it; 'No: it's much handsomer than I can pretend to be', she says, 'besides, the complexion is fair, and mine is dark.' Tossing such inessential details aside, H. insists that the eyes in the picture are just like hers, when she looks up and says 'No, never!' (p. 2). Beginning *in medias res*, *Liber Amoris* presents us with a situation in which Stendhalian crystallization around the image of the beloved has already obscured the underlying object.[37] The picture in question turns out to be a small and delicate copy of some Old Master, whose author and subject remain unknown. 'Some say it is a Madonna', H. says, 'others call it a Magdalene' (p. 3). Like the picture she resembles, S. is beautiful but ambiguous, an angel who is always about to transform into a whore. She is like a proletarian version of Proust's Odette in this respect: tantalizing not so much because of her positive qualities, as because of her resistance to being read.

Much of the literary allusion in *Liber Amoris* has an equally slippery quality, tending to function as 'a goodly temple | That's built on vaults where carcasses lie rotting' (to quote from Middleton's *Women Beware Women*). Part II partakes of that most apparently bright and breezy of forms, the epistolary travel narrative, as H. roams through Scotland – Edinburgh, the Borders, Stirling Castle, the mountains – while waiting for his divorce. But its deep affinities are with Rousseau's *Confessions* (1782–8), Goethe's *Sorrows of Young Werther* (1774) and Mary Wollstonecraft's *Letters from Sweden, Denmark and Norway* (1796), all stories of unhappy love, exile and alienation in which the threat of suicide is prominent. Congratulating P. on his marriage in the last letter of Part II, H. remarks that 'it is just what I proposed to her to do … to have visited Vevai and the rocks of Meillerie, and to have repeated to her on the spot the story of Julia and St. Preux' (p. 122). The great epistolary novel *Julie, ou La Nouvelle Heloise* (1761) was one of the bestsellers of the eighteenth century, and a great favourite of Hazlitt's. It offered an intoxicating picture of passionate, pure (and, by the end of the novel, entirely platonic) love. The reference to Meillerie in Switzerland is interesting in that this landscape forms the backdrop for one of the darkest and most dramatic letters in the novel. Banished from Vevey and his beloved Julie, her former tutor Saint-Preux borrows a telescope from a local priest and climbs the rocks of Meillerie. From there he finds he can see all the way across the lake that divides him from his lover, and right into her house and quarters. 'Here it is', he writes to Julie, 'that your unhappy lover is enjoying to the full perhaps the last pleasures he will taste in this world', before concluding his letter with the words: 'the mountainside is steep, the water deep, and I am in despair.'[38] Returning to *Liber Amoris*, it is interesting to note that even this apparently sunny allusion to *Julie* carries within it a hidden message of forlornness, frustrated sexuality and suicidal thoughts. Like so many of the other bookmarks in Hazlitt's crazed memoir, it carries a sting in its tale.

There are verbal reminiscences of Shakespearean tragedy everywhere in *Liber Amoris*, with *Othello* giving way to *Macbeth* and then to *Lear* as H.'s state of mind worsens. But the most striking allusions of all are to Jacobean drama. Stray images or quotations push us towards tales of domestic suspicion and adultery in middle-class settings: the pretended infidelity of Infelice with her footman in Dekker's *The Honest Whore*, the real adultery of Ann Frankford and her lodger Wendoll in John Ford's *A Woman Killed With Kindness*, and the betrayal of Leantio by Bianca in Middleton's *Women Beware Women*. Slowly but surely S.'s image becomes decorated with suspicious allusions, as the process of crystallization becomes increasingly negative.

THE BUST OF BONAPARTE

Culturally and geographically wide-ranging though it is, the *Liber Amoris* remains an intense, even claustrophobic reading experience, not least because even the most far-flung reference always brings us back to the little lodging-house in Holborn. From the moment S. looks deliberately back at H. before closing the door on their first meeting, it is her extreme proximity that torments him, the maddeningly 'thin partition' that seems to stand between him and success. Perpetually up and down stairs and in and out of his room, she is always around and always – apparently – available. And it is this that fuels H.'s dream of domesticity – and its nightmare opposite. At the beginning of the fifth dialogue in Part I, H. displays the unstable nature of his imaginings, as he questions S. about her behaviour towards the other male lodgers:

H. You are angry with me?
S. Have I not reason?
H. I hope you have; for I would give the world to believe my suspicions unjust. But, oh! My God! After what I have thought of you and felt towards you, as little less than an angel, to have but a doubt cross my mind for an instant that you were what I dare not name – a common lodging-house decoy, a kissing convenience, that your lips were as common as the stairs –
S. Let me go, Sir! (p. 20)

Like a new Rousseau, or like a Robespierre in love, H. develops a Jacobin plot about S. in which either she loves him, and it is only his marital status that prevents her from saying so, or she is actively and poisonously treacherous towards him, a monumental pillar of ill-will. To speak of *Liber Amoris* in terms of the final defeat of revolutionary idealism might seem a little far-fetched, but there are a number of threads that back up this line of interpretation, and which give this very domestic disaster, this crisis of 'commonness', a wider resonance. In Part I of the narrative, S. expresses a passing interest in H.'s little bust of Bonaparte, if only because it reminds her of a former beau. H. gives it to her only too willingly, but in such a manner as makes clear that all his former public hopes are being invested in it for S.'s personal safe-keeping. Later, in despair at the collapse of their relationship, and full of suspicion that S. has started seeing someone else, H. smashes the little Bonaparte on the floor, and the effect of this on the page is simultaneously both frightening and farcical:

> I then dashed the little Bonaparte on the ground, and stamped upon it, as one of her instruments of mockery. I could not stay in the room; I could not leave it; my rage, my despair were uncontrollable. I shrieked curses on her name, and on her false love; and the scream I uttered (so pitiful and so piercing was it, that the sound of it terrified me), instantly brought the whole house, father, mother, lodgers and all, into the room. They thought I was destroying her and myself. (p. 142)

Can it be an accident that the two great texts on frustrated love in the period – Stendhal's *De l'Amour* and Hazlitt's *Liber Amoris* – were both written by disappointed Bonapartists, by militant liberals whose hopes rose and fell with Napoleon? Certainly, what Bonaparte represented to Hazlitt and Stendhal was not simply a body of political ideas – republicanism, equality, meritocracy – but also, more concretely, a certain model of masculinity, a model that did not celebrate aristocracy, breeding or physical stature, but genius, enthusiasm and the individual energy of the man of destiny. The anger and frustration in the passage quoted above is not, I would suggest, directed solely towards Sarah, but also, through and beyond her, to the figure of the 'little Bonaparte', which serves as an ironic reminder of Hazlitt's own failure to rechannel disappointed public hopes into the private realm, and, more painfully, of the pathetic diminution of his middle-aged masculinity. On smashing the Bonaparte to the ground, H. utters a shriek so loud and piercing that everyone in the house assumes it must have come from a woman. He has been unmanned by love and history. This is his personal Waterloo.

In the *Lyrical Ballads* (1798) and the *Poems* of 1807, Wordsworth had made much of the imagination's capacity to attach deep significance to apparently mean or trivial things; a ruined cottage, a withered thorn, leech gatherers, clouds, daffodils. So too in Rousseau's *Confessions* seemingly insignificant objects – ribbons and periwinkles – were often the prompt for the most sublime personal associations. Hazlitt saw a democratic quality in all this. To him such highly individual imaginative investments were a potent antidote to more established – and Establishment – images of sublimity (such as the image of Windsor Keep in Edmund Burke's *Letter to a Noble Lord* of 1796). Characteristically, in the Cockney drama of *Liber Amoris*, the fetish object is not a ribbon or a flower but a kitschy ornament, and its cultivation as a symbolic focus for H.'s hopes is all too easy to deride. But the little Bonaparte is a resonant symbol nonetheless, not merely of the diminutive general's extraordinary career as a man of talent, but also, more generally, of the revolutionary potential of 'sublime little things'.

Not that this potential is borne out by *Liber Amoris*, however. Some time after the Bonaparte-smashing incident, H. and S. come to a kind of rapprochement, and S. agrees to try to see whether the little bust can be mended. In real life there seems to have been a certain ambiguous sweetness in Sarah Walker's behaviour at this time. Fear must have had something to do with it, since, as Patmore points out in the only letter of his to be included in *Liber Amoris*: '[the family] are all of them, every soul, frightened at you; they have *seen* enough of you to make them so; and they have doubtless heard ten times more than they have seen' (p. 114). On a first reading of *Liber Amoris* it is not completely clear why the entire family should have been so frightened by H. *at this stage*, but when one considers that in real life this letter of Patmore's was written some time *after* the terrible confrontation described in Part III, Letter I it is much easier to comprehend. To include this letter at all is evidence of extraordinary candour on Hazlitt's part, and, placed where it is, it does have the virtue of suggesting that from everyone else's point of view the affair had a very different complexion. But the family finances may also have had an influence on Sarah's new manner. It was at this time that Hazlitt told Mrs Walker of his desire to rent all the free rooms in the house, and this may well have led her to bury her misgivings, draw a line under the past and urge Sarah to make one final effort to be friendly. None of the social and economic pressures upon S. are foregrounded in *Liber Amoris*; and even the startling new perspective that is presented by Patmore's Part II letter passes largely without comment. Instead the emphasis is entirely on H.'s misguided sense of entitlement, and on the perceived cruelty of S.'s increasingly distant manner.

FADING INTO THE LIGHT OF COMMON DAY

In the dénouement of *Liber Amoris*, H. briefly turns stalker, following S. on a trip to Somers Town, where she is supposedly going to visit her grandmother. Discovering S. walking in the street with 'a tall, rather well-looking man', H. finds himself ignored by her completely, despite the fact that he twice crosses her path. Later H. recollects him to be 'Mr. C—' (i.e. John Tomkins), one of the family's former lodgers, the man he had been most jealous of a few months before, and soon after he discovers that S. had been carrying on with this man at the same time as she had been trifling with him. Finally, in the closing pages of the book H. becomes self-tormentingly exultant at having torn away S.'s 'mask'.

> Such is the creature on whom I had thrown away my heart and soul – one who was incapable of feeling the commonest emotions of human nature, as they regarded herself or anyone else … My seeing her in the street has gone a good way to satisfy me. Her manner there explains her manner in-doors to be conscious and overdone; and besides, she looks but indifferently. She is diminutive in stature, and her measured step and timid air do not suit these public airings. I am afraid she will soon grow common to my imagination, as well as worthless in herself. Her image seems fast 'going into the wastes of time', like a weed that the wave bears farther and farther from me. Alas! thou poor hapless weed, when I entirely lose sight of thee, and for ever, no flower will ever bloom on earth to glad my heart again! (pp. 191–2)

A possible angel in the house, S. is confirmed (in H.'s mind at least) as a whore in the street – the change of setting and perspective helping to rectify his former error. On first reading, it is difficult to get beyond the sheer hypocrisy and misogyny of this passage, especially when one thinks of Hazlitt's own penchant for street-walkers. But there are other things at work here too. One is the subtle shift, a very painful one for an old-style Jacobin to make, between the positive, rather democratic connotation of 'common' in the phrase 'commonest emotions' and the contemptuous flavour it carries later on. The phrase 'I am afraid she will soon grow common to my imagination' recalls that earlier accusation of H.'s that S. was a 'common lodging-house decoy' with 'lips as common as the stairs'. 'Commonness', it seems, is now no longer something to be celebrated, a meeting-ground, a place of shared understanding; all it evokes is vulgarity, worthless ubiquity, prostitution.

The other thing to notice, with this final bursting of the Cockney bubble, is the changed perspective on smallness. Once S. was H.'s 'little all', but now she is merely 'diminutive'. It is as if Hazlitt's narrator, like the Cockney at the beginning of 'On Londoners and Country People', has been made giddy by too much proximity, coming 'so often in contact with [certain] persons and things', that he has 'rubbed off a little of the gilding, and is surcharged with a sort of second-hand, vapid, tingling, troublesome self-importance'. Unrequited love is like this, one could argue, but so too is

Cockneyism. In 'On Londoners', the redemption from false consciousness comes when the metropolitan is reminded of his political birthright, the fact that 'in London there is a public, and each man is part of it'. Only then, as it were, might he be ready to receive the true lesson of the street, for it is by seeing a tenth part of 'the *People*' moving daily before us, Hazlitt argues, that we gradually come to understand that 'vast denomination', 'and by having our imaginations emancipated from petty interests and personal dependence, we learn to venerate ourselves as men, and to respect the rights of human nature'. There is a similar process at work in the passage quoted above, I would argue, with S.'s charms, 'near, superficial, little' as they are, finally proving no match for the street's 'public airings'. At last H. is freed from 'that world of romance, that fairy land of his own' which had almost been his undoing. The difference is, of course, that whereas the masculine bias at the end of the 'On Londoners' had been relatively implicit ('there is a public, and each man is part of it'), in *Liber Amoris* the affirmation of public space and public life is clearly made at the expense of women.

Liber Amoris is an ironic sequel to Rousseau's *Pygmalion* in that it describes a man who falls in love with a statue only for the statue to fail to come to life. The narrator, H., who is as close to Hazlitt as it is possible to be, clearly thinks that it is an indictment of everything 'common' – common humanity and common people – that S. has failed to respond to him. This is the irony of the story in his eyes. But the *book* itself, which corresponds to that portion of Hazlitt's mind that could see beyond his own feelings, does keep reminding us of just how solipsistic, how *un*common H.'s love was from the beginning – in the dialogues, in the fear of the family towards him, and in that powerful sense of another, alternative history lurking just beyond his consciousness. To look at the narrative from this perspective is to step outside the studio of Pygmalion's imagination and explore the narrowness of *his* sympathy, not hers. Far from showing the world what Shakespeare's women were, *Liber Amoris* ends up showing us what the men of Jacobean tragedy were: foolhardy, jealous and obsessed with sexual corruption. Both perspectives on the story – the romantic and the ironic – are present in the final scene, because by taking S. outside into the street at the end of *Liber Amoris* Hazlitt simultaneously banishes her and frees her – from H.'s love, from the Jacobean drama of the lodging-house and from the pressure of being a statue – so that her drift into the wastes of time is also a return from the world of art to nature, and a 'fading into the light of common day'.

Hazlitt's decision to publish his feelings about Sarah was spectacularly imprudent; the *Liber Amoris* played right into his Tory enemies' hands and caused lasting damage to his reputation. The book also represented a grave slur on Sarah Walker's character, and may have forced her to settle down with Tomkins. But however foolish and destructive we might consider Hazlitt to have been in life, in art he knew what he was doing. Far from being '"vile kitchen stuff", fit only for the midden' (as his Edwardian biographer Augustine Birrell once described it),[39] *Liber Amoris* is one of the first great literary texts to offer a really honest portrayal of romantic obsession, and to display it in its modern aspect, as a lurid hothouse flower fostered alike by history and social setting.

CHAPTER 4

Pierce Egan and Life in London

The Cockney School has been superbly served by criticism over the past twenty years, one of the most essential books on the subject being Jeffrey N. Cox's *Poetry and Politics in the Cockney School* (1998). Cox's leading contention is that we need to consider Leigh Hunt as the central figure of a self-conscious literary coterie, a group that was always highly aware of its status as a radical avant-garde. Not only does this give us a better understanding of these writers' sense of themselves, he argues, it also improves our grasp of what is going on in their work. 'Put simply', he says, 'I believe that if we attend to the Hunt circle the individual works produced within it will speak to us more fully as we hear them speak to and for the group.'[1] Cox's sense of the close interconnections and internal dialogues in the work of Hunt, Keats, Shelley, Byron, Hazlitt, Webb, Horace Smith and others has been deeply invigorating, even if there are occasional difficulties about his conception of them as a movement. The most important difference, however, between his book and the present study, is in the conception of the word 'Cockney'.

For Cox, Cockneyism in this period begins and ends with the 'Cockney School': the term is a name for a particular set of writers, which includes the liberal aristocrats Byron and Shelley. But this is not quite how the Cockney phenomenon played out in the periodicals of the time. To be sure, many conservative magazines of the day saw Leigh Hunt, John Keats and William Hazlitt as the epitome of Cockneyism – its prime examples and leading lights. But they were also inclined to regard it as a broader social contagion that needed constant critical policing. This is one reason why, for *Blackwood's Edinburgh Magazine*, vilifying the *Examiner* set was not the end of the story, for occasionally it became necessary to bring other figures to the bar. Charles Lamb was one such example, as we saw in Chapter 2, and so too were his friends Thomas Hood and Bernard Barton. One obvious thing to note in this context is that, ultimately, the question of whether or not a particular figure had the Cockney disease was less important to the Blackwoodsmen than the fact of their being checked for it, for it was by engaging in this critical practice that the magazine was able to reinforce the term's status as a real criterion of aesthetic and moral judgement, and not merely a nickname for a group.

Figures of the new popular culture were particularly suspect, especially if they had been praised by the *London* or the *Examiner*. Hence it was one of the charges against Edmund Kean, when *Blackwood's* reviewed his autobiography in 1824, that he had been supported and sponsored by the Cockney School. The connection was, as it were, contaminating, and told one everything one needed to know about this ill-bred, upstart actor. 'These were Kean's patrons', it sneered, 'they pronounced him a second Garrick, and the town bent in prostrate reverence before the fetid breath of the oracle.'[2] Interesting as it is to look at the characters that magazines such as *Blackwood's* and the *John Bull* convicted, it is even more absorbing, in a way, to look at the figures they clearly worried about but decided to absolve. Lamb was one of these. So too was the popular writer Pierce Egan, whose spectacular travelogue *Life in London* (1821) was to take the Regency world by storm. Looking at Egan's work from our historical vantage point, it is difficult to conceive of a book that is more completely immersed in the Cockney culture of the period. Yet it managed to escape the wrath of *Blackwood's*. Politics, of course, had a lot to do with it; but the case was still a complicated one. With all this in mind, this chapter will explore a lower-middle-class text that somehow managed to be liberating without being liberal and ambitious without being aspirational; it will look at Cockney literature in Tory form.

How do we explain the phenomenal popularity of *Life in London*? There is no doubt that Tom and Jerry were among the most popular and influential creations of the nineteenth century: not only did the novel run into countless editions during the course of the Victorian age, it was also the subject of innumerable imitations, from street broadsides to theatrical burlesques. The problem is that it has always been rather difficult to see *why*. Critical comparison with later Victorian fiction has never been particularly illuminating, other than to show that, even at the most basic level of cockney comedy, Tom and Jerry simply cannot compete with later works such as *The Pickwick Papers* or *The Yellowplush Correspondence* (both 1838). More importantly, the fact that *Life in London* doesn't seem to respond to literary analysis in the manner of a Dickens classic has always been seen as convincing proof of its lack of critical interest. Readings have always tended to treat the novel as if it were merely an unreflective symptom of 'the spirit of the age', or, less convincingly still, as a baggy source of documentary information about Regency London. Only in the last twenty years or so have more resourceful readings started to appear.[3] What intrigues me is the possibility that it might be precisely our deep familiarity (not to say complicity) with the great Victorian novelists and sociologists that has prevented us from appreciating Tom and Jerry on their own terms. To those of us brought up on Dickens, the social vision of *Life in London* is bound to seem hopelessly simplistic and lacking in definition. But what if a certain degree of indeterminacy, vagueness even, had been an essential part of its appeal?

One has only to look at the frontispiece of *Life in London* (Figure 2) to feel the full force of both its strengths and limitations. The engraving (which, like all the illustrations in the book, is by Robert and George Cruikshank) strives to capture the full range of English society, with its various classes and conditions imagined as different elements in the design of a Corinthian Column. On the uppermost level, serving as the prime ornament of the edifice, are 'the Flowers of Society', that is, the newly crowned George IV, his Lords of the Garter and the fine ladies of the court (the 'Roses, Pinks and Tulips' of the age). Below this are two figures representing the 'Noble' and the 'Respectable', both considered among the 'Ups' of contemporary life. Inside the main oval we find Tom, Jerry and Bob Logic (the three main protagonists of *Life in London*) in their characteristic attitude of drinking and singing. Beneath them, another couple of images depict the 'Downs': on the one hand the 'Mechanical' (an artisan with a hammer and a jug of beer), and on the other the 'Rag, Tag and Bobtail' (a seller of street goods). Beneath them, the Cruikshanks have depicted the 'base' of the column, which is represented by a slum family struggling for existence in a dark basement. The accompanying tag identifies them as the 'Vegetables' of London society, presumably by way of a contrast to the 'Flowers' depicted above. There are two bundles of fasces on either side of this image, labelled 'Bunches of Turn-Ups' and 'Strings and Ingens'. Underneath this runs a carousing quatrain from Burns: 'Here are we met Three Merry Boys | Three Merry Boys I trow are we | And many a night we've merry been | And many mae we hope to be.' Finally, on either side of the main oval, and on a different axis from the 'Ups' and 'Downs', we come across the 'Ins' and 'Outs' of *Life in London*, namely a man holed up in a debtors' prison and one newly released.

In the past, commentators have tended to pass over this opening flourish, and to a certain extent it is easy to see why. As a piece of comic entertainment, it is entirely successful (it is an engaging conceit, with a number of witty oppositions), but as a vision of the social order it is rather limited

Figure 2. George and Robert Cruikshank, Frontispiece to *Life in London*. Engraving. 1821.

and old-fashioned. At first sight, it says nothing interesting about the condition of England in 1821; it has no place for the various new ranks and professions that the industrial revolution was bringing into being, and it is notably neglectful of women. Nor does it invite further analysis, in the way that one might expect of a traditional graphic satire; instead it seems to situate itself firmly within the emergent genre of book illustration, an entertaining but essentially casual form (one might think) at one remove from the realm of 'serious' art. But if one were to try to think differently about the print's apparently slipshod manner one might come to different conclusions concerning its meaning.

In the first place, one might begin to discover something highly suggestive in the very casualness and simplicity of its design. Initially, the Corinthian Column invites us to read it vertically, as a social hierarchy in which each rank has its proper place. But there is also a sense in which society has been laid out like a game of roulette (that recent invention which had come over from France in the early 1800s), as if status were an infinitely unstable thing, a kind of lottery. Simultaneously, class society is depicted as a fixed classical structure and its absolute opposite. How then do we read Tom and Jerry's pivotal position within this design? Potentially, at least, theirs is a highly precarious situation: their bubble of mirth hovers uncertainly between the Ins and Outs and the Ups and Downs, liable to be thrown in any direction at a moment's notice. They are at the centre of the wheel of fortune, and at the crossroads of class. But this effect is offset by their evident air of relaxation and enjoyment. Clearly there is a strong sense in which we are supposed to think of their central position purely as a vantage point from which the rest of society, with all of its violent contrasts and reversals, becomes readable as a form of sporting spectacle. On the ambiguous ground lying between the 'Respectable' and the 'Mechanical', Tom and Jerry have succeeded in raising a hot-air balloon of the imagination, in which all anxieties about fortune and status have been subsumed into a fantasy of visual pleasure. It is my contention that this combination of effects was an essential element in *Life in London*'s enduring appeal, not only the relative indeterminacy of its central protagonists, but also their consistently playful attitude, and that these effects were enabled by the very same qualities that have rendered the novel so impenetrable to modern readers, namely its self-consciously slapdash manner, its 'flash' style.

One of the great virtues of David Cannadine's *Class in Britain* (1998) was the way in which it problematized traditional narratives of the emergence of class consciousness in Britain.[4] One of the important things to recognize, Cannadine argues, is that highly developed concepts of class have always been a feature of English life across the social order. Not only that, they were rather supple and complex from the start. From the late seventeenth century onwards, he argues, successive generations of Englishmen and -women have rarely stuck to one simple model of class. Instead they have always tended to work with three essentially contradictory paradigms co-existing in their minds: class as a finely graded hierarchy (the oldest model of all); class as a three-tiered system of upper, middle and lower; and class as a simple division between the 'nation' and its enemies (the infamous 'us and them'). Without necessarily being aware of it, individuals have shifted from one paradigm to another, as and when it has suited them, according to the social and political needs of the moment. At certain times, and in certain circumstances, one model may have become pre-eminent, but they have all continued to influence the national conciousness, in one way or another. Suitably enough, therefore, in Cannadine's view there has never been any 'right' way of reading English class society: the long-standing cohabitation of these three paradigms indicates that each one has always contained an important element of truth within it, without ever being entirely adequate.

One positive effect of this analysis is to re-emphasize the importance of subjective experience to the historical study of class. My only quibble with *Class in Britain* is that it may not have been subjective enough. While freely acknowledging that class thinking has never been an absolute science, Cannadine still tends to think of it as an essentially secular and rational mode of consciousness, a subdivision of the political understanding. In his eyes, its implicit aim has always been a greater purchase on the reality principle, a firmer grasp on the reins of power. The problem with this emphasis is that there are aspects of class thinking that it doesn't take into account. In the eighteenth and nineteenth centuries, for example, there was always a metaphysical aspect to class consciousness, a strong tendency to conflate issues of social rank with questions of spiritual election and damnation (or death and immortality, as we saw in Chapter 1), and this significantly affected the way in which many people thought about the social order and their own position within it. More broadly, it is possible to argue that Cannadine's model seriously neglects what we might think of as the *fanciful* element in class thinking. Precisely because of the potential for social mobility built into the English class system, and the levelling tendencies of modern metropolitan life, city-dwellers have always been free to cultivate their own highly idiosyncratic (and often deeply irrational) version of their position within the social hierarchy, aligning themselves in the most unlikely of ways. One can simply dismiss these formulations as false consciousness, but it might be better to accept their status as 'real fantasies', that is, as dreams and visions that have always had the potential to influence social reality – to 'come true' in some form or other – however vulnerable to social and institutional prejudice they might also have been.

There has never been a class monopoly on this kind of thought, but there are good reasons for thinking that it finds its natural home in the ranks of the urban petite bourgeoisie. In the early years of the nineteenth century, with the decline of artisanship and the rise of new forms of communication, commerce and bureaucracy, an entirely new species of worker came into being, the semi-professional class. It comprised a heterogeneous assortment of people, taking in clerks, trainee lawyers and industrial apprentices on the one hand, and shopkeepers and craftsmen on the other. What bound them together was the fact that they were all, in their different ways, difficult to place within traditional (i.e. eighteenth-century) categories. Neither entirely 'Respectable' nor straightforwardly 'Mechanical', they were in a certain sense creatures without a home, caught uneasily between different elements, the social amphibians of their age. That this rootlessness could be both painful and ludicrous is amply demonstrated by the Cockney satires we have been looking at. That it could also be interpreted more positively as a licence for free-thinking, for far-reaching dreams and aspirations, is not so well documented, except insofar as such traits were singled out by the likes of *Blackwood's Magazine* for satirical treatment. *Life in London*'s major achievement, I want to argue, was to throw itself into this experience of social indeterminacy and to turn it into a source of pleasure. It rejoices in the role-playing nature of modern urban existence. Unlike many of the 'bourgeois' classics of the High Victorian period, it is more interested in viewing class society as a repertoire of possibilities – of Ins and Outs and Ups and Downs – than in putting individuals in their place.

That such a formulation should have gained such popularity right across the social order, and not merely among the 'uneasy' class described above, has a lot to do with the sporting culture out of which *Life in London* emerged, and its uniquely fashionable status in 1821. Had it not been for the broad appeal of the Regency 'flash style' and its oddly democratic mixture of cant and slang, Tom and Jerry would not have been able to appeal to such a wide range of readers on such a variety of levels. The purpose of this chapter, then, is twofold: first, to attempt to describe what was special and enabling about this style, and, second, to try to identify the uses to which it could be put, in the hope that this might explain what it was that made *Life in London* such a sensation on its first appearance, and so stubbornly popular for generations afterwards.

AN ENGLISH DIORAMA

Success did not come early to Pierce Egan. Born in London in the early 1770s into a family from Tipperary, he started his working life in 1786 as a printer's apprentice. It was not until the Waterloo years, however, that he really began to make a name for himself. Initially this was in the opportunistic world of street literature, of broadsides and street ballads, but gradually he moved into sporting journalism, writing regular boxing columns for the *Weekly Despatch*. The Regency was a fine time for boxing, which was increasingly coming to be seen as *the* sport of English Protestant masculinity. It was phenomenally popular with both the 'highs' and 'lows' of society; only the respectable bourgeoisie and evangelicals found it distasteful. By 1820 Egan was justly celebrated as one of the liveliest and most skilful of writers on 'the fancy'. Both his *Sporting Anecdotes* and his fighting anthology *Boxiana* had gone into numerous editions. In writing *Life in London* Egan was clearly attempting to cash in on his established reputation as 'fancy's child'. But he was also bidding to expand that appeal, and make inroads into the 'respectable' reading public. J. C. Reid, in his classic study *Bucks and Bruisers* (1971), sums Egan up as

> a Protestant Irishman who had exchanged ancestral loyalty to the old sod for a passionate devotion to the British monarchy and British mores, an experienced printer, book-maker and hack, a convivial spirit who loved to mix with not only sportsmen and their noble patrons, but also the humble folks of London's back streets, a militant Cockney for whom London was the centre of the universe, a self-educated man whose tastes had been formed on Shakespeare and eighteenth-century literature, but who knew equally well the ephemera of his day … the kind of person, in fact, both ignored and despised by polite society and polite letters, for whom he and his kind were 'low'.[5]

That this last assertion is not true – or not *quite* true – is the main source of interest in this chapter, for, as we shall see, *Life in London*, like all truly Cockney texts of the period, was actually rather difficult to classify or dismiss, hovering as it did in that uncertain realm between popular and polite literature.

The plot of *Life in London*, such as it is, tells simply of a series of 'sprees' conducted by Corinthian Tom, a young man of fashion, Jerry Hawthorn, his ingenuous country cousin, and Bob Logic, an Oxford scholar turned gambler and debauchee. But this narrative is forever being interrupted and augmented by a wide variety of interpolated matter – poems, songs, jokes and anecdotes, and, perhaps most importantly of all, an endless stream of footnotes explaining the numerous *cant* and *slang* terms that pepper every page. Each chapter tells of a fresh jaunt by Tom, Jerry and Logic to a particular place of entertainment. There are pilgrimages to sites sacred to the sporting fancy, such as 'Gentleman' Jackson's boxing club and Tattersall's stables in Hyde Park Corner. There are visits to Covent Garden Saloon, the Royal Academy exhibition at Somerset House and Almack's. There is even a trip to the *ne plus ultra* of 'life in London', Carlton Palace, the London residence of King George IV. Piquantly enough, however, each fashionable excursion is followed by a late-night trip to a low dive or sleazy haunt. These include dog-pits, gin-shops, cadgers' dens and debtors' prisons – not to mention brothels, although Egan is comparatively discreet about them. The entire narrative is written in a very vivid pictorial style, which is perfectly complemented by an extended series of plates from the Cruikshank brothers, illustrating each and every space on the itinerary.

The dynamic interplay of text and image that fuelled the narrative of *Life in London* was hugely successful from the beginning. Like Combe and Rowlandson's *Dr Syntax in Search of the Picturesque* (1809) it was perfectly suited to the serial format in which it first appeared. Only a couple of months after the publication of the first number in September 1820 it was already being reviewed enthusiastically by some of the more popular magazines. Soon after, a number of imitations began to appear, both serial publications and popular broadsides. Many of these were shamelessly plagiaristic.[6] By the time the book finally appeared in full volume form in July 1821 a series of pirate Tom and Jerrys were already competing with the originals for public attention; and by September of the same year the first dramatic adaptation was being announced. In the years that followed, countless versions of the story were put on in the capital and all over the provinces. The production at the Adelphi Theatre, which was based on a text by W. T. Moncrieff, was performed over a hundred times in 1822.[7] The *Literary Chronicle* was not alone in railing against Egan's 'literary abortion' and its influence on contemporary theatre, but it did so with an implicit acknowledgement that all resistance had become futile.[8]

By the mid 1820s *Life in London* had even crossed the threshold into the legitimate theatre, with a run at Covent Garden. Nor was this pattern of success merely a thing of the moment. Even after the initial craze had died down, Tom and Jerry continued to be popular with the public at large. The book went into countless editions, remaining in print until well into the late 1800s, and theatrical revivals ensured that even in the 1840s audiences were still well acquainted with the formula.[9]

At first sight, there is not much that is really new about *Life in London*. The sporting element was relatively novel. On matters of sex and the city the book was neither wholly respectable nor wholly unrespectable, coyly referencing but never quite recalling eighteenth-century pornography and graphic satire. In more literary terms, as Egan's opening 'Invocation' freely acknowledged, the text drew heavily on past urban classics such as Johnson's *Life of Savage*, Addison's *Spectator* and Ned Ward's *London Spy*. It also sought to capitalize on the growing enthusiasm for 'police' literature, which included slang dictionaries, 'crim con' narratives and the ever-popular *Newgate Calendar*. In many of these texts, the main appeal for the genteel or semi-genteel reader lay in a voyeuristic experience of metropolitan low-life. What rendered *Life in London* distinctive was its spectacularization of this idea:

> The *Camera Obscura* is now at work; the table is covered with objects for the amusement of my readers, and whenever it is necessary to change the scene it is only requisite to pull the string, *i.e.* to turn over leaf after leaf, and LIFE IN LONDON will be seen without any fear or approbation of danger either from *fire* or *water*; avoiding also breaking a limb, receiving a *black* eye, losing a pocket-book, and getting into a watch-house, or picking up a *Cyprian* and being exposed the next morning before a magistrate for being found *disorderly*; likewise in steering clear of all those innumerable rows and troubles incident or allied to 'keeping it up, and the loving of fun.' It would have been fortunate indeed for poor JERRY and CORINTHIAN TOM if they had possessed such advantages. But 'experience makes fools wise;' and, as good-natured HAWTHORN and laughing TOM are now about to relate their *adventures* for the benefit of *fire-side* heroes and sprightly maidens, who may feel a wish to 'see Life' without receiving a *scratch*, it must be considered that the Metropolis is now before them.[10]

Egan makes an explicit comparison between *Life in London* and the domestic camera obscura, but the link with the metropolitan panorama is almost equally striking. It was in 1821 that Louis Daguerre first brought his illuminated dioramas to Regent's Park. They created a sensation on their arrival, primarily because of their use of subtle back-lighting effects to create the illusion of movement and change across the painted surface. The first French translator of *Life in London* certainly had this analogy in mind when he presented the adventures of Tom and Jerry to his readers as 'un diorama anglais'.

One way of interpreting Egan's introductory address is to see it as having been consciously written with a non-metropolitan readership explicitly in mind, to supply provincial readers with a vicarious experience of the city. That would explain why he presumes so little previous knowledge of London, and why he almost always imagines the reader to be (like Jerry Hawthorn) an outsider looking in. But in fact it is highly likely that many inhabitants of London would have been equally attracted to such a treatment. After all, the city was growing at such an unprecedented rate during this period that a significant proportion of the urban population would have been very recent arrivals, adrift in the metropolis without any real sense either of its history or its moral topography.[11] Indeed, the more one thinks about the intended public of *Life in London*, in fact, the more one recognizes the extent to which it would have crossed many of the formal boundaries of its day, in social as well as geographical terms. In part Egan was obviously seeking to capitalize on his popularity among the sporting and gambling contingent of the upper classes, by giving a jaunty account of their favourite haunts and habits; but he must also have been endeavouring to entertain and instruct people in the middle of the social order, by giving them a brief peek at the rich and the criminal classes at play. The picture of the cosy suburban fireside is a crucial element here, positing an overwhelmingly respectable frame for this largely unrespectable subject matter, a deeply inviting image of zero-risk engagement.

There is a similar kind of structural hypocrisy at work in the text proper. In alternating between Tom, the experienced man-about-town, and Jerry, the fresh-faced countryman, *Life in London* is constantly striving to occupy two positions at once, to be both knowing and naive. Every chapter of the book is organized on this principle: Tom introduces Jerry to the various pleasure-haunts of London, helping him to interpret what is going on; meanwhile Bob Logic keeps them both entertained with an endless stream of slang patter, which the footnotes then labour to explain. What is interesting is that this commitment to explication is never allowed to undercut the spirit of playfulness that characterizes the main text. Not everything is spelled out; an atmosphere of moral evasiveness prevails. Partly, this is a function of Egan's literary style, which is unconscionably florid and arch. Witness this description of the old Oxonian Bob Logic:

> In the *Kingdom of Sans Souci* he proved himself a *brilliant* of the first water; and from the figure he had cut in the *Province of Bacchus* and the *Dynasty of Venus*, LOGIC had been pronounced a hero. On the *Plains of Betteris* he had shown himself a general of no mean stamp: and his knowledge of *Navigation* was so

good, that he had been enabled to steer clear of the shoals and rocks of *Dun Territory* and the *River Tick*.

[*Duns* were debt collectors; *tick* referred to bills, debts.]

In passages like this, a fissure opens up between the highly facetious, mock-epic surface of the text and the social reality to which it refers. Wit, here, manifests itself in the form of a secret shared vocabulary, a kind of private running joke. Egan's long list of the things that 'life in London' should *not* be about ends up serving as a positive checklist for his protagonists to pursue:

IT WAS NOT to know, or to pretend to know, all the young ladies in town; and should you discover any one, two or three of them to have conceived an affection for you, to endeavour to *debauch* them all … IT WAS NOT to belong to drinking clubs, sporting clubs or drinking societies. To go often to the playhouses, and there always to distinguish yourself as highly as possible in assuming every freakish air and saucy attitude; and, when profound attention is required for the hearing of any fine and pathetic speech, to be suddenly seized with a loud fit of coughing; to clap like a hero at what you should not, and hiss at what you do not understand … IT WAS NOT to frequent places of fashionable resort, and to *keep it up* all night in drinking, swearing and singing. (p. 128)

It is possible to read statements such as this as an attempt to define the *limits* of healthy hedonism, to keep 'life in London' within proper bounds. But it is also possible to read it as an extended joke addressed particularly to the book's male readership, a statement of libertine complicity. When Tom introduces Jerry to a bevy of 'Cyprians' thronging the saloon at Covent Garden, Egan supplies a footnote bewailing the fate of many young girls in the city. But these concerns are never allowed to intrude into the main text or the accompanying illustration (Figure 3), which both retain a thoroughly carefree attitude to urban prostitution. The authors could never be explicit about sex, of course, but they do find means of implying that Tom and Jerry are enjoying a very active night life, sometimes through craftily inserted songs, sometimes through little cryptic illustrations: 'it is quite immaterial how our heroes eluded the pursuit of the Charleys', Egan writes, after Tom and Jerry have *boxed* a *charley* (that is, trapped a watchman in his box), 'or in what manner they spent the remainder of the night' (the accompanying illustration has Jerry carrying a 'Cyprian' on each arm), 'they were out on a spree and determined to finish it. They were not immaculate' (p. 233).

The ultimate effect of *Life in London*'s elliptical manner, I would suggest, is to open up a gap between Tom and Jerry's genteel appearance and the 'real' life that we might imagine lying behind it. Repeatedly, during

Figure 3. George and Robert Cruikshank, *Tom and Jerry in the Saloon at Covent Garden*, from *Life in London*. Engraving. 1821.

the course of the novel, Egan insists on the extent to which he is describing 'real life', life as it *really* is: there is a continual emphasis on the absolute accuracy of both the text and its illustrations. Curiously enough, however, as I have tried to suggest, the intermittent coyness of the text, its repeated willingness to retreat into playful puns and coded gestures, cannot help but suggest a further layer of experience behind the public surface of the 'real'. One way of interpreting this is to see it as a half-conscious indication, on Egan's part, that there is more to Tom and Jerry than meets the eye. By continually suggesting that there are aspects of their lives to which we don't have access, he can't help but raise the possibility that they themselves are not quite what they seem.

FLASH STYLE

To those *in the know* (such as Moncrieff, the theatrical impresario) it was no secret that the characters of Tom, Jerry and Logic were actually based on George Cruikshank, Robert Cruikshank and Pierce Egan himself, since the trio had been hard-drinking companions in and around the metropolis for some years.[12] Egan was even to take the part of Bob Logic in Moncrieff's stage version of the story. What provincial readers and theatre-goers may not have guessed, however, is that a dramatic social and geographical shift had taken place in the translation from life into art. Corinthian Tom's residence was in the West End, as befitted his status as an independent gentleman; George Cruikshank's was in Amwell Street, Islington, and marked him out as a true Cockney. Amwell Street was close to Sadler's Wells and Merlin's Cave, right in the midst of the assorted pleasure-gardens, glee clubs and private theatres of Clerkenwell, a milieu that was to be brilliantly captured by the young Charles Dickens in his 1830s sketch of two city clerks 'Making a Night of It'. Cruikshank's hard-living rackety lifestyle was already notorious by the 1820s. In his superb *City of Laughter* (2006), Vic Gatrell cites a contemporary source declaring that 'often he would come home with the milk in the morning reeking of tobacco and beer and laugh while his sister-in-law scrubbed his face and his mother belaboured him with her fists'.[13] Indeed, George's carousing had become so well known that in July 1823 *Blackwood's* saw fit to issue him with a warning. Cruikshank, so the rumours went, was a clever but careless creature, he seemed to eat, drink and be merry like one of his own heroes. 'But life is short, and art is long', the reviewer said, 'and our gay friend must pull up.'[14] The magazine lavished praise on the illustrator's 'genius', but left its readers in no doubt that he was, at present, a man 'whose education had been neglected', and whose limited stock of knowledge was in danger of limiting his art.

This desire to place George Cruikshank in his metropolitan milieu was part of a more widespread concern in the respectable periodicals of the period: to highlight and expose Cockney dandies. Egged on by a growing supply of cheap versions of the latest aristocratic fashions, a large number of the London lower middle classes were now regularly dressing up in imitation of their 'betters'. Of course, there was nothing very novel about this in general terms: such sumptuary confusion had long been a leading feature of European city life. The only thing that was new was the scale on which it was happening, and the fact that, with aristocratic styles now changing all the more rapidly in order to keep a step ahead of the masses, an identifiably modern fashion industry was coming into being. *Blackwood's* and the *John Bull* were predictably antagonistic to Cockney interlopers, but the animus was by no means confined to them. In January 1821, with *Life in London* sweeping the town, the *New Monthly Magazine* launched an attack on 'Pseudo-Gentlemen'. 'The Chesterfield gentleman was always *well*-dressed', it opined, 'the pseudo-gentleman is, in appearance and manner, the caricature of a fop, the *Ultima Thule* of extravagant frippery. The real gentleman generally gave his coat a character; the pseudo-gentleman gets his character from his coat.'[15] The pseudo-gentleman has numerous shifts and expedients to keep up his credit, but it will always be his destiny to be found out in the end. 'If he be of plebeian order', the *New Monthly* continued, 'he finishes his career *in Banco Regis*' (p. 306). Given that the King's Bench is exactly where Bob Logic ends up in the second volume of *Life in London*, it is quite possible that this passage was written with Egan's bestseller in mind.

Egan's Tom and Jerry are inordinately fond of disguise: they will use any excuse to dress up, whether it is for the masquerade at Covent Garden or the cadgers' feast at St Giles. There are a number of different examples of this. On most occasions, it seems a simple case of two well-to-do gentlemen of leisure 'dressing down' to fraternize with the poorer classes. But a fruitful confusion sets in, at some points, about where Tom and Jerry's 'real' place might be. In one scene, Tom succeeds in getting Jerry and himself some tickets to Almack's, the exclusive assembly rooms in the West End, a regular meeting-place of the great and the good. Before they set out, Tom tells Jerry that in order to pass the test they will have to be on their best behaviour: 'We must also mind our P's and Q's at ALMACKS; more especially as we have been so free and easy lately among the *flash* part of mankind, or otherwise we shall be in danger of letting the blackguard *peep*' (p. 293). They agree to police one another by giving out the warning shout of 'Lethe!' if ever a slang phrase or cant term threatens to loom on the horizon:

> Indeed, if it were possible to call to your aid the waters of LETHE, to cleanse your pericranium of all ideas of 'the *slang*' for a night, upon entering those regions of refinement, or if it were possible only to obtain a few drops to pour over your tongue, to bury in oblivion all thoughts of vulgarity and coarseness of disposition, it would be highly advantageous towards your attraction. (p. 295)

As things turn out, both Tom and Jerry acquit themselves rather well, but not without resorting to their private shibboleth on a number of occasions.

What is interesting here, I think, is the peculiar role of flash language in this scene. It is at once highly fashionable – one of the things that serve to identify Tom and Logic as cultivated and sophisticated men about town – and yet it is also socially ambiguous – the kind of playful vocabulary that might be resorted to, quite readily, by a number of different ranks of metropolitan masculinity. This is one of the things that renders Tom and Jerry such intriguingly ambiguous figures in socio-cultural terms. Is it really that they have been spending too much time with the criminal and sporting classes, and feel that their language might have been corrupted by them? Or are they 'afraid to let the blackguard peep' because they actually belong to the *flash* part of mankind themselves? There is no easy way of resolving this double vision, because although ostensibly their milieu and movements fit squarely within the tradition of aristocratic libertinism, in many other ways they act in exactly the same way as young 'gents' from the lower ranks would do when seeking to *pass themselves off* as gentlemen of leisure.

Flash language in Egan is a rich cocktail of real Regency cant and slang liberally laced with metaphors of the author's own invention, and, presented to the reader in the form it was, with all of those intrusive CAPITALS and *italics*, it comes across as a kind of literary fancy dress. Whatever its linguistic status, the fact that George IV should have had no trouble in accepting the dedication to *Life in London* shows how fashionable this mode of writing was in 1821. During the Victorian period, though fashionable slang still existed, it had lost the special appeal that it enjoyed in the Regency. In the 1820s there still survived vestiges of that old idea, which was expressed in the original preface to Egan's revision of Grose's *Classical Dictionary of the Vulgar Tongue*, of slang as the characteristic expression of a free people (and hence a means of distinguishing the liberty-loving English from the supposedly servile and rule-bound French).[16] As Egan himself says, in a (slightly defensive) note to *Life in London*:

I am aware that some of my readers of a higher class of society may feel or seem to think, that I have introduced a little too much of the *slang*; but I am anxious to render myself perfectly intelligible to all parties. Half the world are up to it; and it is my intention to make the other half down to it. LIFE IN LONDON demands this kind of demonstration. A kind of *cant* phraseology is current from one end of the metropolis to the other. Indeed, even in the time of Lord Chesterfield, he complained of it. (p. 84)

Egan speaks here as if cant and slang were exactly the same thing. Strictly speaking, 'cant' referred to the language of thieves and vagabonds, while 'slang' was associated with more modern activities and professions. Cant was old; slang was new. As the *Dictionary of Modern Slang* put it in 1859: 'Cant was formed for purposes of secrecy. Slang is indulged in from a desire to appear familiar with life, gaiety, town humour, and with the transient nick-names and street jokes of the day.'[17] During the Regency, however, this distinction seems to have been increasingly confused. This muddying was largely a product of the growing popularity of sport and sporting terms. Sporting life had long provided a meeting ground of the classes, a series of arenas where men of widely different backgrounds could come together as 'equals', enjoying a kind of temporary fellowship in the technical vocabularies of the turf and the ring. As Tom says to Jerry during their visit to Tattersall's:

It is no matter who *sells* or who purchases at this repository. A bet stands as good with a LEG, and is thought as much of, as with a *Peer*, – MONEY, being the touchstone of the circumstance. The 'best judge' respecting sporting events is acknowledged the 'best man' here; every person being on the 'look-out' to see how he *lays* his *blunt*. (p. 238)

[A *leg* is a disreputable sporting character, a *peer* is of course a lord and to *lay one's blunt* is to put down money.]

Because of its close connections both with aristocratic society and with lower-class criminality, sports such as boxing and racing partook liberally of both cant and slang, and, as sport became ever more popular among the higher echelons of society in the early 1800s, so too its extravagant and varied lexicon began to take on an increasingly fashionable status. So much so, indeed, that by 1820 many of these words had become slightly severed from their original context, and hovered in a slightly uncertain space somewhere between the polite and the plebeian. The word *flash* is a perfect expression of this ambiguity. As it came to be used in the 1820s, *flash* referred indiscriminately *both* to the world of sport and fashion and to the world of thieving and prostitution, it gestured towards that which was truly dazzling and spectacular, but also to that which was specious and fraudulent. To be 'flash' was to be 'in the know', but it was also to *seem* to be in the know, to 'appear knowing'. The word itself can be seen to hover between registers, like a kind of optical illusion, functioning both as appearance and reality, aspiration and fulfilment. *Life in London* thrives on this kind of double-meaning, out of which it creates a kind of enabling ambiguity. As Egan says of Tom: 'although *one of the fancy* [a man of the sporting, betting, carousing fraternity] he was not a *fancy-man* [a pimp]: yet [he] was as much at home in blowing a cloud, listening to a night-row charge at a watch-house, as he proved himself an adept in all the luxurian movements when waltzing at Almack's' (p. 42). In Egan's novel the patter of cant and slang terms is absolutely incessant, irritatingly so, in the eyes of most modern readers. But one of the effects of this thick verbal texture was to create what would have been otherwise unimaginable in the context of the time, that is, a kind of classless language, a polyglot vocabulary that was not tied to any particular social milieu.

BLACKWOOD'S ON EGAN AND CRUIKSHANK

One of the main aims of *Blackwood's*, as we saw in the Introduction, was to police the boundary between respectable and vulgar literature at a time when rapid social and cultural expansion was in danger of obscuring the divide. To this end, John Wilson and J. G. Lockhart's repeated attacks on the so-called 'Cockney School' from 1817 until well into the 1820s have often been seen as attempts to re-establish a polite standard by drawing attention to its absence in the work of Hunt, Keats and Hazlitt, writers whom they regularly stigmatized as arrant social upstarts, pretentious and vulgar interlopers in a realm that should only – indeed could only – be inhabited by gentlemen. Specifically, Lockhart saw Hunt's *Story of Rimini* as a poem *apparently* dealing with the lives of Italian Renaissance aristocrats but *actually* pandering to the intellectual tastes and habits of the lower middle class. He saw it as a classic tragic narrative translated into a vulgar Cockney romance. With the 'Cockney School' debate in mind, it is interesting to consider what the Blackwoodsmen made of *Life in London*. Given Lockhart and Wilson's no-nonsense treatment of Hunt's fictional creations, why didn't they go after those two arrant impostors Tom and Jerry?

When it came to muddying the distinctions between high and low, street and salon, *Life in London* was as much of a Cockney hybrid as anything by Keats or Hunt. The production values and the literary and artistic ambitions were high enough, but the songs, the humour and much of the subject matter were never far from broadside. One only has to take a brief look at the pirate *Life in London* that the celebrated James Catnach of Seven Dials rushed out shortly after Tom and Jerry's first appearance to see how easily Egan's heroes could be returned to the fold of street literature. Catnach specialized in many of the same genres as Egan in this period: sporting stories, criminal stories, urban travelogues; the main difference was that the productions of the former were always indubitably 'low'. Catnach's pamphlets and broadsheets were cheap and, although sometimes scarcely legible, would often sell in very large numbers, offering up-to-date news, scandal and entertainment in a readily accessible form. In 1824 his account of the Thurtell–Weare murder case (which was also covered by Egan) sold upwards of 250,000 copies, making its publisher well over £500 in profits. The pirate *Life in London* was scarcely less successful. Retailing at tuppence a copy, it contained twelve woodcuts, all of which were close copies of the original Cruikshank illustrations, and a complete, if condensed, version of the original story. In the eyes of many readers it would have been the 'real' Tom and Jerry.

So *Life in London* effectively blurred the line between the polite and the popular, not only in and of itself but also in terms of the many imitations it generated. Why, then, didn't *Blackwood's* target it in the same way as it had *The Story of Rimini*? Marked differences of literary register aside, the simple answer is that Egan was saved by his politics. Whereas Hunt was always liberal and progressive in his views, the 'Xenophon of the Ring' was an outspoken Tory. When *Life in London* first began to appear in the autumn of 1820, the country was still in the grip of the Queen Caroline controversy. The political tension had lessened considerably by the time the collected volume appeared in 1821, but Egan still made a point of dedicating the book to the newly crowned George IV. He even had the gall to compare him to Prince Hal, suggesting that the king was about to cast off his former peccadilloes now that he had finally assumed the crown.[18] It was almost certainly this, in combination with *Life in London*'s extraordinary popularity, that encouraged the Tory critics to hold their fire.

Significantly, there was no *Blackwood's* review of *Life in London*, instead there was only a 'Letter to Pierce Egan, Esq. from Christopher North' (alias John Wilson), which appeared in March 1821. This made no explicit reference to Tom and Jerry, but was clearly prompted by their success. Ostensibly, the main purpose of the article was to praise Egan for the new edition of his *Sporting Anecdotes*; actually it was designed to give him some pointed advice. The article began by stating that Egan had the *Blackwood's* 'Boxiana' reviews to thank for making him known to the 'literary population', declaring that they had ensured him a larger and more refined audience than he would otherwise have gained 'unpatronised'. It then threw itself into enthusiastic praise for the 'gusto' of Egan's writing. Before long, however, the main object of the essay was disclosed. This was to criticize Egan for having included an extract from Hazlitt's essay on Cavanagh, the fives player, in his latest edition of the *Anecdotes*. The piece had no place in the anthology, 'North' argued, because, like every other effeminate Cockney upstart, Hazlitt knew nothing about sport. After quoting a brief extract the reviewer added: 'Is it not evident to you, that this is a dirty species of slang, my dear Pierce, quite different from the bang up language of the fancy, of which you are the great lexicographer? You see from it at once, that the fellow who could write this puppy sentence never had a heart to play fives.'[19] The rest of the article laboured hard to make an absolute distinction between the good old-fashioned Tory activities of boxing and fives-playing and the sour and spineless habits of Cockney journalists. The concern throughout was to drive a wedge between Egan the popular sports writer and Hazlitt the radical Cockney: 'It would give me inexpressible grief', the reviewer noted, 'were the Cockney crew to be at all read by the Fancy' (pp. 674–5).

Repeatedly 'Christopher North' warns Egan away from Hazlitt's 'garbage' while also suggesting that he himself should refrain from meddling in literature and stick to sport: 'you certainly are a very proper man in your line, Pierce, but you cannot have as much experience of men and books as I, or you never would have polluted your work with any of the impertinent drivellings of this fellow' (p. 672). These patronizing comments, coupled with a brief statement expressing disapproval at the mixing of high and low personages in the *Sporting Anecdotes*, form the basis of the *Blackwood's* review. Taken together they indicate a considerable awareness of the subversive potential lying behind Egan's 'flash style'. The deep fear was clearly that he might form part of a growing army of literary rabble-rousers dead set on putting Cockney self-confidence to political ends. That this fear was ultimately unfounded does not change the fact that it must have seemed plausible in the political atmosphere of the early 1820s.[20] A lesser anxiety had clearly been excited by *Life in London*'s insouciant blending of high and low literary styles, hence the article's continuing concern to re-establish Egan firmly within a certain current of loyalist sporting journalism, where his Cockney tendencies would remain harmless. What makes this piece more intriguing is the fact that *Life in London* was already six months into its run by the time it appeared. In one sense its preventive action was already too late: the boundary between Cockney literature and sporting journalism had already been breached. But from another point of view, the 'Letter to Pierce Egan' can be seen as part of a canny attempt to exert a distant influence on an author while steadfastly refusing to concede his most successful publication any kind of literary status.

Two years later *Blackwood's* adopted an even more patronizing tone in a 'Lecture on the Fine Arts' devoted to 'George Cruikshank'. Both George and Robert had been heavily involved in radical satire in the 1810s, and had been a constant source of annoyance to the Prince Regent and his government. Not that this seems to have prevented them from working, on occasion, for loyalist printsellers as well. The beginning of the 1820s was a watershed in graphic satire, for, as Vic Gatrell has shown, it was then that the king finally succeeded in silencing the artists who had been making his life a misery, essentially by buying them off one by one, or in some cases print by print.[21] The 1823 *Blackwood's* article on George Cruikshank came at a particularly interesting moment in this story, being almost exactly contemporary with the London artist's shift from print satire into book illustration, a renunciation of the grubby, disreputable, controversial world of his youth for more 'respectable' literature.

In its 'Letter to Pierce Egan' *Blackwood's* had striven hard to drive a wedge between the healthy, happy sporting fraternity inhabited by Pierce Egan and the sickly Cockneyism of Hunt and Hazlitt. But in the 'George Cruikshank' article of July 1823 'Christopher North' was to depict the Cockney artist at a crossroads. At present, 'North' suggested, George Cruikshank was leading a vulgar, rackety life, but fortunately there was still plenty of time for him to pull himself together. Tellingly, it was Cruikshank's status as a carefree, careless mercenary, a man 'quite contented to dine off the proceeds of a "George IV" today and those of a "Hone" or a "Cobbett" tomorrow',[22] that was both his problem and his salvation. It was a problem insofar as it showed that Cruikshank was not taking his art seriously enough, but it was a source of potential salvation insofar as it showed that he was not yet a radical Cockney. The *Blackwood's* piece then branched out unexpectedly into a semi-facetious sociological study of the habits of the modern metropolitan artist:

Now what are the painters in general? Capital fellows, no doubt, in their way – a little addicted to turning up their noses at each other – amicably open in their vanities – but, upon the whole, pleasant people – most assuredly so. But what do they know of the world, past, present, or to come? They have never read anything worth speaking of – that, indeed, they scarcely ever pretend to have done – So much for the past. They live among themselves – they marry [most commonly as the modern Pygmalion would fain have married] or they are bachelors – men of the third floor and the mutton chop – cheerful over ale or gin-twist 'of an evening' – smokers of shag, frequenters of the pit, emergers into sunshine on 'clean-shirt day' – dry, yellow, absurd men with fantastic curls or picturesque baldness – the solemn smile of a recluse – the ease of an actor *off the stage* – a shuffling lounging gait – and too often green spectacles. (p. 19)

'Clean-shirt day' alludes to the one day per week in which Ofellus, the impecunious artist in Samuel Johnson's *Art of Living in London*, was able to go out and meet society. 'The modern Pygmalion' is a reference to Hazlitt's *Liber Amoris, or the New Pygmalion* (1823), the story of the author's disastrous infatuation with his landlord's daughter, a thoroughgoing Cockney romance published only a couple of months earlier. And as for those other details – the curls, the baldness, the spectacles – all these seem designed to suggest the so-called 'Cockney Raphael', Benjamin Robert Haydon, who had begun his first stint in the King's Bench debtors' prison in April that same year. Both Haydon's prison experiences and Hazlitt's *Liber Amoris* are treated more substantially in other chapters; for the moment, therefore, the most interesting thing to note about this passage, I think, is the way in which Cockney satire feeds naturally into a developing notion of Bohemia. *Blackwood's* returned to the same idea a few months later in an article titled 'The General Question', painting a similarly vivid, fanciful portrait of the contributors to the *London Magazine*: 'A bang-up contributor or two, peradventure, figures away in white upper toggery and Belcher handkerchief, and throws his hat into the ring. But they are palpable pretenders; and must be the derision of Pierce Egan and Josh.'[23] Once again, Egan is used as a kind of stick with which to beat the Cockneys, an image of good, old-fashioned Tory populism, confident but not counter-jumping, upstanding but not upstart. The earlier article on 'George Cruikshank' had made the same point. Cruikshank's political caricatures were all very well, the magazine conceded, but it is his work for Egan that really shows the way forward: 'But what a start did he make when his genius had received a truer and a diviner impulse from the splendid imagination of an Egan!' (p. 21).

COCKNEY LIBERTINISM

How did Pierce Egan himself feel about his literary reputation? One of the curious things about *Life in London* is that, in his hands, the 'flash style' ends up registering a curious ambivalence about social and professional ambition – functioning simultaneously as both expression and denial. One example of this is contained in the extended 'Invocation' that was incorporated into the first collected edition. In this section Egan makes an elaborate show of seeking the support, the patronage even, of the contemporary literary establishment. He writes an extended paean to literary talent, in which he pays tribute to many of the great figures of the past, from Shakespeare to Sheridan, while advertising his own status as an aspiring 'man of genius'. In this guise, he makes a series of direct addresses to some of the leading publishers of the day, begging them to find room to display his work:

> But thou, O, Murray, whose classic front defies with terrific awe, ill-starred, pale and *shabbily* clad GENIUS from approaching thy splendid threshold, retreat a little from thy frigid reserve, and for once open thy doors, and take the unsophisticated JERRY HAWTHORN by the hand: and although not a CHILDE HAROLD by birth, a CORSAIR bold, or a HARDY VAUX,[24] *wretched* exile; yet let me solicit thee to introduce him to thy numerous acquaintance, that, having once obtained thy *smiling* sanction, JERRY may not only have the honour of being allowed to call again, but to offer his services throughout thy extended circle. (pp. 8–9)

The entire 'Invocation' is presented as the buoyant fantasy of an industrious apprentice. The author represents himself (quite wrongly) as an innocent newcomer to the city, a Dick Whittington figure, full of great expectations: 'The metropolis is now before me … To thee, FAME, my finger-post towards the right road, I once more look up, and if I cannot command success, at least, it shall not be averred that I did not exert myself to deserve it' (p. 17). The tone throughout is humble yet ebullient, aspiring but not impertinent. But in other parts of the book there is a distinct sense of discomfort about Cockney ambition. Egan's depiction of Tom's mistress Corinthian Kate is the key element here, for it is in his consideration of her character that many of his doubts about careerism have their most expressive outlet. Corinthian Tom is represented throughout *Life in London* as every inch the proper gentleman: he has no need to pursue money or status, they have been accorded him from birth (the fact that Tom's father was a self-made man is nevertheless important to Egan, as if he had to advertise the entrepreneurial energy that must have *gone into* a creation like Tom). Kate, on the other hand, is openly in search of money and position. The text is impressively vague about her family background, and indeed about her actual status, but there is absolutely no doubt about the nature of her aspirations:

> The CORINTHIAN was her idol, but it was not from all-powerful LOVE … No, it was her AMBITION that had sealed the *contract*. It was the splendid fortune of TOM, his elegant figure, his superior abilities, his great character, his being the TON, that had fastened upon her eye; and KATE preferred the envy of her sex, in securing such a hero to herself, rather than to be *pitied* for loving him without obtaining a conquest, being lost, as it were, to the world, and sighing and pining in some private corner. PROPERTY, and even CHARACTER, had been leapt over in order to gratify her AMBITION. (p. 244)

At first sight this looks like misogyny of a relatively familiar kind. But there is something else at work here too: in Egan's over-emphatic concern for Kate's sacrifice of 'property' and even 'character' to the gratification of 'ambition' (she has clearly sacrificed her sexual reputation in an attempt to win Tom's affections) one can detect a repressed professional anxiety about the compromises one might have to make in order to become a success in the fashionable world. Everywhere in *Life in London* the link between writing and prostitution is overdetermined by its absence. It is what the 'Invocation' continually gestures towards, but is expressly designed to deny. In Egan's hands, the 'flash style' is a considered attempt to banish such considerations: it presents itself as a kind of universal currency, a means of sidestepping the traditional distinctions of class society, a guarantee of total mobility. But it also tries to pretend that such movements can be made without ambition or the sacrifices attendant upon it. There is no such thing as exploitation or alienation in *Life in London*, there is only the imprudent adventurism of Corinthian Kate.

One way of explaining this ambivalence about ambition is to look into the character of apprentice culture at this time, and of Egan's relation to it. One of the best investigations of the artisanal class at the turn of the nineteenth century is Anna Clark's *The Struggle for the Breeches* (1995). As a result of the industrial revolution, Clark argues, artisans found they could no longer follow the traditional sequence from apprentice to journeyman, and to the status of master and married man. Industrial working practices, and the increased involvement of women and other 'unskilled' workers in the system, had accelerated the demise of the old male 'trades'.

> Unable to afford their own workshops, they focused on creating trade solidarity through a bachelor journeyman culture of drinking rituals and combinations. Unwilling to tolerate lifelong celibacy, an artisan would often marry or cohabit,

relying on the woman's earnings to help support the family. However, artisans' bachelor orientation could be easily warped into misogyny and violence against women, directed both against rival female workers and against wives who complained of time and money spent with workmates in the pub. Artisans followed an exclusivist trade-union strategy directed against not only women but other male workers as well, further contributing to divisions among working people.[25]

In some quarters, this bachelor culture was highly politicized; in others it merely sought to bury its political frustrations in hedonism. What linked this culture to the traditional libertinism of the aristocracy was its comparable rejection of 'respectable' values; what distinguished it was its roots in thwarted ambition. There is good reason for thinking that Egan was deeply sympathetic to this mode of being, probably as a result of his extended apprenticeship to a printer. Indeed, one way of reading *Life in London* is to see it as the utopian text of artisanal libertinism because of the way in which it taps into the characteristic instincts of the young bachelor apprentice, with its commitment to fraternity, its mistrust of respectability and (as we have seen) its complex suspicion of women. But of course there is also evidence to suggest that many of these qualities would also have appealed to people outside the old manual trades. By the 1820s there was a growing army of bachelor clerks and lawyer's apprentices living and working in London, men whose professional experience was in many ways as uncertain and embattled as that of the apprentice artisans, but who did not have the latter's political traditions to draw upon. The libertine element of *Life in London* would have appealed to this class as well, not least because of the way in which it took all of the drawbacks of bachelor life, namely its lack of status and respectability and its uncertain relation to citizenship (as non-property-holders, apprentices were often excluded from political societies and were ineligible to vote), and transformed them into positive virtues, open invitations to freedom and mobility. It is in this sense that *Life in London* can be seen as a truly 'Cockney' text, because of the way in which it reinterprets the insecurity and isolation of the lower-middle-class Londoner as an invitation to overleap all bounds.

From beginning to end, *Life in London* is animated by a fervent enthusiasm for performance and disguise. This is very much a product of its time. One result of the modernization of the textile industry in the early nineteenth century was a significant fall in the price of clothes; so much so, indeed, that little by little the sartorial gap between the classes began to narrow. By the early 1820s cheap imitations of the latest aristocratic fashions had begun to fall within the reach of the lower orders. *Life in London* was very much part of this democratization process, not least because its graphically detailed but essentially uncomplicated version of London high life was so suitable for lower-middle-class imitation. Predictably enough, this phenomenon prompted considerable concern in the respectable periodical press, with a number of commentators complaining about the increasing lack of correlation between status and dress. Egan incorporated a number of statements into *Life in London* designed to fend off criticism of this kind: he has Tom criticize the habit of 'IMITATION' of Almack's, where 'the greatest anxiety with most individuals (the *lovers* and *devotees* of fashion) is to appear what they are not'; he also engages in a number of attacks on dandies, whom he represents as arrant impostors trying to trick their way up the social ladder. Tellingly, however, all of these criticisms are directed not at would-be Cockney upstarts but at fashionable society itself.

If *Life in London* does express misgivings about performance and disguise, it does so *not* on behalf of the established hierarchy, but in pursuit of a certain notion of authenticity, a continued hankering after the 'real'. The low-life scenes of the novel are essential to this pursuit. Once again, as with so much of *Life in London*, there is a twofold purpose to such scenes. On one level, they were clearly intended to assuage the growing social anxiety of the upper and middle classes, that is, to offset the increasing social segregation of early-nineteenth-century London, reassuring the genteel inhabitants of St James's of the fundamental humanity of the denizens of St Giles (a district that urban transformation and demographic change was rendering increasingly off-limits to the well-to-do).[26] But they can also be seen to have had a distinct and separate function for the 'uneasy class' of which Egan himself was still a member, for what they offered was a unique opportunity for the Cockney class to renegotiate its own relation to working-class experience, through the characters of those would-be gentlemen Tom and Jerry.

The poorer parts of central London were undergoing a terrifying transformation at this time. One result of John Nash's much-vaunted programme of metropolitan improvements was a massive displacement of the poor from the Regent Street area to its immediate environs, districts already overcrowded with low-grade housing. To a significant extent, this contributed to the worsening of the slums.[27] None of this finds its way into *Life in London*. Within its pages, the poor are invariably depicted as a remarkably static and stable community, hopelessly depraved but also vigorously happy. One of the best examples of this is the cadgers' den scene towards the end of the book, in which Tom and Jerry disguise themselves as street people in order to witness the fraudulent beggars of the metropolis at play. The challenge posed by the cadgers is that, far from being touchstones of authenticity, they too are merely playing a part. That is why Tom and Jerry must track them down to their hiding place in the 'Holy Land' of St Giles. Characteristically, however, once the two protagonists have witnessed the beggars at their revels, their mission is accomplished (Figure 4). Once the poor have been reaffirmed both as unreflective objects of knowledge and as embodiments of primitive human nature, it then becomes possible for Tom and Jerry to throw themselves enthusiastically into the beggars' merrymaking.

There is something richly ironic in the spectacle of Tom and Jerry putting on a disguise in order to uncover the cadgers' disguise, while on a meta-textual level continuing to be Cockney characters disguised as gentlemen. Or, to put it another way, one reason why Tom and Jerry might feel so 'at home' with the cadgers is that they are also leading a double life themselves. Above and beyond this, one of the most important things to say about the low-life scenes in *Life in London* is that they are entirely devoid of the sociological interest that characterizes High Victorian 'slum' literature, and are almost completely free of the latter's moralizing tone. There is a much simpler and more permissive concept of the social order at work here. The poorer classes, for all their local colour, have a rather basic epistemological function: they are there as embodiments of the real. This is the reason why there are no degrees of poverty in the book, why everyone is pitched at the same level of abjection. The poor are there to serve as a kind of panoramic backdrop to the story, so that the freedom and mobility of Tom and Jerry might stand out in greater relief. That said, it is difficult not to detect a rather wistful and nostalgic element in these scenes as well, for they all represent the lower orders as a united and happy community, untouched by history or by personal ambition; a rueful acknowledgement, perhaps, by an alienated lower-middle-class author of what he has been forced to leave behind.

FINISH TO LIFE IN LONDON

That Egan was intoxicated by *Life in London*'s success is clear from the flurry of literary activity it prompted him into. He immediately sought to cash in on his new-found status as the expert on 'flash' London. In 1822 he brought out a new edition of Grose's *Dictionary of the Vulgar Tongue*, supplying a lengthy introduction of his own and adding his own name to the title page. He also produced a short account of the criminal Samuel

Figure 4. George and Robert Cruikshank, *Tom and Jerry 'Masquerading It' among the Back Slums of the Holy Land*, from *Life in London*. Engraving. 1821.

Hayward, a real-life 'flash' hero whose brief career as a fraud, thief and fancy-man had led him to the gallows. Hayward represented the sociological reality behind the cartoon blackguardism of Tom and Jerry, a man in whom the taste for disguise had its source in a life spent on the run. While Egan was pursuing these projects, pirate copies and theatrical adaptations of *Life in London* continued to flood the market. In January 1823 the *New Monthly Magazine* declared that Tom and Jerry was 'still acting at the Adelphi Theatre, teaching the rising male generation "that great moral lesson" how to patter slang, mill a lamplighter, or box a charley'.[28] The success of these stage productions was a source of considerable frustration to Egan, not least because, try as he might, he could not succeed in getting his *own* dramatized version accepted. In spite of this, however, he continued to look to the theatre for his future success. In 1825 he published his *Life of an Actor*, another blend of picaresque fiction and historical anecdote. But his real ambition remained to write *for* the stage rather than *about* it.

In 1828 Egan finally produced a sequel to Tom and Jerry, which he called the *Finish to Life in London*. A brief glance at this work will make clear how much the moral climate in England had changed since the heady days of 1821–2. Egan's authorial attitude is defensive from the start. There is an extended introduction 'to vindicate characters of the author and artist from the unmerited aspersion of having attempted by the joint efforts of real tales, original anecdotes and animated sketches, to demoralise the rising generation; and likewise to refute the charge of having turned the heads of older folks towards the commission of acts of folly and intemperance'. Further in, Egan transforms the introduction into a protest against the continuing piracy of his work:

> We have been *pirated*, COPIED, *traduced*; but, unfortunately, not ENRICHED by our indefatigable exertions; therefore NOTORIETY must satisfy us, instead of the smiles of FORTUNE. Our efforts have given rise to numerous productions in the market of literature;[29] yet we can assert, with a degree of confidence hitherto unshaken, that none of our imitators have dared to think for themselves during the long period of seven years, neither have they shown any originality upon the subject of LIFE IN LONDON; but who have left it (*disinterested* souls!) to the Author and Artist to put a climax to the adventures of TOM, JERRY and LOGIC. (pp. 7–8)

One can see his point: 1828 found Egan suffering from being at once too much and too little the author of Tom and Jerry. On the one hand, inadequate copyright laws had enabled extensive exploitation of his work; on the other, he himself had become too closely associated with the (increasingly unfashionable) 'flash' style. He was still some distance from literary respectability, and was finding it difficult, in spite of his fame, to break into drama. The *Finish* registers Egan's frustration with this situation. For all its general good humour, it is difficult not to see it as an attempt to revenge himself on his imitators, first by clearing up the playful ambiguities that had surrounded his fictional creations, then by killing them off one by one. Nothing criminal is ever pinned on Tom or Jerry in the *Finish*, but the comparative sordidness of their wild lifestyle is repeatedly revealed. Corinthian Kate is exposed as an unprincipled harlot, and is shown descending into the lowest levels of urban prostitution after being 'cut off' by Corinthian Tom. In Chapter 8 Jerry gets fleeced in a brothel, which is exactly the kind of occurrence that *Life in London* might have hinted at but never shown. Consistently, both the text and the illustrations of the *Finish* can be seen to draw on the precedent of Hogarth's *Harlot's Progress*, as the gently permissive tone of 1821 is replaced by something darker. Bob Logic dies of over-indulgence, Corinthian Tom after being thrown from his horse. Only Jerry is left alive at the end, to offer a kind of apology for his friends: 'APPEARANCES, I am perfectly aware, might be against both of their characters with the fashionable part of society; yet hypocrisy, cant, humbug, or dissimulation, never disgraced their conduct: a love of honour shone conspicuously through their actions, and, by an acknowledgement of their own errors, displayed a noble generosity towards the faults of others' (p. 318). The defensiveness of this is as interesting as its manifest untruth. Times had changed, and the rise of respectable society (to use F. M. L. Thompson's classic phrase) was putting increasing pressure on Tom and Jerry's lifestyle. What is more, the characters themselves had inevitably come to seem more vulgar over time. 'APPEARANCES' had changed so much since 1821, in fact, that Tom, Jerry and Logic had started to become all-too-recognizable as Cockney upstarts, the social 'dissimulation' they once gloried in having been revealed as dissipation in the end.

CHAPTER 5

Charles Lamb and the alchemy of the streets

In the Konvolut on 'Fashion' in his *Passagenwerk*, Walter Benjamin quoted Maurice Talmeyr on posters: 'These images of a day or an hour, bleached by the elements, charcoaled by urchins, scorched by the sun – although others are sometimes collected before they have even dried – symbolize to a higher degree even than newspapers the sudden shock-filled, multiform life that carries us away.'[1] To recapture this sense of shock one needs only to turn to John Orlando Parry's *London Street Scene* of 1835, an image that blends public advertisement and everyday street crime with all the virtuosity of a modern web page (see Figure 5). At first one hardly notices the little frieze of street figures in the foreground – the street buyers and sellers, the chimney-sweep and the delivery boy; the pickpocket picking what looks to be a policeman's pocket – nor indeed the witty cropping of St Paul's on the left. The eye is too dazzled by the virtuosic montage of wall advertisements in the centre, a bewildering array of shapes, colours and texts. Numerous products are being pushed. Headlines include 'Madame Vestris', 'Paganini', 'Mr. Mathews [the famous impressionist] *at home*'; 'Liverpool in 24 hours', 'Chester on the Royal George', 'Jerusalem', 'Paris', 'King Arthur', 'Othello', 'Marino Faliero', 'Tom and Jerry', 'The Destruction of Pompeii – Every Evening', 'Are You Aware Your Hat Is Very Shabby?' and, last but not least, 'Have You Seen The Industrious Fleas?' The posters are crammed together, struggling to impose themselves, like plants competing for the light. Some are scratched or peeling, and have broken up into a wild criss-crossing of letters. One is being pasted before our eyes. There is no order or pattern to this palimpsest, and luck seems the only essential for survival. It is an image of the city as a battleground of competing commodities in which the individual struggle to *be* a spectacle only forms part of a larger, collective spectacle, what Charles Lamb was to call the 'ever-shifting Pantomime' of metropolitan life.

Parry's Darwinian bank of advertisements seems strikingly modern for 1835, but in fact such sights had been commonplace in London for

Figure 5. John Orlando Parry, *A London Street Scene*. Oil on canvas. 1835.

many years. In his *Letters from England* of 1807 Robert Southey had noted that: 'Tradesmen here lose no possible opportunity of forcing their notices upon the public. Wherever there was a dead wall, a vacant house, or a temporary scaffolding erected for repairs, the space was covered with printed bills.'[2] William Wordsworth recalls a similar wall of advertisements in the 1805 *Prelude*, at the beginning of his devastating attack on the city.

> Here files of ballads dangle from dead walls;
> Advertisements, of giant size, from high,
> Press forward, in all colours, on the sight;
> These, bold in conscious merit, lower down,
> That, fronted with a most imposing word,
> Is, peradventure, one in masquerade.[3]

The point about the ads Wordsworth mentions is that, exactly as in Parry's *Street Scene*, there is no correlation between size and significance. Trivial things are just as likely to be spectacularly advertised as coaches, plays or operas. It is advertisements such as these that could be thought of as being 'in masquerade', i.e. fraudulent, pretending to be more important than they really are. That this is only a suspicion ('peradventure') is also significant, for it shows that the poet himself cannot be *quite* sure of where 'pressing forward' tumbles into imposture.

The *Prelude* passage about the wall advertisements comes from the early part of Book vii, when Wordsworth is, relatively speaking, open-minded about London, as sensitive to its attractions as to its alienations. Gradually, however, the poet becomes increasingly bewildered and disillusioned by the city, which he finally comes to consider as nothing but a repository of

> Folly, vice,
> Extravagance in gesture, mien and dress,
> And all the strife of singularity,
> Lies to the ear, and lies to every sense (vii, ll. 571–4)

As many critics have noticed, Wordsworth's notion of 'the strife of singularity' is startlingly prescient, prophetic even, of later representations of the nineteenth-century city. Selfhood, Wordsworth says, becomes a species of self-advertisement in the metropolis; everyone has to perform themselves in order to survive. Fashion, the emulation of others, becomes the only way of being oneself. 'To be in the fashion is to exist, it is existence itself', wrote Henry Southern in the *London Magazine* in August 1825, 'to be out of it, is non-existence; it is oblivion, death and the grave.[4] In *The City in History* (1961), the American architectural historian Lewis Mumford placed special emphasis on the role of fashion in the early-nineteenth-century metropolis: 'In the great capital cities, too large for people to know their neighbours, the standards of the market came generally to prevail. People sought by overt display to make a decisive impression as to their station in life, their taste, their prosperity: every individual, every class, put on a front.'[5]

In the early part of the 1820s, new legislation banning bill-posting on private buildings encouraged a new urban phenomenon into being: the placard man. The German painter Georg Scharf had an obsessive interest in London street life, and produced several friezes of this novel species (Figure 6). And like John Parry he documented every aspect of what he saw. Each placard is clearly legible in Scharf's rendering, and the figures are reproduced with great accuracy too. The ads are for such things as 'The British Diorama at the Royal Bazaar, Oxford Street', 'Battles of the French Army, at the Egyptian Hall Piccadilly', 'A Grand Masquerade, at the Argyll Rooms on Monday', 'Malt Whiskey' and 'Patent Pens'. And Scharf has affixed a date to each example – 1825, 1828, 1833 – as if to acknowledge their fleetingness. Also depicted are the men themselves, hollering, scowling at one another or simply drooping under the weight of their announcements; some are clearly, then as now, urban beggars in borrowed clothes.

This was a common sight in the nineteenth-century city, and was still a feature of Walter Benjamin's Paris of the 1930s: 'Human billboards, they advertised and publicized the products and events (cinemas, store sales) of bourgeois consumer culture', writes Susan Buck-Morss, 'yet they themselves, despite the uniforms they were loaned to give a respectable appearance, were associated closely with poverty.'[6] To Benjamin, as Buck-Morss has brilliantly shown, the sandwich-man offers a dialectical image of modern false consciousness (and thus, in the terms of this book, a valuable lesson to every would-be Cockney upstart). More specifically, he embodies the condition of the modern writer in proletarian form. 'The nineteenth-century writer "goes to the marketplace as flâneur"', as Buck-Morss notes, quoting Benjamin, 'supposedly to take a look at it, but in reality to find a buyer'. The anonymous freelance might like to think of himself as a satirist who wanders the streets as a detached observer, but in reality he functions as 'a sandwich man who advertises its coming attractions' (p. 43). To Benjamin, then, the placard man was the urban writer's uncanny doppelgänger, a constant reminder of his underlying status as a prostitute of modernity.

Figure 6. Georg Scharf, *Placard Men*. Watercolour. 1825–33.

When the poet Wordsworth meets his double, in the latter half of *The Prelude* Book VII, it is a blind beggar with the most simple of placards, stating baldly who he is and what he was. This beggar quickly becomes a symbol of heroic resistance to the city, in Wordsworth's mind, the perfect, and only, antidote to the modern culture of self-advertisement:

> My mind did at this spectacle turn round
> As with the might of waters, and it seemed
> To me that in this label was a type,
> Or emblem, of the utmost that we know,
> Both of ourselves and of the universe;
> And, on the shape of the unmoving man,
> His fixèd face and sightless eyes, I looked,
> As if admonished from another world. (VII, ll. 615–22)

This man is, as it were, the only true placard man, or self-advertiser, and reminds the poet of the natural ground and basis of humanity. He is 'the thing himself … unaccommodated man', as Lear described Poor Tom. Such groundedness and stability are, however, rare things in the metropolis, and Parry's *Street Scene* helps explain why: it offers a mini-essay on what the city does to concepts, on how it desiccates, juxtaposes and flattens them. It is like a street full of people, or the front page of a newspaper, a busy shop window or a list of prices. It provides collisions, not real relations; it deracinates and levels all things. It brings all the world to London – landscapes and battles (through the panoramas), other cities (through improved travel connections), world histories (through lectures, plays and operas) – and it shamelessly appropriates them, re-presenting them to the consumer as free-floating commodities.

Wordsworth's poem represents the extreme agrarian reaction to the metropolis in this respect. To him, the 'blank confusion' of Bartholomew Fair is a hellish emblem for the disorderly life of the city as a whole:

> An undistinguishable world to men,
> The slaves unrespited of low pursuits,
> Living amid the same perpetual flow
> Of trivial objects, melted and reduced
> To one identity, by differences
> That have no law, no meaning and no end. (VII, ll. 699–704)

The 'trivial objects' here are both human aims and inhuman commodities, and indeed Wordsworth's felicitous phrasing cleverly implies that the city blurs the two. The strongest are not free from this pernicious influence, but the poet himself feels he has the power to resist it, largely as a result of his childhood in the Lakes. Ever-changing yet enduring, the mountains of his homeland provide a firm bedrock, a principle of philosophical constancy, with which to counter 'The Destruction of Pompeii Every Evening'.

THE LONDONER

Wordsworth first saw Bartholomew Fair in 1802, with his sister Dorothy and his friend Charles Lamb. It came at the end of a period of particularly intense meditation on the nature of the city, when the seeds of the *Prelude* critique were first being sown. The year 1800 had seen the publication of the famous second edition of *Lyrical Ballads*, with its ground-breaking preface attacking modern urban existence. It also saw the composition of Wordsworth's tragic pastoral *Michael*, in which a faithful old shepherd loses his only son to the temptations of the city. Wordsworth and Coleridge's outspoken attacks on London did not go unopposed, however, for their great friend Lamb took up the gauntlet almost immediately. There is a Romantic Metropolitanism to counter Romantic Primitivism and it was born at the same time. Within a few months of the 'Preface' to *Lyrical Ballads*' first appearance, Lamb had already penned his riposte, first in a series of private letters (to Wordsworth himself, and to another friend, William Manning), and then, later, in a *Morning Post* article entitled 'The Londoner' (dated 1 February 1802). It was twenty years before Lamb was able to expand upon his vision, in the 'Elia' essays he wrote for the *London Magazine*. But even in 1802, at the age of twenty-seven, his conception was powerfully coherent – and modern. Here, in the space of a few short sentences, we have the nineteenth century's first formulation of the writer as *flâneur*, the 'man of the crowd' that became so important to Baudelaire and Benjamin; here also we see the street as a site of strange transformations and alienations in a manner that looks forward to Edgar Allan Poe and Thomas De Quincey.

> This passion for crowds is nowhere feasted so full as in London. The man must have a rare recipe for melancholy, who can be dull in Fleet street. I am naturally inclined to hypochondria, but in London it vanishes, like all other ills. Often when I have felt a weariness or distaste at home, have I rushed out into her crowded Strand, and fed my humour, till tears have wetted my cheek for inutterable sympathies with the multitudinous moving picture, which she never fails to present at all hours, like the shifting scenes of a skilful Pantomime.[7]

Countering Wordsworth's assertions head on, 'The Londoner' celebrates the spectacular nature of London life as a cure for self-absorption and melancholia. The Strand (which was the very type of the busy, mixed thoroughfare in this period) works a curious kind of magic in the narrator's mind. It takes his melancholy humour and 'feeds' it with vivid images of human striving and suffering, so that everyday social observation takes on a theatrical form. Sympathy, here, is not primarily a prelude to communication or philanthropy; it is an unashamedly voyeuristic and self-consoling experience. It moves from pain at someone else's suffering to a pleasure in one's own capacity to sympathize with that suffering. It is a kind of emotional alchemy. Indeed in passages like this, we might conclude, 'sympathy' itself is in danger of becoming a mere screen or shield against social reality, rather than a fuel for improvement.

Lamb was particularly well equipped to write about the early-nineteenth-century metropolis. Born and brought up in London, he was deeply intimate with its rhythms and practices. Committed all his life to nursing his psychologically fragile sister Mary (who had killed their elderly mother in a fit of madness in the 1790s), Lamb rejoiced in the privacy that only living in London could afford. In his time, he was both a full-time worker and a part-time *flâneur*, spending the best of his days clerking at the East India House in the city, and writing plays, poems and journalism in the evenings: 'The enfranchised quill', he wrote in 'Oxford in the Vacation',

> that has plodded all the morning among the cart-rucks of figures and ciphers, frisks and curvets so at its ease over the flowery carpet-ground of a midnight dissertation – it feels its promotion * * * * So that you see, upon the whole, the literary dignity of *Elia* [that is, his literary persona in the *London Magazine*] is very little, if at all, compromised in the condescension.[8]

Nowhere is there a better account of early-nineteenth-century work discipline than in Lamb's essays and letters, and nowhere a more powerful sense of alienation's mingled pains and pleasures. Many times he lamented how much of his life was lost to drudgery, and envied the semi-independence of his friends Wordsworth and Coleridge. 'I grow ominously tired of official confinement', he wrote to Wordsworth on 20 March 1822:

> Thirty years I have served the Philistines, and my neck is not subdued to the yoke. You don't know how wearisome it is breathe the air of four pent walls without relief day after day, all the golden hours of the day between 10 and 4 without ease or interposition … O for a few years between the grave and the desk![9]

'Pent' is a resonant term between the Lakers, as Lucy Newlyn has elegantly shown; for both Coleridge and Wordsworth it is a position, and a posture, that is explicitly identified with city confinement – as in 'This Lime Tree Bower My Prison', 'Frost at Midnight' and, as we shall see, 'The Old Cumberland Beggar'.[10] Here Lamb can be seen temporarily acquiescing in his friends' anti-urbanism by self-consciously invoking a key term from their early poetry.

It is partly Lamb's status, then, as a full-time office worker in the world's first industrial metropolis that gives his city writings bite and value. But it is also the fact that, in common with many men and women of his generation, his attitude to the city was so clearly, and unapologetically, pre-Victorian. Even in Regency London there were many evangelical voices around – voices moralizing and philanthropic, reformist or ruralizing. But these voices were not as dominant as they became in the age of Mayhew and Ruskin. The social and sanitary nightmare of mid-nineteenth-century London had not yet been identified; there were still a number of different ways of thinking about the city. In this way we can see figures such as William Hazlitt, Lamb, De Quincey, the youthful Charles Dickens and E. T. A. Hoffmann in Germany as the true originators of that rich Romantic tradition of city writing that runs in a direct line through Baudelaire and Poe to Benjamin and his followers.

Lamb's metropolitan aesthetic sees the relationship between the Londoner and his surroundings as a form of transaction in which the urban stroller 'lends out' his heart to the streets around him in the hope of a rich return.

> I love the very smoke of London, because it has been the medium most familiar to my vision. I see grand principles of honour at work in the dirty ring which encompasses two combatants with fists, and principles of no less eternal justice in the tumultuous detectors of a pickpocket … Thus an art of extracting morality, from the commonest incidents of a town life, is attained by the same well natured alchemy, with which the Foresters of Arden in a beautiful country
>
> > Found tongues in trees, books in the running brooks,
> > Sermons in stones, and good in every thing.
>
> Where has spleen her food but in London – humour, interest, curiosity, suck at her measureless breasts without a possibility of being satiated. Nursed amid her noise, her crowds, her beloved smoke – what have I been doing all my life, if I have not lent out my heart with usury to such scenes?[11]

One invests one's heart in the grubby spectacle of the city, but precisely in order to receive it back again, like a usurer, with interest. This is sympathetic engagement with the common details of urban life as canny economic investment. This is misanthropic Jaques, who was so adept at 'sucking melancholy' out of rural life, finding a new kind of sustenance in the 'measureless breasts' of the metropolitan picturesque.

JOHN NASH AND THE METROPOLITAN PICTURESQUE

The picturesque was not simply a way of seeing in Lamb's London; it was a principle of urban planning as well. Of all the 'metropolitan improvements' undertaken in the 1810s and 1820s, easily the most ambitious, both architecturally and socially, was Regent Street and Regent's Park. In scale, of course, 'Beau' Nash's project cannot be compared to Baron Haussmann's comprehensive *boulevardisation* of Paris later in the century. But in many respects their aims were similar. Nash's initial 1812 plan proposed the construction of a new thoroughfare through north-west London that would sweep majestically from St James's Park via Pall Mall and Piccadilly to a newly redeveloped Regent's Park in Marylebone. This street was to be built largely on crown land, and would comprise public colonnades, private residences and shops. The prime benefit of this new, wide thoroughfare was commercial: it was intended to encourage luxury retail, and to free up traffic in a highly congested quarter of the city. But it would also, like the great slum-clearance thoroughfares of the Victorian period, act as an agent of social segregation. Neatly dividing Mayfair from Soho, the New Street would serve as 'a boundary and complete separation', as Nash put it, 'between the Streets and Squares occupied by the Nobility and Gentry, and the narrow streets and meaner houses occupied by mechanics and the trading part of the community'.[12] The idea was also, as Nash later expressed it, that all the streets leading east from this New Street into Soho would lead into the more respectable streets, leaving out all the 'bad' ones. And as to the street itself, it was expressly designed with the elite in mind:

> The Balustrades over the Colonnades will form Balconies to the Lodging-rooms over the Shops, from which the Occupiers of the Lodgings can see and converse with those passing in the Carriages underneath, and which will add to the gaiety of the scene, and induce single men, and others, who only visit the Town occasionally, to give a preference to such Lodgings. (p. 16)

Here Regent Street is imagined as a space ruled over by the three urban Graces: mobility, sexuality and shopping. More specifically, it is also envisaged as a place of visual consumption and display, where bold bachelors would 'see and converse with' fashionable young ladies in passing carriages, and where the values of freedom and opportunism would be paramount (Figure 7). Freedom and opportunism were intended to epitomize the finished street, but they also ended up characterizing its construction,

THE QUADRANT, REGENT ST

Figure 7. Georg Scharf, *The Westminster Dairy in the Quadrant, Regent Street.* Watercolour. 1825.

which was conducted throughout in the most piecemeal, improvisatory fashion. Though the grand plan was Nash's, significant portions of the street were built and funded by others, and in allowing for this free development the Prince Regent's favourite architect was, as John Summerson has argued, effectively making a virtue of necessity:

> This curious mixture of *laissez-faire* and spasmodic control reflects Nash's philosophy of street design as it evolved in the unique circumstances with which it was faced. It was nothing if not realistic. It allowed individual expression by different users but at the same time aimed at shuffling the accidental into picturesque coherence. It was a landscape philosophy brought to bear upon townscape. It was business but also a sort of art.[13]

Even after the Regent Street project had been approved, there were still significant obstacles to its completion. Displaced property-owners had to be compensated and private landlords who owned portions of the land en route needed to be bullied into selling. The project progressed rapidly, nevertheless, and Nash oversaw it all with the energy and avidity of a great gambler (he had invested a lot of money in it himself). During the first few years of building, contemporaries were shocked at the level of disruption: 'nothing like it had ever been seen', Summerson says, 'and the obvious conclusion to be drawn was that some kind of disaster had overtaken London' (p. 84). But Nash's extraordinary unpopularity did subside a little after the summer of 1819, when the first portion of the New Street, which ran from St James's Park to Piccadilly, was finally opened.

Critics attacked the street's picturesque theatricality and variety. 'Architecture was architecture once', complained an Old Bachelor (Edmund Carrington), 'but now it is a monster – a mongrel, produced by the illicit connection of Graecisms and Gothicisms.'[14] To some, the new street was a fair-seeming row of flimsy stucco facades, mere brick masquerading as stone. 'In less than half a century', wrote the *London Magazine* in an article entitled 'The Bricks of the Modern Babylon', 'Regent-street will have the ring-worm, the scab, the itch, the leprosy. Its skin will peel off, like the bark of a rotten tree, and the hide will hang in rags and tatters about the rotting carcass.'[15] But there were also some enthusiasts who embraced the street as the epitome of 'modern improvement' and reminded contemporaries of what it was replacing: 'Swallow-street, with all the dirty courts in its vicinity, have been swallowed up, and replaced by one of the most magnificent streets in Europe', said the *Monthly Magazine*.[16] And on Nash's death in 1835, Theodore Hook was to adopt the same line in the *John Bull*:

> Let the readers recollect the huddled mass of wretched streets and houses which twenty years ago covered the site of Regent Street, the Quadrant and Waterloo Place; let the reader recollect the still more wretched courts and alleys, dens of infamy and haunts of thieves, which maze-like spread themselves from St. Martin's Church to the neighbourhood of Covent Garden; let him now look upon the range of buildings and the handsome streets which occupy their places.[17]

During the London building boom of the late 1810s and 1820s, Regent Street was only one large-scale architectural project among many; other examples included the British Museum, the University of London (the so-called 'Cockney College') and the Dulwich Picture Gallery. 'The 1820s was the most momentous decade of change in old London since the 1660s', as Jerry White has recently pointed out.[18] New London Bridge was one of the last major structures to be built during this era, opening in 1831. Thereafter urban development became less about splendour and show and had more to do with managing the poor. Hook himself mentions another Nash initiative in the passage quoted above, the slum-clearance project around lower St Martin's Lane and Covent Garden, which made way for Trafalgar Square and the West Strand. In 1827 James Elmes and Thomas Shepherd published *Metropolitan Improvements*, 'a series of views and illustrations' celebrating the recent transformation of the metropolis. Only briefly, in the opening Preface, did they also acknowledge the shock of it: 'So rapidly indeed are these improvements taking place around us, that the absence of a few months from London, produces revolutions in sites, and alterations in appearances, that are almost miraculous, and causes the denizen himself to feel himself a stranger in his own city.'[19] Along with the strangeness of the new there came a new strangeness to the old: the shadow of improvement changed the appearance and meaning of decay. Georg Scharf, the painter of the placard men, had first arrived in London in 1816, just as the building boom was beginning; his main private interest, as has already been mentioned, lay in recording the everyday life of the metropolis, its people, its streets and its endless rows of shops. Where Shepherd and Elmes loved celebrating the fashionable, the spectacularly uncommercial Scharf preferred recording the outmoded, especially when it had been earmarked for destruction by 'metropolitan improvers'. Aware of Nash's plan to demolish the streets around old St Martin's Lane, he produced a number of different views of the surrounding area. The cover image for this book, which depicts the lane with St Martin's Church in the background, is one of them. Scharf's images are produced in a very different spirit from the dominant current of the urban picturesque in this period, which is epitomized by John Thomas Smith's *Antiquities of London* (1800) and *Antiquities of Westminster* (1807), being far more interested in capturing the everyday look of the streets (see Figure 8). The problem for Scharf was that there was no real market for such pictures in the early nineteenth century, and so even though a fair few of his street scenes were publicly exhibited in his lifetime, none, as far as we know, were ever purchased. The painter's livelihood, such as it was, came almost exclusively from scientific illustrations for professional bodies and learned journals; a small, relatively obscure niche in the London art world. His London paintings remained a private passion, irremediably uncommercial, but also (perhaps precisely for that reason) refreshingly uncompromised by contemporary public taste.[20]

Not only did improvement rub shoulders with decay in Regency London; it also helped bring it about. The great scandal of Regent Street, in hindsight, was not, finally, Nash's bullying of old Swallow Street's shopkeepers and landlords into submission, for these figures did gain some compensation for their losses. It was the complete lack of housing provision for the displaced labouring population. With no replacement dwellings in the vicinity, the working-class poor of the area had little choice but to move to St Martin's Lane and its environs, and then later, when that region became subject to redevelopment, to St Giles in south Bloomsbury, already one of the most cramped and unsanitary regions of the capital.[21] And as increasing pressure came upon the housing stock in these areas, property-owners began subdividing their townhouses into smaller and smaller units to maximize profits. The name that was subsequently given to this process was 'slummification'. In *The Culture of Cities*, Mumford deplored the early-nineteenth-century cult of the picturesque as an aesthetic naturalization of free-market economics. 'In fine', he wrote, 'this cult of the picturesque was a disguised form of laissez-faire – applied wholesale to the environment. The accidental, the unforeseen, and the perverse became new values. Whatever could not be reduced to an orderly pattern, whatever denied man's collective control and defied his organisation and avoided the human measure, was exalted.'[22] Regent Street flaunted its mix of 'Graecisms and Gothicisms', offering a deeply theatrical panorama of historical discontinuity and change. To some contemporaries, indeed, it was a construction that always seemed to be imagining its own ruin, even and perhaps especially in its pristine form. It was in this sense that the street confessed its secret, scandalous link with the new slums of St Giles. Later in the century John Ruskin was to make a striking distinction between the 'true' and the 'false' picturesque;

CHARING CROSS, 1830

Figure 8. Georg Scharf, *Charing Cross in 1830*. Watercolour. 1830.

the former being an authentic image of ruined function and decay, the latter a deliberately contrived aesthetic of harmonious disorder.[23] Both spectacles were available in the London of the 1820s, and there was a dialectical relationship between them.

ON THE DECAY OF BEGGARS

It was in the period after 1810 that the free market really came into its own in Britain: hence the building boom of the late Regency; hence also the dramatic increase in cyclical unemployment, vagrancy and street crime. The mass demobilization of soldiers and sailors after Waterloo only made matters worse, and by 1814–15 the cost of poor relief in Britain had risen to £5.4 million. In keeping with the spirit of the age, most evangelical schemes set up to tackle the problem strove hard to work within the new doctrine of laissez-faire. Efforts were made to replace old-fashioned charity with new systems that regulated the alms-giving process while also keeping it at the level of the individual benefactor. Such, at least, was the aim of the Society for the Suppression of Mendicity, which was a voluntary association of evangelicals and philosophical radicals founded in 1818.

The President of the Society was Nicholas Vansittart, the Board of Management Patrick Colquhoun, Joseph Hume and David Ricardo. This body was prompted into being by what its Honorary Secretary, W. H. Bodkin, described as a 'sudden and alarming increase in the number of vagrants in the metropolis' post-Waterloo.[24] What compounded the problem, Bodkin argued, but also paved the way for a solution, was the fact that, according to his estimates, at least *half* of the 3,284 cases of vagrancy in London in the previous year were so-called 'cadgers', professional beggars who didn't deserve public charity. So the Society proposed a scheme in which the careless alms-giving of the past would be replaced by a system that discriminated between what it called the deserving and the undeserving poor. The plan was for individual subscribers to dole out tickets to the objects of their charity, tickets that could then be exchanged for food, clothing or other relief at the Mendicity Society headquarters in Red Lion Square, Holborn. Aid would be given to beggars, but only after they had undergone extensive questioning, the idea being that by collecting files on each client, the Society would soon be able to identify inveterate 'cadgers'. Charity would be accorded to genuine unfortunates but refused to professional mendicants, and this regardless of whether they had tickets in their hands. By these means, as M. J. D. Roberts has recently argued: 'the principles of the free market were to be extended from the world of business and of labour discipline into the world of charity ... The involuntary subsidy to waste and injustice would be ended, freeing resources for cases of legitimate need.' To us, this scheme looks forwards to the workhouse system, and to the Prison Discipline Society, which was set up in 1817. But, as Roberts argues quite persuasively, it did have a sentimental as well as a utilitarian side, and clear human aims: 'For the Mendicity Society the goal was to strip away the impersonality of existing transfers of resources between rich and poor to reinstate "the gift" as a moralising force in the lives of both givers and receivers.'[25] At bottom, however, the underlying aim of the organization was evident from its title – the Society for the Suppression of Mendicity – and to that end the tendency was always for the careful discrimination between acceptable and unacceptable forms of mendicancy to slide into a war on begging as a whole.

It is with this in view that we must approach one of Lamb's richest and most enjoyable Elia essays, 'A Complaint of the Decay of Beggars in the Metropolis' (1822). Written twenty years after 'The Londoner', it explores much more deeply the complex relationship between urban spectacle and social sympathy, and makes a significant advance upon the earlier essay's somewhat complacent picturesque. The piece begins as a reworking of Wordsworth's 'Old Cumberland Beggar' (from the *Lyrical Ballads*) in a metropolitan context. Lamb's general target, like Wordsworth's, is the utilitarian concept of pauper management. But his specific target is the Mendicity Society, which by the early 1820s was attracting the support of some 1,500 annual subscribers, with its goals and methods of operation already being taken up in other parts of the country.[26] We can tell from Thomas Hood, who took a similar attitude to Lamb on this issue, the impact that this was having on London's streets. In his 'Sentimental Journey' of 1821 he records a Londoner threatening a particularly importunate street-beggar that he will report him to the Society, and there is a beggar clutching a Mendicity ticket in his 1825 print *The Progress of Cant*.

In the first part of the 'Decay of Beggars', Lamb's blithely anti-reformist argument is that beggars are a necessary part of the urban system because they are touchstones of humanity. 'The beggar is', he says, 'never out of the fashion, or limpeth awkwardly behind it ... he is the only man ... who is not obliged to study appearances ... he is the only free man in the universe.'[27] In this section the argument is noticeably reminiscent of the one relating to the Blind Beggar in Book VII of Wordsworth's *Prelude*. Immediately afterwards, however, it takes a distinctly metropolitan turn:

The Mendicants of this great city were so many of her sights, her lions. I can no more spare them, than I could the Cries of London. No corner of a street is complete without them. They are as indispensable as the Ballad Singer; and in their picturesque attire as ornamental as the Signs of old London. They were the standing morals, emblems, mementos, dial-mottos, the spital sermons, the books for children, the salutary checks and pauses to the high and rushing tide of greasy citizenry. (p. 535)

Wordsworth's Cumberland Beggar was not only good in himself but also the cause of goodness in others; he was a semi-oblivious old vagrant whose weekly visits helped bind the village community together. In him the villagers beheld 'a record' of 'past deeds and offices of charity | Else unremember'd'.'[28] He served as an objective reminder of how virtuous they were. Whereas the Cumberland Beggar's beneficial mnemonic effect was clearly related to his mobility – his regular habit of coming and going – in the case of Lamb's urban mendicants it seems to consist in their standing still. Beggars, for Lamb, are like street signs or public monuments in that they rise above the constant traffic of the city, helping to reorient the distracted city-dweller and reinforcing a sense of history and locality. It is in this sense that they can be thought of as 'standing morals'. The one specific example Lamb gives is of a veteran of the Gordon Riots:

Few but must have noticed him; for the accident, which brought him low, took place during the riots of 1780, and he has been a groundling so long. He seemed earth-born, an Antaeus, and to suck in fresh vigour from the soil which he neighboured. He was a grand fragment; as good as an Elgin marble. The nature, which should have recruited his reft legs and thighs, was not lost, but only retired into his upper parts, and he was half a Hercules ... Was a daily spectacle like this to be deemed a nuisance which called for legal interference to remove? or not rather a salutary and a touching object, to the passers-by in a great city? (p. 534–5)

Like Keats's Saturn in *The Fall of Hyperion*, Lamb's street cripple is a giant who has been deposed by a new dispensation, a long-term victim of a long-ago coup. His message is a Centaur-like combination of resilience and obsolescence. In his editorial notes to this essay, E. V. Lucas names this man as Samuel Horsey, and tells us what a well-known figure he was in the early 1800s.[29] Given how easy it would have been for Elia to mention this beggar by name, it is interesting to consider why he chose not to do so (if that is indeed the case). One way of explaining it would be to remind ourselves that this essay is about the decay of beggars, both as landmarks to lay a course by and as unofficial historians of the streets, and by keeping his 'half-Hercules' anonymous Lamb is able to present him as a kind of anti-advertisement, a singular figure in whom ruined meaning is part of the message – in short, a figure of allegory. Susan Buck-Morss has described allegory as the antidote to advertising in her now-classic study of Benjamin's *Arcades* project: 'Within advertising', she writes, 'a new, dissimulating aura is injected into the commodity, easing its passage into the dream world of the private consumer. In contrast, the allegorical intention points backward in time, as if puzzling to remember an original meaning that has been lost.'[30]

The beggar has always been something of an abstract and ideal figure in Western literature, a way of thinking about poverty that is also a way of not thinking about poverty. That Lamb was aware of the other side of poverty, that is, its real social aspect, can be gathered from his essay 'Poor Relations' from 1823: 'A poor Relation – is the most irrelevant thing in nature; – a piece of impertinent correspondency, – an odious approximation, – a haunting conscience, – a preposterous shadow, lengthening in the noontide of your prosperity … a death's head at your banquet … He is known by his knock.'[31] The street-beggar makes no such claims of kinship, and causes no such irritation or embarrassment. What he offers, no, what he sells, is 'humanity', humanity as an abstract commodity, the alienated cure for modern alienation. Lamb's 'Decay of Beggars' essay is an ironic celebration of this transaction, this trade. The question remains, however, as to whether even his irony can comprehend the fact that, like Benjamin's writer as sandwich-man, its author has effectively been duped by the market into celebrating what is (in fact) politically anathema to him, for by the end of his essay 'the defence of poverty' has taken on a decidedly double-edged meaning.

STREET THEATRE

Elia was not the only writer of his generation to celebrate individual beggars in this way. In 1817, with the utter eradication of London's vagrants expected to be imminent, an elegant book of prints appeared with the title *Vagabondiana, or, Anecdotes of Mendicant Wanderers through the Streets of London, with Portraits of the Most Remarkable Drawn from the Life by John Thomas Smith, Keeper of the Prints in the British Museum*. Smith specialized in engravings of London antiquities, and had already produced a series of 'London Cries' (that is, images of metropolitan street-sellers in their traditional costumes). But *Vagabondiana* took this interest in the urban picturesque one stage further, setting out to record the lives and appearances of some of the most 'eminent' mendicants before they vanished forever.

Smith's beggars, like Lamb's, are strongly associated with particular localities. There's the tall blind man who strikes stones by the Whitbread Brewery on Chiswell Street and the Jew in the cart who begs on Petticoat Lane. There's Priscilla, who sits making patchwork quilts by the wall of the New River in Islington, and Taylor the blind shoemaker who lives at No. 6 Saffron Hill. And the fact that so many of the beggars selected are blind only reinforces their status as allegorical emblems of the spirit of place. Eyeless and immobile like the statues of local deities in a ruined classical landscape, they evoke the extreme specificity, tactility even, of a particular spot or corner; and conjure up a notion of urban space as something that can be deeply inhabited and felt. But they also, because of their blindness, cannot help reminding us of its fragility, of how quickly memory can be marooned by the traffic of time. 'In allegory', as Benjamin wrote in his *Origin of German Tragic Drama*, 'the word history stands written on the countenance of nature in the character of transience'.[32]

Evocative though its images undoubtedly are, *Vagabondiana* is not a straightforwardly nostalgic text; indeed it tries to have it both ways as regards the discourse of improvement. In its introduction, which was by Smith's fellow antiquarian Francis Douce, it welcomes the new initiatives to eradicate the 'disgusting nuisance' of begging.[33] But thereafter it spends most of its time reminiscing about its practice, offering a brief defence, in its final pages, of old fashioned face-to-face charity.

The artistic pedigree of beggars is established early on. Many great artists, it is argued, have used them as models, from Michelangelo to Sir Joshua Reynolds. *Vagabondiana*'s first character sketch is of one Jack Stuart, a model of the contemporary sculptor John Flaxman's, who had died on 15 August 1815 aged thirty-five. Stuart's protégé was another blind beggar by the name of George Dyball, who forms the second figure in the book. 'A fellow of considerable notoriety', the text tell us, 'he sometimes dresses as a sailor, in nankeen waistcoat and trousers; but George, like his master, never was a seaman: Stuart taught him to maund, by allowing him to kneel at a respectable distance, and repeat his supplications.' With all this discussion of artists and models, masters and pupils, *Vagabondiana*'s emphasis is very much on begging as a kind of modelling, the art of striking picturesque attitudes. And this is further borne out by the ensuing description of Dyball's dog:

> His business was to make a response to his master's '*Pray pity the Blind*' by an impressive whine, accompanied with uplifted eyes and an importunate turn of the head; and when his eyes have not caught those of the spectators, he has been seen to rub the tin box against their knees, to enforce his solicitations. When money

was thrown into the box, he immediately put it down, took out the contents with his mouth, and, joyfully wagging his tail, carried them to his master. (pp. 26–7)

Text and image stand at cross-purposes in *Vagabondiana*. The text is invariably a celebration (as well as an exposure) of a particular beggar's performance practice, and fits relatively neatly, in tone and perspective, within the 'cautionary literature' tradition. The images, however, are much more straightforwardly picturesque, and represent their subjects with great stillness and pathos, their effect often strikingly different from that of the surrounding anecdotes. In Dyball's case the text is all about the relationship of a particular actor to his audience, but in the image it looks as if this relationship has all but broken down (Figure 9). Not only do the people in the picture have their backs turned to Dyball, as if blind to his blindness, they also appear to be staring at a blind wall themselves. Blindness has become the allegorical subject of this portrait, with Dyball looking much more like the epitome of dignified abjection than a wily street performer.

There is a different kind of ambivalence in Lamb's 'Decay of Beggars'. In the first part of the essay the beggar is celebrated in heroic terms, as a naive figure for unadorned humanity; in the second half, however, he is quickly transformed into a skilled performer. While musing at length on his 'half-Hercules' of the street, Elia starts to contemplate beggary itself as just another kind of urban show, in intention as well as effect: 'Among her shows, her museums, and supplies for ever-gaping curiosity (and what else but an accumulation of sights – endless sights – is a great city; or for what else is it desirable?) was there not room for one Lusus (not Naturae, indeed, but) Accidentium?'[34] And the essay concludes on the same note:

Shut not thy purse strings always against painted distress. Act a charity sometimes. When a poor creature (outwardly and visibly such) comes before thee, do not stay to inquire whether the 'seven small children,' in whose name he implores thy assistance, have a veritable existence. Rake not into the bowels of unwelcome truth, to save a halfpenny. It is good to believe him … When they come with their counterfeit looks, and mumping tones, think them players. You pay your money to see a comedian feign these things, which, concerning these poor people, thou canst not certainly tell whether they are feigned or not. (p. 536)

In the Holy Land scene of Pierce Egan's *Life in London*, as in *Vagabondiana*, it is only when the beggar's mask has been lifted, and his status objectified, that he can be truly enjoyed. But Lamb enjoys allowing his beggar to hover ambiguously, between mock and earnest, a little like an author writing in a persona for a periodical magazine. In their different ways

Figure 9. John Thomas Smith, *George Dyball*, from *Vagabondiana or, Anecdotes of Mendicant Wanderers*. Engraving. 1817.

Life in London, *Vagabondiana* and the Mendicity Society all exemplify the characteristic hypocrisy of the picturesque. Metropolitan spectacle is a one-way street with them. In the case of the Mendicity Society, for example, we are presented with an institution that strove hard to preserve the picturesque experience of the individual alms-giver 'acting a charity' in the London streets, all the while ruthlessly punishing any suggestion of performance in the recipient. This hunting down of imposture was to take on an even more pathological, and preposterous, character in the Victorian age, when the deserving beggar became a kind of vanishing point of authenticity. How is it, Henry Mayhew demanded in *London Labour and the London Poor* (1861–2), that 'a fainting, famished fellow' can walk leisurely up the street, and still bellow out in notes of thunder, 'I am starving!' … If one of my readers will try when faint and exhausted to produce the same tone in the open air, he will perceive the impossibility of shouting and starving simultaneously.'[35] According to this logic, the only really deserving beggar is the one who is incapable of begging, and the only really authentic appeal for relief would be no appeal at all. It seems that for Mayhew the only way for the urban beggar to avoid the grubby connection between speech and commerce is to make himself, like Wordsworth's Blind Beggar, or the Old Cumberland Beggar from the *Lyrical Ballads*, a thing to be seen and not heard.

Writing thirty years before Mayhew, Lamb is more sophisticated about the beggar–bystander relationship, and much more attuned to its innately theatrical nature. In 1825 he wrote an article on 'Imperfect Dramatic Illusion' for the *London Magazine*, in which he argued that it was a crucial component of the audience's pleasure, and, indeed, of their larger moral instruction, that certain characters in comedies should go beyond the bounds of the theatrical illusion and establish a knowing relationship with the audience.

> Why are misers so hateful in the world, and so endurable on the stage, but because the skilful actor, by a sort of sub-reference, rather than direct appeal to us, disarms the character of a great deal of its odiousness, by seeming to engage *our* compassion for the insecure tenure by which he holds his money bags and parchments?[36]

By sharing his character's vice with the spectators through a 'perpetual sub-insinuation' of looks and gestures, a great actor can generate sympathy as well as opprobrium. 'Comedians, paradoxical as it may seem, may be too natural', Lamb says. Their perplexities, to be genuinely involving, must seem 'half-put on' (p. 601). Stage illusion, then, must be somewhat qualified in comedy, which requires for its highest effects 'a sort of compromise … a judicious understanding, not too openly announced, between the ladies and gentlemen – on both sides of the curtain' (p. 601). There is a similar dynamic, I would suggest, in the conclusion to his essay on beggars, which seeks to establish the same 'judicious understanding' between the various parties concerned. In this case poverty is the crime, and begging the skilful performance – a performance that disarms poverty of half its odiousness by being 'half-put on'. 'Pauperism, pauper, poor man, are expressions of pity, but pity alloyed with contempt', Lamb says, near the beginning of the piece, 'but no-one properly contemns a beggar' (p. 532). To Lamb, theatricality was in no way destructive of the moral spectacle of beggary, as it was to Wordsworth and Mayhew, it was an intrinsic part of it.

There is evidently something 'half-put on' in the tone of the 'Decay of Beggars' essay itself, a quality that used to be called Romantic irony, and which is especially present in the penultimate anecdote, a story about a blind beggar and a clerk:

> A clerk in the Bank was surprised with the announcement of a five hundred pound legacy left him by a person whose name he was a stranger to. It seems that in his daily morning walks from Peckham (or some village thereabouts) where he lived, to his office, it had been his practice for the last twenty years to drop his halfpenny duly into the hat of some blind Bartimeus, that sate begging alms by the wayside in the Borough. The good old beggar recognised his daily benefactor by the voice only; and, when he died, left all the amassings of his alms (that had been half a century perhaps in the accumulating) to his old Bank friend. Was this a story to purse up people's hearts, and pennies, against giving an alms to the blind? – or not rather a beautiful moral of well-directed charity on the one part, and noble gratitude upon the other? I sometimes wish I had been that Bank clerk … Reader, do not be frightened at the hard words, imposition, imposture – give, and ask no questions. Cast thy bread upon the waters. Some have unawares (like this Bank clerk) entertained angels. (pp. 535–6)

Beautiful moral or no, this story is a fantastical imposition on Elia's part – and his cleverly 'sub-insinuating' tone confesses it. But it is also, one feels, an allegory of some personal significance for Lamb, in spite of the facetiousness of its presentation. Essentially it is a story about commuting, and about the new time–work discipline of the early nineteenth century. The life of the city clerk, as Lamb knew only too well, was all prudence and punctuality, buffed shoes and book-keeping, and in giving his daily halfpenny to the Borough beggar, his Peckhamite protagonist is, in some small way, rebelling against this strait-jacket. He is paying a small tribute to the time-freedom of the wayside, and to the mysterious usury of the streets. The irony is, of course, that far from being a disorderly figure, the beggar is, in his way, as regular and as prudent as the clerk himself – he acts all along as the bank clerk's banker, and is at his station, and his office, every morning. He has come not to destroy accounting but to transfigure it, first recommending heedless charity by encouraging his clients to 'give and ask no questions', and then, quite unexpectedly, redeeming it through his own Christ-like book-keeping.

THE SUPERANNUATED MAN

Throughout Lamb's professional career, he exhibited a healthy interest in what Michel de Certeau has called *la perruque*, the spirit of tactical resistance at the heart of everyday life.[37] His jokes and puns are of this nature; so too his habit of writing long private letters on the firm's time. Beggars are, in a sense, the patron saints of *la perruque*; they are all tactics and no strategy, theirs are the innumerable little victories of the dispossessed. It was for this reason, perhaps, that Lamb wanted to celebrate beggars as being actors as well as emblems, recorders as well as instances of metropolitan history.

Wordsworth was interested in the beggar as a double of the poet; Elia was chiefly preoccupied with him as the opposite of the clerk. Earlier we quoted a letter to Wordsworth of 20 March 1822, in which Lamb penned an eloquent lament on his 'pent' condition. It is a fine piece, strikingly modern in feeling, and made all the more interesting when we consider that it was produced only a couple of months before the 'Decay of Beggars'. 'O for a few years between the grave and the desk', he had written,

> I do not whisper to myself a Pension on this side of absolute incapacitation and infirmity, till years have sucked me dry. *Otium cum indignitate.* I had thought in a green old age (O green thought!) to have retired to Ponder's End – emblematic name how beautiful! in the Ware road, there to have made up my accounts with Heaven and the Company, toddling about between it and Cheshunt, anon stretching on some fine Izaac Walton morning to Hoddesdon or Amwell, careless as a Beggar, but walking, walking ever, till I fairly walked myself off my legs, dying walking! (VII, 563)

As for Hunt and Keats, so too for Lamb: the suburban space, the ideal space of freedom and recreation, is also a literary space, in this case strongly associated with Marvell, Walton and seventeenth-century 'retirement'. Nor was Lamb quite able to keep his fantasies of being 'free as a beggar' private, for when a generous retirement package did come his way three years later, he composed one of his most interesting essays trying to come to terms with the consequences. 'The Superannuated Man' is about the 'eight, nine, and sometimes ten hours' a-day attendance at a counting-house', and how its hangover effectively ruined those few golden moments – the one day a week, the one week a year, that one was permitted to call one's own: 'Where was the quiet, where the promised rest? Before I had a taste of it', Elia says, 'it was vanished.'[38] The essay touches on the very same issue, then, as Leigh Hunt's 'Country Houses Near Town' and Cyrus Redding's August 1822 essay 'The Tea Garden', namely, the seeming inability of the Cockney to embrace and enjoy his leisure. But it deals with it from the inside, from the perspective of the Cockney himself. After much grumbling about the pains of work, Elia then goes on to describe how one day, quite unexpectedly, the firm suddenly decided to retire him on a generous pension. The shock was extraordinary. For the first day or two, he felt 'stunned, overwhelmed':

> I could scarce trust myself with myself. It was like passing out of Time into Eternity – for it is a sort of Eternity for a man to have his Time all to himself. It seemed to me that I had more time on my hands than I could manage. From a poor man, poor in Time, I was suddenly lifted up into a vast revenue; I could see no end of my possessions; I wanted some steward, or judicious bailiff, to manage my estates in Time for me. (p. 69)

'The Superannuated Man' is, in this way, the story of a fortunate Cockney Triptolemus who *does* leave behind 'the weariness, the fever and the fret' to make the painful transition to bourgeois 'immortality'. But this being Lamb, the narrator's success story is inevitably framed by a rich, controlling irony. 'I am to be met with in trim gardens', he says, as the essay relaxes towards its conclusion, 'I am already come to be known by my vacant face and careless gesture, perambulating at no fixed pace, nor with any settled purpose.' 'They tell me, a certain *cum dignitate* air, that has been buried so long with my other good parts, has begun to shoot forth in my person. I grow into gentility perceptibly' (p. 73).

CHAPTER 6

John Martin, John Soane and Cockney art

The 'Cockney School' debate of the late 1810s and early 1820s has long been familiar to Romanticists. Less often remarked upon is the fact that the language of Cockneyism as a mode of cultural abuse continued to have critical purchase well into the 1820s and 1830s, and that its influence went beyond the literary. This chapter is devoted to two men who attracted this type of criticism – the first an artist and the second an architect – and is prompted by the recognition that, in this period at least, the term 'Cockney', far from being a simple class insult, actually registers a complex awareness of, and discomfort with, the aesthetics of modernity. Cockneyism, in these instances, is more of a cultural than a social slur, and gestures towards everything that is most amphibious and uncertain about early-nineteenth-century metropolitan life. It is concerned, among other things, with questions of scale and perspective, and with the challenge that the city poses to traditional forms and categories, ways of seeing and modes of representation. Hence to review the charges that were laid against John Soane and John Martin is also to remind ourselves of what was seemingly most incongruous and challenging in their work, helping us to recover a sense of these highly idiosyncratic (and still relatively neglected) artists as 'painters of modern life'.

In 1821 the notion of London as a 'New Babylon' was more compelling than ever. Since medieval times, Babylon had been the epitome of the worldly city, a legendary metropolis of great monuments and great impiety, drawing its Christian meaning from the fact that hardly any of it remained. With the increased archaeological activity of the Romantic period, however, some flesh was being put on these bones. There was renewed speculation as to the exact lineaments of the first great brick city of antiquity, and the look and shape of its famous structures – the Hanging Gardens, the Temple of Jupiter Belus, the Tower of Babel. In 1815 Claude James Rich, resident for the East India Company at the Court of Baghdad, published his *Memoir on the Ruins of Babylon*, proposing that the public edifices of the old city were probably 'remarkable more for vastness of dimensions than elegance of design', and the following year Thomas Maurice, assistant librarian of the British Museum, published some of his own observations on Rich's memoir, speculating further on Babylon's appearance and dimensions.[1] This new interest in Babylon coincided with a post-Waterloo construction boom in England, which led to a spectacular wave of public building in the West End of London. By 1821 the Burlington Arcade was open, John Nash's Regent Street and Regent's Park were nearly completed and plans were afoot to remodel the King's Mews (now Trafalgar Square) and Buckingham House. Fashionable, showy and built of brick rather than stone, Nash's Regent Street invited comparison with the great hubristic city of antiquity, of which it was sometimes seen to be a throwaway modern version.[2]

Historical parallels between the British and Babylonian Empires reached a height in 1821, with the final demise of the mad King George III. Since the onset of his illness, George had invited covert comparison with Nebuchadnezzar, the Babylonian king who had gone insane after bringing the Jews into captivity. William Blake's 1795 print of *Nebuchadnezzar* can be read in this way; so too Keats's 'Nebuchadnezzar's Dream' of 1817. The historical successor to Nebuchadnezzar's kingdom was his son (or in some accounts his grandson) Belshazzar, another vain and impious king – at least according to Judaeo-Christian tradition – whose decadence eventually brought about Babylon's downfall. John Martin first unveiled his spectacular history painting *Belshazzar's Feast* at the British Institution in the spring of 1821, only a few months before the coronation of George IV and in the very midst of the Queen Caroline controversy. At the centre of this composition we see a vain king surrounded by beautiful concubines, with a magnificent feast set before him, and the opulent grandeur of a newly constructed palace and capital city providing an evocatively oriental, and yet also (as we shall see) curiously contemporary-looking backdrop (see Figure 10). The Prince Regent, a notorious voluptuary and spendthrift, as well as being the foremost patron of Nash and his Brighton Pavilion, was only too easy to see as a modern Belshazzar, and so the satirico-political resonances must have been deafening. So deafening, indeed, that even Martin's later dedication of the 1826 mezzotint of *Belshazzar's Feast* to the king looks suspiciously like a negative confirmation of the painting's original impulse rather than a refutation of it.

Belshazzar's Feast commemorates that moment in the Bible when Daniel interprets the words MENE, MENE, TEKEL and PARSIN, written in Aramaic by a mysterious hand on the wall of Belshazzar's palace, as

Figure 10. John Martin, *Belshazzar's Feast*. Oil on canvas. 1821.

a prophecy of Babylon's imminent downfall.[3] The narrative had long been a popular one in Christian art, registering a powerful critique of vanity and idolatry. So powerful and direct was its message, indeed, that many treatments concentrated solely on its three central elements: Belshazzar, Daniel and the writing on the wall. Such was the case with Rembrandt's celebrated 1635 canvas, which quickly became the most authoritative rendering. The originality of Martin's version lay in the fact that the main elements of the story were set against a vast architectural backdrop, a huge square and a colonnade, a distant temple and towering ramparts, with a violent thunderstorm overhead and everything illuminated by a lurid glow.

What the artist had done, in effect, was bring the new aesthetic of the urban panorama to bear upon traditional history painting, combining a dazzling overall spectacle with minute local detail in a manner strongly associated with the new medium. 'The picture is a bold attempt at composition', wrote the *Monthly Magazine*, 'uniting architecture, sculpture, furniture, feasting, drapery, revelry, thunder and lightning. The conception is grand, but extravagant, the air and costume theatrical, and the colouring not of the best or most harmonious. The picture is in bad taste, but the best perhaps of its style that was ever painted.'[4] There were many contemporary panoramas portraying contemporary city-spaces, and a good number that reimagined lost classical ones, but the wonder of Martin's painting was that it somehow managed to do both at the same time, for his Babylon was not only convincing in itself, as a scholarly reconstruction of an ancient city, it also had strong resemblances with modern Regency London.

Belshazzar's Feast's architecture would have struck a chord with many Londoners. To West End gallery-goers in particular, it would have been almost impossible to see the great triple arch at its centre without thinking of the new Burlington Arcade (Figure 11), or the great receding columns of the Temple of Astarte without recalling the recently completed Regent Street colonnade just around the corner. The former was to become so fashionable that it had an entire song devoted to it in *Tom and Jerry*, W. T. Moncrieff's surprise theatrical hit of 1822. To some observers this curious mixture of the historical and the contemporary may have enhanced *Belshazzar's Feast*'s satirical purchase, but to many of the cognoscenti it was a disastrous distraction from the main theme. The main problem was that, for certain critics at least, the showiest and most vulgarly fashionable element in the painting was not the architecture, or even the court, but the spectacle of divine intervention. To one reviewer, looking back some

Figure 11. Burlington Arcade from Shepherd and Elmes's *Metropolitan Improvements.* Engraving. 1828.

years later, *Belshazzar's Feast* was a mere compendium of the popular stage techniques of the day, and looked exactly like a spectacle designed by Philippe de Loutherberg, put on by Covent Garden, and starring one of the most celebrated popular preachers of the day in the role of Daniel:

> Belshazzar is Wallack, the actor, in affected attitude, with a commonplace look of fear; the prophet is the Reverend Mr Irving; the soothsayers resemble the vocal priests of the opera, arrayed in cumbrous draperies; and the concubines are a mob of females with preposterous trains, fainting in the most extravagant postures. Instead of 'the fingers of a man's hand writing over against the candlestick on the plaster of the wall of the king's palace' there is a pyrotechnic display of colossal hieroglyphics on the marble frieze of a stupendous temple.[5]

In a similar fashion, Charles Lamb considered the overall architectural effect of the composition 'stupendous' but its main event, the prophet's reading of the writing on the wall, reminded him of nothing so much as a theatrical trick got up by the Prince Regent himself for a party at the Brighton Pavilion.[6]

There is undoubtedly, however one chooses to read it, a topical element in *Belshazzar's Feast*, but there is also evidence of an earnest antiquarian interest in the painting that went far beyond any purely fashionable or satirical requirements. Martin had been inspired to paint the subject in the first place by reading a prize poem written by a fellow of Emmanuel College Cambridge, Thomas Hughes.[7] Hughes's *Belshazzar's Feast* began with a vivid poetic retelling of the salient events as described in the Book of Daniel. But by far the greater part of his slender volume had been devoted to an extensive series of accompanying notes on Babylonian religious beliefs and architectural practices. Hughes cited Maurice and Rich enthusiastically, quoting the former on a Mexican temple thought to resemble the Babylonian Temple of Belus: 'The temple stood in the midst of an immense court, enclosed by a wall, which was adorned externally with sculpture, representing serpents interlaced one with another, a symbol of the ancient fire-worship.'[8] In Hughes there was a tension between the highly moral Christian message of the poem itself and the deep fascination and scholarly affection for pagan culture in the notes. So too, in the case of Martin's *Belshazzar's Feast*, both the timeless message of the painting and its modern-day satirical inflection were partially overridden by the sheer enthusiasm with which the artist had reconstructed this fabled 'city of sin'.

All that was needed for the main story of *Belshazzar's Feast* could have been drawn from chapter 5 of the Old Testament Book of Daniel. But the painting's catalogue description, which was written anonymously by

Martin himself, revealed a deep scholarly engagement not only with contemporary experts such as Maurice and Rich, but also with Josephus, Strabo, Herodotus and Diodorus, the ancient writers who had written extensively on the material reality of the ancient city. Martin knew from his researches that Babylon had been an architecturally eclectic place, with influences from all over the Near and Far East, and he made sure that this was evident in the painting and its accompanying description, which listed all the architectural and ornamental details in the painting – the hall of Astarte (the Babylonian Venus), the golden statue of Jupiter Belus, the Temple of Belus and the Tower of Babel.[9] Where the recent excavations of Babylon did not help, Martin looked to the Elgin Marbles for his inspiration, and to the many Egyptian artefacts that could be seen around London. The Babylonians hadn't known how to construct arches, Martin pointed out, and so he had tried to show how the stones of the triple colonnade would have been arranged 'in such a manner as to give the apparent strength of an arch without being one' (p. 2). Zodiacal signs lined the walls of the central square and starry portents decorated the firmament, to commemorate the fact that it was the Chaldeans, or Babylonian priests, who were thought to have invented both astrology and astronomy.

Even the theatrical element of the painting was couched in archaic terms, with Martin dividing the narrative action into three moments, the Protasis, the Epitasis and the Catastrophe. This last detail is telling, because it shows how keen he was for viewers to read his static image as if it was a moving spectacle, exactly in the manner of de Loutherberg's *eidophusikon* and the panoramas:

> First Act, or Protasis: The mysterious writing on the wall has just been completed – the hand therefore is withdrawn – the characters, in strokes of the most intense light, send forth an undescribable effulgence, such as would be the blaze of lightnings, could they be fixed on the dark ground of the angry clouds from which they emanate. Their scintillating beams fill the whole of the Atrium with awful resplendency, and the whole assembly with horror and distress. (p. 4)

On one level, *Belshazzar's Feast* was a daring attempt, on the part of a maverick painter who had fallen foul of the Royal Academy, to produce an original and important work in the highest pictorial genre – the historical sublime. But it was also shot through with a more populist panorama-style desire to captivate its audience with historical learning. This pedagogical impulse had one further aspect to it as well. Like another Daniel interpreting the writing on the wall to Belshazzar's court, Martin's over-elaborate *Description* also took upon itself the task of explaining the strange, comet-like ways of genius to the public:

> Like supernatural beings, whose visits are 'few and far between' [men of genius] wheel their brilliant course above contemporary rivals, and though, being mortals, they soon disappoint the widowed sight of their admirers, their works, if well understood, still secure for them, a sort of immortality on earth, while they repose in the bosom of HIM who breathed life into their bodies and enthusiasm into their souls. (p. 1)

Martin was an artistic outsider, the product of a strict Calvinist background in the North East of England, and he had a rich seam of fanaticism and millennialism in his family. His elder brother William was a visionary philosopher and failed engineer, who seems to have become increasingly delusional in later life, and his younger brother Jonathan became famous for setting fire to York Minster.[10] There was a potent mix of religious zeal and personal ambition in John Martin's career too, especially in the great series of Biblical disasterscapes that he produced in the 1820s and 1830s, including *The Fall of Babylon*, *The Fall of Ninevah*, *The Seventh Plague* and *The Flood*. But in his work the religious vision is effectively subsumed into its artistic context, becoming a metaphor for his own originality and independence as a painter. Here already, in the passage quoted above, we can see how keen Martin was to see the story of Daniel as an allegory for the way in which divine inspiration speaks in and through the individual genius, offering the figure of the artist up to the reader as the archetypal outsider, a being almost supernatural, a spectacular object of 'holy dread'.

COCKNEY HISTORY PAINTING

Hung low like a panorama in the main gallery of the British Institution, *Belshazzar's Feast* was to prove an immediate and resounding success with gallery-goers, and with many of the critics that followed in their wake. The *New Monthly Magazine* hailed it as a 'magnificent picture' before adding that 'the governors of the Institution have added to the admiration of the public, the weight of their high and encouraging approval of this noble work, by conferring upon Mr. Martin the reward of two hundred guineas, besides leaving to him the produce of its sale'.[11] The picture was then bought for a thousand pounds by William Collins, a former employer of Martin's, and exhibited at his shop in the Strand. This was the beginning of that meteoric rise in Martin's reputation which would lead Edward Bulwer-Lytton to hail him, twelve years later, as 'the greatest, the most lofty, the most permanent, the most original genius of the age'.[12] Benjamin Robert Haydon's friend, the Academician David

Wilkie, also considered the painter a 'phenomenon', noting that 'although weak in all those points in which he can be compared with other artists, [Martin] is eminently strong in what no artist has attempted'.[13]

Not everyone was blown away, however. To Wilkie's fellow Royal Academician John Constable, *Belshazzar's Feast* was nothing but 'a pantomime',[14] a view with which Janus Weathercock (alias Thomas Griffiths Wainewright) concurred in his extended review of the exhibition for the *London Magazine*:

> The whole scene seems to me rather a theatrical pageant – a presentment of unknown fire works, before a barbaric Prince (a king of Ashantee for instance), of which the old black figure standing on the table, like a speaker at the Freemason's, is showman – than the arena of a real courage-blasting portent. There is too much bustle, noise, hubbub, and screaming for any real supernatural awe. It is either common affrightment or mere simulation. The groups are only groups in the last scene of a melodrama. These gaudy minions have self-possession enough to hurry, and scamper, as if from a mad ox or dog.[15]

At the beginning of his review Wainewright had made a lot of how difficult it had been to catch a glimpse of the painting, such were the crowds continually blocking his view. 'It is the fashion', as a fellow viewer declares (p. 437). The implication was that the British Institution had been transformed, for the occasion, into a vulgar street show, an effect that mirrored exactly what went on in the painting itself. After quoting the story of Belshazzar from the Book of Daniel, Wainewright concluded by asking: 'Has Mr. Martin anything in this picture which harmonizes with this noble passage? Does it not at once render his women Bartlemy dolls, and men, wire-strung puppets?' (p. 443). John Scott, that real-life victim of the 'Cockney School' debate, was only a couple of months dead when this article was written, and the notion of Cockneyism had been a problematic one for the *London* (as we have seen) some time before that. So it is not surprising that 'Janus Weathercock' doesn't invoke the concept outright. Nevertheless, it is clear enough what he is getting at. His strictures on the anachronistic feel of the painting – its inability to evoke anything but contemporary Regency London – cannot help but recall *Blackwood's Edinburgh Magazine*'s much-publicized attacks on 'faulty costume' in Cockney School poetry, most specifically in relation to Keats's *Endymion* and Hunt's *Story of Rimini*. So too Weathercock's attack on Martin's incongruous blend of the microscopic and the macroscopic also has a distinctively anti-Cockney flavour, culminating as it does in the assertion that the painter has transformed the men and women in his composition into 'little Bartlemy [i.e. Bartholomew Fair] dolls'. As with Hunt and

Keats, so too with Martin; it seems that an acquaintance with inferior street spectacle has so infected his Cockney imagination that the true sublime is now beyond him. Of the painter's earlier *Macbeth* Weathercock had insisted 'the tone was feeble and without *gusto*':

> It had none of that vast, illimitable-black-level barrenness which stamps on the mind such a chilling image of bleakness and desolation, mingled with curdling awe; but, on the contrary was cut up into a thousand littlenesses, which peremptorily arrested the sweep of the eye. Some of the hollows looked like gravel pits; – there were bare patches whence turf had been cut for Mr Any-Body's Garden; and bating the mountains and lake, which seemed very much ashamed of themselves, it put me in mind of Hampstead Heath in the winter. (p. 442)

The grand assumption here, and it is one that was shared by most members of the artistic establishment, was that it was the great duty of history painting, that most high and heroic of forms, to capture the great sweep of events, and not to get bogged down in petty details. Put simply, it was the genre's burden to represent History but not the historical; costume was always to take second place to Character.[16] But what Martin had done in *Belshazzar's Feast* was precisely the opposite. Gone was the humanist emphasis on individual power and virtue: his personages were mere puppets in a storm. Instead of concentrating on the sublimity of the divine power, the painter had allowed himself to become preoccupied by everything else, with the result that his *Belshazzar's Feast*, like his *Macbeth*, had finally devolved into 'a thousand littlenesses', as broken up and inconsequential as a new view of the London suburbs. For once the *Blackwood's* critic found himself in agreement with his opposite number at the *London*: 'In short', their reviewer said,

> the figures can only be looked on as accompaniments to the scene, and ought not to be regarded as historical, any more than those introduced in the landscapes of Wilson or Claude Lorraine. – It is perfectly ridiculous, therefore, to consider the picture as an attempt at the highest styles of art – The class to which it belongs is the ornamental.[17]

Weathercock was no straightforward Cockney-basher; indeed, in making use of the word 'gusto' as an artistic term he was borrowing from none other than the 'Cockney Aristotle' himself, William Hazlitt. But there were clearly elements in the *Blackwood's* attacks that he had picked up on, and which he was now directing towards a new target. Cockneyism, in this period, was simply too useful a concept to be completely monopolized by the Tories: liberal writers, and writers for the London magazines, couldn't help resorting to it as well. It was as if there was something present in the culture of modern metropolitan spectacle, something peculiarly discrepant and disconcerting, and Cockney criticism was the best means of gesturing towards it, whether or not that particular nickname was invoked.

Charles Lamb prided himself on his metropolitan imagination, as we saw in Chapter 5, but that didn't stop him from objecting to Martin's *Belshazzar's Feast* in what were (for him at least) unusually outspoken terms. His critique was first registered privately, in a letter to his friend Bernard Barton in 1827. It was then considerably expanded upon in his late 'Elia' essay, 'On the Barrenness of the Imaginative Faculty in the Productions of Modern Art' (1833), which was first published in parts in the *Athenaeum*. In his letter to Barton, Lamb reiterated a judgement that had already been made by a number of people before, which was that while its 'stupendous architectural designs' were undoubtedly of the 'highest order of the material sublime', the people – the human figures – were mean and commonplace. In addition, he suggested that, however good the historical and architectural detail was, it should not have had such a central place in a history painting, because in the end such detail could only distract from the main theme. Characters present at the great moment depicted would not have had eyes for the diverse architectural forms, the dishes on the banqueting table, etc., and therefore nor should the viewer. Miracles in Biblical times had only appealed to the senses, Lamb argued, in order to overthrow their tyranny. Their entire purpose was to *go beyond* materialism and idolatry – that was why Christians did not need miracles any longer. But in Martin's painting, he hinted, there was a paganism of vision that effectively reversed this historical process. As he said in his letter to Barton:

> What *one* point is there of interest? The ideal of such a subject is, that you the spectator should see nothing but what at the time you would have seen, the *hand*, and the *King* – not be at leisure to make tailor-remarks on the dresses, or Doctor-Kitchener-like[18] to examine the good things at table … Still [Martin] is showy in all that is not the human figure or the preternatural interest: but the first are below a drawing school-girl's attainment, and the last is a phantasmagoric trick.[19]

In Lamb's view *Belshazzar's Feast* was both too historical and not historical enough. Martin had failed to realize that the real purpose of history painting was to *transcend* history, to capture the timeless moment, the moment in and out of time. It was not to engage in a painstaking reconstruction of a particular historical occasion that, precisely because of its intent concern with scene-setting, also seemed hopelessly tangled up in the fashionable tastes of the present. *Belshazzar's Feast* should have been about God exposing the foolish vanity of the Babylonian kings and their futile attempts to purchase immortality through architecture. Its main intention ought to have been to show the light of the divine word revealing the truth about pagan structures – namely, their absolute fragility. But the very elaborateness, the very concreteness of Martin's material structures meant that, in direct contrast to some of J. M. W. Turner's great classical cityscapes, exactly the opposite effect was conveyed. The objective trumped the subjective, Babylon, the city of fashion, was exalted, and the writing on the wall was made to look like a cheap party trick.[20]

After Wainewright, Hazlitt was the next of the *London Magazine*'s contributors to criticize Martin's *Belshazzar's Feast*, contrasting the painter unfavourably with the sculptor of the Elgin Marbles:

> [Martin] strives to outdo nature. He wants to give more than she does, or than his subject requires or admits. He subdivides his groups into infinite littleness, and exaggerates his scenery into absolute immensity. His figures are like rows of shiny pins; his mountains are piled up one on the back of the other, like the stories of houses. He has no notion of the moral principle in all art, that a part may be greater than the whole. He reckons that if one range of lofty square hills is good, another range above that with clouds between must be better. He thus wearies the imagination, instead of exciting it. We see no end of the journey, and turn back in disgust. We are tired of the effort, we are tired of the monotony of this sort of reduplication of the same object.[21]

Hazlitt does not say so explicitly, but the suggestion is that Martin's imagination has been so warped by city spectacles ('rows of shiny pins', 'stories of houses') that constant visions of accumulation and accretion have finally corrupted his taste. Critically speaking, it is only a short step from Hazlitt's notion of Martin's compositions as being full of 'reduplications of the same object' to that High Victorian judgement of John Ruskin's that his paintings were, in effect, mass-produced. 'Workmen such as John Martin … I do not regard as painters at all', he wrote, in an early draft of *The Stones of Venice*, 'Martin's works are merely a common manufacture, as much makeable to order as a tea-tray or a coal scuttle.'[22] The money that Martin had made from mezzotints of his paintings, which *were* indeed mass-produced, must have been at the back of Ruskin's mind here, and this in spite of the fact that he was by no means the only artist to flourish through cheap engravings.

What Ruskin says, Hazlitt only implies: that Martin is a mere manufacturer of visions, not a true artist. There is also the further suggestion, in Hazlitt's attack, that by bringing the aesthetics of the modern panorama to bear upon the field of classical history painting, Martin has compromised traditional notions of emphasis and perspective. To the reviewer's mind, he has created a form of sublimity that is mathematical rather than moral, and which disrupts the traditional relation between part and whole. 'This craving after quantity', Hazlitt insisted, 'is a morbid affection' (p. 418). Benjamin Haydon, who was the other 'great' artist of the period operating in defiance of the Royal Academy, could only concur. Of Martin's *Creation* he wrote that

> There is nothing grand in a man stepping from York to Lancaster; but when he makes a great Creator fifteen inches, paints a sun the size of a bank token, draws a line for the sea and makes one leg of God on it and the other above, and says: 'There! That horizon is twenty miles long, and therefore God's leg must be sixteen relatively to the horizon,' the artist really deserves as much pity as the poorest maniac in Bedlam.[23]

There was even a kind of Babylonian hubris, Hazlitt hinted, in Martin's continual attempt to outbuild nature, with the results being at once vertiginous and absurd: 'A landscape is not an architectural elevation. You may build a house as high as you can lift up stones with pulleys and levers, but you cannot raise mountains into the sky merely with the pencil' (p. 448). Interestingly enough, the suspicion that Martin was nothing but a frustrated architect-engineer at heart (like his brother William) was only to be exacerbated during the 1820s and 1830s, as he submitted plan after plan to the British government calling for the building of a Thames embankment. He had become aware, while researching his apocalyptic cityscape *The Fall of Ninevah* in 1828, that it was a failure of the urban water supply that had caused the demise of Ninevah and Babylon, and he began a campaign to renovate London's abject sewer system to save the 'Modern Babylon' from a similar destiny. Tellingly, the embankment design he submitted to the government in his 1828 *Plan for Supplying with Pure Water the Cities of London and Westminster* drew heavily on the elegant promenades he had laid out on either side of the River Euphrates in his 1819 painting *The Fall of Babylon*. This is the central paradox of Martin's career: the fact that so many of his Biblical disaster paintings can be read as self-advertisements, millennial visions of death and destruction that also served as architectural flyers. Martin bombarded the establishment with sewer plans over the course of the 1830s, but none of them were ever taken up; nor was he ever fully accepted by the British art establishment. So, as with Leigh Hunt, there remained an idiosyncratic, unprotected, resolutely amateur quality about John Martin, and like Hunt he was to spend many of his later years doggedly defending his record as a progressive. One of his last statements to this effect was in a poignant letter to the *Illustrated London News* of March 1849:

> In 1832, 1834, 1836, 1842, 1843, 1845 and 1847 I published and republished additional particulars [of his Thames sewer and embankment plan] – being so bent upon my object that I was determined never to abandon it; and though I have reaped no other advantage, I have, at least, the satisfaction of knowing that the agitation thus kept up, constantly, solely by myself, has resulted in a vast alteration in the quantity and quality of water, supplied by the companies, and in the establishment of a Board of Health, which will, in all probability, eventually carry out most of the objects I have been so long urging.[24]

SOANE, GANDY AND THE 'BOEOTIAN' ORDER OF ARCHITECTURE

If there was an anxiety among fine art critics in 1821 that history painting was being subsumed into architectural drawing, there was also an equal and opposite fear doing the rounds in architectural circles, which was that architectural drawing was becoming ever more fantastical and picturesque. *Belshazzar's Feast* looked original when placed on the walls of the British Institution, in close proximity to other, more conventional landscapes and history paintings. But if it had been displayed at the Royal Academy as part of their annual exhibition of architectural perspective paintings, its indebtedness to this sub-genre would have been only too evident. One of the leading practitioners in this field for many years, and one who certainly had an influence upon Martin, was Joseph Michael Gandy.[25] By 1821 Gandy was a failed architect who had nevertheless made a kind of alternative career for himself as a producer of architectural drawings, most notably for John Britton, the antiquarian publisher, and his friend the architect John Soane.[26] Gandy excelled in intricately constructed and theatrically lit resurrections of ancient cities and shrines; he was also a brilliant illustrator of Soane's own buildings, both real and projected.[27] What Gandy shared with Soane in particular was a bitter sense of the Regency period as one inimical to the production of truly great architecture, with both men considering the quest for purity, whether by Greek Revivalists or those of the Gothic persuasion, as a disastrous shackling of the imagination.

Soane was no rank outsider in the field of architecture, as Martin was in painting; indeed he was elected to the Royal Academy, along with Turner, in February 1802. But he was a man from a humble background with a highly eccentric and fiercely independent streak. Born the son of a Reading brickmaker, he was by 1821 an eminent and successful figure by all the usual standards, who had built a considerable reputation for himself as the architect of the new Bank of England. But he was, for all that, a disappointed man – disappointed at his comparative lack of involvement in London's new metropolitan improvements, disappointed also at the lack of ambition being exhibited by (more successful) contemporaries such as Nash and Smirke. Increasingly, Soane's professional disappointment drove him to cultivate his House Museum at Lincoln's Inn Fields, and to indulge his shamelessly eccentric imagination in the process.

In 1821 the Royal Academy exhibited a *Bird's Eye View of a Design for a Royal Residence* (Figure 12) and plans of four new churches, all designed by Soane and lavishly illustrated by Gandy. Practical considerations had never been foremost in this genre of painting, for as with architectural examination pieces, its main purpose was to allow architects to display their originality. That said, in the eyes of some of the reviewers of the period, Soane and Gandy were beginning to take this tradition of architectural fantasy too far. There was something both arrogant and facetious, it was felt, in their repeated insistence on presenting buildings that not only *would* never but *could* never be built. Together they had developed a preposterous, overblown style that was in danger of transforming architectural perspective drawing into a new category of picturesque painting.[28]

In May and June 1821 there was a series of attacks on Soane and Gandy in *The Guardian* newspaper, all prompted by, but by no means restricted to, the recent *Royal Residence* design. Soane was characterized as a man who had sacrificed 'nature, common sense, propriety and simplicity' to his idol 'Novelty', while Gandy was dismissed as one whom the anonymous critic 'had long ceased to consider as an architect'. '[Soane] has not the slightest conception of the chaste, the grand, or the sublime of his art', the reviewer continued, before implying that the architectural value of his palace design stood in an inverse ratio to the sublimity of the Gandy drawing: 'The tasteful style of the drawing of the Palace, and its bird's eye perspective, produce a very pleasing, and even magnificent effect, which we are sorry to say is not supported by an examination of the architecture. To a spectator on the ground, the principal points of the building would be low, lengthy and monotonous.'[29] Soane's royal palace was impractical and overblown; there was no access to the central courts and not a single chimney to be seen. And the style as a whole, even when seen purely on its own terms, was simply too eclectic in ornament and design: 'It was most fortunate for the good taste of the country that the knowledge of the Grecian style became general just at the time it did', *The*

Figure 12. Joseph Michael Gandy, for John Soane, *Bird's Eye View of a Design for a Royal Residence.* Oil on canvas. 1821.

Guardian continued, 'it acted as an antidote to the deleterious mixture of Mr Soane, and saved us from the scorn of the world.'[30]

Soane was by no means the only architect to be attacked for his eclecticism; according to one 'Old Bachelor' the disease had become widespread: 'They are no neat simple Churches now: you see Christian edifices stuck all over with the sacrificial emblems of paganism, bullocks' heads, and rams' horns: in one quarter you see great sprawling uncouth Caryatides – in another an extinguisher by way of spire, hoisted on the top of a Greek balcony.'[31] The caryatids were propping up the new St Pancras church at Woburn Place, which was built by the Inwood brothers between 1819 and 1822. The 'extinguisher by way of spire' was, of course, on top of Nash's All Souls Church in Langham Place, one of the more controversial constructions of period. Even Britton's short-lived *Magazine of the Fine Arts*, a publication otherwise friendly to Gandy and Soane, found itself quietly influenced by such reactions, joining in the criticism of the Greek and Gothic mix at the newly completed St Pancras, and, in an article that could only have been directed at Soane and Gandy, urging a sober retreat from 'impossible' perspectives in architectural paintings.[32]

In 1815 John Scott's *Champion* had published two long and vicious articles in which the writer attacked Soane's work on the Chelsea Hospital as a 'monster in the art of building'. 'Disproportion', he insisted, 'is the most striking feature of the works of this artist.' His House Museum 'looked like a record of the Departed'. The architect's mixed style came in for even more criticism a few years later, with the unveiling of the Dulwich Picture Galley in South London: 'What a thing – What a creature it is!' said the critic of the *London Museum*, 'a Maeso-Gothic … Semi-Arabic, Moro-Spanish, Anglico-Norman – a what-you-will production! It has all the merit and emphatic distinction of being unique.'[33]

Attacks on Soane in the press frequently focused on a gloomy, egotistical element in his work, as well as a perceived lack of fit between form and function. His Bank of England was to attract more than its fair share of criticism on that score. 'We can neither understand nor admire the horizontal lines which *score* the walls of the Bank', said the *Eclectic Review*, 'and while we admire, in part, the semblance of a temple which looks out on Prince's Street and Lothbury, we are unable to discern either the felicity of its adaptation, or the coherence of such a member with the general design.' 'Fancy there may be', the reviewer concluded, 'and ingenuity, but to our view there is a complete lack of tangible principle.'[34] Nobody was keener on fancy than Leigh Hunt, and his newspaper *The Examiner* was to publish an eloquent defence of Soane after the *Champion* attacks of

1815.[35] But even a liberal eclectic like Hunt couldn't help expressing a kind of consternation at some of the Professor's more contrary visions:

> Mr. Soane, a theoretical master of his art, wished to be original when he repaired the Bank; and how did he effect his purpose? Merely by giving his edifice the look of a different object – merely by giving us a title page contradictory to the contents of the book; the Bank has the air of a mausoleum, as if its builder intended to be ironical on our departed gold.[36]

That there was indeed a deep vein of Romantic irony in Soane can be seen from the canvas Gandy painted for him in 1830, which shows a cut-away perspective of the Bank of England as a ruin. In *Belshazzar's Feast* John Martin had brilliantly reconstructed Ancient Babylon in order to commemorate the moment of its destruction. Nothing better summed up the towering ambition and alienation of the modern artist. Soane and Gandy's architectural fantasies had a similarly perverse quality, a kind of self-cancelling Bonapartism of the imagination, the architectural equivalent of Wordsworth's 'levelling muse'.

Soane's Bank of England improvements had been completed in the 1810s, but the exhibition of several Gandy 'Views' of the new building at the Royal Academy in the spring of 1824 seems only to have succeeded in stirring up a new cloud of criticism. The *Literary Gazette* thought the improvements worse than the former structures of Sir Robert Taylor.[37] So too did the *Literary Magnet*, which returned once more to the discrepancy between form and function in the Lothbury corner. It having been rumoured that Soane prided himself on 'turning the corner of a building well', the *Magnet* concluded sharply that 'The architect may "turn" buildings into whatever forms he thinks proper; but we cannot forgive his attempts to "turn" Architecture into ridicule.'[38]

Controversial as Soane had always been, it was only at this moment, in the spring of 1824, that public criticism gelled into an accusation of Cockneyism. In its April issue the *Knight's Quarterly Magazine* published a satire on Soane's style which it identified as the 'Sixth or Boeotian Order of Architecture'.[39] This article (which is suspected to have been by Thomas Whitwell, a former pupil of Soane's),[40] argued that in the Boeotian school, 'singularity of ornament' was always more important than propriety, and all notions of relative proportion were considered 'chimerical and absurd'. It then went on to make fun of the sheer variety of Soane's obsessions – his theatrical taste for funeral monuments, top-lighting, stained glass, etc. – implying that they were all, in a sense, eccentric and egotistical distractions from the proper concerns of architecture:

Is he an Astronomer? His science will lead him to surmount his roofs with unglazed apertures, that he may *coolly* trace the course of the midnight stars. Is he an Undertaker? He will know the proper construction of *Mausolea*, a feel the just altitude of Sarcophagi, and supersede the use of iron coffins ... Is he an Optician? He will understand all the varieties of opake and stained glass, and so apply their colours in a Court of justice (for instance)[41] as to shed the yellow hue of guilt on the face of a criminal, and the rosy tint of modesty on the face of a barrister. (p. 459)

The *Knight's Quarterly* article concluded with an imitation of Thomas Gray's 'Eton College Ode', purportedly composed by Soane himself, in which the architect celebrated his new Dulwich Picture Gallery and Mausoleum in its suburban setting, 'whose dusty paths, whose lanes among, | Wander the cockney crowds along, | Their Sunday-sauntering way'.

Ah, *sightless roof*! Ah, *Chimney-block*!
Ah, *Mauseoleum* grand!
Where late I lavished all my stock
With bold and practis'd hand;
I see the fame that round ye flies,
I hear the plaudits as they rise,
As Art's dull precepts scorning,
My critic-hating soul they soothe,
And speak of 'Visions of my Youth,'
Dreams of 'my early morning.'[42] (pp. 460–1)

The influence of the 'Cockney School' attacks can palpably be felt here, not only in the powerful blend of savage criticism and playful parody, but also in the identification of Soane as another self-aggrandizing Rousseau of the suburbs. Begun in 1817 by *Blackwood's Magazine*, this vein had been picked up by a number of periodical publications in the ensuing years, with varying degrees of serious or satirical intent. Only in October the previous year the *Knight's Quarterly* had published an article called 'Cockney Balaam, A Dinner at the Johnson's Head', which was an extended and often very funny parody of Hunt's best fireside manner.[43] Like Hunt in the contemporary satires of the period, Soane emerges in the 'Boeotian' article as a pert amateur of everything, an inveterate flouter of rules and disciplines, a misguided Romantic egotist. And by slyly linking Soane to Cockney crowds and the South London suburbs, the *Knight's Quarterly* further reinforces his proximity to Hunt, the Hampstead-based 'King of the Cockneys', with his absurd delusions of grandeur.

A COCKNEY ELEUSIS

Soane was incensed by the *Guardian* and *Knight's Quarterly* attacks, and in the latter case took out an unsuccessful suit for libel. Throughout his life he remained a suspicious, paranoid man, who took criticism very badly. Mindful of his patron's 'critic-hating soul', Gandy had risen instantly to Soane's defence after the *Guardian* articles in 1821, submitting two intriguing but rambling articles 'On the Philosophy of Architecture' to Britton's *Magazine of the Fine Arts*. In these he defended the principle of architectural eclecticism, and the creative freedom that went with it:

> The taste and genius of a nation is not confined to a single possessor; a comprehensive mind will select from all sources: and perhaps societies of builders, like the original Free Masons ... were more likely to characterise a country, by the results of free discussion, than the jarring, isolated, interested builders, speculators, or architects of modern times.[44]

The rest of Gandy's text was taken up with a brief, elliptical exploration of the symbolic unity of architectural history, that is, of architecture as a universal symbolic language that had proliferated and diversified from a single source. Taken together, these essays were closer to the spirit of Romantic mythography and late-Enlightenment freemasonry than they were to traditional architectural history. But this tallied admirably with his patron's own feelings. It was only relatively late in life that Soane became a freemason. Having been engaged to work on the Freemasons' Hall in Great Queen Street in 1813, he became a member of the same lodge shortly after. But for a number of years previously he had been an enthusiastic admirer of texts in which the iconography and ideals of freemasonry had figured prominently, most notably the eminent French architect Claude-Nicolas Ledoux's *Architecture considerée sous le rapport de l'art, des moeurs and de la legislation*, first published in 1804.[45] David Watkin has even gone so far as to speculate on the significant influence Masonic thought may have had on Soane's later life and projects:

> It is even possible to consider whether there are Masonic overtones to the intense struggle which is visible throughout Soane's mature work as he attempted to reconcile apparently contradictory elements in Greek, Gothic, Tudor and Baroque architecture, as well as to unite senses of sight and sound with the worlds of structure and illusion. We may, perhaps, find in these endeavours an echo of the Masonic ideal of harmonizing discordant features in the sphere of human history and society.[46]

Soane's interest in synthesis, both historical and aesthetic, was a lasting one. In 1827 he commissioned Britton to write a guide to his House

Museum at 13 Lincoln's Inn Fields, entitled *The Union of Architecture, Sculpture and Painting*. In the introduction Britton described how architecture had migrated from nation to nation through history, offering Soane's collection as a record of this process. In the text itself he celebrated the museum's highly picturesque quality, noting Soane's skilful manipulation of mirrors, candles and top-lighting. To Soane's critics this combination of pedagogy and theatricality was specious and vulgar, but to the architect himself their conjunction was crucial. As Helen Furjan points out, Lincoln's Inn Fields was intended to operate on a number of levels:

> It was a model townhouse, demonstrating a proper gentlemanly abode and a diversity of architectural invention within a restricted space. It was a connoisseurial collection, demonstrating Soane's taste and discernment. It was a didactic collection, in which the house itself provided as much instruction as the objects it contained. It was an antiquarian collection, displaying inscriptions of culture and history. And it was a catalogue of architectural detail and form. But above all, 13 Lincoln's Inn Fields was a collection of spectacular spaces designed to leave a lasting impression on the visitor.[47]

As Furjan suggests, the Soane Museum was a complex, layered space that was built up over time, an assemblage of different impulses and narratives. It housed classical busts and sculptures by John Flaxman, Piranesi landscapes and Hogarth's *Rake's Progress*. There was a collection of Napoleonic memorabilia in the Breakfast Room and a Shakespeare Recess halfway up the stairs. On the ground floor at the back there was a classical atrium with ornaments, fragments and copies of antique sculpture. In the basement the theme was death and burial, with roman funerary urns, an Egyptian sarcophagus, cork models of Etruscan tombs, a monument to Soane's own dead wife and a little Gothic parlour in the corner somewhat facetiously dedicated to a fictional medieval monk 'Padre Giovanni'. As the Prussian architect Karl Schinkel noted in his *English Journey* of 1826, 'medieval, antique and modern works are intermingled at every level; in courtyards resembling cemeteries, and in chapel-like rooms, in catacombs and drawing-rooms, ornamented in Herculanean and Gothic styles. Everywhere little deceptions'.[48] But in spite or perhaps even because of all this heterogeneity and theatricality, it is possible to see a Masonic ethos, albeit of a highly individual and non-exclusive kind, superintending the whole.

The Soane Museum was opened to professional men and amateurs in 1821. There was a very positive review of it in the *London Magazine* for April of that year – the very same number that carried Janus Weathercock's eloquent critique of Martin's *Belshazzar's Feast*. 'Certain we are', the reviewer said, 'that whatever may have been [Soane's] occasional errors and delinquencies in matters of taste, no one has displayed greater energy, zeal and perseverance in the cause of architecture, or has more warmly advocated its interests.'[49] By the mid 1820s the museum had become a minor feature on the London scene, despite being continually subject to expansion and refurbishment. But the candlelit party that Soane threw in 1825 to celebrate the acquisition of the Belzoni sarcophagus was, even by his standards, rather spectacular. In the first place, it took place over three days (23, 26 and 30 March). Second, all the great and the good attended: leading aristocrats, men of letters, artists and patrons of the arts. Coleridge was there, and Dr Spurzheim the famous phrenologist, as well as the Cockney Raphael himself, Benjamin Haydon.

'Only the ground floor and basement were illuminated', Soane's biographer Gillian Darley tells us, 'with over one hundred specially ordered lamps, chandeliers and candelabra.'[50] In a letter of 1825, Soane's friend James Christie voiced deep regret that he wouldn't be able to attend the nocturnal exhibition, not least because it would have fitted so well with his sense of the lamplight ceremonies that had taken place at Eleusis. For years Christie had been fascinated by the Eleusinian mysteries, that series of ancient, secret rites designed to initiate the chosen few of classical Greece into the hidden truths of paganism.[51] He saw the higher mysteries as a prefiguration of Christianity, preaching monotheism and immortality to the chosen few, while also upholding what he considered to be paganism's grand principle: the admission of all religious ideas.[52] Richard Payne Knight's *Inquiry into the Symbolical Language of Ancient Art and Mythology* (1818), was to go further still with this line of reasoning, regarding the mysteries as an initiation into the symbolic nature of things, with the pagan gods, in all their variety, being revealed for the first time as mere metaphors or 'emanations', an eclectic mix of forms and fictions concealing a hidden unity.

One did not have to be a freemason or a mythographer to be interested in initiation mysteries at this time. The curiosity about them was more widespread than that, especially among what we might consider to be 'Cockney' artists. In Keats's unfinished poem of 1819, *The Fall of Hyperion*, the main action of the poem was presented as a kind of rite-of-passage for the poet, introducing him into the new religion of humanity. That said, Soane and Gandy's interest was more intense than most. Only four years previously Gandy had produced a reconstruction of the ancient *Mystic Temple of Ceres at Eleusis*, which looks uncannily like an idealized, outdoor version of Soane's Museum (Figure 13). And his brother John Peter Gandy was to produce a painting on the same subject a couple of years

Figure 13. Joseph Michael Gandy, *Mystic Temple of Ceres at Eleusis*. Oil on canvas. 1815.

later. But the main evidence to suggest that the Lincoln's Inn museum might have been intended to function (surreptitiously) as a temple of initiation is culled from the revised *Description* of it that was published by Soane in 1835.

Dissatisfied by Britton's commentary, the architect commissioned a new one from his friend Barbara Hofland, and the account that she gave of the space was much more impressionistic and picturesque, placing a clear emphasis on the actual experience of the individual making his or her way through the museum:

> Deep masses of shadow, faint gleams that rise like *ignes fatui* from the adjoining crypt, lights that shine like lustrous halos round marble heads, others more vague and indistinct, yet beautiful in their revealings, present appearances beheld as in a dream of the poet's Elysium; and without enlarging the objects, the scene itself, under this artificial illumination, appears considerably expanded. By degrees this space becomes peopled – figure after figure emerges from the crypt and corridors, where they had loitered in the gloom; they assemble round the sarcophagus, which sheds from within a pale, unearthly light upon the silent awe-struck beings that surround it. Fair and lovely they appear, the sons and daughters of a high-born race, exempt from the common evils of life, but awake to all its generous sensibilities and higher perceptions. Pensive is every countenance, and soft is every falling footstep; yet in gentle accents many a voice breathes thanks to him who hath rolled back the current of time to show them glorious visions of the past, yet taught them to feel, even in the hour of pleasure itself, that
>
> 'The paths of glory lead but to the grave.'
>
> Such, I believe, were the feelings of all who had the gratification of witnessing the most impressive scene in the year 1825, when Sir John Soane had it thus prepared for three evenings, during which the rank and talent of this country, to an immense number, including many foreigners of distinction, enjoyed an exhibition as striking as it must ever be unrivalled. Had any one of that gay company been placed *alone* in the sepulchral chamber, at the 'witching hour of night,' when
>
> 'Churchyards yawn and give up their dead,'
>
> when the flickering lights become self-extinguished, and the last murmuring sounds from without ceased to speak of the living world, – it is probable that even the healthiest pulse would have been affected with the darker train of emotions which a situation so unallied to common life is calculated to produce. The awe ameliorated by beauty, and softened by tender reminiscence, would be exchanged for the mysterious expectation of some terrific visitant from the invisible world; and the very strongest mind would explain with Hamlet:–
>
> 'There are more things in heaven and earth, Horatio,
> Than are dreamt of in your philosophy.'[53]

For Hofland, to enter Soane's basement was to descend, like Aeneas, into the 'poet's Elysium' and mingle with the dead. Her description then shifted seamlessly into a reminiscence of the 'high-born' elite of the day being ushered around the museum in 1825, moving from the ground floor to the basement-crypt and then back again, in an implicit allegory of life, death and resurrection. The powerful effect of the lamplight was a leading feature of her account. Somehow or other, 'without enlarging the objects' the lighting made Soane's small basement 'appear considerably expanded', with the whole scene taking on the enchantment of a theatrical show or ritual ceremony. There is also the suggestion that under this artificial illumination new truths could suddenly become visible, especially to those of 'generous sensibilities and higher perceptions'.

In 1784 one of Gandy's favourite authors, the 'English Platonist' Thomas Taylor, had lectured at the Freemasons' Tavern in London on the properties of phosphorus lamps. In ancient temples, Taylor argued, the slow-burning lamps of sepulchral shrines had functioned as neo-Platonic metaphors, signalling to initiates that the descent into the realm of the dead was in fact a sublime ascent into 'the temple of intellectual illumination'.[54] Soane's friend James Christie had been similarly preoccupied by the lamps of the ancients in his *Disquisition upon Etruscan Vases* of 1806, arguing that one of the central features of the Eleusinian mysteries had been a symbolic re-enactment of the death and rebirth of Bacchus, in which the god had been depicted travelling across the Styx in the guise of a lantern. He also corroborated Taylor's view, as expressed in his *Dissertation on the Eleusinian and Bacchic Mysteries*, that Book VI of Virgil's *Aeneid* was essentially a faithful representation of some of these Eleusinian shows. Given Soane's great familiarity with the works of Taylor, Christie, Payne Knight and others, it is perhaps not too fanciful to think of the Soane Museum itself as a kind of Cockney Eleusis, offering a teasing, covert initiation into the 'higher truths' of nature.

To anybody who has visited the Soane Museum by candlelight (and one is still able to do so, at the time of writing, on the first Tuesday of every month), it is tempting to think of this sublime effect as something unique and achieved. Certainly the *Literary Chronicle* thought so. 'There are mansions in this metropolis more extensive', it admitted, in an article on Soane's soirée, 'more splendid, as regards furniture and upholstery, but, perhaps, not one exhibiting so much taste, and picturesque arrangement, such a happy economy of room, and such richness, yet chastity, of decoration.'[55] To many contemporaries, however, the house was, rather like Martin's *Belshazzar's Feast*, a deeply curious mixture of the hubristic and the petty. Benjamin

Haydon was present at Soane's 1825 extravaganza, and offered a coy but telling account of the general atmosphere of the evening:

> Soane's house is a perfect Cretan labyrinth: curious narrow staircases, landing places, balconies, spring doors, and little rooms filled with fragments to the very ceiling. It was the finest fun imaginable to see the people come in to the library after wandering about below, amidst tombs and capitals, and shafts and noiseless heads, with a sort of expression of delighted relief at finding themselves again among the living, and with coffee and cake! Upstairs stood Soane, spare, thin, caustic, and starched, 'mocking the thing he laughed at,' as he smiled approbation for the praises bestowed on his magnificent house.[56]

Haydon's account does offer further circumstantial evidence for the Eleusinian mystery theory – the idea that, in some playful way, the museum did function as a kind of ritual journey of death and resurrection, with people beginning their journey in the basement and then later coming up for air. But it does also suggest a degree of supercilious sniggering among Soane's social superiors. While at the party, Haydon has a conversation with a leading dandy, a sly, smirking exchange in which insinuations are repeatedly made about the sheer oddness of Soane's residence. And at the end of his anecdote, Haydon himself takes a last look at his host, 'smiling and flushed by flattery', and offers one final, damning judgement on the whole evening: 'There was not a soul then around him who would not, ere they put on their night-caps, envy him his assemblage of rank, and talent, and fashion; sneer at his antiques, quiz his coffee, and go to sleep, pitying his affected superiority, his delusion and vanity.' No man was more vainglorious or more addicted to shameless self-advertisement than Haydon, and so it is interesting to see him diagnose such an absurd discrepancy between aspiration and achievement in Soane. Whether the architect of the Bank of England really was guilty of such self-complacent Cockney vanity is quite another matter. There is plenty of evidence, in the architect's various sayings and doings, to suggest a complex mixture of enthusiasm and cynicism in his character; certainly any man who could raise a classical monument in his back garden 'To the memory of my dog Fanny' was possessed of a sly humour. But to those of conservative or classical tastes, Soane's Cockney eclecticism remained a problem, not least when it exhibited its facetious, playful side.

Even in later years, visitors to the house were often struck by the cramped incongruity of it all. In his *English Journey* Karl Schinkel marvelled at the complexity of the labyrinthine arrangements within what was, after all, little more than a 'second rate' London terraced house.[57] Some of the praise that Soane received was astonished but reluctant, as we can see from this review of the *Union of Architecture &c.* in the *Eclectic Review*:

With the help of skylights, galleries, domes, recesses, folding-shutters, arches, crypts, catacombs, corridors, mirrors, stained glass, vistas, vestibules, heights and depths, Mr Soane has created, in little more than the cribbed and confined superficies of a London ground-plan, a succession of scenery, somewhat fantastic, it may be, and irreducible to strict classical canons, but picturesque, ingenious and of infinite variety. Even where law and rule are absent there is *meaning*.[58]

THE ECLECTIC CITY

Between 1837 and 1841, in the immediate aftermath of Soane's death, the newly founded *Civil Engineer and Architect's Journal* was consistently contemptuous about the museum and the Act of Parliament by which it had been bequeathed to the nation, arguing that the building had much in it 'that looks no better than a temporary experimental trial or model of what was intended to be executed on a larger scale: for at present, not a few effects partake far too much of the petty and the peep-show'.[59] In 1838 the German art historian G. F. Waagen granted it a certain picturesque charm in his *Works of Art and Artists in Great Britain*, but also felt compelled to conclude that, when all was said and done, the house's 'arbitrary mixture of heterogeneous objects' had 'something of the unpleasant effect of a feverish dream'.[60] In 1840, with the dust finally settling on Soane's career, his former pupil George Wightwick remembered how his master had been 'continually subject to the censure of the press', and called the House Museum 'a perfect illustration of that playful fancy and whimsicality, which, at the same time, contributed to his celebrity as a master, and subjected him to much ridicule as a madman'.[61]

As with Martin, so too with Soane; there is something quite overdetermined about these critical objections, as if both men were being used as scapegoats for a larger phenomenon. Reviewing the museum in 1837 shortly after Soane's death (and shortly before it was due to be opened to the public), *Fraser's Magazine* offered a typically irreverent but insightful judgement. For the reviewer in question the house constituted a terrible mismatch of ambition and scale. 'It's not for us to say', he commented, 'that this is all in singularly bad taste, – in the style of a Cockney tea-garden, or the bills of a puppet show.'[62] He then drew particular attention to the absurd gap between Hofland's grand description of the house (and, he might have added, Gandy's equally sublime drawings, see Figure 14) and its tiny actuality:

Figure 14. Joseph Michael Gandy, *Soane Museum Interior*. Oil on canvas.

Nevertheless, we can't help agreeing with the old and homely adage which says, 'fine words butter no parsnips,' and are, accordingly, of opinion that these transcendently fine names do not at all improve the little rooms and closets they are intended to dignify: on the contrary, they are likely to beget expectations that will be strangely disappointed when the public shall be admitted into this raree-show, and behold the Soanean Museum in all its – littleness. (p. 338)

One way of explaining the reaction against Soane and Martin is that as the nineteenth century wore on and the Romantic period passed into the Victorian, they both came to be seen as representatives of an outdated amateur antiquarianism. With reference to the Soane Museum in particular, Rosemary Hill remarks that 'as archaeological knowledge grew and the systematic categorisation of objects in public museums developed, such arrangements came to seem inauthentic, to some extent naïve'.[63] What made the position of men such as Soane and Martin seem even more exposed from the 1820s onward was their continued commitment to a rather Napoleonic conception of genius, that is, of genius as an impossibly grandiose anti-establishment quality single-handedly capable of creating and destroying empires. Hence that element of egotism and demagoguery in their work, hence also the anti-Cockney criticism that it tended to provoke. References to Bartlemy puppets and raree-shows were quite apposite in this respect, because what they drew attention to was that element of arrant street showmanship, of smoke and mirrors, in both men's art. The trait the critics didn't catch, however, was that fascination with initiation and election that Soane and Martin were also to share with fellow Cockneys Keats, Hunt and Lamb. Only a few months before the *London*'s review of the Soane Museum, Hunt had staged his own homespun Eleusinian mystery in 'The Nurture of Triptolemus', in which a visionary hero, envied and mocked by the priestly establishment, had been initiated into the mysteries of nature, before going on to become a great, though regrettably mortal, philanthropist. It was in the nature of Cockney outsiders to set up complicated allegories about their relation to the establishment. In Martin's *Belshazzar's Feast* the artist had pictured himself as another Daniel, staging God's word, as a spectacle, for a corrupt and benighted court; so too Soane had set up a close, bewildering little temple of initiation in his own parlour, meant partly to educate the social elite into the 'higher mysteries' of life, and partly to confuse and alienate them if they proved unsympathetic to his vision.

Prominent among those unsympathetic to the vision of Soane and Martin in this chapter have been the Cockneys themselves: Hunt and Haydon in the case of Soane; Hazlitt and Lamb in the case of Martin.

This might be seen as surprising, given that they all moved in the same circles, and stood in a similar relation to the critical establishment. Martin counted William Godwin as a friend, and played chess with Hunt's brother John; he also knew Haydon and Washington Allston. Soane knew Haydon well enough to invite him to his museum, and knew Hazlitt from the Surrey Institution. *The Examiner* had also defended both Soane and Martin. But all this goes to prove, I think, is that Cockneyism was not an issue that always separated cleanly on party lines. When Tory critics wanted to address something troublingly modern or metropolitan about Soane or Martin they were only too willing to invoke the accursed nickname. But this was not the case, for obvious reasons, with Hunt or Hazlitt. Still, when it came to modern developments in the fine arts in particular, the so-called 'Cockney School' writers had many of the same anxieties as their conservative counterparts, and couldn't help expressing themselves in similar, often markedly anti-metropolitan, terms. Cockneyism, one could argue, had descended deep into the critical subconscious by the 1820s, not so much as a class notion, but as an aesthetic idea. Discrepancies, disproportions, egotistical protrusions and dissolutions, these were the phenomena that put the idea in mind, and London liberals showed themselves as apt to be swayed by it as Tories from Edinburgh or the West End.

Soane and Martin were both, in their different ways, urban artists. Whether one thinks of the narrow corridors and distorting mirrors of the Soane Museum or the bewildering mixture of depth and detail in Martin's *Belshazzar's Feast*, theirs is a theatre of metropolitan vertiginousness and heterogeneity. That characteristic jumbling of dimensions, genres and perspectives that takes place in the modern city is mimicked in their work. More or less impelling the viewer to read their art as one would read a panorama, a busy street or a wall of advertisements, they insist upon an eclectic, dynamic, inescapably urban view of things. And this urban view is one in which world history itself comes to be seen as something both layered and coterminous, a mosaic of ruins concealing a mysterious living unity.

To the *Fraser's* critic, the excruciating gap between the rhetoric in the Soane Museum *Description* and the material actuality reminded him of the impressive-sounding advertisements outside a Strand exhibition or Smithfield raree-show: it was pure Cockney vanity and false consciousness. But for Soane and Hofland the museum was conceived of as a form of ritual theatre, a setting in which all notions of perspective, both spatial and historical, had been fruitfully and edifyingly confused. Downstairs in the crypt, perusing miniature casts and models, one had a God's-eye view of the forms in question; yet when looking up through the atrium to the huge glass skylight, one felt buried alive. Upstairs in the picture gallery one could move back in time by peeling away the wooden panels to reveal earlier and earlier paintings. Behind the last layer there stood a full-size classical statue. By such means the history of art and architecture was revealed by Soane not as an orderly succession or collection, but as an eclectic city, a city of the mind, a city that was constantly rearranging and rebuilding itself, with each object standing in a dramatic and dynamic relationship to its neighbour. Similarly, such was the enthusiasm with which Martin had painted that most famous of fallen (and about-to-fall) cities, ancient Babylon, that Babylon itself was vividly resurrected in his hands, and (in a manner completely counter to the ostensible message of the picture) its pagan eclecticism unconsciously indulged.

Ascendent in the 1820s, neither Soane's nor Martin's reputation survived the 1830s. By 1824 Martin's painting career was already running out of steam, only to be dramatically revived a couple of years later when he started producing his own mezzotints.[64] When Soane died in 1837 there was at last an opportunity to reassess his achievements. But it wasn't until the twentieth century that his and Gandy's mystic eclecticism really began to be appreciated. Back in the 1830s the current of opinion was moving fast in the other direction, as is indicated by the other book being discussed by the *Fraser's* reviewer in that March issue of 1837: the first edition of A. W. Pugin's *Contrasts*. At the same time Gandy was labouring long and hard over an enormous, unpublishable comparative history of world architecture, writing of 'pantheistic emanations and regenerative geologies', Pugin was returning to true principles and the authority of the Catholic tradition. Nor was there any doubt in the latter's mind of Soane's place in the new Gothic world order. In the first (1836) edition of *Contrasts*, the 'The Professor's Own House' (the museum at Lincoln's Inn Fields) had been contrasted unfavourably with the Rue de l'Horloge, Rouen. And in the main text Pugin railed passionately against the sheer whimsicality of Regency buildings, their utterly incongruous relationship with the surrounding country and each other:

> Let us look around and see whether the Architecture of this country is not entirely ruled by whim and caprice. Does locality, destination, or character of a

building, form the basis of a design? no; surely not. We have Swiss cottages in a flat country; Italian villas in the coldest situations; a Turkish kremlin for a royal residence; Greek temples in crowded lanes; Egyptian auction rooms; and all kinds of absurdities and incongruities: and not only are separate edifices erected in these inappropriate and unsuitable styles, but we have only to look into those nests of monstrosities, the Regent's Park and Regent's Street, where all kinds of styles are jumbled together to make one mass.[65]

CHAPTER 7

B. R. Haydon and debtors' prisons

In June 1827 Benjamin Robert Haydon was imprisoned for debt in the King's Bench Prison in Southwark. It was not the first time Haydon had been behind bars, but on this occasion it gave rise to one of his most successful canvases, a comic genre piece called *The Mock Election* (Figure 15). The picture was inspired by a real event that took place during his stay. Donning bedsheets, curtain rings, mopsticks and ribbons, a number of the debtors had spent days staging a political masquerade in the main yard of the prison, and sparked off a jocular riot as a result. Haydon was released from the Bench at the end of July,[1] but he was back again within a fortnight, sketching faces for a picture, 'a sort of Beggar's Opera', as he put it, 'a Polly and Macheath affair' to commemorate the event.[2] Completed during the autumn of that year, *The Mock Election* was first exhibited at the Egyptian Hall, Piccadilly in January 1828, with Haydon's accompanying *Explanation* offering a typically fulsome account of its genesis:

> To the last day of my life I shall ever remember the impression I received – baronets and bankers; authors and merchants; painters and poets, dandies of rank in silk and velvet, and dandies of no rank in rags and tatters; idiotism and insanity; poverty and affliction, all mingled in indiscriminate merriment, with a spiked wall, twenty feet high, above their heads![3]

One purpose of the project was to contribute to the growing protest, which was to reach its climax in the Victorian period, against the long-standing institution of imprisonment for debt. 'I earnestly hope', as Haydon said towards the end of his *Explanation*,

> that not only my creditors, but all creditors, will see how much more just it is to let a man, honourably inclined, work his way out of debt, than double their charges, if they see him embarrassed, send him worse goods, bring him in enormous bills, deliver him to a lawyer if he is unable to pay them, then hurl him to a prison, and let him rot in sloth and vice, useless to his family, the world, and even themselves. (p. 9)

Figure 15. B. R. Haydon, *The Mock Election*. Oil on canvas. 1828.

But intriguingly enough this message was almost lost in the painter's sheer fascination with the debtors' prison as a pictorial subject. What Haydon liked above all about the King's Bench was that it appeared to present 'real life', life at its most various and vivid, frozen in a frame. He was not alone in this feeling. 'The world itself is a queer *mélange*', wrote one veteran of the place many years later, 'and in the Bench you have its most salient points, its most striking features, the most prominent of human faults, passions, vices, and virtues, concentrated in a small space convenient for contemplation by those who are fond of studying the world.'[4]

Debtors' prison, as many writers of the 1820s agreed, was a place in which class society was framed as a spectacle, with each class placed in theatrical proximity to its neighbours. But it was also a space that exposed imposture and performance, a space in which faces were at their most legible and types at their most transparent. So much so, indeed, that in Egan and Cruikshank's celebrated travelogue of 1821, *Life in London*, and in its numerous imitations and theatrical adaptations, the debtors' prison always had a central function as the ultimate hiding-place of the 'real'.

It was this modish enthusiasm that overtook Haydon in 1827. So enthused was he by the Hogarthian nature of his project, indeed, that within a few days of his release he was out in the West End looking at the satirist's work. Characteristically though, he came away less than impressed, considering that 'occasionally [Hogarth] bordered on caricature'.[5] To Haydon, the great strength of the King's Bench as a subject was that, precisely because 'real life' seemed to present itself more expressively there, a painter could draw out his moral without needing to exaggerate. As he wrote in his diary on 26 August 1827:

> What a set of heads I shall have in this extraordinary picture! ... What a set of beings are assembled in that extraordinary Place – that temple of Idleness and debauchery. Good God! When you walk amongst them you get amongst faces that are all marked by some decided expression, quite different from the people you meet in the street.[6]

It should be of no surprise then, that all of the characters in *The Mock Election* were based on real people, and drawn from the life.[7] This was vouchsafed by the fine arts reviewer for the *Mirror of Literature*, who claimed to have made 'a few hourly visits to the spot' in order to corroborate the accuracy of the portraits.[8] The main action of Haydon's painting depicts the Lord High Sheriff of the King's Bench Prison, his officers and several electors all preparing to elect an MP to voice the prisoners' grievances in the House of Commons. Taking the central group first, the artist introduces us to the pivotal figure of the Sheriff, who is begging the candidate on the left, a red-ribboned Tory, not to fight with his Whig rivals. Appropriately enough, given the strong links between Toryism and violent sports in this period, the angry candidate is being egged on by Harry Holt the pugilist, who was well known in Regency London as 'the Cicero of the Ring'.[9] The gentleman who took the part of the angry candidate was, Haydon tells us, a man called Meredith, a navy lieutenant of considerable fortune in Ireland, who behaved that day as if he really did see a dazzling political career ahead of him. 'The belief was real', the painter noted in his diary, 'he thought the Election genuine and at the conclusion of every speech promised to fight up to his knees in blood for the rights of his fellow prisoners.'[10] Opposite him, dressed in a yellow turban and quilt, is his main rival, one Robert Stanton, the MP for Penrith from 1824 to 1826, a has-been to the Irishman's presumptuous wannabe. 'Stanton died in a mad-house', Haydon wrote, in the margin of his own copy of the catalogue description, 'he became after spending £80,000 a clerk to Charles Pearson, saved money, became mad & died.'[11] This figure was the moving spring in the whole masquerade, the painter writes, inviting us to note the expression of 'sarcastic mischief' that was on his face throughout (p. 6). Between the Lord High Sheriff and the candidate in the quilt is the third candidate, a man named Birch, who like Stanton is sporting the Whig colours of blue and buff.

Immediately below the Sheriff is the head poll clerk swearing in the three citizens before their vote. The three voters are holding a bit of deal, the first being 'a dandy of the first fashion just imprisoned', Haydon tells us, 'with a fifty-guinea pipe in his right hand, a diamond ring on his finger, dressed in a yellow silk dressing gown, velvet cap and red morocco slippers'. To the left of him stands 'an exquisite, who has been imprisoned three years, smoking a threepenny cigar, with a hole at his elbow, and his toes on the ground'. And the third elector is 'one of those characters of middle age and careless dissipation, visible in all scenes of this description, dressed in a blue jacket and green cap' (p. 6). To the right of the dandy is another poll-clerk, entering the names of the electors. Above the clerk is the assessor, 'suppressing a laugh', and finally, to the right of the assessor, is a short red-nosed man, another fake official, dressed in the red curtain of his room and proudly sporting his mace of office.

The Mock Election presents a vivid picture of dandies both high and low, fresh and faded, of political aspirants and political failures, of metropolitan performers of every kind, all unexpectedly levelled by debt and imprisonment. It takes the burlesque spirit of an image such as Robert

Cruikshank's 1825 graphic satire of King's Bench prisoners giving a lawyer the bumps and subjects it to a closer analysis (Figure 16).[12] And such is the brilliant exposure of Cockney self-delusion in the painting that one cannot help but be reminded of Haydon's friend William Hazlitt's 1823 essay 'On Londoners and Country People': 'A real Cockney is the poorest creature in the world, the most literal, the most mechanical, and yet he too lives in a world of romance – a fairy-land of his own.'

The figures to the left of this colourful main group constitute a good, plain family in affliction, respectable people for whom all this facetiousness is folly. They are mostly dressed in black. There is a wife, 'devoted, melting, clinging to her husband', and her eldest boy, 'with all the gaiety of a child', cheering the voters. The father and mother are in mourning for the loss of their second boy, for 'troubles never come in single files', Haydon says, 'but whole battalions'. Behind is the old nurse sobbing over a new baby, while the husband, virtuous and in trouble, is contemplating the merry electors with pain. In his hand he holds a paper which says: 'Debt £26, 10s. *paid* – costs £157, 14s. *unpaid*. Treachery, Squeeze and Co., *Thieves' Inn*.' Behind this group, Haydon tells us, is a group of electors with flags and trumpets, and all the bustle of an election. On one flag is written 'The Liberty of the Subject'; on the other, 'No Bailliffs'. The Bench's spiked wall and state house complete the background (p. 8).

The final group, two men and a woman, have a sunnier, more Mediterranean look, and are dressed mainly in white. The man sitting at the table is, Haydon tells us, a well-born soldier, who distinguished himself in Spain, and then was imprisoned for running away with a ward in Chancery. 'Embarrassment followed', says Haydon, 'and nine years of confinement have rendered him reckless and melancholy.' 'He was one of the most tremendous heads I ever saw in nature', the artist continues, 'something between Byron and Bonaparte'. 'It was affecting to see his pale determined face and athletic form amongst the laughing afflicted, without a smile! Without an emotion! Indifferent to the humour about him, contemptuously above joining the burlesque. He seemed like a fallen angel, meditating on the absurdities of humanity!' (p. 7). Haydon then describes how he has finished off the portrait by putting this hero at his ease, talking with a companion, while champagne bottles, a dice box, dice, cards and a racket bat and ball on the ground testify to the manner in which he has been spending his time. In the painter's own copy of the catalogue description there is a little pencil annotation identifying this man as 'Campbell, nephew of Sir Neil',[13] and indeed there was a Major Campbell who spent fourteen years in the King's Bench Prison during

Figure 16. Robert Cruikshank, *Surrey Collegians Giving a Lift to a Limb of the Law*, from *The English Spy*. Engraving. 1825.

this period – a man who appears in Egan's *Book of Sports* (1832) as one of the finest rackets players in the country.[14] Leaning over him is an 'interesting girl' who has apparently become attached to him 'in his reverses' – a figure who, like many of Haydon's women, bears a striking resemblance to his own wife, the long-suffering Mary Hyman.

To the Victorians, Haydon was a pitiful figure, a man of high ambition, reckless expense and a blustering belief in his own genius, who had spent a lifetime trying to convert the rest of the world to this conviction, while all the time driving both himself and his family ever more deeply into debt.[15] In 1846, with his finances in intractable disarray, he finally reached the end of his tether, committing suicide in his studio on Cavendish Road. In 1853 Tom Taylor published his *Life of Benjamin Robert Haydon*, which included the painter's autobiography and large chunks of his diaries, and Haydon's reputation grew as one of the nineteenth century's most colourful failures. Back in January 1828, however, Haydon's fortunes looked to be on the up. Not only was he out of prison, *The Mock Election* was getting favourable reviews in the press, more favourable certainly than he was to receive in later years, and shortly after its exhibition in Piccadilly, it was bought by King George IV for 500 guineas.[16] The irony here is that *The Mock Election* and its sequels *Chairing the Member* (1828) and *Punch, or May Day* (1829) weren't really in Haydon's preferred style of painting. He always saw himself as a history painter, in the heroic tradition, not a comic genre painter like Rowlandson or Hogarth. His preferred mode was painting enormous canvases, with no expense spared, over a long period; certainly these were the conditions in which he produced his grandest works, *The Judgment of Solomon* (1814), *Christ's Entry into Jerusalem* (1820) and *The Raising of Lazarus* (1823). Hence *The Mock Election* was, for Haydon, a temporary sojourn into a more vulgar Cockney realm – and yet it was among his most successful efforts.

HAYDON'S RELUCTANT COCKNEYISM

A number of friends had rallied round Haydon in the summer of 1827 and helped secure his release from prison. Of these, by far the most energetic was J. G. Lockhart, who ten years earlier had been the anonymous author of the famous 'Cockney School' attacks in *Blackwood's Edinburgh Magazine*. Lockhart's main targets in those days had been the London liberals Leigh Hunt, the so-called 'King of the Cockneys', John Keats and Hazlitt. But he had also found time for a few casual swipes at their close friend Haydon, whom he had dubbed 'The Cockney Raphael'. When

Lockhart actually met Haydon in Edinburgh in 1821, the Scot immediately realized his mistake. Far from being a radical upstart like Hunt or Hazlitt, Haydon was clearly a man of his own stamp, that is, a high-minded but pugnacious Tory. Thereafter the writer seems to have gone out of his way to help the painter, for as Haydon noted in his autobiography, 'L[ockhart], when we became acquainted, felt so strongly how little I deserved what had been said of me, that his whole life has since been a struggle to undo the evil he was at the time party to.'[17]

On Haydon's first imprisonment for debt in July 1823, *Blackwood's* had tried its utmost to be constructive. The painter's difficulties, it argued, had arisen directly from two main causes, 'his idle scorn of following the common courses of his profession, and his determination to paint only Scripture-pieces, and those on the most colossal and hazardous scale'.[18] By turning his nose up at the lucrative practice of portrait painting and devoting all his time to gigantic, costly masterpieces, Haydon had been courting disaster. Rehearsing a mantra that was to be repeated many times in the newspapers and magazines of the 1820s, the reviewer paid homage to the painter's high principles and undoubted talents, while also insisting that 'no individual can triumph by resisting the taste of a civilized age'. In an article the following year, however, *Blackwood's* was to invoke that other line on Haydon gaining currency among the critics of the period, which was that the painter had gone backwards since painting his *Solomon*. Of his *Silenus Preaching to Ariadne*, the magazine complained that it was 'bad beyond belief – a complete Cockneyism in conception, and a daub of daubs in its most coxcombical execution'.[19]

In spite of these differences of opinion, support from people of money and influence continued to be forthcoming. When Haydon was incarcerated again in 1827 it was Lockhart who organized the public meeting (which was held at the Crown and Anchor Tavern on the Strand) to co-ordinate his rescue. And only a few months later Lockhart urged Haydon to distance himself from the Cockney School once and for all by writing a vituperative review of Hunt's *Lord Byron and His Contemporaries* (1828). Haydon did pen an attack on Hunt but then retracted it at the last moment, resolving to guard himself in future against what he called Lockhart's 'tricks':

March 2 1828. The more I reflect, the more I see the gulph I have escaped. I will venture to say it would have infallibly branded me for ever. Lockhart showed me a review by Lord Byron of Keats's work, in which Lord Byron called him a dirty little blackguard. I said 'This is shocking' & Lockhart took his pen and scratched it out. He said he had scratched out a good deal; Lord Byron called

> Keats 'The Masturbator of the human mind – the Onan of Literature'. The review came after Gifford's death, and now Lockhart is using it in his Review of Hunt's Byron. It will be out next. The fact is, the cause of all the Cockney School of Poetry being so full of the daisies and posies is because the Poets were brought up in brick walls and London fogs, and their minds fly to the very reverse for enjoyment.[20]

In the event, Lockhart wrote the review of Hunt's *Byron*, and it turned into one of the longest and most devastating of *Blackwood's* attacks on the author, reopening old wounds and reigniting the 'Cockney School' debate. The mid 1820s had seen Hunt and Hazlitt travelling on the continent for extended periods, at one remove from domestic controversy, and this, when combined with the reduced political tension of the time, had led to a lull in hostilities. But *Lord Byron and His Contemporaries* was just the thing to set them off again, brimming as it was with Hunt's characteristic self-complacency and with repeated, ignominious insights into Byron's deeply flawed character. To Lockhart, Hunt's book was a piece of arrant class warfare – an attack not merely on a particular aristocrat, but on the whole principle of aristocracy – and he was suitably incensed.

It was Hunt who had first urged Haydon to write complaints about the Royal Academy in *The Examiner* in the 1810s, thus encouraging the controversialist in him.[21] But in the painter's own mind at least, he was no Cockney radical. Politically he had a profound respect for rank and title and aesthetically he was steadfastly devoted to that most classical of forms, large-scale history painting. This was the reason for his continued criticism of the Royal Academy: it was not that it was too conservative, as a body, but that it wasn't conservative enough. It refused to accept that proper public support was needed to preserve and support the art of history painting in England; it was too willing to acquiesce in the taste of the times. But in spite of Haydon's ever more apparent distance from his Cockney friends on matters of politics and aesthetics, the spring of 1828 found him residually resistant to dishing them in public.

Before Haydon penned his 2 March diary entry on the plight of the Cockney School he had the idea for another metropolitan genre painting, *Punch, or May Day*, and shortly afterwards he started working on a sequel to *The Mock Election*, entitled *Chairing the Member*. With this in mind, it is tempting to think that Haydon had his own recent prison experiences in view when he wrote so feelingly of 'brick walls and London fogs' and the desire to transcend them. Admittedly, Haydon's 'Cockney Moment' was a brief one, for when the king subsequently declined to purchase either *Punch* or *Chairing the Member*, the painter flounced back to history painting, feeling that he had prostituted his talents. But in spite of all this, *The Mock Election* remains one of his most significant and characteristic performances: characteristic in its conscious assertions, which are Romantic and heroic; characteristic also in its underlying style, which is richly if reluctantly 'Cockney'. In their reviews, *The Examiner*, the *New Monthly Magazine* and the *Literary Gazette* all praised Haydon's new manner, and the painter himself was to wonder in his diary whether 'this Picture has not awakened a faculty which has been dormant'.[22] The same opinion was also expressed in that old Cockney rag the *London Magazine*, with one reviewer even going so far as to suggest that 'common life' might prove Haydon's salvation:

> If … Mr Haydon can look upon common life as he has looked upon this singular carnival of a prison, and delineate the ideas and follies of this great metropolis with a similar spirit, he may earn a fame – not quite so high perhaps, as that of being the first historical painter of the age – but a fame that will infallibly protect him from any further acquaintance with these scenes, which are quite unsuited for the dwelling place of talent, however they may add to that knowledge of human nature upon which practical talent must work.[23]

The *New Monthly* expressed similarly optimistic sentiments: 'We trust', it said, 'this is but the commencement of a series of pictures of modern life and society. There is a vast field open.'[24] But of course the sad truth is that, one or two exceptions aside, Haydon did not move on from this 'singular carnival' to look abroad into 'common life', but was to remain doggedly (and self-destructively) committed to history painting. Quite how successful he would have been had he chosen the path of Augustus Egg or W. P. Frith we shall never know. What is more certain, however, is the role of these 'singular scenes' in the painter's brief revival, for as we shall see in the rest of this chapter, the debtors' prison was a place of unique appeal in this period, not least because of its status as a Cockney microcosm, a place of extraordinary paradox and incongruity, a veritable 'world within walls'.

DEBTORS' PRISONS AND THE DEBTOR ETHOS

Despite repeated calls for its abolition, imprisonment for debt remained an important part of English civil law in the early nineteenth century. Indeed, it wasn't until the late 1860s, with the introduction of a new set of bankruptcy laws, that its role began to be reduced. Before that, in these islands as elsewhere, everyday economic activity relied upon a vast network of personal credit relations, which bound and connected everyone.

And in an age without formal financial institutions, such as banks or building societies, the legal procedures governing indebtedness were seen as absolutely crucial to preserving confidence in the national economy. As *The Times* put it on 6 May 1793: 'Imprisonment for debt is virtually a part of the British Constitution, and without that, or some other strong mode to compel justice to be done to the creditor, our trade, commerce and, in short, the source of all our wealth, must soon be destroyed.'[25]

Two kinds of imprisonment for debt were possible: pre-trial and post-trial, the first called imprisonment on mesne process and the second imprisonment on final process, with the debtor detained on final process being, in normal circumstances, entirely dependent upon his creditor for his discharge. Because of this, as the historian Joanna Innes has pointed out, 'the process is less well described as a system of court-supervised arbitration than as a system of legalized bullying'.[26] But the law was not completely biased on the side of the creditor. There were certain loopholes that the debtor could exploit. First, the bailiffs' power of arrest was fairly limited: they could not make arrests at night or on Sundays; a fact that Thomas De Quincey made use of when slipping into Edinburgh to visit his family in the 1830s. Nor could they break into a house in order to make an arrest. Second, even when captured, the debtor was under no legal compulsion to surrender what he had, unless the creditor attempted the difficult course of proceeding against his property. So, given that imprisonment for debt actually offered the debtor legal protection for his assets, it was not unusual for people to arrange to have themselves detained by 'friendly actions'. Naturally enough, this only exacerbated creditors' frustrations, and led to frequent complaints during the eighteenth century that debtors' prisons were nothing but 'a haven for the spendthrift'.[27]

Generally speaking, it was not penniless or even especially poor people that were imprisoned for debt, but people who had incurred substantial obligations that they had repeatedly failed to discharge; and normally incarceration came only after a long series of threats and appeals on the part of the creditor, culminating in a night or two in the local 'sponging-house'.[28] Some minor improvements had been made to the law of creditor and debtor by the time Haydon fell foul of it in 1827: in 1813, for example, a Court of Relief for Insolvent Debtors had been established which gave 'honest' insolvents some of the benefits normally reserved for bankrupts, and it was this court that came to the painter's rescue during his first incarceration in 1823.

Nor was the life of an imprisoned debtor necessarily a miserable one. Officers would generally allow them out of the prison on day trips to help sort out their affairs. In the King's Bench debtors could actually live outside the prison: several square miles called 'The Rules' had been designated as an area in which prisoners and their families might settle, on payment of a weekly stipend. There were opportunities for debtors, especially tradesmen, to try to dig their way out of difficulty. Within the walls, debtors called meetings with their creditors and sought legal advice; this advice helped create what Innes describes as 'a debtor ethos'. Debtors told themselves that the state of the law of debt was so weighted against them that their creditors had been able to make an arbitrary assault on their property and liberty, and that their own efforts to resist such tyranny were, by contrast, a vindication of the spirit of English law.[29] There was a lot of sympathy for this 'debtor ethos' in the eighteenth century especially; hence debtors were often on the receiving end of both public and private charity. They were also generally successful in presenting themselves to the world not as criminals but victims.

By the late 1820s there was a growing consensus towards reform in the literature surrounding debtors' prisons, and increasing calls for the abolition of imprisonment for debt. It is this movement that prison veteran R. P. Gillies gave added impetus to, first in a story for *Fraser's* entitled 'O'Hanlon and his Wife' (1836), and then in an article 'On the Law of Debtor and Creditor' for the *British and Foreign Review* (1837), and which Dickens publicized further in the Fleet Prison section of his 1837 novel *Pickwick Papers*.[30] In the short term, this campaign led to the dissolution of some of the smaller debtors' prisons (the Fleet and the Marshalsea were closed down in 1842). But it wasn't until the late 1860s, with the introduction of new bankruptcy laws, that imprisonment for debt was seriously curtailed.

In this extract from an anonymous memoir, *Prison Reminiscences, or Whitecross Street and the Law of Imprisonment for Debt* (1859), the oft-repeated argument for abolition is put very powerfully and succinctly:

> As the law of imprisonment for debt now stands, its operation saps the very foundations of honour and morality. It involves the honest and dishonest, the truthful and the habitually false, the accidentally unfortunate and the predetermined cheat, in the meshes of the same net, returning them back upon society, in due time, all of the same colour … rogues all, in fact.[31]

There was, however, another current of feeling that ran alongside and even counter to this abolitionist position. It had been present in the eighteenth century, but seemed to gain in power during the Romantic period, perhaps because the world-view it expressed was so self-consciously archaic and sentimental. This current celebrated debtors' prisons as entertaining, instructive, strangely inviting places. Such sentiments were not necessarily in conflict with those of a reformist nature, but focused less on the prison as a breeding ground of vice and misery, and more on its status as a place of refuge, of freedom-in-imprisonment, an ironic paradise.

In his autobiography of 1860 the hack journalist turned pub-owner and comedian Renton Nicholson struck a delicate balance between the cautionary and the celebratory in his treatment of the King's Bench. Listing the extraordinary social mix of liars and cheats among the inmates, he offered a facetious homage to the place as a 'little republic of ingenuity' and 'a commonwealth made up of errant and fugitive talent'. But he did also note how one could get addicted to the conviviality of the place, and that it had functioned for him personally as both a school and a shelter: 'The King's Bench, or Queen's Prison', he wrote, 'is a great instructor. My knowledge of refined life has been mostly gleaned, and materially improved, by relations therein.'[32]

In the 1840s Nicholson shot to fame as the founder of the so-called 'Judge and Jury Society', which staged mock-trials before paying audiences in the Garrick's Head, Covent Garden. The proceedings were riotous in the extreme, abounding in vulgarity, double entendre and coarse mirth.[33] Comic actors were enlisted to play eminent politicians, and the formula became so popular that many prominent legal and literary men came to see it. Given Nicholson's close acquaintance with the King's Bench, it is quite possible that this taste, and this talent, for political burlesque may have been fostered during his time in prison – especially as we know that the mock election of 1827 was by no means a unique event.[34]

In the 'World within Walls' chapter of *Real Life in London* (1822), which was a rather lively plagiarism of Egan's Tom and Jerry, there was a similarly facetious mock-celebration of the King's Bench debtors as speculative over-reachers who had let their fantasy get the better of them:

> It is generally speaking not your empty-headed fellows who can arrive at the honour of a residence here, it is rather those of brilliant imagination, of aspiring talent, who have been determined to have money for a time, without heeding the source from which it was derived – who have been up to snuff, till they have reduced themselves to the necessity of resting contented with the marrowbone stage instead of a phaeton or a curricle, and twopenny in lieu of claret.[35]

Debtors' prison is here represented as a particular type of urban spectacle, a place where metropolitan ambition comes to ground, and is subject to innumerable ironies. But it is also viewed, with a certain paradoxical wit, as a haven for birth and talent, boasting a real community united by 'brilliant imagination'.

In the various prospectuses that were sold to prisoners on their arrival there was a strong emphasis upon the debtors' prison as a friendly and much-needed resting-place. 'The King's Bench', insisted a guide from 1823, 'is for most debtors a happy and welcome asylum.'[36] The Marshalsea doctor who delivers Amy in Dickens's *Little Dorrit* (1855–7) expresses the same opinion to her bewildered father:

> A little more elbow-room is all we want here. We are quiet here; we don't get badgered here; there's no knocker here, sir, to be hammered at by creditors and bring a man's heart into his mouth. Nobody comes here to ask if a man's at home, and to say he'll stand on the door mat till he is. Nobody writes threatening letters about money, to this place. It's freedom, sir, it's freedom![37]

Dickens had first-hand knowledge of debtors' prisons, his own father John having been imprisoned for debt in the Marshalsea in 1824. This is well known now, but was a closely guarded secret during most of the novelist's lifetime, such were the feelings of shame that this childhood trauma provoked. But although Dickens could not endorse the doctor's position, as we shall see in the next chapter in relation to the Fleet Prison sections of *Pickwick Papers*, his understanding of it did grow with the years. Indeed, according to his biographer John Forster, Dickens claimed that 'in every respect indeed but elbow-room ... [his own] family lived more comfortably in prison than they had done for a long time out of it'.[38] Moreover, the sentiments that Dickens puts in the doctor's mouth did form part of a long-standing tradition of celebrating debtors' prisons as little suburban utopias, bohemian backwaters miraculously freed from the commercial concerns of the outside world. This was such a strong current, particularly in the visual representations of the period, that one is tempted to think of debtors' prison imagery in the early 1800s in terms of a poetics of denial. Witness the golden glow of Pugin and Rowlandson's print of the King's Bench for Ackermann's *Microcosm of London* (1808) and the similarly Arcadian, and crepuscular, feel of their picture of the racket grounds of the Fleet. This latter image was of such attractiveness, it seems, that it was still being copied well over seventy years later, long after the Fleet itself had vanished, and debtors' prisons in general were on the way out.

A LITTLE REPUBLIC

In chapter 15 of his *Book of Sports*, Egan writes of 'Banco Regis' in the 1820s that it 'was one continued scene of *gaiety* and *dash* – indeed, it was like anything else but a place of confinement'.[39] The King's Bench was the largest and most socially respectable of the London debtors' prisons,[40] but as Ackermann's illustration and Haydon's painting clearly shows, its architecture and layout were still pretty basic. Put simply, the prison consisted of a number of brick buildings standing in an open ground, which was surrounded on all sides by a high brick wall decorated by *chevaux-de-frise*. Most of the prisoners' rooms were contained in a large dormitory block. There was also a kitchen, tap-house, coffee-house, bake-house and chapel, and a large open space called the 'yard' or 'parade' containing the prison pumps, which also served as the scene for all kinds of social and sporting activities, most notably skittles and 'rackets'. Rackets – or squash, as it was later to be called – was actually invented in the Fleet Prison, which was another prison for 'the better sort of debtor'.

Debtors' prisons like the Fleet, the Marshalsea, Whitecross Street and the King's Bench were all privately run. Each institution was headed by a marshal and administered by a series of officers, or turnkeys. Normally, the turnkeys were remarkably few in number, and had limited official duties that included escorting prisoners to trial and making sure that inmates did not leave without permission. The rest of their time was spent supplying the prisoners with goods and services, often at extortionate prices. Apart from that, their role in the prisons was rather small, since much of the day-to-day running of these institutions was generally left to the prisoners themselves.[41]

Prisoners frequently resumed their trades in prison. 'Nearly all the lower or ground floor rooms were occupied by men who had turned them into places of business – into shops in fact', the author of *Prison Reminiscences* tells us, 'here were cobblers – I beg their pardon, boot and shoe makers – tailors and barbers, who worked for inmates of the prison.'[42] Some prisoners even got chronically in arrears to their fellow prisoners, opening up a new realm of debt within debt. Printers, journalists and poets committed to the King's Bench (sometimes for seditious libel) often continued to work, sometimes selling pamphlets and newspapers from their rooms.[43] There were hierarchical elements in prison society: different classes had different living conditions, purchasing power and living habits, with the gentleman's world tending to revolve around the prison coffee-house, and that of the lower classes, the beer-house or tap. But if King's Bench society was hierarchically structured, it was also knit together with bonds of community and mutual aid. Nicholson was not being entirely facetious, therefore, when he referred to it as 'a commonwealth made up of errant and fugitive talent'.[44]

The most important manifestations of the King's Benchers' sense of community were the corporate bodies established among the prison population, one for the 'masterside' of the main prison block, which looked out on the main yard and contained the richer debtors, and the other for the 'commonside', which faced the perimeter wall. The masterside corporation was called the King's Bench 'college', and each member a 'collegian'. The college was a representative institution that facilitated good order and harmony among the prison population by providing a formal mechanism for making decisions and settling disputes. It met out in the open, in the main yard of the prison. The officers of the college, who were elected by the prisoners in general assembly, included the president (also described as chairman, steward and lord mayor), the clerk or secretary, and the treasurer; there were also sheriffs, aldermen and constables. Hence, whether Haydon knew it or not, some of the titles sported by the mock-electioneers in 1827 did correspond, in some sense, to 'real' positions within the prison administration.

Nor is it necessary to assume that their prison-yard politicking was purely facetious. The King's Bench college had actually petitioned parliament a number of times in the previous century, one of its aims having been to encourage the government in its occasional habit of freeing large groups of honest debtors in single ad hoc gestures of amnesty – the so-called 'Insolvency Acts'.[45] There were also more distant connections between the King's Bench Prison and outdoor political protest, which had to do with its rather inadvertent role in both the Wilkesite and Gordon riots (of 1768 and 1780 respectively). In neither case had the disturbance in question been precipitated by the debtors, but in each the prison had been chosen as the perfect place from which to assert the liberty and property rights of the English subject. When the Bench was burnt down during the Gordon disturbances, the debtors themselves were in fact rather reluctant to leave, and spent a good deal of their time trying to secure their property before vacating the premises. It is incidents like this that has prompted historians to conclude that, in spite of its democratic traditions, the political ethos of the King's Bench Prison was ultimately more like that of a medieval guild than a modern-day radical organization. 'Defensive conservatism' is the term Margot Finn uses to describe it, a phrase that perfectly sums up both its admirably stubborn yet also fundamentally static nature.[46]

Debtors' prisons were in many ways extraordinary places of paradox and even of inversion. The King's Bench in particular was an open prison, a prison that you could walk out of, a prison where you were, to some extent at least, looked after by your fellow prisoners, and could, if you chose, carry on your life very much as you would have done outside. It was a prison which was also a haven – and sometimes a hustings – and which was run, for the most part, by the prisoners themselves. As even the most reluctant inmate of Whitecross Street Prison in the City of London was forced to admit, 'it appeared that the little community was a pure democracy, universal suffrage being the order of the day'.[47] Equally, the debtors' prison was a genuinely bohemian space, a place with its very own rhythm and humour, and, as such, offered a powerful, if implicit, resistance to the new time and work disciplines of the nineteenth century. Most intriguingly of all, the debtors' prison was a place in which losing might suddenly begin to look a little like winning – if you were capable of playing *misère*.

DEBTORS' PRISONS IN THACKERAY AND DICKENS

It was precisely because of the romantic air that continued to linger around debtors' prisons, one could argue, that some Victorian novelists used them as a space for thinking critically about Romanticism, and Romantic-period literature more generally. Such was the case with both Thackeray's *Pendennis* (1848–50) and Dickens's *Little Dorrit* (1855–7). In *Pendennis* the debtors' prison becomes an objective correlative for the true condition of the modern writer. The writer in question is one Captain Shandon, a man of genius and learning but also a drunkard and a spendthrift, who is holed up in the Fleet Prison with his devoted wife and daughter. Based on Thackeray's own former mentor William Maginn, the virulent anti-Cockney of *Blackwood's* and *Fraser's*, Shandon perfectly exemplifies the structural hypocrisy at the heart of anonymous journalism, writing a prospectus for the *Pall Mall Gazette* – a new High Tory journal to be written by and for gentlemen – while himself leading a hand-to-mouth bohemian existence in the taprooms of the Fleet. Thackeray's own attitude to the prison is one of studied ambivalence: Pendennis, the protagonist, finds the main yard teeming and claustrophobic, but is pleasantly surprised by the 'not uncheerful' look of Captain Shandon's room. Fecklessness is rife in the Fleet, but so too are generosity and conviviality, and Shandon is loving to his family, if also incorrigibly forgetful. Tellingly, Shandon's publisher Bungay (who was supposedly based on Henry Colbourn) is initially reluctant to secure his release from prison, afraid of losing the benefit of his captive genius.

If Thackeray's portrait of Shandon in *Pendennis* is, in a sense, all about the secretly Cockney conditions that afflicted one of the most virulent anti-Cockneys of the age, then *Little Dorrit*'s take on debtors' prisons can be seen as a retrospect on the 'Cockney School' itself. Much has been written on *Bleak House*'s Harold Skimpole as a satirical portrait of Leigh Hunt. The resemblance was widely noted at the time and left Hunt suitably offended. But there was also a role for Hunt in *Little Dorrit*, Dickens's other big novel of the 1850s. In this story William Dorrit is 'the Father of the Marshalsea', a shabby genteel king of the debtors and a virtuoso in denial. The character is partly based on Dickens's own father, but there are elements that were inspired by other, more recent reminiscences, notably Hunt's 1850 *Autobiography*. In this work the writer revealed that his earliest memory had been of the inside of a prison, his father having been incarcerated for debt in the 1780s. He also talked of how his own son, Thornton Hunt, had scampered obliviously around the jail during his own incarceration in 1813–15. Such images would have fed naturally into Dickens's conception of the Dorrit children; and Hunt's obvious pride at being visited by the great and the good in prison may well have given him the idea of William Dorrit's daily 'Levee'. Still closer to the composition of *Little Dorrit* was the publication of Haydon's 1853 autobiography. This book, with its extended descriptions of the painter's King's Bench sojourns of 1823, 1827 and 1830, may also have helped Dickens write *Little Dorrit*, encouraging him to explore the paradoxical draw of debtors' prisons in a way that he had found impossible in *Pickwick Papers*.

Metaphors of prison and imprisonment, and the notion of society itself as a prison, are everywhere in *Little Dorrit*; nevertheless there are a few key moments when Dickens's meditations reveal their influences. Dickens's portrait of John Chivery, for example, is, in its way, a wonderful little essay on Cockney consciousness, pitched delicately between sympathy and satire. Chivery is the son of the Marshalsea turnkey, and helps his mother run a tobacco shop around the corner. He is also a Cockney dandy, who dresses up in a plum-coloured coat to impress the Dorrits. Ever since they were children, John has been in love with Amy Dorrit, and at the beginning of chapter 18 Dickens has him brimming with great expectations:

> Say things prospered, and they were united. She, the child of the Marshalsea; he the lock-keeper. There was a fitness in that. Say he became a resident turnkey. She would officially succeed to the chamber she had rented for so long. There was a beautiful propriety in that. It looked over the wall, if you stood on tiptoe; and, with a trellis-work of scarlet beans, and a canary or so, would become a very Arbour. There was a charming idea in that. Then, being all in all to one another, there was even an appropriate grace in the lock. With the world shut out (except

that part of it which would be shut in); with its troubles and disturbances only known to them by hearsay, as they would be described by the pilgrims tarrying with them on their way to the Insolvent Shrine; with the Arbour above, and the Lodge below; they would glide down the stream of time, in pastoral domestic happiness.[48]

This 'standing on tiptoe' recalls Keats, of course, as does the name of Chivery, which makes us think simultaneously of chivalry ('The Eve of St Agnes' perhaps, or even 'La Belle Dame Sans Merci') and shivery, reminding us of Keats's chronic tuberculosis and tragic early demise. Physically and emotionally, Chivery is close to Keats, being 'small of stature, with very weak legs and very weak light hair' and yet also 'gentle', 'great of soul', 'poetic, expansive, faithful'. But in the arbour he constructs in his mind's eye he also reminds us of Hunt, and the famous prison room and garden that was described in *Lord Byron and His Contemporaries* and the *Autobiography*. What is interesting about Chivery, I think, is the extent to which he is right in his great expectations: not only socially, but also in terms of temperament and upbringing; he and Amy really do belong together. The story, however, for reasons to do with the Victorian novel's bourgeois bias as well as Dickens's own complicated attitude to Cockneys, cannot and will not allow it. Chivery is permitted to play a chivalric role in helping Amy's family recover their fortunes, but the girl herself is ultimately destined for the middle-class 'hero', Arthur Clennam. Clearly one of the ways in which Dickens tries to excuse his exploitation of Chivery, as it were pre-emptively, is by forcing us to see the limitations of his vision (the novelist describes him, incidentally, as having one eye that was weaker and looked larger than the other, 'as if it couldn't collect itself'). The jailer's son's pastoral fantasy is clearly a prime example of Cockney false consciousness. It is also (a little like Keats's 'Nightingale' Ode) based on a death-wish. At the end of the passage quoted above, John finds himself looking forward, with profound satisfaction, to a time when he and Amy will die and be buried together in the prison, having scarcely ever set foot outside. This impulse towards retreat and denial is a very strong one in the novel, and only in the closing paragraph does the High Victorian Dickens definitively reject it, describing how Amy and Arthur finally take their leave of the Marshalsea and go 'quietly down into the roaring streets'.

THE MOCK ELECTION

Haydon's *The Mock Election* registers a similar ambivalence about debtors' prisons, while coming to a markedly different conclusion. Compositionally it presents the viewer with three groups placed on a dirty triangle of ground in the main prison yard. In the background, between the two apartment blocks, is a blustery blue patch of sky. The walls have not been insisted upon, and the prison's space is made to seem like a large one, as if it is the very idea of imprisonment that we are meant to focus upon, not its iron-and-brick reality. Regarding the prison itself, Haydon presents it as a space in which the distinction between public and private has all but ceased to exist. The masqueraders use the yard as a stage for their public meeting; Major Campbell treats it like a drawing room. The respectable couple, however, could not look less at home; to them the prison is clearly a kind of purgatory, a realm of the unburied dead. By this means, Haydon gives a powerful sense of imprisonment for debt as a kind of blank slate, like a theatre stage, an open space of the imagination that could be furnished, and inhabited, in a variety of ways.

Regarding the actual burlesque upon which Haydon's painting was based, the initial media response was one of amusement. On 17 July 1827 *The Times* reported that 'for some days past a great deal of fun and merriment have been going forward within the walls of the King's Bench prison in consequence of a mock election'.[49] But a couple of days later, as the unruliness of the festivities became evident, one of the paper's correspondents finally decided that enough was enough:

> It is with great regret that we have observed the recent proceedings in the King's Bench Prison. Is it by mock elections, and the excesses attendant on such scenes, that the persons removed to that place of confinement mean to satisfy their honest creditors, and (in many cases we fear) make compensation to those they have wronged? … What has the inside of a prison to do with elections?[50]

The writer then went on to praise William Jones, the marshal of the prison, for taking a firm hand with the carnival when it threatened to get out of hand, calling in the Grenadier Guards and quick-marching all three candidates, the High Sheriff and his poll-clerk to the King's Bench strong-room. Not surprisingly, the prison collegians vehemently rejected this view of things; and indeed in the very same issue of *The Times* there was news of a prisoners' petition calling for Jones's resignation. The King's Bench college was outraged at his Peterloo-like introduction of the military, and of his having treated their fellow debtors like criminals.[51]

What *has* the inside of a prison to do with elections? Fundamentally facetious though it was, the King's Bench mock election of July 1827 was clearly drawing on a long-standing tradition of the debtors' prison as a site of political theatre and protest. What is interesting, however, is how very unsympathetic the commentators of the day were to this late flowering of the carnivalesque. Possible explanations are not hard to find. First, the politics of political representation had become very heated by 1827: the campaign for Catholic Emancipation was reaching its height, with the political plight of poor Irish Catholics being remarkably similar, in certain respects, to those of unjustly imprisoned debtors. The participation of several Irishmen in the King's Bench festivities may well have alerted people to this connection. More generally, the mock election may also have served as an unwelcome reminder of the general riotousness and corruption surrounding the typical 'rotten borough' election, a state of affairs that was becoming increasingly embarrassing to the establishment in the late 1820s. But at bottom the comparative lack of public sympathy for the King's Bench burlesque was probably due to the changed economic circumstances of the period. This was a time, after all, of burgeoning national debt. The king himself, George IV, was a notorious debtor, and there had been a great financial crash – the crash that ruined Sir Walter Scott – a couple of years before. There was a new puritanism in the attitude to insolvency during these years. Debtors were still viewed as unfortunate, but it was no longer so easy to celebrate them as martyrs to English liberty. The criminalization of debt that became so prevalent in the Victorian period was beginning to take hold.

Nor is this feeling absent from Haydon's painting: one has only to look at the soberly dressed middle-class family on the left-hand side of the canvas. As honest and industrious citizens who have been imprisoned under a corrupt legal system, they offer a powerful visual embodiment of the abolitionist argument, and in their evident disapproval at what is going on around them, they also represent respectable society's increasing distaste for the 'flash style' of the unreformed debtors' prison.[52] This links in with a strain of moralizing that runs through the painter's diaries at the time, which saw the Bench as 'a temple of idleness and debauchery' whose very depravity must serve to inspire all respectable inmates 'to develop virtues, eradicate Vices, & render deeper religious feelings, improve morals, enlarge understandings, & excite industry'.[53] It was this dual attitude that was to prevail in the later nineteenth century, for as the campaign to abolish debtors' prisons intensified, so too did the stigma of criminality surrounding debt. By the 1870s imprisonment for debt had ceased for everything except small debts, which meant that it was only the poor who were still subject to incarceration, and those convicted were no longer being sent to the King's Bench or the Fleet, but to small, grubby Whitecross Street or, worse still, modern-style reformist penitentiaries like

Holloway. This is one of the reasons cited by Finn for the disappearance of debtors and debtors' prisons from English fiction after *Little Dorrit*: it was not that such places had ceased to exist, but that they no longer contained middle-class people (p. 63).

On this left side of the canvas Haydon shows a growing family rendered suddenly and dramatically abject by a mere accident of debt, and the fact that there are no names attached to these figures in the annotated catalogue only increases the suspicion that it is the painter's own family that has provided the model. While Haydon was working on *The Mock Election* his wife, Mary, gave birth to their sixth child, and, despite being vehemently anti-Malthusian in theory, his burgeoning brood often left him anxious and depressed in practice. But if the group portrait on the left represents Haydon's intermittent acknowledgement of the brute facts of economic reality, the rest of the composition reflects his strenuous defiance of them.

In the central portion Haydon celebrates not only the debtors' burlesque spirit but also the vulgar self-advertisement that he himself always relied upon as a tool to get out of trouble. For the painter was not only the dejected father of a brood of children, he was also, like the Tory candidate in the picture, a vigorous petitioner and polemicist, with a gift for Cockney self-promotion. In 1819 William Carey wrote an eloquent attack on Haydon and his anonymous self-puffing, making him sound like a street performer at Smithfield's Bartholomew Fair. '[He is] a sort of *pictorial Mountebank* on a stage', Carey wrote, 'with his *anonymous Bill-sticker, Hornblower* and *Merry Andrew*, placarding the walls. Sounding the blasts of astonishment, or playing a solo on his salt-box to attract the eyes and ears of the amazed Multitude.' Under Haydon's influence, the author continued,

> The Press is to be converted into an engine for Disappointed Vanity and Envy, to work their unholy purposes, and all contemporary merit, every living British Artist, is to be thrown out of sight, or only brought forward as a mere background and inferior figure to Mr. Haydon; or this scribbling Jack-pudding, his Trumpeter, Showman, and Puff-master general is to be let loose upon us.[54]

Only the year before painting *The Mock Election*, Haydon had begun a concerted campaign to mend his reputation with the Royal Academy, aggressively courting those members with whom he had argued in the past. He was also a regular petitioner of parliament, calling for English history painting to receive state support. Haydon always found public appeals and debates of this kind hugely energizing; through them he indulged his idealism, his vanity and his vulgarity. But to many of his artistic brethren they provided a grave distraction from his painting, and even in their own terms they rarely had the desired effect. In 1826 and 1827 Haydon had tried to cash in on his courtship of the Academy by putting himself up for election, but on neither occasion did he receive a single vote.[55] While working on *The Mock Election* at the end of 1827, he joked in his diary that the Academicians might well see a satirical impulse in his current project, an attempt to bring elected authorities – all elected authorities – into contempt by painting mock Sheriffs and mock Mayors.[56] Nor, one might add, would they necessarily have been wrong to do so, for in the epigraph to the catalogue description Haydon had made a point of quoting *Measure for Measure* on 'man, proud man, dressed in little, brief, authority, most ignorant of what he's most assured'.

On the right-hand side of the painting, with the figure of the war hero Major Campbell, the painting moves beyond self-promotion to heroic defiance. In the catalogue Haydon links Campbell with Bonaparte, Byron and Milton's Satan, all brilliant over-reachers, 'men of aspiring talent' who finished their careers in exile. One indication of Haydon's strong identification with this figure is the latter's striking profile, which closely resembles the painter's own; another is the following passage from the catalogue description, which exalts Cockney frustration into a Byronic brand of post-Napoleonic disappointment:

> We gaze after the eagle in his flight, and are bound by gravitation to the earth we tread on; we sail forth in pursuit of new worlds, and after a year or two return to the spot we started from, we weary our imaginations with hopes of something new, and find, after a long life, we can only embellish what we see; so that while our hopes are endless and our imagination unbounded, our faculties and being are limited; whether it be six thousand feet, or six thousand miles, a limit still marks the prison! (p. 4)

Major Campbell had spent nine years in prison by 1827, but Haydon himself had been in debt for even longer, and this passage is a painful, though oblique, acknowledgement of that fact. The eagle here, like the figure of Campbell in the painting, is a perfect image of the independent history painter, a man both heroic in himself and committed to heroic subjects, who has somehow found himself imprisoned in the world of genre painting. Genre, here, can be construed aesthetically as that mode of low Dutch realism in which the artist is condemned to 'only embellish what he sees', and also economically, as the grubby world of everyday economic reality. Similarly, the Campbell figure registers Haydon's own contemptuous attitude to material difficulty, and his determination to go it alone, independently of parliaments or academies. He is in that sense an image of the painter's ideal self.

Pictorially, the Major is portrayed in a broader, brighter, less detailed style than everyone else. His physique is strongly reminiscent of the Ilissus, one of the largest of the Elgin Marbles, and recalls Haydon's vehement championship of them in the previous decade. It was the Elgin Marbles, Haydon had argued, that were going to inspire a whole new generation of English artists, with the Illissus in particular representing a perfect synthesis of the natural and the ideal. The treatment of the respectable couple, by contrast, is much closer to that of contemporary genre painting, a point made by George IV himself when he pointed to the left-hand side of the canvas during his first perusal of the painting and said 'This is our friend Wilkie out-and-out.'[57] The Royal Academician David Wilkie was one of Haydon's life-long friends, a brilliant genre painter who had first made his name in 1806 with a superbly conceived rustic scene called *Village Politicians*, and then soared to even greater heights in 1822 with his history-cum-genre painting *Chelsea Pensioners reading the Waterloo Despatch*. Not long before his second incarceration, Haydon had made an entry in his diary comparing himself to Wilkie, in which he employed a favourite analogy between artistic and military endeavour:

> Wilkie's system was Wellington's: principle and prudence the groundwork of risk. Mine that of Napoleon: audacity, with defiance of principle, if principle was in the way. I got into prison. Napoleon died in St. Helena. Wellington is living and honoured, and Wilkie has had a public dinner given him in Rome, the seat of art and genius, and has secured a competence, while I am as poor and necessitous as ever.[58]

In his diary Haydon balanced a long-standing respect for Wilkie's gifts with an equally enduring contempt for the genre his friend specialized in. And its manifold popularity with the public only increased his anger. 'Nothing bold, or masculine, or grand, or powerful touches an English connoisseur', he wrote in 1824, 'it must be small and highly wrought, and vulgar and humorous, and broad and palpable.'[59]

Haydon's *Mock Election* possesses many of the latter qualities, and owes a considerable amount to Wilkie's example, not only in the sober realism of the respectable family but also the energy and naturalness of the central group, which is, in fact, something of a Cockney translation of *'Village Politicians'*, with the posturings of the impotent now transferred to the city. It is also, in its way, an ironic sequel to Wilkie's heart-warming image of veteran patriotism in the *'Chelsea Pensioners'*. Aesthetically, then,

The Mock Election is a deliberate confusion of genre painting, history painting and Hogarthian graphic satire; something *The Times* reviewer may have been gesturing towards when he accused it of 'coarseness'.[60] But narratively the painting is clear enough, with the visual composition describing what is in effect a left-to-right progress from abjection through protest to stoic defiance, a movement that is also, in its way, a progression from genre painting to history painting and from a purely economic understanding of things to a purely political.

In Haydon's hands, history painting was a genre that specialized in extreme, even foolhardy acts of will. In his first major painting, which was exhibited in 1809, he depicted Dentatus at the point of death still vigorously defending himself against his assassins, and in one of his last he showed Marcus Curtius leaping into the gulf to save the Roman republic. Haydon's favourite subjects are often creatures of suicidal heroism and self-sacrifice, and to that extent they appeal to the purest form of the political understanding. They appeal, that is, not to the party-political, but to politics as a pure discourse of the will. In *The Mock Election*, Campbell's absolute refusal to negotiate with his creditors – even at the cost of remaining in the Bench for the rest of his life – is just such an act of pure voluntarism, and constitutes a heroic defiance of economics. And as in *Marcus Curtius*, so too in *The Mock Election* there is a politics of profile: by gazing directly off stage and refusing to meet anyone's eye, the hero dramatizes the extent to which his thoughts are, quite literally, on a different plane from everyone else's. He alone, it seems, can see beyond the material confines of the canvas.

Such a defiant gesture was only possible, one could argue, because of the 'debtor ethos' that continued to surround early-nineteenth-century debtors' prisons, for it rendered the King's Bench, ironically enough, the perfect place from which to insist upon the primacy of the political over the economic, the will over circumstance, personality over history. Three years after *The Mock Election*, Haydon was imprisoned in the Bench once more, but by this time, as his biographer Eric George points out, he seems to have treated it almost as a second home.[61] His main discovery on his return was that Major Campbell was dying. The painter went to see him in his rooms. 'C[ampbell] lay on the bed sound asleep', as Haydon remembered 'his grand Satanic head grander than ever, black matted hair tumbled about his white pillow; his cheeks hollow, his mouth firm as if dreaming, while his teeth grated a little.' The painter, too affected to speak, folded his arms and watched 'this grand heroic fellow fast sinking into the grave, the victim of pride and passion'. King George IV had apparently been so moved by his splendid appearance in *The Mock Election* that he had sent Campbell a note begging him to state his wishes, but, 'too conscious of his fallen state', the Major had never replied. In spite or perhaps even because of this, something of the spirit of Ackermann's *Microcosm* engraving seems to have descended upon Haydon during those July days of 1830, with George IV's death the previous month now mingling with news of a new revolution in Paris. 'Waterloo Heroes absolutely abound here', he wrote enthusiastically in his diary. 'On the racket ground at night [Major Bacon], I, and Colonel La Tour walk & talk. I excite them about Waterloo, and I never passed pleasanter evenings.'[62]

CHAPTER 8

Charles Dickens and Cockney adventures

> The shops are now completely opened, and apprentices and shopmen are busily engaged in cleaning and decking the windows for the day. The bakers' shops in town are filled with servants and children waiting for the drawing of the first batch of rolls – an operation which was performed a full hour ago in the suburbs: for the early clerk population of Somers and Camden Towns, Islington, and Pentonville are fast pouring into the city, or directing their steps towards Chancery Lane and the Inns of Court. Middle-aged men, whose salaries have by no means increased in the same proportion as their families, plod steadily along, apparently with no object in view but the counting house; knowing by sight almost everybody they meet or overtake, for they have seen them every morning (Sundays excepted) during the last twenty years, but speaking to no one.[1]

This piece, 'The Streets – Morning', was first published in the *Evening Chronicle* on 21 July 1835, and then included in the *Sketches by Boz* second series as the first of its 'Scenes'. Contemporary reviews of the *Sketches* praised its extraordinary purchase on life among the 'lower classes', but what they didn't do is discriminate – or show how Boz had discriminated – between these mysterious ranks. There are a number of treatments of the very poor in *Boz*, and they tend to be among the best-known pieces. The essay on 'Gin Shops', for example, which gives a study of life in the St Giles Rookery, or 'The Pawnbroker's Shop' which does the same for Drury Lane. What is not often mentioned, however, is how untypical they are of the collection as a whole, which is more substantially concerned with life among the lower middle classes and, in particular, with the specific constellation of types described above. Shopkeepers, seamstresses, apprentices and clerks: these are the professions that the young Dickens knew best and chose to concentrate on, having identified them as the true barometers of modern life.

> Small office lads in large hats, who are made men before they are boys, hurry along in pairs, with their first coat carefully brushed, and the white trousers of

last Sunday plentifully besmeared with dust and ink. It evidently requires considerable mental struggle to avoid investing part of the day's dinner money in the purchase of the stale tarts so temptingly exposed in dusty tins at the pastry cooks' doors; but a consciousness of their own importance and the receipt of seven shillings a week, with the prospect of an early rise to eight, comes to their aid, and they accordingly put their hats a little more on one side, and look under the bonnets of all the milliners' and staymakers' apprentices they meet – poor girls! – the hardest worked, the worst paid, and too often, the worst used class of the community. (pp. 31–2)

When Dickens employs the word 'class' in the *Sketches* he generally means 'profession' or, even more often, 'type'. Nevertheless, he does tend to group semi-respectable white-collar workers together, and represent them in the same kinds of ways. The poor in *Boz* tend to be identified with a specific locality (Seven Dials, Monmouth Street, St Giles), a locality that effectively imprisons them in a kind of violent still-life. In the case of the lower middle classes, however, the impression is one of limited mobility. The clerks' daily commute from Islington and Camden Town to the counting houses in the City is just one example of this – a form of shuttling stasis, a dynamic routine. According to Geoffrey Crossick, this experience of limited movement (both social and geographical) only left the petite bourgeoisie wanting more: 'This persistent ideology of personal mobility was characteristic of the lower middle class and a dominant element in its values', he writes, 'it was an ambition quite distinct from that of the artisan for whom there was far less scope, and often far less desire, for a mobility structured into the job.'[2] In this way 'The Streets by Morning' captures many of the salient features, and ironies, of early-nineteenth-century Cockney life. The image of the 'stale tarts' is a covert reminiscence of the writer's own daily commute, when still quite a boy, from Camden Town to the blacking warehouse on Hungerford Stairs. But it also conjures up a broader vision of the lower middle classes as the natural consumers of the newly-out-of-fashion. In the movement from 'stale tarts' to 'milliners' and staymakers' apprentices' Dickens perfectly captures the characteristically lower-middle-class choice between instant – and inferior – gratification and temporary, possibly even indefinite, deferral; the hint being, in this case, that it is only by saving one's pennies for a long while that one might finally be able to win a milliner's or staymaker's apprentice. The modern historian Anna Clark has written of the way in which London clerks and apprentices were 'feminized' by industrialization, their social positions having become even more precarious and powerless than they had been at the turn of the century.[3] Nor is this merely a retrospective judgement. In 1833 Edward Gibbon Wakefield was already making reference to an 'uneasy class' in England made up of at least two-thirds of professional men; an early attempt, we might say, to diagnose the lower middle class in terms of a particular kind of social and economic fix: 'Now, a great proportion of men in the uneasy class dread marriage', wrote Wakefield, 'as the surest means of increasing their embarrassment. This is one of the most important features in the social state of England.'[4]

THE PERIODICALS AND THE COCKNEY CLASS

The 1830s was the decade in which the lower middle classes entered literature en masse. The phenomenon was noted at the time. Reviewing *Sketches by Boz* in book form in July 1837, the *Westminster Review* rather solemnly noted that 'a taste for depicting their manners and humour has long been gaining ground in our lighter literature'.[5] Critiques of Cockneyism and the Cockney School aside, there had been a regular sprinkling of Cockney sketches and comic vignettes in the periodical magazines of the 1820s, but that number was to increase considerably in the ensuing years. Many of these stories expanded upon already-existing sub-genres. When Thomas Hood published his *London Magazine* sketch 'A Cockney's Rural Sports' in December 1822 he was working within a long-established vein of Cockney sporting comedy, and this was given new life in the 1830s by Robert Surtees's Jorrocks stories and the rural numbers of Dickens's *Pickwick Papers*.[6] Some of these developments showed the influence of the 'Cockney School' controversy. Caroline Bowles's 'Letter from a Washerwoman' of 1824 had been a satirical response to Leigh Hunt's infamous 'Washerwomen' article in the *Round Table*, and yet it also prepared the ground for later lodging-house satires such as Dickens's 'The Boarding-House' in *Boz*.[7] The latter may also have been influenced by Theodore Hook's *Sayings and Doings* (1824), which contained some snide accounts of social faux pas among the Bloomsbury semi-genteel. But it was not only Tories who engaged in Cockney comedy; several writers connected with the *Examiner* circle were regular dabblers as well. Not counting Hood, perhaps two of the liveliest Cockney writers on Cockneyism in this period were Horace and James Smith, the joint authors of *Rejected Addresses*, a much-celebrated book of parodies from the 1810s. Less *parti pris* than Hook or Bowles, the Smith brothers were still pointedly satirical about Cockney pertness, and knew a lot about it because of their background in the City. 'The Hebdomadary of Mr Snooks the Grocer' by James Smith appeared in the *New Monthly Magazine* in January 1824.[8] This relates a week in the life of a naive Cheapside shopkeeper who plays the markets at Capel Court, gets excited as his stocks grow, starts lording it over his social superiors, and then loses everything when the market crashes. 'Cit' comedy had its place, but the comedy of Cockney recreation was much more popular. Not long after 'Mr Snooks', James's brother Horace came up with 'Dinner in the Steam-Boat', which was later collected in his *Gaieties and Gravities* of 1825.[9] This delightful piece, which was also published in the *New Monthly*, captured all the pretension and hilarity of a lower-middle-class pleasure jaunt down the Thames.

What these sketches suggest, and what was certainly borne out in the later 1830s (in the work of Dickens, Nicholson, Thackeray and others), is that there was a natural affinity between the periodical magazines, the form of the urban sketch and the representation of the Cockney classes. The lower middle classes had been bit-part players in English literature before 1820, and they were to be bit-part players again, especially after the rise of the Great Victorian Novel in the 1840s and 1850s. But for a brief moment – the moment when the periodical magazine held centre-stage in British culture – they did come into a special kind of prominence. In an important article on the subject, Arlene Young has shown how 'a variety of marginal social and occupational types populate the comic sketches of the *New Monthly Magazine* and *Bentley's Miscellany* – grocers, apothecaries, hack journalists, booksellers, various kinds of shop assistants'.[10] What distinguished the 1830s in particular was that, as ever more people continued to pour into the metropolis, and as the British state, the national economy and the periodical press continued to grow in ambition and size, a new interest began to develop in what we could call urban sociology, the identification and classification of the various types of metropolitan man. Nor is it surprising that the Cockney or lower middle class should have become an object of special interest in this analysis, since it was this class, above all others, that was muddying the waters, bringing a new kind of uncertainty to those fundamental urban questions of who one was and where one belonged. Too limited in mobility to be the hero of a novel, the Cockney could, nevertheless, be the anti-hero of a sketch, the sketch form being ideally suited to the peculiar freedom-in-imprisonment of modern metropolitan life.

It must be said that the spirit in which this analysis was conducted was not quite the same as that which had animated *Blackwood's Edinburgh Magazine* in their 'Cockney School' attacks of 1817–24. One result of the 1832 Reform Act, which had extended the franchise to all men living in property worth at least £10 a year, was that many members of the lower middle class now found themselves admitted to full citizenship, especially in London, where rents were high. But there were also a large number of white-collar workers – junior clerks, shopmen, journeyman apprentices and so on – who did not make the cut. One way of thinking about the effect of 1832 on the lower middle class, indeed, is to consider that, instead of fixing its free-floating neither/nor quality in one direction or the other class-wise, what it effectively did was institutionalize it, consecrating this class as the class that would always be uneasy, *in transit*, caught between two worlds. This might help to explain why the Cockney class, whose potential radicalism had been an object of such anxiety in the 1820s, was to prove so politically timid – as a class – in the decades that followed, and why it became less feared by the bourgeoisie proper as a result. Such was the English lower middle class's proximity to full citizenship and respectability and so close was it, at least in its own mind, to worldly advancement that it was invariably its default impulse to identify with the class above it and to dissolve its own real social identity in a middle-class dream. For Arno Mayer, in his now-classic essay 'The Lower Middle Class as a Historical Problem', 1848 was the crucial year for what he called that 'critical swing group', the European petite bourgeoisie, this being the year in which it finally emerged in its true colours as a conservative, and reactionary, force.[11] Certainly, even by the late 1830s in England, the clerkly and shopkeeping classes were no longer the object of quite the same suspicion that they had been in the 'Cockney School' period, as the sense began to grow that their constant experience of being 'tossed about between the hope of entering the ranks of the wealthy class and the fear of being reduced to the state of proletarians or even paupers',[12] as Friedrich Engels memorably put it, was so all-absorbing as to be politically debilitating. Surrounded and subdued by the deferred promises of modernity, the lower middle class was to become tantalized into immobility, the perfect living embodiment of a transitional age. Writing in 1847, Albert Smith had summed up the figure of the Cockney 'Gent' in exactly these terms – as a short-lived creature of history: 'We trust the day will come – albeit we feel it will not be in our time – when the Gent will be an extinct species; his "effigies" as the old illustrated books have it, being alone preserved in the museums. And then this treatise may be regarded as those zoological papers are now which treat of the Dodo.'[13]

THE PHILOSOPHY OF CLOTHES IN *SKETCHES BY BOZ*

Economics is a leading feature of Dickens's 'The Streets – Morning', with Malthusian preoccupations dominating each clerk's thoughts. But the emphasis on clothes – the clerks' smart coats but stained trousers and the seamstresses' bonnets – is an equally telling ingredient, and has a special resonance in relation to early-nineteenth-century Cockneyism. Such were the revolutions in the fashion industry in the 1810s that cheap imitations of respectable polite clothing were becoming generally available, for the first time, to the better class of plebeian worker. So lower-middle-class workers who aspired to bourgeois values of politeness and respectability could fulfil them through transforming their appearance. Bourgeois accumulation of other kinds, such as property or luxury commodities, were not so readily open to this class, hence clothes did come to have a special value in the formation of lower-middle-class identity. This was especially true in London where clothes-making, although not fully industrialized in the manner of the North West of England, was still a huge employer of people, and found an eager market among young Cockneys and Cockneyesses.[14]

Clerks and apprentices could not wear fashionable clothing in the workplace, but in the evening, or on their days off, they were free to transform themselves into dandies, complete with elaborate waistcoats, hats and canes. Polite periodicals were full of ridicule for such practices in the early 1820s. At first glance these pieces say the kinds of things about urban upstarts that are always being said in every historical period. What distinguishes it is the scale of the phenomenon, and its social specificity: often it is a particular set of white-collar workers – clerks and shopkeepers and shopkeeper's apprentices – that are singled out for criticism. Conservative critics, as one might expect, were deeply disapproving of such counter-jumping; but even radicals like William Hazlitt could weigh in against it: 'What a strange infatuation', he wrote in his January 1821 article 'On the Look of a Gentleman', 'to live in a dream of being taken for what one is not, – in deceiving others, and at the same time ourselves.'[15]

In the 1820s many of the most significant criminal cases in the news – criminal cases that were intensely covered and even celebrated in the popular and broadside literature of the period – were singularly Cockney in character, that is, they were crimes of performance and disguise. James Hardy Vaux was a clerk in the City before embarking upon his spectacular career in crime; Fauntleroy had been a fraudulent banker.[16] Pierce Egan wrote histories of both these men in 1824, and was also responsible for a colourful account, published two years earlier, of the life of Samuel Hayward, a Cockney fraudster whose brief but dazzling career had been all about posing as a gentleman of leisure:

> Mrs Burnett now began to inspect the apartments of Hayward, and she perceived that his wardrobe was very scantily furnished, and a false collar, frill, and cuffs, with a *well coaxed* cravat, were almost daily worn by our hero as substitutes for a clean shirt: and he was still more depreciated in his land-lady's opinion on her ascertaining that he painted his cheeks and wore false cork ankles; and, in addition to this, he had passed on her a forged Bank-note in such a way as to raise a strong presumption in her mind that he was connected with forgers.[17]

Counterfeit clothing, counterfeit money, even a counterfeit body: these are the characteristics of the Cockney as fake. Egan's memoir of Hayward concludes on a note of the most perfunctory moralizing, but in doing so it demonstrates some of the real anxieties of the time:

> Yet it is quite lamentable to see so many young men in London anxious to *cut a dash*, and to ape the manners and appearance of gentlemen, without having any property at all; to be thought 'knowing ones', – to be viewed as men of the world, – to laugh at advice, &c. looking only, as it were, upon one side of the picture, and not calculating that the 'men on the town' are far from leading happy lives; their existence completely chequered; living by their wits; no regular habits; and a distinct race of beings from the moral part of society. (pp. 204–5)

In *Sketches by Boz* the connection between Cockneyism and fashion is comic rather than criminal. In 'Miss Evans and the Eagle', Samuel Wilkins is a journeyman carpenter who takes Miss Evans, a shoe-binder and straw-bonnet-maker, to the Eagle pleasure-gardens on the City Road. Miss Evans sports a white muslin gown for the occasion, and Mr Wilkins a gilt-knobbed dress cane. Fuelled by 'shrub', Wilkins soon gets into a fight with two other young men – 'swells out o' luck' as he calls them, but whom Boz refers to only as 'waistcoat' and 'whiskers' (pp. 140–2). Cockney rivalry is here fuelled by, and indeed represented as, the conflict between fashion accessories. And poor old Wilkins is shown singularly failing to live up to his dress cane when 'whiskers' and 'waistcoat' eventually move in and beat him up. Items of fashion and clothing are often metonymic in *Boz* – the part that speaks for the whole. In 'Meditations on Monmouth Street' Dickens regards Monmouth Street – a street of old-clothes sellers near Covent Garden – as the 'burial place of the fashions' (p. 43). The street had also made an appearance in Carlyle's *Sartor Resartus*, published only a few years before. But whereas in Carlyle Monmouth Street is the place where clothes, having been at long last separated from the body, are free to resume their ideal form, Dickens is mainly preoccupied by the messy relationship between the two. Boz cannot see an array of men and women's boots without imagining a gallant dance between them, but for him it is the human traces left on Monmouth Street's old clothes that really bring them to life. Seeing a series of shabby outfits dangling on a rack outside one of the shops, the narrator suddenly realizes that this series is also a progress, and follows the contour of one man's life. Like Sherlock Holmes in 'The Sign of Four', Boz deduces social background, personality and even biographical trajectory from the slightest of material traces, sticky substances about the pockets and rusty, threadbare suits. Tellingly, the story that he unearths is one of Cockney aspiration and disappointment, a life beginning in decency and respectability but ending in loneliness and squalor. Boz's imaginative reconstruction is highly detailed and compelling, and reminds us once again of how impressive he must have seemed, to his contemporaries, as a detailed, detached observer of modern metropolitan life. But at a deeper level one cannot help but notice how far Boz's mental habits reproduce those of Hazlitt's typical Cockney, the man who 'sees everything near, superficial, little, in hasty succession' but who also inhabits 'a world of romance – a fairy land of his own'. Seen this way, it is not merely the plot of Dickens's reverie – i.e. its tale of downward mobility – that strikes us as characteristically Cockney. The imaginative method is as well.

Perhaps the best treatment of fashion in the *Sketches* is 'Horatio Sparkins', which was one of the earliest stories that Dickens published (first appearing in the *Monthly Magazine* in February 1834). It focuses on a family of nouveaux riches 'cits' called the Maldertons, and their desperate attempts to find a fashionable husband for their twenty-eight-year-old daughter Teresa. Considerable excitement is felt by all when Teresa begins to receive attention from one Horatio Sparkins, a well-dressed and well-spoken young dandy to whom she is introduced at a party. The Maldertons duly invite him to their suburban villa in order that he can be inspected more closely. There is a mystery about Sparkins that is truly delightful, for although everyone finds him engaging, no one really knows what he does:

> Was he a surgeon, a contributor to the magazines, a writer of fashionable novels, or an artist? – No; to each and all of these surmises there existed some valid objection. – 'Then,' said everybody, 'he must be *somebody*.' – 'I should think he must be,' reasoned Mr Malderton with himself, 'because he perceives our superiority, and pays us so much attention.' (p. 218)

Burning with curiosity, the Maldertons allow their imaginations to run riot. Miss Marianne even begins to suspect that he might be a prince in disguise. Throughout this period of speculation, an air of romantic glamour surrounds Sparkins, and the family refers to him in secret as 'the great unknown'. But this atmosphere of excitement is rudely banished when one day the Malderton women go shopping in central London and pop into an establishment on the Tottenham Court Road, only to discover Horatio serving behind the counter as a lowly linen-draper's assistant. Hints are given throughout the story that Horatio is not all that he might seem. On one occasion his countenance is described as 'brightening up like an old hat in a shower of rain', a heavy hint at the superficial quality of Sparkins's sparkle (p. 219). The fact that he is always talking pretentious nonsense also puts us on our guard. The most interesting thing about him, though, is that although he is clearly acting under an assumed name, he never actually lies about his condition. When asked if he knows Mr Delafontaine of Bedford Square, he says that he has 'exchanged cards' with him, 'since when, indeed, I have had the opportunity of serving him considerably' (p. 224). The fact that this must have been in his capacity as a shopkeeper's assistant is presumably what makes Horatio blush; but the Maldertons choose not to notice, so firmly fixed are they on their aspirational fantasy. In this way the social satire of the piece works in two directions at once, depicting Horatio as a semi-educated Cockney libertine in pursuit of money and marriage, and the Maldertons as a motley crew of suburban Cockneys excruciatingly eager to consort with the genteel. There are references to anonymous writing and periodical journalism sprinkled throughout 'Horatio Sparkins', and Horatio himself is made to talk in the manner of a pretentious essayist, a little like Leigh Hunt. One is reminded of an article on 'The Proof-Sheet' published in the *New Monthly Magazine* in 1821: 'An author in MS is a half-fledged sloven', it said, 'but, when turned out from the various hands, who conspire to dress and powder him for the public, what an Adonis he walks forth! What a typographical dandy!'[18] In this way 'Horatio Sparkins' keeps inviting us to think of the relation between Horatio and the Maldertons as a kind of allegory for the relationship between the anonymous writer and his audience, with both sides doing everything they can to conceal or deny their Cockney roots.

ARTIFICIAL EDENS

Dickens's *Sketches* is full of pieces that, like 'Miss Evans and the Eagle', draw their comedy and energy from places of lower-middle-class recreation and pleasure. There is Vauxhall Gardens, once the resort of the fashionable and wealthy, now a far less pristine and exclusive venue. There is also the Thames, the Islington Tea Gardens that appear in 'London Recreations', Astley's the horse circus in Lambeth and the annual Greenwich Fair. The piece on 'Private Theatres' describes those places where members of the public could pay to indulge their thespian fantasies, taking the big parts in Shakespearean tragedies for the price of a few shillings. Cockney recreation often has something a little desperate about it in Boz, a very modern desire to extract the maximum degree of 'transport' from one's very limited free time. Of an evening dance at Greenwich Fair, for example, he writes in the most vivid and supercilious terms: 'There is no master of the ceremonies in this artificial Eden – all is primitive, unreserved, and unstudied. The dust is blinding, the heat insupportable, the company somewhat noisy, and in the highest spirits possible' (p. 71). There are a number of the essays that function like this, delighting to explore but also to expose the limited charms of these 'artificial Edens'. On occasion, details of Boz's upbringing are quietly slipped in. In 'Greenwich Fair' it is suggested that one of the reasons why Boz can feel superior to this particular site of Cockney pastoral is because he was a 'constant frequenter' of it in his 'earlier days' (p. 67). The theatre at Astley's is another not wholly contemptible spectacle that the narrator has nevertheless thoroughly outgrown.

Cockney consumers; cockney spectacles: there is from the very beginning of *Sketches by Boz* a rather neat fit between the naive imposture of the former and the pasteboard thinness of the latter. Of 'Vauxhall Gardens by Day' Dickens writes: 'We paid our shilling at the gate, and then we saw for the first time, that the entrance, if there had been any magic about it at all, was now decidedly disenchanted, being, in fact, nothing more nor less than a combination of very roughly-painted boards and sawdust' (p. 76). Once inside, the narrator comes across a 'small party of dismal men in cocked hats "executing" the overture to *Tancredi*', and witnesses a balloon ascent that, though diverting, will still be identical in a year's time. Cockneys are at the centre, it seems, of a new age of inauthentic imitation and reproducible wonder: 'A change of performance takes place every day during [Greenwich] Fair', Boz writes, 'but the story of the tragedy is always pretty much the same' (p. 70). One is reminded of the diorama advertisement in John Parry's *London Street Scene* of 1835: 'See the Destruction of Pompeii – Every Evening'.

'The wish of persons in the humbler classes of life, to ape the manners and customs of those whom fortune has placed above them', Boz writes, at the beginning of 'London Recreations', 'is often the subject of remark, and not infrequently of complaint' (p. 55). But by the time he gets to the conclusion of this piece, which focuses on the various 'Sunday pleasurers' that thicken the groves of the Islington tea-gardens, he has made it clear that he is not writing Cockney satire: 'Some of the finery of these people provokes a smile, but they are all clean, and happy, and disposed to be good natured and sociable' (p. 57). In 'Sunday in the Suburbs', which was written only a year or so before (and discussed earlier in Chapter 1), Leigh Hunt had pitied the Cockney classes their meagre recreations, but looked forward to them moving onwards and upwards into the outer suburbs. What is more, the movement that he had imagined was implicitly both a geographical and a social one, an improvement in visual outlook that would also be an improvement in status. In Boz, by contrast, we see a stronger urge to defend the Cockneys' tea-garden pleasures, but also far less inclination to see them as a class in motion. He does not preach to 'these people', in the way that Hunt had done, but nor does he have the same hopes for them either. Clearly, this is the difference between being a liberal educator and an anonymous *flâneur*. Whether or not this tallied with Dickens's own private feelings on the matter, it was a crucial element in Boz's relationship with his polite readers that, deeply knowledgeable about lower-middle-class manners as he was, he should not appear to be a champion of Cockney ambition. Though a product of the 'lower orders' himself, it was essential that Dickens should write as if the social ladder had been pulled up after him, and he was writing about a rank quite different from his own. One result of this is that his Cockneys do come across as hopelessly class-bound, their aspirations and ambitions always doomed to ignominious failure.

One such example is Miss Amelia Martin, the protagonist of 'The Mistaken Milliner' who is a dressmaker to servants in Euston Square. Like the Cockney in Hazlitt's 'On Londoners', it seems that Miss Martin 'comes so often in contact with fine persons and things' (albeit at one remove) that she herself becomes 'surcharged with a sort of second-hand, vapid, tingling, troublesome self-importance'; put simply, she has delusions of grandeur. Not only does she look down on clerks (her most appropriate suitors), she also has ambitions to be a singer, and when her dressmaking business starts to fall off, she manages to persuade an ornamental painter's journeyman to get her a debut concert at the White Conduit Tavern. Predictably, Miss Martin's performance is a complete disaster:

> The symphony began, and was soon afterwards followed by a faint kind of ventriloquial chirping, proceeding apparently from the deepest recesses of the interior of Miss Amelia Martin. 'Sing out' – shouted one gentleman in a white great-coat. 'Don't be afraid to put the steam on, old gal,' exclaimed another.

'S-s-s-s-s-s-s' – went the five-and-twenty bottled ales. 'Shame, shame!' remonstrated the ornamental painter's journeyman's party – 'S-s-s-s' went the bottled ales again, accompanied by all the gins, and a majority of the brandies. 'Turn them geese out,' cried the ornamental painter's journeyman's party, with great indignation. (p. 156)

DICKENS AND RENTON NICHOLSON

The question of Dickens's own relation to his Cockney roots is (of course) a fascinating one, and particularly piquant with respect to *Boz*. Dickens was born in Portsmouth, but spent many of his formative years in Camden Town, Somers Town and Bloomsbury, and like many Cockneys of his status and position, was forced out early into the world of work, becoming a solicitor's clerk in Gray's Inn at the age of fifteen. Soon after he became a shorthand reporter in Doctors' Commons in the City, a parliamentary reporter, and then a journalist at the *Morning Chronicle*. This takes us up to the mid 1830s, when *Sketches by Boz* first burst upon the literary scene. The details of the early life are very well known – my only reason for rehearsing them briefly here is simply to emphasize the fact that, in early-nineteenth-century terms at least, Charles Dickens was the *archetypal* Cockney. A product of North London and a member of the clerkly classes, he was precisely the kind of figure that had been satirized and fought over in the periodical debates of the 1820s, which meant that he grew up with a Cockney literature that was, to a remarkable extent, both for and about him.

Dickens was not the only North London Cockney to emerge as a writer in this period. The figure of Renton Nicholson offers an interesting point of comparison. Nicholson was only three years older than Dickens, and grew up in Islington while the latter was only a mile or so to the west in Camden. And, like Dickens, he did not have much formal education, becoming an assistant to a pawnbroker while still in his teens. Nicholson led an extremely rackety life in the 1820s and 1830s. He knew many of the 'flash' criminals and popular entertainers of the period, and was interned in the King's Bench on a couple of occasions.[19] By 1837 Nicholson had fallen on decidedly hard times when the opportunity suddenly arose to set up *The Town*, a popular weekly journal that was very much in the mould of the *John Bull*, *The Age* (both of which had attacked Hazlitt in the 1820s) and Barnard Gregory's *Satirist*. *The Town* was a satirical and scandalous publication in the tradition of its predecessors, but its target audience was much less socially exclusive, largely consisting (as Donald J. Gray has suggested) of 'apprentices, shop assistants and clerks'. The journal was full of in-jokes about London Cockneys and their fashions, and had a startling (and very un-Evangelical) preoccupation with sex. As Gray points out:

> Its back page, especially in its last couple of volumes, was mostly made up of advertisements for the publications of H. Smith of Holywell Street, whose list included *Venus's Album, or, Rosebuds of Love*, *Wilson's Rum Codger*, a collection 'of the best double-entendre, flash, and comic songs', the memoirs of Harriet Wilson, the works of Paul de Kock, *Onanism Unveiled*, and *Marriage Physiologically Discussed*.[20]

Both Nicholson and Dickens were to find success in the late 1830s, Dickens by producing works of great freshness and originality (*Boz*, *Pickwick Papers*, *Oliver Twist*, *Nicholas Nickleby*), Nicholson largely by imitating (and vulgarizing) Dickens's example, writing essays, sketches and comic portraits for *The Town*. Given the similarity of these writers' backgrounds, and the fact that they both emerged on the literary scene at more or less the same time, critical comparison between them, especially with regard to their early work, is highly stimulating, not least because it shows the particular choices they both made when it came to representing their Cockney roots.

Nicholson's *The Town* was an unstamped Saturday journal, beginning in 1837 and lasting until 1842. Like *Boz* it was obsessed with the Cockney class, but it was also, to a far greater extent than the magazines that published Dickens, written *for* that class, and this led to a marked difference in its tone and perspective. Formally, the contents of *The Town* were very similar to *Sketches by Boz*, being generally composed of metropolitan vignettes, character portraits and stories. But its tone was much closer to the easy, evasive libertinism of Egan's now legendary *Life in London*. On its launch, it offered itself as a reformist paper, an information-gathering service to help clear up the vices of the city. But in fact, barring the occasional rather perfunctory condemnation of crime or street prostitution, it had almost no crusading impulse at all. Its main concern was always to alert and advertise rather than to reprove. Nevertheless, in throwing itself so energetically into such a hedonistic agenda, it was well placed to offer a very cogent and powerful critique of the Evangelical movement in the capital, which it saw as a vindictive campaign to clamp down on popular pleasure.

The Town had regular features on such topics as 'Board and Lodging Houses – Their Keepers and Inmates', 'Police Officers', 'Licensed Victuallers, Their Manners and Their Parlours' and 'Cigar Shops and Pretty Women', offering a 'flash' guide to the leading pleasure-grounds, personalities and prostitutes of the metropolis. But there were also comic tales, which Nicholson later collected together in book form under the title *Cockney Adventures, or Tales of London Life* (1838). These tales are very similar in subject matter to Dickens's *Sketches*, following the antics of apprentices, lawyer's clerks and shop assistants on their days off. But the humour was much broader and more seasoned with sexual innuendo than anything in *Boz*. 'The Man with the Huge Umbrella', which appeared in the second issue, is a racier reworking of 'Miss Evans and the Eagle', and even takes its Cockney protagonists to the same pub. So too 'The Adventures of Ned Shankey' recalls the comic duel in *Pickwick Papers*, and is another example of the instant impact Dickens's work was having on his contemporaries. There are subtle differences, however, in social vision and reach. Some of the heroes of Nicholson's stories are greengrocers, artificial flower manufacturers and journeyman tailors, and often shade into the realms of the 'proper' working class. The young women are mantua-makers, seamstresses and the daughters of clerks. As with Dickens, Nicholson's Cockneys are always getting drunk, getting their best clothes dirty and being trivially humiliated; but generally their indignities are treated carelessly, and in a comradely spirit. Stylistically, Nicholson is intriguing because he doesn't make a distinction between characters who speak dialect and characters who don't; what he does instead is sprinkle his texts with little Londonisms which help to conjure up a broad milieu:

> The learned gentleman concluded a speech, fraught with immense intelligence and ability, by observing, that Mr Home Fag had recently purchased the whiskers of Whittington's cat, at a very enormous cost: he was but an humble individual, but he most humbly conceived that such rare commodities could not be purchased out of the simple income, adequate as it was to the duties, of a mere westry clerk. Mr Baker Doughty conceived, that if the individual as had jist set down was a humble man, he was a much more humbler, yet he would say that the conduct of the westry clerk in wearing satin breeches was very indecent; while many of the most respectable of the inhabitants of this ere parish were content with welveteens and corderoys.[21]

In many respects Nicholson's representations of Cockney life are not very different from the periodical representations of the 1820s – he loves nothing better than to make fun of young Cockneys and explode their ambitions. The difference is that in the easy tone and flash knowingness of his style, a new kind of indulgence is being proffered. What is more, his 'Cockney Adventures' were only part of a larger periodical concern, *The Town*, an insider's guide to London that was expressly, and permissively, addressed to those very clerks and apprentices that were being represented within its pages. As *Fraser's Magazine* couldn't help noticing in 1838:

> The *Town* forms the *délices* of the servant-maid, who grins over the pages along with sly John Footman; the text-book of the apprentice, who doles it out to his comrades; the hidden treasure of the charmed schoolboy, who, by this excellent medium, knows as much about town as the oldest rake in it. Blessed, then, be the press, and the fruits thereof! In old times (before education grew general), licentiousness was considered as the secret of the aristocracy. Only men enervated by luxury, and fevered by excess of wealth, were supposed to indulge in vices which are now common to the meanest apprentice or the poorest artisan.[22]

Written by a Cockney entrepreneur, for a predominantly Cockney readership (although libertines of all classes would have found its contents interesting), *The Town* had a powerful purchase on the milieu it described. Like the French *physiologies* of the 1830s discussed by Walter Benjamin, it set out to solve the mystery of various urban types – showing its readership how one could infer the background and profession of a fellow Londoner by a careful assessment of his appearance. Like Henry Mayhew ten years later, Nicholson had a sociological passion. Unlike Mayhew, however, his concern was not really with the street proletariat and its under-class, but with the indeterminate creatures floating immediately above it: with Cockney miscreants, in all their shapes and sizes. Each issue of the paper began with a 'Characteristic Sketch', which usually focused on a creature from this class: The City Man; East-End Man; The Man of the South; Cabmen; Hackney Coachmen; English Prostitutes; Female Tobacco Dealers; Beadles; The Maidservant; The Cockney Swell; The Swell in Luck; The Swell out of Luck; The Police Officer, etc.

Like the *Sketches by Boz*, *The Town*'s interest in classification was decidedly non-hierarchical and non-Marxist: its aim was to identify people, but not to put them in their place. Many of the typological categories that Nicholson set up cut across class lines: there was, for example, a long-running series on 'flats' and 'sharps', where the word 'sharp' was used to refer to anyone engaged in 'sharp practice', whether an unemployed dock-labourer or a lord; so too with 'swells' there was a seemingly infinite number of types. Of Cockney swells, Nicholson wrote that 'the tip-top Cockney swell is really and truly a fashionable person', before adding that 'the most *nobby* class are the linen-draper's shopmen' (in other words, the Horatio Sparkinses of this world), 'they set the fashions and lead the Cockney van'. 'Class' here, as in the *Sketches by Boz*, is more or less synonomous with 'type'. It implies nothing about broader class allegiances or identities; indeed it might even be said that one of the characteristic traits of the lower middle classes – the Cockney realm in which both Dickens and Nicholson loved to roam – was that its inhabitants did not and could not think of themselves as a class (in the Marxist sense) with a class interest, at all. The salient characteristic of Cockneys, as we have discovered, is that they never really know their place, and one of the leading traits that Nicholson shares with Egan is that he got as much enjoyment from building them up as from putting them down.

The main interest of *Cockney Adventures* for us is Nicholson's energetic engagement with the very same positions and professions that Dickens had so recently made his own. *Cockney Adventures* No. 17 treats of a 'lawyer's clerk' called Tim Mops, whom Nicholson refers to as a 'member of the reading public', almost certainly in facetious reference to *Fraser's Magazine*'s recent jibes: 'Now, Tim Mops was what is, in the literary world, termed one of the reading public – at least, he was fond of public reading; and we may, if we like, presume that to be the same thing.'[23] What happens in the story is that Tim and a fellow clerk are overheard bad-mouthing a senior lawyer, who then gets his revenge by delivering them into the hands of some local blackguards. It is as if Jaggers had chosen to get his own back on a couple of Wemmicks by leaving them to the mercy of some of his criminal clients. The comedy in this story is twofold; there is some limited enjoyment to be had at Tim's various embarrassments and discomforts; but there is also the larger irony of the established lawyer's unscrupulous ways. One way of distinguishing between Dickens and Nicholson on subjects such as this would simply be to say that the former writes comedy while the latter writes farce. But another would be to compare the two authors' attitudes to their characters. Nicholson can be physically brutal to his Cockneys, but his general attitude towards them implies no moral distance. Boz is often more sympathetic, but he is always also more detached. It is for this reason, I think, that Dickens escaped the kind of criticism that the old Cockney-bashers at *Fraser's* were meting out to Nicholson and to Harrison Ainsworth of *Jack Sheppard* fame.

One recurrent theme of the early reviews of Dickens is a kind of wonder on the part of the critics that they were not more repelled by his 'low' subject matter. Sometimes the astonishment is palpable. 'He moves as naturally and easily amongst his favourite characters', noted the High Tory *Quarterly Review*, 'as if there were no such things as conventional proprieties to offend against.'[24] The *Court Magazine* went even further, observing that it was

> a curious and remarkable trait in these whimsical outlines of low and middle life, that while 'Boz' brings before you with a graphic pen, the express image

of the poorest and most ignorant orders, he never descends into vulgarity. The ordinary conversations of the loose and ribald multitude are faithfully reported, but by an adroit process of moral alchemy all their offensive coarseness is imperceptibly extracted.[25]

Sometimes the praise was more complicated. For the *Monthly Review* Dickens was a new phenomenon but a limited one, a Londoner writing above all for a London audience. 'This originality', it insisted, 'specifically strikes at Cockneyland, and has only that sort of sly satire which can be understood in the more vulgar fields of that broad region of life and humour.'[26] Later on, as if for the benefit of a provincial public, the reviewer went on to testify to the truth of Dickens's vision. Quoting a large chunk of 'The Mistaken Milliner', he then concluded by arguing that the reader could 'say what he chooses about the vulgarity of the parties who appear in this picture', the picture itself was 'a faithful and not unattractive one' (p. 159). Fond as Dickens was of his Cockney background, and of the legacy of *Life in London*, it is clear that in tone and manner *Boz* always had far more in common with the polite sketches of the 1820s and 1830s, pieces such as the *New Monthly*'s 'Dinner in the Steam-Boat' and 'Mrs. John Jones's Pic-Nic', in which Cockneyism had been treated engagingly, even a little affectionately, but always with a kind of anthropological curiosity.[27] Such was the pose made possible by the institution of anonymous authorship; such was the social hypocrisy that enabled the Cockney *flâneur*.

COCKNEYS AND THE CRITIQUE OF EVERYDAY LIFE

Dickens's *Boz* articles appeared serially, in various newspapers, over the course of the mid 1830s. But they are also *about* seriality: the drudgery of work routine – commuting and accounting, and then, on one's day off, the ever-recurring spectacle of reproducible wonders. The 'everydayness' (that is, the circularity) of many of Boz's plots is one of the things that have kept lovers of the novel away from this collection. Viewed in the light of subsequent literary history, *Sketches by Boz* must always be regarded as apprentice-work (as well as being a work about apprentices). Certainly, it is a work jostling with anticipations of Dickens's later fiction. But it might be interesting to reflect, for a moment, on the possible losses, as well as gains, in moving from the essay form to that of the novel. In the subtitle Boz's *Sketches* advertised themselves as being 'Illustrative of Everyday Life and Everyday People', and it is precisely this deep grasp on the patterns – one might almost say the politics – of the everyday that makes Dickens's first book truly distinctive.

There has been some excellent work done recently, by writers such as Michael Sheringham and Ben Highmore, on the notion of the everyday in modern literature and society.[28] Drawing upon the writings of such people as Walter Benjamin, Michel de Certeau and Henri Lefebvre, this body of theory sees 'everyday life' as an important category for exploring both the alienation of the modern subject under late capitalism and the continuing resistance to it. Of central interest to this inquiry is the very problem of defining and representing what 'everyday life' and 'the everyday' is in the first place, with the suspicion being that the utopian element of the everyday might lie precisely in its tendency to escape, or evade, official representation and control. In his 2006 study *Everyday Life: Theories and Practices from Surrealism to the Present*, Michael Sheringham plays with the notion that, in spite of all appearances, realist fiction might be a 'poor conductor' of everydayness, not because of its fictionality, but because of its deep-seated tendency to abstraction, its preference for knowledge over practice. There is something in the functionalist logic of narrative, so the argument goes, that is at odds with a true recognition of the everyday and always striving to turn it into 'background'. Against this Sheringham sets Benjamin's figure of 'The Storyteller', who emerges as a kind of narrative artisan, still part of the human community, who tells stories that are full of know-how and that stem from lived experience. To be fair to Dickens, such is the episodic nature of his fiction, and particularly the fictions that were sold in serial instalments, that there is more of the everyday in his work than in many of his contemporaries. The possibility remains, however, that the notoriously hybrid form of the periodical sketch might be ultimately better placed to capture the elusive flight of everydayness than the High Victorian novel. 'No genre can lay claim to the everyday', Sheringham argues, 'but subversive practices that cut across generic divisions have often been productive.'[29]

Paradoxically, the focus on poverty, disease and the 'Condition of England' in Dickens's mature fiction does help feed a narrative of progress, if only in the sense of there being *work to be done*. The secret reward for bourgeois philanthropy in identifying realms of social benightedness is that it can continue to represent history as a prospective mission. A somewhat different emphasis is produced by *Boz*. Stories in this collection regularly focus on ruin (as in 'Scotland Yard') or forms of succession that are not progression. Indeed, for the most part Boz seems to use the word 'progress' in its Hogarthian – that is, ironic – sense. In 'Shops and their Tenants', for example, he says that 'one of our principal amusements is to watch the gradual progress – the rise and fall – of particular shops'

(p. 36). Progress as rise and fall; reincarnation as failure – these are recurrent themes in this work. The experience of modernity is by and large one of brief rapture followed by disappointment. In 'Shabby Genteel People' Dickens focuses on that habit among the not-so-well-to-do of trying to bring their threadbare coats back to life through the use of a liquid 'reviver', whose effect is that of temporary sparkle quickly followed by rapid decline (p. 162). Similarly it is said of Horatio Sparkins that 'his countenance brightened up like an old hat in a shower of rain'. Despite his youthful cheek, Horatio has (it seems) already got the mark of the soon-to-be-shabby-genteel all over him: an artificial creature who will only ever be subject to the most superficial, and short-lived, of renovations. One way of interpreting these similes, and these stories, is to consider the extent to which they represent allegories of lower-middle-class ontology, and of the lower-middle-class experience of modernity in general, as being, essentially, one of *dynamic stasis*, the frequent, and predictable, return of the same.

Eternal juvenility; arrested development: in this way the Cockneys of the *Sketches* can be seen to epitomize the experience of waiting at the heart of the modern everyday, an experience that the High Victorian novel would invariably strive to transcend with its quasi-religious commitment to 'progress'. In 'Thoughts About People', which was first published in the *Evening Chronicle* on 23 April 1835, we can see many of the distinctive oppositions that characterize Dickens's *Sketches* as a whole. 'There is a numerous class of people in this great metropolis,' Boz writes, 'who seem not to possess a single friend, and whom nobody appears to care for.'

> We were seated in the enclosure of St. James's Park the other day, when our attention was attracted by a man whom we immediately put down in our own mind as one of this class. He was a tall, thin, pale person, in a black coat, scanty gray trousers, little pinched-up gaiters, and brown beaver gloves. He had an umbrella in his hand – not for use, for the day was fine – but, evidently, because he always carried one to the office in the morning. He walked up and down before the little patch of grass on which the chairs are placed for hire, not as if he were doing it for pleasure or recreation, but as if it were a matter of compulsion, just as he would walk to the office every morning from the back settlements of Islington. It was Monday; he had escaped for four-and-twenty hours from the thraldom of the desk; and was walking here for exercise and amusement – perhaps for the first time in his life. We were inclined to think he had never had a holiday before, and that he did not know what to do with himself. (p. 131)

Once again, as in 'Meditations on Monmouth Street', Boz deduces a whole life from a few stray details, and once again, as in the 'Streets – Morning' essay, time-discipline and the compulsive habits that it engenders are brought to the forefront. In its interest in institutionalization, this essay looks forward to later nineteenth-century fiction – particularly that of Edgar Allan Poe and Herman Melville. But it also looks back to Lamb, whose *Last Essays of Elia* had been published only a couple of years before. Specifically, the dialogue is with 'Oxford in the Vacation' where Elia had acknowledged himself 'a votary of the desk – a notched and cropt scrivener – one that sucks his sustenance, as certain sick people are said to do, through a quill',[30] and with 'The Superannuated Man', that late essay on the bittersweet pleasures of clerkly retirement.[31]

There is a gentle, autumnal tone to 'The Superannuated Man', but earlier, and in his letters, Lamb had complained bitterly about not knowing what to do on Sundays. Dickens's 'Thoughts about People' explores this predicament, as it were, from the outside, guessing or inferring the clerk's inner alienation from his outward habits. If the experience of the urban poor, as described in 'Seven Dials', is akin to that of hell, always intense, always local and always inescapable, then the experience of the white-collar Cockney is much closer to that of limbo. It is an everyday life of structured shuttling, of pure repetition and routine. Crucial to an account of his condition is Geoffrey Crossick's sense of the lower middle class as being painfully pitched between old-style community, on the one hand, and the freedom of the bourgeois individual on the other. Isolated without being freed, they are always in danger of degenerating, like the South Sea clerks in Lamb's first 'Elia' essay, into a class of bachelor-drones, taking no part in (because they have already been superseded by) history. Cut off from the future, they are also, to a significant degree, alienated from the past, with the dull round of the years having effectively erased it from their memory, replacing older forms of social or communal identity with nothing but a bare set of day-to-day working habits.

This is the closest Dickens comes in *Sketches by Boz* to an intellectual critique of Cockneyism – to a detached analysis of modern-day metropolitan life. It is in this sense broadly comparable with Hazlitt's essay 'On Londoners and Country People'. It has a similar structure too, beginning with the negative side of lower-middle-class metropolitan life before moving on to something more positive. In his 1823 essay Hazlitt had segued from an attack on Cockney vanity and presumption to a discussion of a few colourful individuals to an affirmation of the independent and democratic spirit that still prevails in big cities. It is a suggestive and subtle movement. In his sketch, by contrast, Dickens moves from an analysis of his solitary bachelor clerk to a brief portrait of a rich, selfish bourgeois bachelor before ending with a flamboyant celebration of some Cockney apprentices walking down to the West End on a spree.

> Each of the gentlemen [they are young apprentices] carried a thick stick, with a large tassel at the top, which he occasionally twirled gracefully round; and the whole four, by way of looking easy and unconcerned, were walking with a paralytic swagger irresistibly ludicrous. One of the party had a watch about the size and shape of a reasonable Ribstone pippin, jammed into his waistcoat pocket, which he carefully compared with the clocks at St. Clement's and the New Church, the illuminated clock at Exeter 'Change, the clock of St. Martin's Church, and the clock of the Horse Guards. (p. 133)

'Great men by proxy', these apprentices have time on and in their hands, for the next few hours at least, and are enjoying every minute of what is (in effect) an anti-commute.

> When they at last arrived in St. James's Park, the member of the party who had the best made boots on, hired a second chair expressly for his feet, and flung himself on this two-pennyworth of sylvan luxury with an air that levelled all distinctions between Brooks's and Snooks's, Crockford's and Bagnigge Wells.

'Your Cockney is your only true leveller', as Hazlitt had said in 1823, metropolitan fantasy making up the shortfall between Islington and St James's. Dickens's essay ends, as it began, in St James's Park – one of the city's first great pleasure-gardens, a place of recreation and resort since the seventeenth century. The interesting thing, of course, is that the solitary clerk and the party-going Cockney are, in a sense, two sides of the coin, they are not different types but two different aspects of the same type, or, to put it another way, the one is what the other may yet become. Other stories in *Boz* hint at the secret link between the buoyant young gent and the disappointed bachelor. 'The New Year' is particularly interesting in this respect, functioning as a chillier version of *A Christmas Carol*, for it is made very clear that no matter how much effort Mr Tupple puts into ingratiating himself with the boss's family and friends at their New Year party, there is still no prospect of him marrying his daughter. (Recent memories of Dickens's own experiences of the Beadnell family are clearly in the background to this story.) Cockney dandyism, in stories such as this, is an escapist fantasy of the lower middle class, a performative distraction from everyday social reality, a brief pantomime of belonging. In 'Thoughts about People', however, this satirical pessimism is carefully controlled, so that just when the amusement at the apprentices in question seems about to spill over into open ridicule, Boz steps in to remind himself, and us, of how even

Cockney vanity is still preferable to the 'precocious puppyism' and 'whiskered dandyism' of West End youth.

'What a strange infatuation', Hazlitt had written in 'On the Look of a Gentleman' (1821), 'to live in a dream of being taken for what one is not – in deceiving others, and the same time ourselves.'[32] In this formulation Hazlitt puts his finger on the central irony of lower-middle-class man, the fact that, for him, cultural and political confidence expressed itself in nothing so much as an overwhelming desire to disguise himself as someone else, so that social ambition becomes paradoxically synonymous with a will-to-disappear. Dickens, young dandy that he was, can be seen to have understood this caterpillar mentality better than most, and it is a mark of *Boz* and *Pickwick Papers* that all treatments of costume, performance, anonymous authorship and disguise are always shot through with a peculiar intensity, probably because they were so close to home. Fanciful imaginings and false consciousness shackle the Cockney at the beginning of Hazlitt's 'On Londoners', but in its conclusion he discovers a democratic consciousness that turns all these vices into virtues. In Dickens's *Sketches*, however, politics, and political thinking, is not part of the Cockney repertoire. The only choice is between dandy and drone.

Pickwick Papers

Thinking back on the time when he first embarked upon *Pickwick Papers*, Dickens remembered that his friends had tried to warn him against it, saying that 'it was a low, cheap form of publication', by which he should 'ruin' all his 'rising hopes'.[33] It was 'cheap' because it was published in illustrated serial format, like *Life in London*. It was 'low', one presumes, because it started out as part of the well-worn genre of Cockney sporting literature, made famous by the Jorrocks novels of Surtees, comic tales of clueless metropolitans cavorting about the country. That Dickens transformed the original plan completely, and with astonishing success, is well known. But it is still worth remarking on the extent to which friends thought it a come-down from the (relatively) respectable world of the newspaper sketch, and a dangerous flirtation with a hybrid form. What is noticeable, however, is how much this freed up Dickens's comic imagination. *Pickwick* is almost identical in subject matter to the *Sketches by Boz*: its focus is still primarily on the Cockney milieu – on bachelors, clerks, medical students and servants, on public houses and lodging houses, on the mobile and the misplaced. But its tone is markedly different.

Where the *Sketches* are consistently supercilious, *Pickwick* is comic and celebratory, and the humour has to do with character as well as class.

One way of regarding *Pickwick* is to think of it as a kind of wish-fulfilment in fictional form. The novel is full of London bachelors eating and drinking, having a good time and getting into scrapes. It is also a kind of hall-of-mirrors in which all of the characters are variations on one another. Even the mock-villains, Mr Jingle, the strolling actor, and his servant Job Trotter, are, at bottom, nothing but fraudulent, feckless versions of Mr Pickwick and Sam, a mirroring which is reinforced by the fact that they are continually ghosting one another's movements, as in the famous moment towards the end of the novel when Pickwick discovers Jingle alongside him in the Fleet Prison. Most of the central characters of the novel are easily placed within the Cockney universe: Pickwick is a retired businessman from Goswell Street, Benjamin Allen and Bob Sawyer are bibulous medical students from Lant Street in the Borough (which is where Dickens's family had stayed when his father was in the Marshalsea). The two main exceptions to this rule are Sam Weller and Alfred Jingle. And it is in relation to these two social amphibians that Dickens was to express both his dreams, and his anxieties, about Cockney ambition.

Sam Weller's speech is unmistakeably vulgar from the start: he mixes up his 'v's and 'w's like a low character from an eighteenth-century comedy, and speaks in a common dialect.

> 'Wotever is, is right, as the young nobleman sveetly remarked wen they put him down in the pension list 'cos his mother's uncle's vife's grandfather vunce lit the king's pipe vith a portable tinder-box.'
>
> 'Not a bad notion that, Sam,' said Mr Bob Sawyer approvingly.
>
> 'Just wot the young nobleman said ev'ry quarter-day arterwards for the rest of his life,' replied Mr Weller.[34]

Clever and cocky as he is, Sam's speech fixes him in the realm of the London labouring class, and at the end of a long tradition of popular wisdom. His Wellerisms are the metropolitan equivalent of rural proverbs, an odd mixture of the sagacious and the streetwise. It is the self-same form that Lear's Fool had used in the anecdote about the Cockney who put the eels into the paste alive. Mr Jingle, however, is not so easily placed. Indeed, when he introduces himself to the Pickwick Club, he gives his address as 'No Hall, Nowhere'. And his speech is similarly idiosyncratic too:

> 'Heads, heads – take care of your heads!' cried the loquacious stranger, as they came out under the low archway, which in those days formed the entrance to the coach-yard. 'Terrible place – dangerous work – other day – five children – mother – tall lady, eating sandwiches – forgot the arch – crash – knock – children

look round – mother's head off – sandwich in her hand – no mouth to put it in – head of a family off – shocking, shocking! Looking at Whitehall, sir? – fine place – little window – somebody else's head off there, eh, sir? – he didn't keep a sharp look out enough either – eh, sir, eh?' (I, ch. 2, p. 9)

There is always a moral to Sam's monologues, but with Jingle's little shorthand essays – Pickwick actually describes his manner of speech as a 'system of stenography' – we are always left up in the air. As his name suggests, Jingle's sharp speech give us a chain of loose links, a quick jangle of associations. He reminds us of P. G. Patmore's automaton writer. There is something very funny, and exhilarating, about the speed with which Jingle leaps from one thing to another, bypasses difficulties, cuts to the chase. But does he, as Sam Weller surely does when delivering a Wellerism, get the joke? Is he aware of the dangerous insouciance of his guillotine style? Is that why he draws our attention to Charles I, and why Dickens has him claiming to have been a combatant in the Paris Revolution of 1830? Or is it simply a species of pathological expression in him – the pronoun-free patter of someone who doesn't understand what is proper either to himself or to anybody else? Either way, it is the perfect medium for a Cockney confidence man, coming hard upon the heels of Fauntleroy, Hayward and Hardy Vaux.

The collective quest of the characters in *Pickwick Papers*, although it is never stated as such, is to get married, but it is also their collective nightmare as well. Becoming hooked up to a rich widow is one of the text's leading fantasies – that's what Mr Jingle is all about – but it is also its deepest fear. Tony Weller, Sam's father, has an implacable aversion to widows, having been bitten rather badly in the past. What distinguishes the novel from the *Sketches by Boz*, in fact, is the enthusiasm with which it embraces the bachelor life. Where Boz had been as interested in ambitious milliners' girls and seamstresses as he had been in rowdy lawyer's clerks, the *Pickwick Papers* is interested in women only insofar as they represent the final destination of one's rambles, whether it be a heaven or a hell. There is nothing salacious in *Pickwick* but of all Dickens novels it is perhaps the one that seems the most frank about sexuality, and the most openly amused by it. At the Great White Horse in Ipswich, Mr Pickwick ends up getting into a single woman's bed by mistake, and is terrified when he sees her on the other side of the room, heavily festooned with yellow curl papers, getting ready to join him. There are various entanglements and elopements in the novel. Mr Jingle attempts to make off with a rich spinster quite early on. And then, of course, there is the famous case of Bardell and Pickwick, in which Mrs Bardell, Mr Pickwick's landlady, takes him to court for breach of promise (having become convinced that he proposed to her in his rooms one morning, when he was in fact talking about Sam Weller). There is a certain fear of women in *Pickwick Papers*, and indeed one of its underlying suggestions is that the strongest, most romantic relationships are actually those between men. When the sincerely repentant Mr Jingle and Job Trotter set off for Demerara at the end, they are described as 'a worthy couple' by Pickwick's solicitor Mr Perker. So too the two hard-drinking medical students Tim Allen and Bob Sawyer, the latter having been beaten to the hand of Arabella Allen by Pickwick's friend Mr Wardle, are shown going off to India together in the closing pages. Last but not least, there is the love affair between Sam and Pickwick, which Dickens describes as being 'a strong and reciprocal attachment which nothing but death will terminate' (and this in spite of the fact that Sam does find himself married at the end). The overall fantasy here, it seems to me, is homosocial rather than homosexual, it is a dream of companionable rambling and mobile belonging.

In spite or perhaps even because of this, however, it is very important to Dickens that the gently libertine atmosphere of *Pickwick Papers* should be brought to an end at some point, partly, perhaps, because it is all about young men at a particular stage of life (before marriage and Malthus step in to stake their claims), but also because the space it opened up for the writer was as anxiety-ridden as it was enticing. The very indeterminate quality of the vagabond life worried him. And it is during the scenes in the Fleet Prison, towards the end of the novel, that this is most forcibly pressed upon us. In chapter 40 Pickwick is imprisoned for debt because he has refused, on principle, to pay the costs of his trial in the Bardell and Pickwick affair. But once locked up in the Fleet, a larger set of issues rushes in to confront him. In effect, the Fleet serves as a warning of the final destination of a 'rambling' life-style. It is also, as it were, a kind of acid test of bourgeois respectability. In Dickens's mind, as in Sam Weller's, no honest person can ever feel at home in a debtors' prison. It is not so much that the Fleet represents the nadir of abjection – although the 'poor side' of the prison is clearly not pleasant to behold – but rather that it is a place in which all bounds and divisions have been lost, in which there is no cleanliness and no privacy, and in which all boozy bonhomie is revealed, most noticeably through the character of Mr Smangle, as parasitical pretence. What Dickens only barely acknowledges, and is never concerned to indulge, is the climate of raffish gentility that continued to surround debtors' prisons, and it is in this sense that *Pickwick Papers* really is one of the first Victorian novels.

However much the young Dickens may have been aware of debtors' prisons as a rich site of metropolitan fantasy and theatricality, it was impossible for him to savour it positively, even for a moment. Not to have experienced it as a constant hell was, for him, a sign of moral depravity. In this way the Fleet Prison in *Pickwick Papers* functions as a kind of bonfire of Cockney vanity, burning away all imposture and false consciousness to get close to the real. It exposes a lot of what had been celebrated and enjoyed earlier on in the novel – the fluid and the feckless – as fraudulent and wrong. It is a mark of Dickens's complicated feelings for Mr Jingle that when he turns up in the Fleet, having been arrested for debt himself, he is but a shadow of his former self. Strictly speaking, he ought to be in his element, but when Pickwick comes across him, he is full of remorse for his former (in many ways rather minor) crimes, and his characteristic jauntiness and self-possession are nowhere to be seen. The links in his chain have been severed, and his discourse is now truly a kind of broken jingle. In Dickens's eyes, Mr Jingle had to be punished for his Cockney elusiveness and presumption. Which means that all we are left with is the insubordinate loyalty of Sam. To a far greater degree than the members of the Pickwick Club proper, it is Weller who comes up trumps when Pickwick is imprisoned. At first, Pickwick orders him away, thinking it no place for an uncorrupted young man, but then Sam immediately marches off and arranges to get himself arrested, so that he can continue to be at his master's side.

Like Egan's Peregrine Proteus, Mr Jingle is a strolling actor, and hence someone whose very being is supposed to consist in performance and disguise. But it is one of the more wilful elements of the novel that he is invariably described as sporting only the most ragged, shabby clothing, even before his failure as a con-man becomes fully apparent. The contrast with Sam Weller could not be more striking, for it seems to be part of his reward for being a loyal servant of Pickwick, both in the text and in Phiz's incomparable illustrations, that he always appears as the absolute epitome of the Cockney Swell. Sam's livery is clearly a bit 'flash' – rather dapper, in an upstart Cockney way. But it is also, Dickens makes a point of telling us, very heterogeneous and idiosyncratic, effectively blurring his servant identity.

> Mr Weller was furnished with a grey coat with the 'P.C.' button, a black hat with a cockade to it, a pink striped waistcoat, light breeches and gaiters, and a variety of other necessaries, too numerous to recapitulate. 'Well,' said that suddenly transformed individual, as he took his seat on the outside of the Eatanswill coach next morning; 'I wonder vether I'm meant to be a footman, or a groom, or

a game-keeper, or a seedsman. I looks like a sort of compo of every one on 'em. Never mind; there's change of air, plenty to see, and little to do; and all this suits my complaint uncommon, so long life to the Pickvicks, say I.' (1, ch. 12, p. 119)

'Good', dialect-speaking, salt-of-the-earth Cockneys (the safely low figures of early-modern comedy) had been pitted against 'bad' Cockney upstarts before. One recalls Tom Tug and Mrs Bundle in Charles Dibdin's *The Waterman* (1774). One also recalls the opposition between Caroline Bowles's washerwoman and her 'Cockney School' poet lodgers in the February 1823 issue of *Blackwood's Magazine*. But what is interesting about the opposition in *Pickwick* is the way in which many of their respective qualities have been confused. It is in the extremity of this transfusion that we can see how far Dickens felt he had to repudiate the Mr Jingle in himself – and to transform it into a tribute to Sam Weller. For Sam is not, finally, a true picture of a working-class Londoner, but rather a Cockney Swell who has had all his upstart qualities removed. Early on in the novel Sam expresses a desire to be a gentleman, but he seems to have completely forgotten this ambition by the end. And indeed, in many respects, he is a genie who has been put back in the bottle, a bright, energetic young Cockney who, quite absurdly, chooses to remain low.

In *Sketches by Boz* the kind of cool impudence displayed by Sam had been the sole property of young swells and omnibus cads: here it is bestowed upon a mere 'boots', a lowly tavern menial – because that was what Sam was before Pickwick found him. To Renton Nicholson this was the only thing wrong with the novel – the fact that Sam Weller was, frankly, impossible: 'Although Sam Weller was a quaintly drawn character, as a component part of a highly finished novel', he wrote in *The Town* for 10 February 1838,

yet, with due deference to Mr Dickens – for whose abilities, by the way, we entertain the highest respect – he was anything but a genuine *boots*. As a flash groom, Mr Weller was a perfect picture – rather out of place as a footman, and wholly so as a tavern menial. That thorough knowledge of the world which he is made to evince, could never have been acquired in such a situation, and a man possessing it could never have become the drudge at the Borough Inn.[35]

A more snobbish and less sociologically acute version of the same suspicion was expressed in the *Quarterly Review*, where the reviewer 'constantly' detected Sam and his father 'in the nice and even critical use of words and images borrowed from sources wholly inaccessible to them'. Sam and Tony were, it seems, too clever for their class; revisions, rather than reflections, of reality. But in spite or perhaps even because of this, the *Quarterly* liked what it saw, and marvelled at the broad appeal of Dickens's Cockney invention: 'We once', the reviewer continued, 'heard a celebrated beauty jocularly propose a party to which none were to be admissible who did not consider Sam Weller essentially a gentleman.'[36]

There is indeed a mythic quality about Sam Weller, which looks forward to some of the equally impossible Cockney caricatures of late-nineteenth-century music hall. In Sam, Dickens had taken the figure of the Cockney, which had been a signifier for all that was ambiguously threatening about the free-floating city-dweller in the 1820s and 1830s, and miraculously transformed it into a reassurance against such anxieties, a synonym for everything rooted, loyal and content to be low. *Pickwick Papers* can be seen to mark the transition from the Romantic to the Victorian period in this respect, and the end of the 'Cockney Moment' as we have chosen to describe it. For even though it begins with a thoroughgoing celebration of Cockney amphibiousness, by the end it makes an elaborate point of tossing the infernal creature back into the water, first by banishing all its fakes and swells (Jingle and Trotter, Sawyer and Allen), and second by remaking the Pickwick–Weller connection into one of the most old-fashioned of master–servant relationships.

Many years later John Forster was to wax lyrical about the 'perfect naturalism' of Sam Weller in his *Life of Dickens*. But the manner in which he did so only serves to suggest the exact opposite:

> When indeed the relish has been dulled that makes such humour natural and appreciable, and not [Sam Weller's] native fun only, his ready and rich illustration, his imperturbable self-possession, but his devotion to his master, his chivalry and his gallantry, are no longer discovered, or believed no longer to exist, in the ranks of life to which he belongs, it will be worse for *all of us* than for the fame of his creator.[37]

Never has Sam Weller's mythic status been pointed up so eloquently and yet so inadvertently, with the consequence being that, as we read this statement over, we can't help but start thinking about all the bourgeois anxieties, about the lower orders generally and about Cockneys in particular, that Sam's character might have helped to allay.

Great Expectations

In their different and sometimes complicated ways Hunt, Hazlitt and Lamb had all been supportive of lower-middle-class identity. They had also been seen as such by their conservative antagonists. To the *Examiner* set, the situation and even the shortcomings of the lower middle were now at the very centre of modern life. They represented 'the people' in its most liberal and aspirational aspect. Dickens, who was in many ways the culmination of this tradition, clearly felt this too, but such were the times and his own position as a popular novelist that, even had he wanted to, he could not have written with the same kind of Cockney assertiveness that Hunt had adopted in the late 1810s. He was forced to pay tribute to the emergent bourgeois norm.

In a splendid article, written some fifteen years ago, Arlene Young reminds us of where the bourgeois animus against the lower middle classes lay: 'When the *parvenu* appears', she writes, 'bourgeois identity is threatened because of the overall similarity of the two classes, a problem that is exacerbated by the rapid growth of the lower middle class.'[38] The middle-class technique for dealing with this, she argues, was one of disparagement and belittlement, a consistent insistence on the essentially *petty* nature of the petty bourgeoisie. To this end, representations of the lower middle classes in the High Victorian period often fell into one of two main categories. They tended to be either Swells – that is, cheap, fake dandies a little like Hunt – or they were Clerks – cowed, feminized office workers a little like Lamb's Elia. *Punch*'s 'Natural History of the Gent' (1847) is an example of the former; and its portrait of 'The Clerk' in its 'Guide to Servants' is the epitome of the latter. Dickens himself had played quite a major role in consolidating these stereotypes – as we can see from 'Thoughts about People' – but that didn't mean that his mature novels always upheld them. Or, if they did, it was often with a strong sense that some of these characteristics might not always be quite as ridiculous, or pitiable, as was usually assumed.

Dickens struggles within his shackles, playing many variations on Clerk and Swell. Newman Noggs, Ralph's odd-eyed bibulous assistant in *Nicholas Nickleby* is a sympathetic version of the poor bachelor clerk; Dick Swiveller from *The Old Curiosity Shop* is a feckless swell who finally reforms himself. Mr Guppy, the lawyer's clerk in *Bleak House*, is a pert and shallow Cockney of the first water, but Bob Cratchit, Scrooge's poor clerk in *A Christmas Carol*, is something very close to Dickens's ideal. The novelist's lower-middle-class characters were too low, and too circumscribed, to qualify as full-blown protagonists, at least according to the cultural and political norms of the period. But his heart's home was always with them, as was occasionally noticed at the time. There are of course one or two exceptions to this rule. Walter Gay, the young clerk in *Dombey and Son*, does get to marry the boss's daughter, but this is only after he has spent a large chunk of the novel at sea and had his Cockney cobwebs, and, in effect, his class identity, blown away. Without this experience he would have been in the same position as John Chivery, the dandyish turnkey's son in *Little Dorrit*, who, however close he might be to the bourgeois hero Arthur Clennam in character and disposition, still lacks the latter's outgoing moral vision.

Of course, the best-known portrait of a Cockney in Dickens's mature fiction is John Wemmick in *Great Expectations*, and in some ways Wemmick expresses the ambivalence Dickens felt about the lower middle class in its fullest and richest form. By day Wemmick is clerk to Jaggers, the criminal lawyer in Little Britain in the City; in the evenings and on Sundays he is the suburban Cockney par excellence. Pip the narrator is invited to Wemmick's little cottage in Walworth on the strict understanding that a clear separation be made between his host's life as a professional man and what he calls his 'Walworth sentiments', the romantic, familial and ruralizing propensities that he displays when at his own property. *Great Expectations* was written in 1859–60 but the action of volume II is set in 1823. Wemmick's suburban ideology is thus precisely contemporary with the *Essays of Elia*. It is also clear from Dickens's manuscript notes that Wemmick is nearly fifty when Pip first meets him – which was Lamb's vintage in 1823. The novel silently draws on the literature of the Cockney School then, but it also recalls early 1820s anti-Cockney satire. It was in Walworth that Christopher Cockney had unsuccessfully tried to settle himself in his 'Rural Recollections' of August 1822: 'I managed however to scrape enough together to enable me to leave the smokey metropolis', Cockney writes, 'and retire to Walworth, to a neat cottage, with about twelve yards of garden ground behind, and a fine view of a cow-field in front. I was a whole month in altering, improving, and decorating.'[39] In this way Dickens's portrait of Wemmick, like his treatment of Cockneys generally, can be seen to owe as much to conservative traditions as it does to the essays of Hunt, Lamb and Hazlitt; indeed in many ways it can be seen as a brilliant synthesis of the two. There is a special comic gravity in his rendering of such characters, a unique balance of judgement and enjoyment, sympathy and satire.

Pip develops a real affection for Wemmick and his way of life at Walworth; but this doesn't prevent him from being very funny about his Cockney false consciousness. Wemmick's cottage is, let us remember, made of wood, 'with the queerest gothic windows' and a gothic door, 'almost too small to get in at', with the top cut out and painted like a battery mounted with guns. The house itself is set in a sea of allotments, and connected to a makeshift 'bower'. 'I am my own engineer, my own carpenter, my own plumber and my own gardener', says Wemmick proudly. His father, the Aged P., describes the whole property as a 'pretty pleasure ground', and says that 'this spot and these beautiful works upon it ought to be kept together by the Nation … for the people's enjoyment'.[40] Not only is Walworth close to Dulwich, and Soane's Cockney Picture Gallery, it also seems that Wemmick's house, like Soane's House Museum, is intended for public bequest. While narrating his first stay, Pip can't help making a number of jokes about the diminutive size of everything at Walworth, from the garden fountain to the little moat that surrounds the cottage. As his own life in London becomes increasingly insecure, however, he comes to love the cottage and his inhabitants, and stands as best man at Wemmick's deceptively impromptu wedding.

In many ways, the manner in which Wemmick has arranged his life looks suspiciously like success: he is the Cockney Triumphant – a man of pure private cultivation – a lower-middle-class hero. Tight-lipped and mechanical at work, he is relaxed and amiable in the suburbs, having created a kind of harmless fantasy world for his own and his old father's enjoyment. Seen purely in terms of the politics of the everyday, Wemmick is an unsung hero, picking playfully out of the open pockets of the morning and evening a little freedom and a little fantasy. The Aged P. functions as Wemmick's own Borough beggar-in-residence in this respect – and their little nine o'clock cannon is a regular tribute to the pleasures of the moment. Placed where they are in Dickens's novel, the Walworth scenes are clearly meant for our enjoyment and endorsement, functioning as they do as welcome light relief from the dark Magwitch–Compeyson plot that is all the while gathering pace on the other side of the water. But however admirable and amusing he might be, and however much he might speak to our own modern suburban sensibilities, Wemmick does have his moral limits – limits that are not made evident in anything Dickens says of him directly, but which become quite evident when we think of him in relation to the novel's central narrative.

Seen in the broadest terms, the Pip–Magwitch relationship can be read as an allegory of modern capitalist society, and its secret, suppressed links between labour and capital, production and consumption, crime and money, the bourgeois self and its dirty plebeian origins. Pip is made to feel bad about all of this. He feels guilty about wanting to leave the forge, ashamed when Estella draws attention to his dirty hands at Satis House, guilty to have been embarrassed by Joe's behaviour in London, and guilty that he is ashamed of his benefactor Magwitch. Snobbishness is only part of the point here. Guilt and shame, especially when directed towards the past, and to the people in one's past, are in many ways the natural responses of a person whose life has been riven by ambition, or split by a movement from one place, or set of allegiances, to another. Bad feelings are what recall, and yet also stand in place of, old repressed connections, overgrown paths. What happens to Pip, in the course of his story, is that the disparate elements of his life are constantly being brought into painful proximity: Magwitch and the forge, the forge and Satis House, Joe and London, Estella and Magwitch. What is more, it is his duty, as protagonist, to 'come to terms' with these discrepancies, to find a way of bringing them together. It is this aim, and this achievement, that renders Pip a true hero, for it is his best, indeed his overriding ambition to try to see the whole.

Pip's hard lesson in the novel is the extent to which the 'taint of Newgate' lies upon everything, himself, his money, even Estella. What is interesting, of course, is the extent to which exactly the same might be said of Wemmick. As clerk to a criminal lawyer, he makes all of his money from crime. His salary is paid by Jaggers's criminal defendants, and the mourning rings he wears on his fingers are a continual reminder of their dying tributes. But such is the absolute separation he has made between work and home, city and suburb, that all connection between his Little Britain existence and his Walworth idyll has been ruthlessly suppressed. His entire life, then, is built upon a kind of structural hypocrisy – the absolute denial of all connection between his profession and his recreation, his suburban home and the salary that made it possible. He is a monster of privatized imagination and privatized feeling.

It is one of the functions of Dickens's lower-middle-class characters, I would argue, to act as foils for his bourgeois protagonists, to present an alternative vision of modernity, and modern subjectivity, in which there is no transcendent vision, only blinkered awareness, and no infinite mobility, only shuttling stasis. Modern history emerges, in this parallel model, not as the endlessly unfurling progress beloved of Victorian bourgeois ideology, but as a form of arrested development. This is Dickens's way of registering a kind of scepticism about nineteenth-century progress, and of showing the pleasures, and limits, of cultivating one's (suburban) garden. Nowadays, the socio-cultural category 'lower middle class' no longer seems quite relevant to us, in spite or perhaps even because of the fact that, strictly speaking, it is the stratum to which most people now belong. But the structural ironies and ambiguities that dogged this class's existence in the nineteenth century still continue to apply. Suburbanism, upstartism and the effect of the metropolis upon mental life have all continued to be discussed right up until our own day, but it was during the 'Cockney Moment', I would argue, that the conversation was at its freshest, as many of the most characteristic discrepancies and disproportions of modern life were put under the microscope for the first time.

One example of this is contained in the January 1824 issue of the *New Monthly Magazine*. The article is entitled, amusingly and provocatively, 'The Upstarts', and is addressed to the prejudices of an unnamed London bourgeois, who sees his neighbour, a great Cockney tallow-chandler, pass by his window in a new coach and four. 'The very aristocratic pride in which these prejudices arise is itself founded on the thing it derides', the narrator explains, 'the first founders of the oldest families were upstarts.'[41] What follows is a piece very delicately balanced between mock and earnest. 'Truly', the writer acknowledges, 'an upstart has his uses … at the present moment, the paltry extravagance of the mere estated spendthrift, cannot waste and dilapidate half fast enough to keep industry in employment. It is the upstart alone who can spend like a gentleman' (p. 432). There is, of course, a satirical volte-face, but even when it arrives, there is a surprising sense of the Cockney upstart as a significant figure, a new presence in society, a comic neighbour and ironic double for the 'hypocrite lecteur': 'As a foil they set off; as a rival, they stimulate; but, best of all, as a neighbour, they supply a perpetual fund of never-failing awkwardnesses and absurdities, to glad your heart, amuse your company, feed your malignity, and banish your *ennui*' (p. 433).

Notes

Abbreviations
Blackwood's Edinburgh Magazine = *Blackwood's*
New Monthly Magazine = *NMM*
London Magazine = *LM*

INTRODUCTION

1 Leigh Hunt, *Autobiography*, 2 vols. (New York: Harpers, 1850), I, p. 292. Subsequent page references will be given after quotations in the text.
2 Anthony Holden, *The Wit in the Dungeon: The Life of Leigh Hunt* (London: Little, Brown, 2005), p. 73. For further details on Hunt's life in prison, see chapters 16–18 of Nicholas Roe's *Fiery Heart: The First Life of Leigh Hunt* (London: Pimlico, 2005).
3 There was a marked contrast, in this respect, between Hunt's attitude and that of his older brother John, who had been imprisoned on the same charge in Coldbath Fields Prison in Islington.
4 But however ground-breaking 'A Day by the Fire' might have seemed on its first outing, the great prominence it later came to enjoy, in the minds of friends and enemies alike, was largely due to its reappearance in the second volume of Hunt and Hazlitt's *Round Table* (1817).
5 Leigh Hunt, *The Reflector*, 2 vols. (London: John Hunt, 1811), I, p. 400. Subsequent references will be reproduced after quotations in the text.
6 Thomas De Quincey, 'Confessions of an English Opium-Eater, Being an Extract from the Life of a Scholar: Part II', *LM* (October 1821), 367–9.
7 Leigh Hunt, 'Sonnet to Hampstead', *Examiner* (29 August 1813), 556.
8 'The Bard of Horsemonger Lane', *The Satirist* (October 1813), 302–7.
9 'And when this jape is tald another day | I sal been halde a daffe, a cokenay!'; Geoffrey Chaucer, 'The Reeve's Tale', in *The Canterbury Tales*, ed. F. N. Robinson (Oxford University Press, 1985), p. 58, ll. 4207–8.
10 All of these possibilities are discussed in Samuel Pegge's *Anecdotes of the English Language, Chiefly Regarding the Dialect of London* ... (London: J. Nichols, 1803), pp. 23–34.
11 'The Cockney', *New London Magazine* (September 1788), 495.
12 'The Genius', *London Magazine, or Gentleman's Monthly Intelligencer* (August 1761), 424.

13 'The Bard of Horsemonger Lane', 306–7.
14 'Theatrical Examiner No. 131', *Examiner* (14 March 1813), 170.
15 In a letter to *The Athenaeum* of 11 February 1832, Charles Lamb bore witness to this character's continuing fame when he compared it unfavourably with one of Munden's Cockneys, from a little-known farce called *Johnny Gilpin*: 'The thing ran but one night', Lamb writes, 'but when I say that Liston's *Lubin Log* was nothing to it, I say little; it was transcendent' (p. 96)
16 Theoretically, the term Cockney might include anyone who came from London who was not an aristocrat; in practice, however, the appellation seems to have been restricted to those people, or fictional characters, upon whom the influence of the metropolis had been seen to 'rub off' in one way or another.
17 See Gareth Stedman Jones, 'The "Cockney" and the Nation 1780–1988', in *Metropolis London: Histories and Representations since 1800*, ed. by David Feldman and Gareth Stedman Jones (London and New York: Routledge, 1989), pp. 272–324.
18 Charles Dibdin, *The Waterman, or, the First of August, a Ballad Opera in Two Acts* (London: James Pattie, 1838).
19 William Matthews's *Cockney Past and Present: A Short History of the Dialect of London* (London: George Routledge and Sons, 1938), pp. 25–61 offers an interesting survey of this field, albeit one that focuses almost exclusively on the way in which the Cockney was represented linguistically.
20 In *The Connoisseur* No. 79, there is a portrait of a likeable, if idiosyncratic Cockney egotist who invites the correspondent to the *Cockney's Feast*, where, he assures him, 'you'll be mighty merry, and hear a good many good songs'; (July 1755), 469–74.
21 Geoffrey Crossick, 'The Emergence of the Lower Middle Class in Britain: A Discussion', in *The Lower Middle Class in Britain 1870–1914*, ed. by Geoffrey Crossick (London: Croom Helm, 1977), p. 12.
22 Edward Gibbon Wakefield, *England and America*, 2 vols. (London: Bentley, 1833), I, p. 102.
23 Pegge, *Anecdotes*, p. 2.
24 Holden, *The Wit in the Dungeon*, pp. 95–9; Roe, *Fiery Heart*, pp. 241–2, 268–75.
25 Leigh Hunt, 'On Periodical Essays', *Examiner* (10 January 1808), 26.
26 'Social Genealogy', *The Indicator* No. 6 (17 November 1819), 41. All page references to this work are taken from the collected edition, 2 vols. (London: Appleyard, 1822).
27 Jane Stabler has written splendidly on this sonnet in 'Leigh Hunt's Aesthetics of Intimacy', *Leigh Hunt: Life, Poetics, Politics*, ed. Nicholas Roe (London: Routledge, 2003), pp. 95–117.
28 Leigh Hunt, 'To Robert Batty, M.D., on His Giving me a Lock of Milton's Hair' – 'To the Same, on the Same Subject', in *Foliage, or Poems Original and Translated* (London: C. and J. Ollier, 1818), p. cxxxii.
29 See Marilyn Butler, 'The Cult of the South', in *Romantics, Rebels and Reactionaries* (Oxford University Press, 1981), pp. 113–37; Nicholas Roe, *John Keats and the Culture of Dissent* (Oxford University Press, 1997).

30 Leigh Hunt, 'Household Gods of the Ancients', *Indicator* No. 5 (10 November 1819), 38.
31 Leigh Hunt, 'Pleasant Recollections Connected with Various Parts of the Metropolis', *Indicator* No. 3 (27 October 1819), 23.
32 Leigh Hunt, 'Mists and Fogs', *Indicator* No. 8 (1 December 1819), 59.
33 'Godiva', *Indicator* No. 3 (27 October, 1819), p. 19.
34 Leigh Hunt, *Companion* No. 2 (16 January 1828), 10. All page references to this periodical are taken from the collected edition (London: Hunt and Clarke, 1828).
35 Lord Byron, *Journal*, 1 December 1813, in *Letters and Journals of Lord Byron*, ed. Thomas Moore (Frankfurt, 1830), p. 197.
36 William Hazlitt, 'Mr T. Moore – Mr Leigh Hunt', in *The Spirit of the Age* (London: Colbourn, 1825), p. 390.
37 John Keats, 'To George and Georgiana Keats', 16 December 1818–4 January 1819, in *Selected Letters*, ed. Robert Gittings (Oxford University Press), p. 181.
38 [J. G. Lockhart], 'Letter from Z. to Leigh Hunt, King of the Cockneys', *Blackwood's* (May 1818), 200–1.
39 This is a phrase from Greg Kucich's impressive essay, 'Cockney Chivalry: Hunt, Keats and the Aesthetics of Excess', in *Leigh Hunt: Life, Poetics, Politics*, ed. by Nicholas Roe (London: Routledge, 2003), p. 125.
40 Ostensibly referring to the *Story of Rimini*, Z. recalled 'those many melancholy prison hours, when [Hunt] sought to beguile the punishment inflicted on him for the outrage he had committed against his sovereign by the whisper of that Italian muse who "visited his slumbers nightly", and breathed into his ear all the agonies and all the transports of an incestuous passion'. *Blackwood's* (May 1818), 197.
41 'On the Cockney School of Poetry No. I', *Blackwood's* (October 1817), 39.
42 Anna Clark, *The Struggle for the Breeches: Gender and the Making of the British Working Class* (Berkeley: California University Press, 1995), ch. 2.
43 Richard Altick, *The English Common Reader: A Social History of the Mass Reading Public 1800–1900* (Chicago University Press, 1957), p. 83.
44 'On the Cockney School of Poetry No. IV', *Blackwood's* (August 1818), 519.
45 'Cockney School of Poetry No. I', 39.
46 J. G. Lockhart, 'Extracts from Mrs. Wastle's Diary', *Blackwood's* (March 1820), 690.
47 Kevin Gilmartin, *Print Politics* (Cambridge University Press, 1996), p. 220.
48 Roe, *Fiery Heart*, p. 46.
49 In a poem of 1811 entitled 'Politics and Poetics', Hunt represented himself as a poet temporarily diverted from his vocation by political necessity. See Gilmartin, *Print Politics*, p. 197.
50 'Cockney School of Poetry No. I', 40.
51 'On the Cockney School of Poetry No. II', *Blackwood's* (November 1817), 198.
52 'Cockney School of Poetry No. II', 198.
53 'Cockney School of Poetry No. I', 39.

54 'Cockney School of Poetry No. I', 39.
55 Leigh Hunt, 'To Horatio Smith', in *Foliage*, pp. cxxviii–cxxvix.
56 'Hunt's *Foliage*', *Eclectic Review* (November 1818), 493.
57 'The Drama', *Literary Chronicle* (17 November 1821), 733.
58 'This whimpering, maudlin Philosopher is as tenacious of innovation as the late Mr. Burke, and as great an admirer of *the good old times* as the Editor of a modern journal'; [William Hazlitt?], *Examiner* (28 July 1816), 474.
59 *British Stage* (September 1817), 193.
60 *British Stage* (September 1817), 200.
61 Tokely died young in 1821, a victim of intemperance, but he was still being remembered more than twenty years afterwards. See 'Outpourings', *Bentley's Miscellany* (July 1845), 450: 'Poor Tokely! His Cockneys were excellent!'
62 *Theatrical Inquisitor* (September 1820), 238.
63 'Theatrical Examiner No. 409', *Examiner* (1 October 1820), 632.
64 That there was an interest in Cockneys outside London and Edinburgh is not hard to demonstrate. To give but one example, not only did the Liverpool-based *Kaleidoscope* reprint several of Hunt's *Indicator* essays in 1820, it also maintained a lively interest in Cockney satire. See 'Literary Recollections of London', *Kaleidoscope* (8 February 1820), 123 and 'The Cockney Sportsman', *Kaleidoscope* (18 September 1821), 84.
65 One notable non-*Blackwood's* example is the series 'The Cockney School of Prose Writers' in the *NMM*, which attacked Hazlitt's recent lecture series at the Surrey Institution. No. I (October 1818) 198–202, No. II (November 1818) 299–304, No. III (January 1819) 487–492.
66 'Pleasant Walks: A Cockney Pastoral, in the Manner of Leigh Hunt, Esq.', *Literary Journal* (March 1819), 192. Other non-*Blackwood's* examples include 'A Cockney Pastoral', *NMM* (March 1819), 133; 'Cockney Balaam: A Dinner at the Johnson's Court, Bolt-Court, Fleet-Street', *Knight's Quarterly Magazine* (October 1823), 331–5; 'A Visit from a Wit', *Literary Magnet* (January 1824), 183–5.
67 Sporting satires of the period include 'The Cockney Sportsman', *Kaleidoscope* (18 September 1821), 84; Thomas Hood, 'A Cockney's Rural Sports', *LM* (December 1822), 498–507; 'Philosophy in a Punt, or the Delights of Cockney Angling', *Literary Gazette* (4 October 1823), 636; 'The Cockney's Journal', *Mirror of Literature* (6 September 1824), 251–2; 'The First of September, or the Confessions of a Cockney', *Mirror of Literature* (9 September 1826), 147–8.
68 'The First of September', 147.
69 See, for example, 'Wine and Walnuts, or After Dinner Chit Chat, by a Cockney Greybeard', *Literary Gazette* (21 October 1820), 680–2; 'London Lanes', *Literary Chronicle* (August 1823), 541–2.
70 Some non-*Blackwood's* examples include 'A Description of a Voyage to Gravesend, by Caleb Cockney, Esq.', *Literary Speculum* (April 1822), 420–6; 'Rural Recollections of Christopher Cockney, Gentleman', *Literary Speculum* (August 1822), 151–9; and 'The Last of the Cockneys!' *Literary Magnet* (July 1824), 125–7.

71 'The London 'Prentices', *NMM* (August 1822), 172.
72 'Dinner in the Steam-Boat', *NMM* (September 1824), 258.
73 Theodore Hook, *John Bull* (14 February 1825).
74 'The London University and the "Smutty Gazette"', *Examiner* (17 July 1825), 447.
75 William Hazlitt, 'On Nicknames', *Edinburgh Magazine* (September 1818), 243.
76 See Dror Wahrman, *Imagining the Middle Class: The Political Representation of Class in Britain c.1780–1840* (Cambridge University Press, 1995).
77 On the construction of middle-classness as the invisible middle in the polite periodicals of the period, see Jon Klancher, *The Making of English Reading Audiences 1789–1832* (Madison: Wisconsin University Press, 1987).
78 Leigh Hunt, 'Autumnal Commencement of Fires – Mantel-Pieces – Apartments for Study', *Indicator* No. 2 (20 October 1819), 10. Further references to this issue are given after quotations in the text.
79 Of those works not cited so far, the following have been particularly crucial to this study: Kim Wheatley, 'The *Blackwood's* Attacks on Leigh Hunt', *Nineteenth-Century Literature*, 47 (June 1992), 1–31; Elizabeth Jones, 'Keats in the Suburbs', *Keats–Shelley Journal*, 45 (1996), 23–43; Richard Cronin, 'Keats and the Politics of Cockney Style', *Studies in English Literature*, 36, 4 (1996), 785–806.
80 An event that is brilliantly discussed in the opening chapter of Richard Cronin's recent *Paper Pellets, British Literary Culture after Waterloo* (Oxford University Press, 2010).
81 'Hood's Whims and Oddities', *Blackwood's* (January 1827), 45.
82 For a classic discussion of the political ambiguity of the lower middle class, see Arno J. Mayer, 'The Lower Middle Class as Historical Problem', *Journal of Modern History*, 47, 3 (1975), 409–36. Jonathan M. Wiener countered Mayer's sense of the lower middle class as an increasingly reactionary agent in his 'Note: Marxism and the Lower Middle Class – A Response to Arno Mayer', *Journal of Modern History*, 48 (1976), 666–71.
83 'A Batch of Architects', *Fraser's Magazine* (March 1837), 338.
84 W. T. Moncrieff, *Gypsy Jack, or the Napoleon of Humble Life* (London: Cumberland, 1835).
85 See Stedman Jones, 'The "Cockney" and the Nation', pp. 272–324.

1 LEIGH HUNT, JOHN KEATS AND THE SUBURBS

1 *Indicator* No. 1 (13 October 1819), 1. This introductory section appeared in the original weekly issue only. See *The Indicator* BL. 5382, p. 1, in the British Library.
2 F. M. L. Thompson, *The Rise of Suburbia* (Leicester University Press, 1982), p. 2.
3 Ann Bermingham, 'Middle Grounds and Middle Ways', in *Landscape and Ideology: The English Rustic Tradition 1740–1860* (New York and London: Thames and Hudson, 1986), p. 168.
4 'The Last of the Cockneys', *Literary Magnet* (June 1824), 127.
5 Bermingham, *Landscape and Ideology*, p. 170.

6 Jones, 'Keats in the Suburbs', 27.
7 Hunt, *Foliage*, p. 18.
8 Elizabeth Jones, 'Suburb Sinners: Sex and Disease in the Cockney School', in Roe, ed., *Leigh Hunt: Life Poetics, Politics*, pp. 78–94.
9 Leigh Hunt, *The Story of Rimini* (London, Edinburgh and Dublin: John Murray, 1816), Book III, ll. 485–6, p. 71.
10 See Jones, 'Keats in the Suburbs' and 'Suburb Sinners'.
11 'Cockney School of Poetry No. IV', 521.
12 *The Works of Lord Byron with His Letters and His Life*, 14 vols., ed. by Thomas Moore (London: John Murray, 1832), V, p. 171.
13 'A Cockney Pastoral', *NMM* (March 1819), 133.
14 'Letter from a Contributor in Love', *Blackwood's* (October 1823), 472.
15 James Stevens Curl, *Spas, Wells and Pleasure-Gardens of London* (London: Historical Publications, 2010), p. 39.
16 Cyrus Redding, 'The Tea-Garden', *LM* (August 1822), 138–9.
17 W. S. Scott, *Bygone Pleasures of London* (London: Marsland, 1948), p. 15.
18 *Bagnigge Wells, a Satirical Poem* (London, 1779). British Library, General Reference Collection T.660.(12.)
19 Warwick Wroth, *The London Pleasure Gardens of the Eighteenth Century* (London: Macmillan, 1896), p. 7.
20 One has only to compare Wilkinson's *London Directory* map of 1811 with Greenwood's map of 1827 to see the dramatic change that had taken place in this area. A number of the London maps of the period are well displayed at www.oldlondonmaps.com.
21 'Original Correspondence: Sketch', *Literary Gazette* (August 1822), 517.
22 'Four Views of London', *NMM* (June 1833), 195.
23 'Review of *Hints on Ornamental Gardening*', *Literary Chronicle* (July 1823), 437.
24 'Rural Recollections', 158–9.
25 'Crockery's New Lamentations', *Literary Chronicle* (22 March 1823), 188.
26 'London Lanes', *Literary Chronicle* (23 August 1823), 541.
27 William Clarke, *Every Night Book, or Life After Dark* (London: Richardson, 1827), p. 36.
28 Leigh Hunt, *The Descent of Liberty, A Mask* (London: Gale, Curtis and Fenner, 1815), p. 23.
29 Leigh Hunt, 'The Political Examiner: Disturbances in the Metropolis', *Examiner* (8 December 1816), 769.
30 Leigh Hunt, 'Country Houses Near Town', *Indicator* No. 1 (13 October 1819), 6.
31 Leigh Hunt, 'Far Countries', *Indicator* No. 9 (8 December 1819), 72.
32 Leigh Hunt, 'On the Realities of the Imagination', *Indicator* No. 24 (22 March 1820), 190.
33 Leigh Hunt, 'Objects of the London Journal', *Leigh Hunt's London Journal* No. 23 (3 September 1834), 177. Quoted in Kevin Gilmartin's *Print Politics*, p. 226.

34 Leigh Hunt, 'Sunday in the Suburbs', *Leigh Hunt's London Journal* No. 51 (18 March 1835), 84.
35 Redding, 'The Tea-Garden', 139.
36 Leigh Hunt, 'The Nymphs', in *Foliage*, pp. vi–vii.
37 'Foliage; or, Poems Original and Translated by Leigh Hunt', *NMM* (September 1818), 163.
38 'Hunt's *Foliage*', *Eclectic Review* (November 1818), 488.
39 *Indicator* No. 15 (19 January 1820), 114.
40 Sergei Ouvaroff, *Essay on the Mysteries of Eleusis*, trans. by J. D. Price, with observations by James Christie (London: Rodwell and Martin, 1817), p. 125.
41 S. T. Coleridge, *Biographia Literaria*, ed. by Nigel Leask (London: Dent, 1997), p. 175.
42 Leigh Hunt, 'The Stories of Lamia &c. as Told by Mr Keats', *Indicator* No. 43 (2 August 1820), 341.
43 Leigh Hunt, 'Young Poets', *Examiner* (1 December 1816), 761–2.
44 'Cockney School of Poetry No. IV', 522.
45 Hunt, *Autobiography*, II, p. 240.
46 Thomas Hood, *Hood's Own, or Laughter from Year to Year* (London: Baily, 1839), p. 289.
47 Most notably in 'On the Aristocracy of Letters', published in vol. II of *Table-Talk* (1822).
48 'Cockney School of Poetry No. IV', 521.
49 *Endymion, A Poetic Romance* (London: Taylor and Hessey, 1818), Book I, ll. 320–31, pp. 18–19.
50 Leigh Hunt, *The Poetical Works of Leigh Hunt* (London: Moxon, 1832), p. 124.
51 Scott, *Bygone Pleasures of London*, pp. 16–19.
52 'Cockney School of Poetry No. IV', p. 522.
53 John Keats, 'Ode to a Nightingale', in *Lamia, Isabella, The Eve of St. Agnes and Other Poems* (London: Taylor and Hessey, 1820), pp. 107–12.
54 Hunt, *Foliage*, p. vi.
55 Marjorie Levinson, *Keats's Life of Allegory* (Oxford University Press, 1988), p. 9.
56 See especially David Trotter, *Paranoid Modernism* (Oxford University Press, 2001) and 'The Invention of Agoraphobia', *Victorian Literature and Culture* (2004), 463–74.
57 Leigh Hunt, 'More News of Ulysses', *Indicator* No. 9 (8 December 1819), 65.
58 Leigh Hunt, 'The Nurture of Triptolemus', *Indicator* No. 50 (20 September 1820), 393. Further page references are given after quotations in the text.
59 It is interesting, in this light, to consider that only a few days before the publication of 'The Nurture of Triptolemus', Hunt had been writing a piece in *The Examiner* on the recent Portuguese Revolution: 'These are certainly the times for novelty and great excitements', he wrote, 'Let us hope, as we do, that they are the times for great and lasting improvements.' *Examiner* (17 September 1820) p. 593.

60 James Christie, *A Disquisition upon Etruscan Vases Displaying Their Probable Connection with the Shows at Eleusis* (London: William Bulmer, 1806), p. 78.
61 Thomas Taylor, *The Eleusinian and Bacchic Mysteries* (Amsterdam, 1790), p. 130.
62 Leigh Hunt, 'November', in *The Literary Pocket-Book, or Companion for the Lover of Nature and Art* (London: C. & J. Ollier, 1819), pp. 120–1. The copy in the British Library (BL Mark C.60.b.7) belonged to Mary Russell Mitford and is in effect her diary for 1819.
63 A John Tomkins, Esq. had also been invoked, in a very similar context, in the Preface to *Foliage*, p. 13. It is intriguing to note the liberal use that Dickens was to make of such surnames in the Cockney satires in *Sketches by Boz*, especially when one considers their similarity to his own.
64 Leigh Hunt, 'Sprit of the Ancient Mythology' *Indicator* No. 15 (19 January 1820), 113.
65 Leigh Hunt, 'The Stories of Lamia &c.' [part 2], *Indicator* No. 44 (9 August 1820), 345.
66 Hunt, 'The Stories of Lamia &c.' [part 2], 350.
67 Crockery Junior, 'Nature Outdone', *Literary Chronicle* (24 May 1823), 331.

2 WILLIAM HAZLITT AND THE PERIODICAL PRESS

1 William Hazlitt, 'Table Talk No. VII: On Londoners and Country People', *NMM* (August 1823), 171. Further references are given after quotations in the text. The essay was republished in *The Plain Speaker* of 1826.
2 His most extended attack on the Hartleyan philosophy is contained in his early *Essay on the Principle of Human Action* of 1805.
3 Hunt, 'Country Houses Near Town', 7.
4 Hunt, 'Far Countries', 72.
5 [Evans Eyre Crowe], 'Hazlitt's Table-Talk', *Blackwood's* (August 1822), 159.
6 Jon Klancher, 'Reading the Social Text', in *The Making of English Reading Audiences*, pp. 47–75.
7 Lee Erickson, 'Ideological Focus and the Market for the Essay', in *The Economy of Literary Form: English Literature and the Industrialization of Publishing 1800–1850* (Baltimore: Johns Hopkins University Press, 1996), p. 89.
8 Hazlitt himself was briefly arrested for debt in February 1823. See Stanley Jones *Hazlitt: A Life* (Oxford University Press, 1989), p. 343.
9 'The General Question', *Blackwood's* (September 1823), 338.
10 See William Maginn's 'Profligacy of the London Periodical Press', *Blackwood's* (August 1824).
11 P. G. Patmore, 'On Magazine Writers', *LM* (July 1822), 25. Further references are given after quotations in the text.
12 John Mullan, *Anonymity, A Secret History of English Literature* (London: Faber & Faber, 2007), p. 190.
13 John Scott, 'Blackwood's', *LM* (November 1820), 511–12.

14 'Town Conversation: Cockney Writers', *LM* (January 1821), 69–70. Further references are given after quotations in the text.
15 Theodor Adorno, 'The Essay as Form', in *New German Critique* (Spring–Summer 1984) p. 152–3.
16 In the 'Letter from Dr. Olinthus Petre to Christopher North Esq', *Blackwood's* (November 1820), 208.
17 'The Works of Charles Lamb', *Blackwood's* (August 1818), 599.
18 Leigh Hunt, 'On the Sight of Shops', *Indicator* No. 34 (31 May 1820), 265–2; 'A Nearer View of the Sight of Shops', *Indicator* No. 35 (7 June 1820), 273–8.
19 'Works of Charles Lamb', *Blackwood's* (August 1818), 600.
20 William Hazlitt, 'The Periodical Press', *Edinburgh Review* (May 1823), 349–50.
21 'Letter of Timothy Tickler to Eminent Literary Characters No. VIII', *Blackwood's* (August 1823), 219. Further references are given after quotations in the text.
22 William Hazlitt, *Table-Talk, or Original Essays on Men and Manners*, 2 vols., 2nd edn (London: Colbourn, 1824), II, p. 63. Further references are given after quotations in the text.
23 William Hazlitt, 'Table Talk No. I: On Going a Journey', *NMM* (January 1822), 73–9. Intriguingly, this essay appeared in the very same issue of the *NMM* as Redding's 'London and the Country'.
24 Hazlitt, *Table-Talk*, II, p. 72.
25 Hazlitt, *Table-Talk*, II, p. 235.
26 See the last chapter of John Barrell's *The Political Theory of Painting from Reynolds to Hazlitt: The Body of the Public* (New Haven, CT: Yale University Press, 1986) p. 320–38; also John Whale, 'Hazlitt on Burke', *Studies in Romanticism*, 25 (1986), 465–81.

3 *LIBER AMORIS* AND LODGING HOUSES

1 William Hazlitt, *Liber Amoris, or the New Pygmalion* (London: John Hunt, 1823), p. 64. Further references are given after quotations in the text.
2 Roland Barthes, 'Ravishment', in *A Lover's Discourse: Fragments*, trans. Richard Howard (Harmondsworth: Penguin, 1990), p. 190.
3 Bryan Waller Proctor (Barry Cornwall), *An Autobiographical Fragment and Biographical Notes* (London: George Bell and Sons, 1877), p. 181.
4 Hazlitt, *Table-Talk*, II, p. 391–2.
5 For biographical discussion of the Sarah Walker affair, see especially Duncan Wu, *William Hazlitt: The First Modern Man* (Oxford University Press, 2008), chs. 17–20; Jon Cook, *Hazlitt in Love* (London: Short Books, 2007); A. C. Grayling, *The Quarrel of the Age: The Life and Times of William Hazlitt* (London: Weidenfeld & Nicolson, 2001), pp. 252–92; Jones, *Hazlitt*, pp. 319–42; and P. P. Howe, *The Life of William Hazlitt* (London: Hamish Hamilton, 1947), pp. 306–33.
6 See Sarah and William Hazlitt, *Journals 1822–1831*, ed. by W. Bonner (University of Buffalo Press, 1959), pp. 171–271.

7 Jones, *Hazlitt*, pp. 336–7.
8 William Hazlitt, 'The Fight', *NMM* (February 1822), 102.
9 William Hazlitt, 'On Great and Little Things', *NMM* (February 1822), 135.
10 P. G. Patmore, *My Friends and Acquaintances* (London: Saunders and Otley, 1854), II, p. 311.
11 Hazlitt, *Table-Talk*, II, p. 299.
12 Hazlitt, *Table-Talk*, II, p. 343.
13 Hazlitt, *Table-Talk*, II, pp. 354–5.
14 Haydon, *The Diary of Benjamin Robert Haydon*, 5 vols., ed. by W. B. Pope (Cambridge, MA: Harvard University Press, 1960–3), II, pp. 375–6.
15 Proctor, *An Autobiographical Fragment*, pp. 180–1.
16 The 'Journal of F' is reproduced in *Letters of William Hazlitt*, ed. by H. M. Sikes and W. H. Bonner (New York University Press, 1978), Appendix A, pp. 379–89. Stanley Jones supplied emendations to this some years later in *The Library*, 5, 26 (1971), 325–6.
17 See Hazlitt, *Letters of William Hazlitt* p. 257, p. 265.
18 'Liber Amoris', *Literary Gazette* (31 May 1823), 339.
19 'The Confessions of an English Glutton', *Blackwood's* (January 1823), 86.
20 *Examiner* (11 May 1823), p. 314.
21 William Hazlitt, 'The Round Table', *Examiner* (14 April 1816), 237, reproduced as 'Character of Rousseau', in *The Round Table* (1817).
22 William Hazlitt, 'Simplicius on the Poor Laws', *Cobbett's Political Register* (January–June 1807), 402.
23 See Gregory Dart, 'Sour Jacobinism: William Hazlitt and the Resistance to Reform', in *Rousseau, Robespierre and English Romanticism* (Cambridge University Press, 1999), pp. 209–46.
24 *Literary Register* (17 May 1823), 305.
25 *The Times* (30 May 1823); *Country Literary Chronicle and Weekly Review* (28 June 1823).
26 *Literary Register* (17 May 1823), 307.
27 'Liber Amoris; or the New Pygmalion', *Blackwood's* (June 1823), 645.
28 'Lectures on the Fine Arts, No. 1: George Cruikshank', *Blackwood's* (July 1823), 19.
29 'The General Question', 337.
30 Leigh Hunt, *Examiner* (15 September 1816), 588. The essay was reproduced later as 'On Washerwomen' in *The Round Table* (1817).
31 The August number had included the 'Letter from Timothy Tickler No. VIII' (by Lockhart and Maginn) which had taken issue with Hazlitt's *Edinburgh Review* article 'The Periodical Press'. This article is discussed in Chapter 2. The September issue had included 'The General Question'.
32 [Henry Thomson], 'Letter from a Contributor in Love', *Blackwood's* (October 1823), 472.
33 Caroline Bowles Southey, 'Letter from a Washerwoman', *Blackwood's* (February 1823), 235.
34 William Hazlitt, 'On Great and Little Things', *NMM* (February 1822), 128.
35 Redding, 'London and the Country', 275.

36 Leigh Hunt, 'Rousseau's Pygmalion', *Indicator* No. 31 (10 May 1820), 241.

37 Hazlitt was almost certainly aware of Stendhal's *De l'amour* (1822), in which his famous theory of crystallization was first presented, as it was reviewed in the very same issue of the *NMM* that carried 'On Great and Little Things' and 'The Fight' (February 1822).

38 Jean-Jacques Rousseau, *Julie, or the New Heloise*, trans. Philip Stewart and Jean Vaché (Hanover, NH: New England University Press, 1997), Part 1, Letter XXVI, pp. 74–6.

39 Augustine Birrell, *William Hazlitt* (London: Macmillan, 1902), p. 167.

4 PIERCE EGAN AND *LIFE IN LONDON*

1 Jeffrey N. Cox, *Poetry and Politics in the Cockney School: Keats, Shelley, Hunt and their Circle* (Cambridge University Press, 1998), p. 15.

2 'Auto-Biography of Edmund Kean', *Blackwood's* (September 1824), p. 276.

3 See Deborah Epstein Nord's *Walking the Victorian Streets: Women, Representation and the City* (Ithaca, NY and London: Cornell University Press, 1995), pp. 31–51; Roger Sales, 'Pierce Egan and the Representation of London', in *Reviewing Romanticism*, ed. by Philip W. Martin and Robin Jarvis (Basingstoke: Macmillan, 1992); and Jane Rendell, *The Pursuit of Pleasure: Gender, Space and Architecture in Regency London* (London and New Brunswick, NJ: Rutgers University Press, 2002).

4 David Cannadine, *Class in Britain* (Harmondsworth: Penguin, 1998).

5 J. C. Reid, *Bucks and Bruisers: Pierce Egan and Regency England* (London: Routledge, 1971), p. 11.

6 See, for example, *Real Life in London* (by an Amateur), 2 vols. (London, 1822).

7 W. T. Moncrieff, *Tom and Jerry; or Life in London: An Operatic Extravaganza, in 3 Acts* (London: Richardson, 1828).

8 'The Drama', *Literary Chronicle* (13 April 1822), 238.

9 A good account of this phenomenon is given in Charles Hindley's *The True History of Tom and Jerry, or Life in London from the Start to the Finish* (London, 1890).

10 Pierce Egan, *Life in London, Or the Day and Night Scenes of Jerry Hawthorn, Esq. and his elegant friend Corinthian Tom accompanied by Bob Logic the Oxonian, in their Rambles and Sprees Through the Metropolis* (London: Sherwood, Neely and Jones, 1821), pp. 19–20. Further page references given after quotations in the text.

11 On the rapid growth of London at this time, Chapter 3 of Lewis Mumford's *The Culture of Cities* (London: Routledge, 1938) still offers one of the most frightening and compelling accounts.

12 Reid, *Bucks and Bruisers*, p. 55.

13 Vic Gatrell, *City of Laughter: Sex and Satire in Eighteenth-Century London* (London: Atlantic Books, 2006), p. 539.

14 'Lectures on the Fine Arts, No. 1: George Cruikshank', 18.

15 'Pseudo-Gentlemen', *NMM* (January 1821), 305.

16 Pierce Egan, ed., *Grose's Classical Dictionary of the Vulgar Tongue*, 3rd edn (London: Sherwood, Neely and Jones, 1822) pp. v–vi.
17 *A Dictionary of Modern Slang, Cant and Vulgar Words … by an Antiquary* (London: John Camden Hotten, 1859), p. vii.
18 Of course, it should be pointed out that a dedication such as this would not necessarily have alienated contemporary radicals. Indeed, in some ways it tallied only too well with what many of them were saying about George even at the height of the Caroline affair: that he had been misled by evil advisers, and was not in himself incapable of reform. See Thomas Laqueur, 'The Queen Caroline Affair: Politics as Art in the Reign of George IV', *Journal of Modern History*, 54 (1982), 417–66.
19 'Letter to Pierce Egan, Esq. from Christopher North', *Blackwood's* (March 1821), 673.
20 On the limits of Hunt and Hazlitt's radicalism, see Gilmartin, *Print Politics*, pp. 194–223.
21 Gatrell, *City of Laughter*, pp. 530–46.
22 'Lectures on the Fine Arts, No. 1: George Cruikshank', 18.
23 'The General Question', 338.
24 James Hardy Vaux was a Cockney criminal of the period, whose *Memoirs* created a great stir in 1819.
25 Clark, *The Struggle for the Breeches*, p. 5.
26 See David R. Green, *From Artisans to Paupers: Economic Change and Poverty in London 1790–1870* (London: Scolar Press, 1995), p. 8.
27 See H. J. Dyos, 'Urban Transformation: A Note on the Objects of Street Improvement in Regency and Early Modern London', *International Review of Social History*, 2 (1967), 259–65; David R. Green, 'The Geography of Economic Change', in *From Artisans to Paupers*, pp. 140–80; and Donald Olsen, *The Growth of Victorian London* (London: Batsford, 1976).
28 'Annus Mirabilis! Or a Parthian Glance at 1822', *NMM* (January 1823), 21.
29 At this point Egan gives a long list of all the various copies and adaptations of his work since 1821.

5 CHARLES LAMB AND THE ALCHEMY OF THE STREETS

1 Walter Benjamin, 'Fashion', in *The Arcades Project*, ed. by Rolf Tiedemann, trans. Howard Eiland and Kevin McLaughlin (Cambridge, MA: Harvard University Press, 1999), p. 65.
2 Robert Southey, *Letters from England*, ed. by Jack Simmons (London: The Cresset Press, 1951), p. 51.
3 William Wordsworth, *The Prelude*, 1805 text, in *The Prelude: A Parallel Text*, ed. by J. C. Maxwell (Harmondsworth: Penguin, 1971), Book VII, ll. 193–8, p. 262.
4 Henry Southern, 'On Fashions', *LM* (August 1825), 586.
5 Lewis Mumford, *The City in History: Its Origins, Its Transformations, and Its Prospects* (New York: Harcourt Brace, 1961), p. 433.

6 Susan Buck-Morss, 'The Flâneur, the Sandwichman and the Whore: The Politics of Loitering', in *Walter Benjamin and the Arcades Project*, ed. by Beatrice Hansen (London: Continuum, 2006), p. 41. First published in *New German Critique*, 39 (Fall 1986), 99–140.
7 Charles Lamb, 'The Londoner, No. 1', *Morning Post* (1 February 1802).
8 Charles Lamb, 'Oxford in the Vacation', *LM* (October 1820), 365.
9 *Works of Charles and Mary Lamb*, 7 vols., ed. by E. V. Lucas (London: Methuen, 1903), VII, p. 563.
10 See Lucy Newlyn, '"In City Pent": Echo and Allusion in Wordsworth, Coleridge and Lamb 1797–1801', *Review of English Studies*, 32, 128 (November 1981), 408–28.
11 Lamb, 'The Londoner, No. 1' (1 February 1802).
12 *The Universal Magazine* (July 1813), 16. A large extract from Nash's *First Report on the Projected Improvements of Marylebone Park* (1812) was reproduced in this magazine on pages 14–19 of its July issue. On the class politics of Regent Street, see Dana Arnold, *Rural Urbanism* (Manchester University Press, 2005), ch. II.3 and III.2.
13 John Summerson, *The Life and Work of John Nash, Architect* (London: HarperCollins, 1980), p. 132.
14 Edmund Carrington, *Confessions of an Old Bachelor* (London: Colbourn, 1827), p. 16.
15 'The Bricks of the Modern Babylon', *LM* (September 1825), 75.
16 'Metropolitan Improvements', *Monthly Magazine* (February 1827), 122.
17 *John Bull* (18 May 1835), reproduced in the *Gentleman's Magazine* (October 1835), 438.
18 Jerry White, *London in the Nineteenth Century* (London: Vintage, 2008), p. 26.
19 Thomas Shepherd and James Elmes, *Metropolitan Improvements, or London in the Nineteenth Century* (London, 1827), p. 2.
20 See Peter Jackson, *George Scharf's London: Sketches and Watercolours of a Changing City 1820–1850* (London: John Murray, 1987); F. S. Schwarzbach, 'George Scharf and Early Victorian London', in *Victorian Artists and the City*, ed. by I. B. Nadel and F. S. Schwarzbach (London and New York: Pergamon Press, 1980).
21 See J. H. Stallard, *London Pauperism amongst Jews and Christians …* (London: Saunders and Otley, 1867), p. 271.
22 Mumford, *The Culture of Cities*, p. 204.
23 John Ruskin, 'Of the Turnerian Picturesque', in *Modern Painters* (London: Smith, Elder and Co., 1856), IV, pp. 7–14.
24 W. H. Bodkin, *The First Report of the Society Established in London for the Suppression of Mendicity* (London: Warr, 1819), p. 9.
25 See M. J. D. Roberts, 'Taming the Masses, 1815–34', in *Making English Morals: Voluntary Association and Moral Reform in England 1767–1886* (Cambridge University Press, 2004) and 'Reshaping the Gift Relationship: The London Mendicity Society and the Suppression of Begging in England 1818–1869', *International Review of Social History*, 36 (1991), 201–31.
26 Roberts, *Making English Morals*, p. 108.

27 Charles Lamb, 'A Complaint of the Decay of Beggars in the Metropolis', *LM* (June 1822), 533.
28 Wordsworth, 'The Old Cumberland Beggar. A Description', *Lyrical Ballads*, 2nd edn, 2 vols. (London: Longman and Rees), II, 156.
29 See E. V. Lucas's note to 'The Decay of Beggars', in his *Works of Charles and Mary Lamb*, II, p. 386.
30 Susan Buck-Morss, *The Dialectics of Seeing: Walter Benjamin and the Arcades Project* (Cambridge, MA and London: MIT Press, 1991), p. 184.
31 Charles Lamb, 'Poor Relations', *LM* (May 1823), 533.
32 Walter Benjamin, *Origin of German Tragic Drama*, trans. John Osborne (London: Verso, 1998), p. 177.
33 John Thomas Smith, *Vagabondiana, etc.* (London: J. McCreery, 1817), p. 14.
34 Sport or freak of nature (or of accident).
35 Henry Mayhew, ed., *London Labour and the London Poor*, 4 vols. (London: 1861–2), IV, p. 47.
36 Charles Lamb, 'Imperfect Dramatic Illusion', *LM* (August 1825), 600.
37 Michel de Certeau, *The Practice of Everyday Life*, trans. Stephen Rendall (Berkeley: California University Press, 1984), chs. 2 and 3 especially.
38 Charles Lamb, 'The Superannuated Man', *LM* (May 1825), 68.

6 JOHN MARTIN, JOHN SOANE AND COCKNEY ART

1 See Claude Rich, *Memoir on the Ruins of Babylon* (London: Longman, 1815), p. 58 and Thomas Maurice, *Observations on the Ruins of Babylon as Recently Visited and Described by Claudius James Rich Esq.* (London: John Murray, 1816).
2 See 'The Bricks of the Modern Babylon', *LM* (September 1825), 75.
3 The Aramaic writing is interpreted by Daniel as MENE, MENE = God hath numbered thy kingdom and finished it, TEKEL = thou art weighed in the balance and found wanting, and PARSIN = thy kingdom is divided and given to the Medes and the Persians. See 'The Book of Daniel', *The Oxford Bible Commentary*, ed. by John Barton and John Muddiman (Oxford University Press, 2001), p. 566.
4 'The British Institution', *Monthly Magazine* (March 1821), 175. For a more positive view of Martin's bringing together of 'nearly all the branches of painting' see *NMM* (March 1821), 108.
5 'Illustrations of the Bible', *Westminster Review* (April 1834), 455.
6 Charles Lamb, 'Barrenness of the Imaginative Faculty in the Productions of Modern Art', in *Last Essays of Elia* (London: Moxon, 1833), pp. 172–3.
7 Hughes's poem was first recommended to Martin by his fellow painter Washington Allston, who was also at work on his own version of *Belshazzar*.
8 T. S. Hughes, *Belshazzar's Feast* (Cambridge: J. Smith, 1818), p. 26.
9 John Martin, *A Description of the Picture Belshazzar's Feast* (London: J. Robins and Co., 1821), p. 2.
10 Mary L. Pendered, *John Martin, Painter, His Life and Times* (London: Hurst and Blackett, 1923), p. 24.
11 'Fine Arts: British Institution Gallery', *NMM* (March 1821), 108–9.

12 Edward Bulwer-Lytton, *England and the English*, 2 vols. (London: Bentley, 1833), II, p. 211.
13 Allan Cunningham, *Life of Sir David Wilkie* (London, 1843), pp. 56–7.
14 John Constable, *Memoirs of the Life of John Constable, Composed Chiefly of His Letters*, ed. by John Leslie (London, 1845), p. 86.
15 [Thomas G. Wainewright], 'The British Institution', *LM* (April 1821), 443.
16 In 1834 the art critic of the *Westminster Review* said of Martin that 'the time is not far distant when his merits will find their true level, and his pictures be appreciated as the inventions of an ingenious scene-painter' (April 1834), 452.
17 'The British Gallery', *Blackwood's* (March 1821), 685.
18 William Kitchener, M.D., was the author of *Apicius Redivivus, or the Cook's Oracle*, 1817.
19 Lamb, *Works*, VII, p. 731.
20 On Martin as an 'objective' and Turner as a 'subjective' painter of sublime history paintings, see Martin Meisel, 'The Material Sublime: John Martin, Byron, Turner and the Theater', in *Images of Romanticism: Verbal and Visual Affinities* (New Haven, CT: Yale University Press, 1978).
21 William Hazlitt, 'On the Elgin Marbles: The Ilissus', *LM* (May 1822), 448.
22 John Ruskin, *Works of John Ruskin*, 39 vols., ed. by E. T. Cook and Alexander Wedderburn (London: Allen, 1904), X, p. 223.
23 Benjamin Robert Haydon, *Life of Benjamin Robert Haydon*, 3 vols., ed. by Tom Taylor (London: Longman, 1853), II, p. 100.
24 *Illustrated London News* (17 March 1849), 177.
25 On the stylistic links between Martin and Gandy see, for example, the *Westminster Review* (April 1834), 458.
26 On John Britton's connections with Soane and Gandy, see J. Mordaunt Crook, 'John Britton and the Genesis of the Gothic Revival', in *Concerning Architecture*, ed. by John Summerson (Harmondsworth: Penguin, 1968), pp. 98–120.
27 See Brian Lukacher's *Joseph Gandy: An Architectural Visionary in Georgian England* (London: Thames and Hudson, 2006).
28 The point was still being made about Gandy's drawings some thirteen years later: 'We really wish Gandy would descend a little from his ultra-classicism, ultra-poetry, and monstrous sublimities, and favour us with something approaching nearer to the realities of architecture'; 'Exhibition of the Royal Academy: Architectural Drawings', *Arnold's Magazine of the Fine Arts* (June 1834), 150.
29 'T.C.', *The Guardian* No. 77 (27 May 1821), n.p.
30 On Soane's genuine eclecticism as an architect, see Peter Collins, *Changing Ideals in Modern Architecture* (London: Faber & Faber, 1965), p. 22.
31 *Confessions of an Old Bachelor* (London: Colbourn, 1827), p. 17.
32 'On the Architecture of the New Churches', *Magazine of the Fine Arts*, I (1821), 130–8; 'Architectural Portraiture', *Magazine of the Fine Arts*, I (1821), 459–63.
33 The quotations in this paragraph are taken from Gillian Darley, *John Soane: An Accidental Romantic* (New Haven, CT and London: Yale University Press, 1999), pp. 175, 234–5, 272.

34 *Eclectic Review* (April 1829), 312.
35 'Mr Soane', *Examiner* (10 December 1815), 794.
36 Leigh Hunt, 'Remarks on the Past and Present State of the Arts in England', *Reflector* (1811), 1, 230.
37 'Fine Arts: Royal Academy', *Literary Gazette* (5 June 1824), 362.
38 'Modern Architecture', *Literary Magnet* (January 1824), 62.
39 [Thomas Whitwell?], 'The Sixth or Boeotian Order of Architecture', *Knight's Quarterly Magazine* (April 1824), 456–7. The stupidity of the inhabitants of Boeotia in Ancient Greece was proverbial. In November 1830 *Fraser's* made the same connection in its list of a dozen 'Nuisances of London': '111. Soane. See the Bank of England – his own house in Lincoln's Inn Fields – the Treasury – the whole of the Boeotian order of architecture'; *Fraser's* (November 1830), 450.
40 Whitwell, whom Soane had once turned down as an architectural assistant, is also suspected of writing the *Guardian* attacks three years previously. See Darley, *John Soane*, p. 278.
41 A reference to Soane's new Insolvent Debtors' Court, 33 Lincoln's Inn Fields, built 1823–5.
42 In 1820 Soane and Gandy had exhibited a painting entitled *Architectural Visions of Early Fancy, in the Gay Morning of Youth, and Dreams in the Evening of Life.*
43 'Cockney Balaam', *Knight's Quarterly* (October 1823), 331–5.
44 Joseph Michael Gandy, 'On the Philosophy of Architecture', *Magazine of the Fine Arts*, 1 (1821), 292–3.
45 Darley, *John Soane*, p. 23.
46 David Watkin, 'Freemasonry and Sir John Soane', *Journal of the Society of Architectural Historians*, 54, 4 (1995), 402–17.
47 Helen Furjan, 'Sir John Soane's Spectacular Theatre', *AA Files, The Journal of the Architectural Association School of Architecture*, 47 (2002), 12.
48 Karl Schinkel, *English Journey*, ed. by David Bindman and Gottfried Reiman (New Haven, CT: Yale University Press, 1993), p. 114.
49 'Mr Soane's Museum', *LM* (April 1821), 431–2.
50 Darley, *John Soane*, p. 275.
51 See, for example, Christie's *Disquisition upon Etruscan Vases* (1806) and *The Worship of the Elements* (1814).
52 Ouvaroff, *Essay on the Mysteries of Eleusis*, p. 125.
53 John Soane, *Description of the House and Museum* (London: Levey, Robson and Franklin, 1835), pp. 38–9.
54 Lukacher, *Joseph Gandy*, p. 122. Years later Taylor had added a long footnote to his translation of *Pausanias' Description of Greece*, a favourite text of Gandy's, in which he had speculated further on the ancients' use of slow-burning lamps, 3 vols., (London, 1824) 1, 215–9.
55 'Mr Soane's Soiree', *Literary Chronicle* (2 April 1825), 221.
56 Letter to Miss Mitford, quoted in Olney Clarke, *Benjamin Robert Haydon: Historical Painter* (Athens: Georgia University Press, 1952), pp. 161–3.
57 Darley, *John Soane*, pp. 280–1.

58 'The Union of Architecture &c', *Eclectic Review* (April 1829), 312.
59 'The Soanean Museum', *Civil Engineer and Architect's Journal* (October 1837–December 1838), 44.
60 G. F. Waagen, 'Sir John Soane's Museum', in *Works of Art and Artists in Great Britain*, 3 vols. (London: John Murray, 1838), II, p. 181.
61 George Wightwick, *The Palace of Art and Architecture* (London: Fraser, 1840), p. 192.
62 'A Batch of Architects', (March 1837) 338. *Fraser's* had targeted Soane before. See 'The Election of Editor for Fraser's Magazine' which takes place outside the architect's house (May 1830), 496ff., and 'A Dozen Nuisances of London' (November 1830), 451.
63 Rosemary Hill, 'Cockney Connoisseurship and Keats's Grecian Urn', *Things*, 6 (Summer 1997), 6.
64 William Feaver, *The Art of John Martin* (Oxford: Clarendon Press, 1975), pp. 72–88.
65 A. W. Pugin, *Contrasts, or a Parallel between the Noble Edifices of the Middle Ages, and the Corresponding Buildings of the Present Day, Showing the Present Decay of Taste* (London, 1836), pp. 30–1.

7 B. R. HAYDON AND DEBTORS' PRISONS

1 Haydon, *Life of Benjamin Robert Haydon*, II, 162.
2 Haydon, *Diary of Benjamin Robert Haydon*, III, p. 215, 22 August 1827.
3 [Benjamin Robert Haydon], *Explanation of the Picture of the Mock Election Which Took Place at the King's Bench Prison, July 1827* (London: James Bullock, 1828) (BL. 1044. e. 15. 3), p. 5. Further references are given after quotations in the text.
4 [Edward Callow], *Whitecross and the Bench: A Reminiscence from the Past* (London: 1879), p. 148.
5 Haydon, *Diary*, III, p. 216, 30 August 1827.
6 Haydon, *Diary*, III, pp. 215–16, 26 August 1827.
7 We know this because the British Library has Haydon's own copy of the 1828 *Explanation* of the picture, in which all the names, and some biographical details, have been supplied. See *Explanation*, pp. 6–7. See also the article 'King's Bench Prison' in *The Times*, 17 July 1827.
8 'The Mock Election in the King's Bench Prison', *Mirror of Literature* (22 March 1828), 193.
9 Haydon, *Diary*, III, p. 218n.
10 Haydon, *Diary*, III, p. 216n.
11 Haydon, *Diary*, III, p. 215n.
12 Robert Cruikshank's 'Surrey Collegians Giving a Lift to a Limb of the Law (Banco Regis, or King's Bench)' appeared in a *Life in London*-style metropolitan travelogue called *The English Spy: An Original Work, Characteristic, Satirical and Humorous, Comprising Scenes and Sketches in Every Rank of Society etc. with Illustrations by Robert Cruikshank* (London: Sherwood, Jones, 1825).

13 Sir Neil Campbell, the uncle of the Major Campbell in Haydon's picture, was in the Peninsular Campaign, and was the senior officer in charge of Napoleon when he was exiled to Elba. Napoleon escaped during one of Campbell's frequent trips to Italy, although, officially at least, Campbell was not to blame.

14 'It is too true that the Major had rather a "long innings", nearly fourteen years in the situation of a lodger to Mr. Jones [the Marshall of the King's Bench]. The high spirit of the Major – his fine stamina – his great activity – and his attachment to rackets – united with considerable experience, and his "long practice" in the Racket Court, rendered him a first-rate player in every point of view.' Pierce Egan, *Book of Sports and Mirror of Life*, 2nd edn (London: Tegg, 1836), p. 228.

15 Reckless with money in general, Haydon was especially extravagant in his outlay on props and models for his pictures. See William Bewick, *Life and Letters of William Bewick*, ed. by T. Landseer, first published in two volumes in 1871 (London: EP Publishing Limited, 1978), I, pp. 267–9.

16 This is just one of the details inked into Haydon's own annotated copy of the *Explanation* (p. 3).

17 Haydon, *Life of Benjamin Robert Haydon*, I, p. 350.

18 'London Oddities and Outlines', *Blackwood's* (July 1823), 12.

19 'Buchanan's Memoirs of Painting: British Galleries of Art', *Blackwood's* (November 1824), 505.

20 Haydon, *Diary*, III, pp. 257–8, 2 March 1828.

21 Holden, *The Wit in the Dungeon*, pp. 69–70.

22 Haydon, *Diary*, III, p. 219, 12 September 1827; 'Fine Arts', *Examiner*, 12 January 1828), 29; 'Haydon's Picture of the Mock Election', *Literary Gazette* (15 December 1827), 811; 'Chairing the Member', *Literary Gazette* (11 October 1828), 651.

23 'Mr Haydon's Picture of Chairing the Members', *LM* (November 1828), 507.

24 'Fine Arts: Mr Haydon's Picture', *NMM* (January 1828), 18.

25 Quoted in Hugh Barty-King, *The Worst Poverty: A History of Debt and Debtors* (Phoenix Mill: Budding Books, 1997), p. 100. The best recent treatment of this theme, and one to which this chapter is indebted, is Margot Finn, *The Character of Credit: Personal Debt in English Culture 1740–1914* (Cambridge University Press, 2003).

26 Joanna Innes, 'The King's Bench in the Later Eighteenth Century: Law, Authority and Order in a London Debtors' Prison', in *An Ungovernable People*, ed. by J. Brewer and J. Styles (London: Hutchinson, 1980), p. 253.

27 The phrase is from Innes, 'The King's Bench', p. 255. Innes points out that on at least one occasion in the eighteenth century, creditors got so frustrated about debtors using the prison as a refuge that they sought statutory powers to compel them to come out and make a settlement.

28 That said, it does also seem that the majority of people imprisoned at any one time were actually detained on mesne process, that is, simply because they couldn't put up bail.

29 Innes, 'The King's Bench', p. 257.

30 [R. Gillies], 'O'Hanlon and His Wife', *Fraser's Magazine* (August 1836), 184–202; 'Law of Debtor and Creditor', *British and Foreign Review* (July–October 1837), 64–89. Gillies was also the author of the *Memoirs of a Literary Veteran*, 3 vols. (London, 1851), which gives an extensive account of his experiences in debtors' prison.

31 Anon., *Prison Reminiscences* (London: A. W. Bennett, 1859), p. 4.

32 Renton Nicholson, *Rogue's Progress: The Autobiography of 'Lord Chief Baron' Nicholson*, ed. by J. Bradley, first published 1860 (London: Longman, 1966), pp. 114–18.

33 See the introduction to *Rogue's Progress*, and also Donald J. Gray, 'Early Victorian Scandalous Journalism: Renton Nicholson's The Town', in *The Victorian Periodical Press: Samplings and Soundings*, ed. by M. Wolff and J. Shattock (Leicester University Press, 1982), pp. 317–48.

34 There was another mock election, in Whitecross Street Prison, only a month after the one that Haydon witnessed in the Bench, and some years later Robert Cruikshank produced an engraving of *The Evening after a Mock Election in the Fleet Prison, June 1835*. This image can be seen in the Guildhall library print room, and is reproduced in Finn's *Character of Credit*.

35 Anon., *Real Life in London*, 2 vols. (London: Jones, 1822), p. 11, 95.

36 Anon., *A Description of the King's Bench Prison, Being a Brief Review of Its Constitution, the Prison Itself, the Day Rules &c.* (London: John McShee, 1823), p. 1.

37 Charles Dickens, *Little Dorrit*, 4 vols. (Leipzig: Tauchnitz, 1857), 1, ch. 6, p. 91.

38 John Forster, *Life of Charles Dickens*, 2 vols. (London: Dent, 1966), 1, p. 26.

39 Egan, *Book of Sports*, p. 228.

40 Barty-King, *The Worst Poverty*, p. 114.

41 Officers tended to think of their prisoners as customers, or clients, rather than reprobates, an ambience accurately captured in the relationship between Chivery the turnkey and Dorrit the long-term debtor in Charles Dickens's *Little Dorrit* (1855–7).

42 *Whitecross and the Bench*, p. 133.

43 See Thackeray's portrait of Captain Shandon (William Maginn) in *Pendennis* (Leipzig: Tauchnitz, 1848–50), chs. 31–3.

44 Nicholson, *Rogue's Progress*, pp. 115–6.

45 See Innes, 'The King's Bench', p. 260.

46 Finn, *Character of Credit*, p. 145.

47 Anon., *Prison Reminiscences*, p. 28.

48 Dickens, *Little Dorrit*, 1, ch. 18, pp. 308–9.

49 'And to show the mirth that has been going forward amongst the inmates of the gaol, nothing will give a better idea than the following occurrence, which took place on Saturday. On that day, at the height of the contest, a creditor called at the gaol, and observing so much amusement going forward,

and meeting but smiling countenances, he remarked that it was no punishment to place a man there, he had him released immediately, adding that he thought he would have a better chance of getting his money than before.' 'King's Bench Prison', *The Times*, No. 13333 (17 July 1827), p. 3.

50 *The Times*, No. 13335 (19 July 1827), 2.

51 *The Times*, No. 13335 (19 July 1827), p. 3. Eventually, both sides came to a peace, and things went on very much as before. Nor was the prisoners' taste for mock elections overly diminished thereafter. Only a month later a similar event took place at Whitecross Street Prison, the main difference being that on this occasion the authorities in question made an explicit promise not to intervene upon the merriment as long as peace was maintained.

52 For Haydon in abolitionist mood, see *Diary*, III, p. 231, 9 November 1827.

53 Haydon, *Diary*, III, p. 273, 28 April 1828.

54 William Carey, *Desultory Exposition of an Anti-British System of Incendiary Publication &c.* (London: Elmes, 1819), pp. 74–5.

55 See Clarke, *Benjamin Robert Haydon* (Athens: University of Georgia Press, 1952), pp. 165–6. p. 15.

56 Haydon, *Diary*, III, pp. 233–4, 14 November 1827.

57 Haydon, *Life of Benjamin Robert Haydon*, II, p. 184.

58 Haydon, *Diary*, III, p. 182, 9 February 1827. See also Eric George, *The Life and Death of Benjamin Robert Haydon* (London: Oxford University Press, 1948), p. 180.

59 Haydon, *Life of Benjamin Robert Haydon*, II, p. 69.

60 'Fine Arts', *The Times*, No. 13483 (8 January 1828), 3. See also the *Athenaeum* review from the following day: 'The seriousness of the prominent figures in the foreground greatly assists the effect of the caricature of the middle of the picture, but whose comic character is less happily expressed' (9 January 1828), 30.

61 George, *Life and Death of Benjamin Robert Haydon*, p. 202.

62 Haydon, *Diary*, III, p. 448, 3 June 1830.

8 CHARLES DICKENS AND COCKNEY ADVENTURES

1 Charles Dickens, *Sketches by Boz* (London: Chapman and Hall, 1850), p. 31. Further references will be given after quotations in the text.

2 Crossick, *The Lower Middle Class in Britain 1870–1914*, p. 22.

3 See especially chapter 2 of Clark's *The Struggle for the Breeches*.

4 Edward Gibbon Wakefield, *England and America*, I, p. 103.

5 'Sketches by Boz', *Westminster Review* (July 1837), 196.

6 Thomas Hood, 'A Cockney's Rural Sports', *LM* (December 1822), 498–507.

7 Bowles, 'Letter from a Washerwoman', 232–6.

8 James Smith, 'The Hebdomadary of Mr Snooks the Grocer', *NMM* (January 1824), 436–40.

9 Horace Smith, 'The Steam-Boat from London to Calais', *Gaieties and Gravities*, 3 vols. (London: Henry Colbourn, 1825), pp. 277–93.

10 Arlene Young, 'Virtue Domesticated: Dickens and the Lower Middle Class', *Victorian Studies*, 39, 4 (Summer 1996), 486.
11 Mayer, 'The Lower Middle Class as a Historical Problem', 418.
12 'Germany: Revolution and Counter Revolution', quoted in Mayer, 'The Lower Middle Class as a Historical Problem', 416.
13 Albert Smith, *The Natural History of the Gent* (London: Bogue, 1847), p. 104.
14 Clark, *The Struggle for the Breeches*, p. 15.
15 [William Hazlitt], 'On the Look of a Gentleman: Table Talk No. VI', *LM* (January 1821), 41.
16 *Memoirs of James Hardy Vaux* (London: Knight and Lacey, 1824); *Pierce Egan's Account of the Trial of Mr. Fauntleroy for Forgery, 30 October 1824* (London: Knight and Lacey, 1824).
17 Pierce Egan, *The Life and Extraordinary Adventures of Samuel Denmore Hayward* (London: Sherwood, Neely and Jones, 1822), p. 85–6.
18 'The Proof-Sheet', *NMM* (January 1821), 233.
19 See Renton Nicholson's own account of his early life in *Rogue's Progress*, Chapters I–XIII.
20 See Gray, 'Early Victorian Scandalous Journalism', pp. 330–1.
21 Renton Nicholson, *Cockney Adventures and Tales of London Life* (London: W. M. Clark, 1838), No. 4: 'Parishocracy, or, A Tale of an Antiquary', p. 31.
22 'Half-a-Crown's Worth of Cheap Knowledge', *Fraser's Magazine* (March 1838), 290.
23 Nicholson, *Cockney Adventures* No. 17: 'A Lawyer's Clerk', p. 134.
24 'Sketches by Boz, Pickwick Papers (Review)', *Quarterly Review* (October 1837), 507.
25 'Some Thoughts on Arch-Waggery, and, in Especial, the Genius of "Boz"', *Court Magazine and Monthly Critic* (April 1837), 187.
26 'Review of Sketches by Boz and Pickwick Papers', *Monthly Review* (February 1837), 153.
27 'Mrs. John Jones's Pic-Nic', *NMM* (December 1833), 433–46.
28 See especially Michael Sheringham, *Everyday Life: Theories and Practices from Surrealism to the Present* (Oxford University Press, 2006); de Certeau, *The Practice of Everyday Life*; and Ben Highmore, *Everyday Life and Cultural Theory: An Introduction* (London: Routledge, 2002).
29 Sheringham, *Everyday Life*, p. 45.
30 Lamb, 'Oxford in the Vacation', 365.
31 Lamb, 'The Superannuated Man', 67–69.
32 Hazlitt, 'On the Look of a Gentleman', 41.
33 Peter Ackroyd, *Dickens* (London: Sinclair-Stevenson, 1990), p. 186.
34 Charles Dickens, *The Posthumous Papers of the Pickwick Club*, 2 vols. (London: Chapman and Hall, 1837), ch.2, 543.
35 'Characteristic Sketches: The Boots', *The Town* (10 February 1838), p. 289.
36 'Sketches by Boz, Pickwick Papers (Review)', 506.
37 Forster, *Life of Charles Dickens*, I, p. 74.

38 Young, 'Virtue Domesticated', 491. See also the larger book of which this article forms part: Arlene Young, *Culture, Class and Gender in the Victorian Novel* (Basingstoke: Macmillan, 1999).
39 'Rural Recollections', 155.
40 *All the Year Round* (16 March 1861), 529–30.
41 'The Upstarts', *NMM* (January 1824), 431.

Bibliography

PERIODICALS USED

All the Year Round
Arnold's Magazine of the Fine Arts
The Athenaeum
Beau Monde, or Literary and Fashionable Magazine
Belle Assemblee, or Court and Fashionable Magazine
Bentley's Miscellany
Blackwood's Edinburgh Magazine
British Critic
British and Foreign Review
British Magazine
British Stage
Chambers's Edinburgh Journal
The Champion
Civil Engineer and Architect's Journal
The Companion
The Connoisseur
Court Magazine
Drama
Eclectic Review
Edinburgh Review
Englishman's Magazine
European Magazine
The Examiner
Fraser's Magazine
Gentleman's Magazine
The Guardian
The Hive
Illustrated London News
Imperial Review
John Bull's Magazine
Kaleidoscope; or the Literary and Scientifice Monitor
Knight's Quarterly Magazine

Lady's Monthly Museum
Leigh Hunt's London Journal
Literary Chronicle
Literary Gazette
Literary Journal
Literary Lounger
Literary Magnet
Literary Register
Literary Speculum
London Magazine
London Magazine, or, Gentleman's Monthly Intelligencer
Magazine of the Fine Arts
The Metropolitan
Mirror of Literature
Monthly Magazine
Monthly Review
Morning Chronicle
New London Magazine
New Monthly Magazine
New Sporting Magazine
Penny Magazine
Quarterly Review
The Reflector
Robin's London and Dublin Magazine
The Satirist
Saturday Magazine
The Seer
Theatrical Inquisitor
The Times
The Town
Town and Country Magazine
Universal Magazine
Westminster Review

SELECTED PRIMARY SOURCES

Anon., *Real Life in London*, 2 vols. (London, 1822)

A Description of the King's Bench Prison, Being a Brief Review of Its Constitution, the Prison Itself, the Day Rules &c. (London: John McShee, 1823)

The English Spy: An Original Work, Characteristic, Satirical and Humorous, Comprising Scenes and Sketches in Every Rank of Society etc. with Illustrations by Robert Cruikshank (London: Sherwood, Jones, 1825)

A Dictionary of Modern Slang, Cant and Vulgar Words … by an Antiquary (London: John Camden Hotten, 1859)

Prison Reminiscences, or Whitecross Street and the Law of Imprisonment for Debt, with Facts Showing Its Cruelty and Impolicy (London: A. W. Bennett, 1859)

Ackermann, Rudolph, *The Microcosm of London* (London: Ackermann, 1808)
Bee, John, *Slang, A Dictionary of the Turf, the Ring, the Chase, the Pit, of Bon-Ton, and the Varieties of Life*, (London: T. Hughes, 1823)
Bewick, William, *Life and Letters of William Bewick*, ed. by Thomas Landseer (London: EP Publishing Limited, 1978)
Bodkin, W. H., *The First Report of the Society Established in London for the Suppression of Mendicity* (London: F. Warr, 1819)
Fourth Report of the Society for the Suppression of Mendicity (London: F. Warr, 1822)
Brenton, Edward Pelham, *A Letter to the Committee of Management of the Society for the Suppression of Mendicity in Red Lion Square* (London: C. Rice, 1830)
Britton, John, *Brief Memoir of Sir John Soane* (London: Fisher's, National Portrait Gallery, 1834)
The Union of Architecture, Sculpture and Painting (London: Longman, 1827)
Byron, George Gordon, Lord, *Letters and Journals*, ed. by Thomas Moore (Frankfurt, 1830)
The Works of Lord Byron with His Letters and His Life, ed. by Thomas Moore, 14 vols. (London: John Murray, 1832)
Callow, Edward, *Whitecross and the Bench: A Reminiscence of the Past* (London: 1879)
Christie, James, *A Disquisition upon Etruscan Vases Displaying Their Probable Connection with the Shows at Eleusis* (London: William Bulmer, 1806)
Dibdin, Charles, *The Waterman, or, The First of August, a Ballad Opera in Two Acts* (London: James Pattie, 1838)
Dickens, Charles, *Great Expectations*, ed. by Charlotte Mitchell and David Trotter (Harmondsworth: Penguin, 2003)
Little Dorrit, 4 vols. (Leipzig: Tauchnitz, 1857)
The Posthumous Papers of the Pickwick Club (London: Chapman and Hall, 1837)
Sketches by Boz (London: Chapman and Hall, 1850)
Egan, Pierce, *Book of Sports and Mirror of Life*, 2nd edn (London: Tegg, 1836)
The Finish to the Adventures of Tom, Jerry and Logic (London: Reeves and Turner, 1828)
The Life of an Actor (London: C. S. Arnold, 1825)
The Life and Extraordinary Adventures of Samuel Hayward (London: Sherwood, Neely and Jones, 1822)
Life in London, or the Day and Night Scenes of Jerry Hawthorn, Esq. and His Elegant Friend Corinthian Tom Accompanied by Bob Logic the Oxonian, in Their Rambles and Sprees Through the Metropolis, 2 vols. (London: Sherwood, Neely and Jones, 1821)
Pierce Egan's Account of the Trial of Mr. Fauntleroy for Forgery, 30 October 1824 (London: Knight and Lacey, 1824)
Recollections of John Thurtell (London: Knight and Lacey, 1824)
Sporting Anecdotes (London, 1808)
Egan, Pierce, ed., *Grose's Classical Dictionary of the Vulgar Tongue* (London: Sherwood, Neely and Jones, 1822)
Forster, John, *Life of Charles Dickens*, 2 vols. (London: Dent, 1966)

Haydon, Benjamin Robert, *Correspondence and Table-Talk*, ed. by Frederick Wordsworth Haydon (London, 1876)

The Diary of Benjamin Robert Haydon, 5 vols., ed. by W. B. Pope (Cambridge, MA: Harvard University Press, 1960–3)

Life of Benjamin Robert Haydon, 3 vols., ed. by Tom Taylor (London: Longman, 1853)

Hazlitt, William, *Complete Works*, 21 vols., ed. by P. P. Howe (London: Dent, 1932)

Journals of Sarah and William Hazlitt, 1822–1831, ed. by W. Bonner (University of Buffalo Press, 1959)

Letters of William Hazlitt, ed. by H. M. Sikes and W. H. Bonner (New York University Press, 1978)

Liber Amoris, or the New Pygmalion (London: John Hunt, 1823)

Table-Talk, 2 vols., 2nd edn (London: Colbourn, 1824)

Hood, Thomas, *Hood's Own, or Laughter from Year to Year* (London: Baily, 1839)

Thomas Hood and Charles Lamb: The Story of a Friendship, Being the Literary Reminiscences of Thomas Hood, Edited with Certain Additions by Walter Jerrold (London: Ernest Benn, 1930)

Hughes, T. S., *Belshazzar's Feast* (Cambridge: J. Smith, 1818)

Hunt, Leigh, *Autobiography*, 2 vols. (New York: Harper and Brothers, 1850)

The Companion (London: Hunt and Clarke, 1828)

Foliage, or Poems Original and Translated (London: C. and J. Ollier, 1818)

The Indicator (London: Appleyard, 1822)

The Literary Pocket-Book, or Companion for the Lover of Nature and Art (London: C. and J. Ollier, 1819)

The Reflector, 2 vols. (London: John Hunt, 1811)

Selected Writings, 7 vols., ed. by Robert Morrison, Michael Eberle-Sinatra *et al.* (London: Pickering and Chatto, 2003)

The Story of Rimini (London, Edinburgh and Dublin: John Murray, 1816)

Keats, John, *Endymion, A Poetic Romance* (London: Taylor and Hessey, 1818)

Lamia, Isabella, The Eve of St. Agnes and Other Poems (London: Taylor and Hessey, 1820)

Selected Letters, ed. by Robert Gittings (Oxford University Press, 1986)

Kenney, James, *Love, Law and Physic: A Farce in Two Acts* (London: John Cumberland, 1813)

Lamb, Charles, *Works of Charles and Mary Lamb*, 7 vols., ed. by E. V. Lucas (London: Methuen, 1903)

Martin, John, *A Description of the Picture of Belshazzar's Feast* (London: J. Robins and Co., 1821)

Mr Martin's Plan for Supplying with Pure Water the Cities of London and Westminster and of Materially Improving and Beautifying the Western Parts of the Metropolis (London, 1828)

Maurice, Thomas, *Observations on the Ruins of Babylon as Recently Visited and Described by Claudius James Rich Esq.* (London: John Murray, 1816)

Mayhew, Henry, ed., *London Labour and the London Poor*, 4 vols. (London, 1861–2)

Moncrieff, W. T., *Tom and Jerry; or Life in London: An Operatic Extravaganza, in 3 Acts* (London: Richardson, 1828)
Nicholson, Renton, *Cockney Adventures and Tales of London Life* (London: W. M. Clark, 1838)
Rogue's Progress: The Autobiography of 'Lord Chief Baron' Nicholson (London: Longman, 1965)
Ouvaroff, Sergei, *Essay on the Mysteries of Eleusis*, trans. J. D. Price, with observations by James Christie (London: Rodwell and Martin, 1817)
Parsons, Charles Edward, *Clerks: Their Position and Advancement* (London: Provost, 1876)
Payne Knight, Richard, *An Inquiry into the Symbolical Language of Ancient Art and Mythology* (London: J. Moyes, 1818)
Pegge, Samuel, *Anecdotes of the English Language, Chiefly Regarding the Local Dialect of London and Its Environs, Whence It Will Appear that the Natives of the Metropolis Have Not Corrupted the Language of Their Ancestors* (London: J. Nichols, 1803)
Place, Francis, *The Autobiography of Francis Place*, ed. by Mary Thale (Cambridge University Press, 1972)
Proctor, Bryan Waller (Barry Cornwall), *An Autobiographical Fragment and Biographical Notes* (London: George Bell and Sons, 1877)
Charles Lamb: A Memoir (London: Moxon, 1866)
Pugin, A. W., *Contrasts, or a Parallel between the Noble Edifices of the Middle Ages, and the Corresponding Buildings of the Present Day, Showing the Present Decay of Taste* (London, 1836)
Rich, Claude James, *Memoir on the Ruins of Babylon* (London: Hurst, Rees, Orme and Brown, 1815)
Ruskin, John, *The Complete Works of John Ruskin*, ed. by E. T. Cook and Alexander Wedderburn (London: George Allen, 1903)
Modern Painters, vol. IV (London: Smith, Elder and Co., 1856)
Scharf, George, *Drawings of Westminster* (London: London Topographical Society, 1994)
Journals and Notebooks, 14 vols. (1833–59)
Shepherd, Thomas, and James Elmes, *Metropolitan Improvements, or London in the Nineteenth Century* (London, 1827)
Smith, Albert, *The Natural History of the Gent* (London: Bogue, 1847)
Smith, John Thomas, *Vagabondiana* (London: J. McCreery, 1817)
Soane, John, *Civil Architecture: Designs for Completing Some of the Public Buildings in Westminster and for Correcting Defects in Others, Humbly Submitted to His Majesty* (London: J. Moyes, 1829)
Description of the House and Museum (London: Levey, Robson and Franklin, 1835)
Designs in Architecture, Consisting of Plans, Elevations and Sections for Temples, Baths etc. (London: I. & J. Taylor at the Architectural Library, 1790)
Designs for Public Improvements in London and Westminster (London: J. Moyes, 1827)
Southey, Robert, *Letters from England*, ed. by Jack Simmons (London: The Cresset Press, 1951)

Stallard, J. H., *London Pauperism amongst Jews and Christians, an Inquiry into the Principles and Practice of Out-Door Relief in the Metropolis and the Result upon the Moral and Physical Condition of the Pauper Class* (London: Saunders and Otley, 1867)
Taylor, Thomas, *The Eleusinian and Bacchic Mysteries* (Amsterdam, 1790)
Thackeray, W. M., *Pendennis* (Leipzig: Tauchnitz, 1848–50)
Waagen, G. F., *Works of Art and Artists in Great Britain*, 3 vols. (London: John Murray, 1838)
Wakefield, Edward Gibbon, *England and America*, 2 vols. (London: Bentley, 1833)
Wightwick, George, *The Palace of Art and Architecture* (London: Fraser, 1840)
Wordsworth, William, *The Prelude: A Parallel Text*, ed. by J. C. Maxwell (Harmondsworth: Penguin, 1971)

SELECTED SECONDARY SOURCES

Aaron, Jane, *A Double Singleness: Gender and the Writings of Charles and Mary Lamb* (Oxford University Press, 1991)
Altick, Richard, *The English Common Reader: A Social History of the Mass Reading Public 1800–1900* (Chicago University Press, 1957)
The Shows of London (London: Belknap Press, 1978)
Andrews, Malcolm, 'The Metropolitan Picturesque', in *The Politics of the Picturesque*, ed. by Stephen Copley and Peter Garside (Cambridge University Press, 1994)
Arnold, Dana, *Rural Urbanism* (Manchester University Press, 2005)
Balston, Thomas, *John Martin 1789–1854* (London: Whitechapel Art Gallery, 1970)
John Martin 1789–1854, His Life and Works (London, 1947)
'John Martin and Metropolitan Improvements', *Architectural Review*, 102, 612 (1947)
'John Martin: New Discoveries', *Burlington Magazine*, 93, 582 (1951)
Barrell, John, *The Political Theory of Painting from Reynolds to Hazlitt: The Body of the Public* (New Haven, CT: Yale University Press, 1986)
Benjamin, Walter, *The Arcades Project*, ed. by Rolf Tiedemann, trans. Howard Eiland and Kevin McLaughlin (Cambridge, MA and London: Belknap Press, 1999)
Origin of German Tragic Drama, trans. John Osborne (London: Verso, 1998)
Bennett, Andrew, *Keats, Narrative and Audience: The Posthumous Life of Writing* (Cambridge University Press, 1994)
Bermingham, Ann, *Landscape and Ideology: The English Rustic Tradition 1740–1860* (New York and London: Thames and Hudson, 1986)
Bewell, Alan J., 'The Political Implications of Keats's Classicist Aesthetics', *Studies in Romanticism*, 25 (1986), 220–9
Blunden, Edmund, *Charles Lamb and His Contemporaries* (Cambridge University Press, 1937)

The Examiner Examined (New York: Archon Books, 1967)
Bourdieu, Pierre, *The Field of Cultural Production* (Cambridge: Polity Press, 1993)
The Rules of Art: Genesis and Structure of the Literary Field (Cambridge: Polity Press, 1996)
Breslow, Julian W., 'The Narrator in Sketches by Boz', *ELH*, 44, 1 (Spring 1977), 127–49
Brewer, John, 'Sensibility and the Urban Panorama', *Huntington Library Quarterly*, 70, 2 (2007), 229–49
Briggs, Asa, *The Age of Improvement* (London: Longman, 1959)
'The Language of "Class" in Early Nineteenth-Century England', in *The Collected Essays of Asa Briggs* (Urbana: Illinois University Press, 1985)
Brown, David Blayney, *Benjamin Robert Haydon 1786–1846: Painter and Writer, Friend of Wordsworth and Keats* (Kendal: Wordsworth Trust, 1996)
Bruhn, Mark J., 'Cognition and Representation in Wordsworth's London', *Studies in Romanticism*, 45, 2 (2006), 157–80
Buck-Morss, Susan, 'The City as Dreamworld and Catastrophe', *October*, 73 (Summer 1995), 3–26
The Dialectics of Seeing: Walter Benjamin and the Arcades Project (Cambridge, MA and London: MIT Press: 1991)
'The Flâneur, the Sandwichman and the Whore: The Politics of Loitering', *New German Critique*, 39 (Fall 1986), 99–140
Burton, Sarah, *A Double Life: A Biography of Charles and Mary Lamb* (London: Viking, 2003)
Butler, Marilyn, 'Culture's Medium: The Role of the Review', in *The Cambridge Companion to Romanticism*, ed. by Stuart Curran (Cambridge University Press, 1993)
Romantics, Rebels and Reactionaries (Oxford University Press, 1981)
'Satire and the Images of the Self in the Romantic Period: The Long Tradition of Hazlitt's *Liber Amoris*', in *English Satire and the Satiric Tradition*, ed. by Claude Rawson (Oxford: Blackwell, 1984)
Cannadine, David, *Class in Britain* (Harmondsworth: Penguin, 1998)
Carretta, Vincent, *George III and the Satirists from Hogarth to Byron* (Athens: Georgia University Press, 1990)
de Certeau, Michel, *The Practice of Everyday Life* (Berkeley and Los Angeles: California University Press, 1984)
Chandler, James, *England in 1819* (Chicago University Press, 1998)
Chandler, James and Kevin Gilmartin, eds., *Romantic Metropolis: The Urban Scene of British Culture 1780–1840* (Cambridge University Press, 2005)
Chesterton, G. K., *Charles Dickens* (London: Methuen, 1956)
Chilcott, Tim, *A Publisher and His Circle: The Life and Work of John Taylor, Keats's Publisher* (London: Routledge & Kegan Paul, 1972)
Clark, Anna, *The Struggle for the Breeches: Gender and the Making of the British Working Class* (Berkeley: California University Press, 1995)

Clarke, Olney, *Benjamin Robert Haydon: Historical Painter* (Athens: Georgia University Press, 1952)

Collins, Peter, *Changing Ideals in Modern Architecture* (London: Faber & Faber, 1965)

Collison, Robert, *The Story of Street Literature* (London: Dent, 1973)

Connell, Philip and Nigel Leask, eds., *Romanticism and Popular Culture in Britain and Ireland* (Cambridge University Press, 2009)

Connor, Stephen, *Charles Dickens* (London: Addison Wesley, 1996)

Cook, Jon, *Hazlitt in Love* (London: Short Books, 2007)

Courtney, Winifred F., *Young Charles Lamb 1775–1802* (London: Macmillan, 1984)

Cox, Jeffrey N., *Poetry and Politics in the Cockney School: Keats, Shelley, Hunt and Their Circle* (Cambridge University Press, 1998)

Cronin, Richard, 'Keats and the Politics of Cockney Style', *Studies in English Literature*, 36, 4 (1996), 787–806

Paper Pellets, British Literary Culture after Waterloo (Oxford University Press, 2010)

'Peter Bell, Peterloo, and the Politics of Cockney Poetry', in *Essays and Studies 1992*, ed. by Kelvin Everest (Cambridge: D. S. Brewer, 1992)

The Politics of Romantic Poetry: In Search of the Pure Commonwealth (Basingstoke: Palgrave, 2000)

Romantic Victorians (Basingstoke: Palgrave, 2002)

Crook, J. Mordaunt, *The Greek Revival* (London: John Murray, 1995)

'John Britton and the Genesis of the Gothic Revival', in *Concerning Architecture*, ed. by John Summerson (Harmondsworth: Penguin, 1968), pp. 98–120

Cross, Nigel, *The Common Writer: Life in Nineteenth-Century Grub Street* (Cambridge University Press, 1985)

Crossick, Geoffrey, ed., *The Lower Middle Class in Britain 1870–1914* (London: Croom Helm, 1977)

'The Petite Bourgeoisie in Nineteenth-Century Britain: The Urban and Liberal Case', in *Shopkeepers and Master Artisans in Nineteenth-Century Europe*, ed. by Geoffrey Crossick and Heinz-Gerhard Haupt (London and New York: Methuen, 1984)

Curl, James Stevens, *Spas, Wells and Pleasure-Gardens of London* (London: Historical Publications, 2010)

Darley, Gillian, *John Soane: An Accidental Romantic* (New Haven, CT and London: Yale University Press, 1999)

Davidoff, Leonore and Catherine Hall, *Family Fortunes: Men and Women of the English Middle Class 1780–1850* (London: Routledge, 1987)

Davis, Terence, *John Nash: The Prince Regent's Architect* (London: David and Charles, 1973)

Donald, Diana, *The Age of Caricature: Satirical Prints in the Reign of George III* (New Haven, CT: Yale University Press, 1996)

Dunlop, C. R. B., 'Debtors and Creditors in Dickens's Fiction', *Dickens Studies Annual*, 19 (1990)

Dunn, William Newton, *The Man Who Was John Bull: Biography of Theodore Hook* (London: Allendale Publishing, 1996)

Dyos, H. J., 'The Objects of Street Improvement in Regency and Early Victorian London', in *Exploring the Urban Past*, ed. by David Cannadine and David Reeder (Cambridge University Press, 1982)

'The Speculative Builders and Developers of Victorian London', *Victorian Studies*, 11 (1968), 641–77

'Urban Transformation: A Note on the Objects of Street Improvement in Regency and Early Modern London', *International Review of Social History*, 2 (1967), 259–65

Dyos, H. J. and Michael Wolff, eds., *The Victorian City: Images and Realities* (London and Boston: Routledge & Kegan Paul, 1973)

Easson, Angus, 'Who is Boz? Dickens and His *Sketches*', *The Dickensian*, 81 (March 1985), 13–22

Ellis, Markman, 'Spectacles within Doors: Panoramas of London in the 1790s', *Romanticism: Special Issue on Re-imagining the City*, ed. Gregory Dart, 14, 2 (2008), 133–48

Erickson, Lee, *The Economy of Literary Form: English Literature and the Industrialization of Publishing 1800–1850* (Baltimore: Johns Hopkins University Press, 1996)

Feaver, William, *The Art of John Martin* (Oxford: Clarendon Press, 1975)

John Martin 1789–1854: Artist, Reformer, Engineer (Newcastle: Laing Art Gallery, 1970)

Feinberg, Susan, 'The Genesis of Sir John Soane's Museum Idea 1801–1810', *Journal of the Society of Architectural Historians*, 43 (1984), 225–37

Finn, Margot, *The Character of Credit: Personal Debt in English Culture 1740–1914* (Cambridge University Press, 2003)

Flynn, Nicholas, 'Seers and Seers Not: John Martin's "Belshazzar's Feast" and the Sublimation of Self', *Word and Image*, 16, 2 (April–June 2000), 163–76

Fox, Celine, ed., *London: World City 1800–1840* (New Haven, CT: Yale University Press, 1992)

Furjan, Helen, 'Sir John Soane's Spectacular Theatre', *AA files, The Journal of the Architectural Association School of Architecture*, 47 (2002), 12–22

Gatrell, Vic, *City of Laughter: Sex and Satire in Eighteenth-Century London* (London: Atlantic Books, 2006)

George, Dorothy M., *Hogarth to Cruikshank: Social Change in Graphic Satire* (London: Penguin, 1967)

George, Eric, *The Life and Death of Benjamin Robert Haydon* (Oxford University Press, 1948)

Gilmartin, Kevin, 'Popular Radicalism and the Public Sphere', *Studies in Romanticism*, 33 (1994), 549–57

Print Politics (Cambridge University Press, 1996)

Grayling, A. C., *The Quarrel of the Age: The Life and Times of William Hazlitt* (London: Weidenfeld & Nicolson, 2001)
Green, David R., *From Artisans to Paupers: Economic Change and Poverty in London 1790–1870* (London: Scolar Press, 1995)
Halevy, Elie, *England in 1815* (London: Ernest Benn, 1961)
Heffernan, James A. W., 'Wordsworth's London: The Imperial Monster', *Studies in Romanticism*, 37, 3 (1998), 421–43
Hibbert, Christopher and Ben Weinreb, *The London Encyclopaedia* (London: Macmillan, 1983)
Higgins, David, *Romantic Genius and the Literary Magazine* (London: Routledge, 2005)
Highmore, Ben, *Everyday Life and Cultural Theory: An Introduction* (London: Routledge, 2002)
Hill, Bridget, *English Domestics in the Eighteenth Century* (Oxford University Press, 1996)
Hill, Rosemary, 'Cockney Connoisseurship and Keats's Grecian Urn', *Things*, 6 (Summer 1997)
Hindley, Charles, *Curiosities of Street Literature* (London: Seven Dials Press, 1969)
The Life and Times of James Catnach (London: Seven Dials Press, 1970)
The True History of Tom and Jerry, or Life in London from the Start to the Finish (London, 1890)
Holden, Anthony, *The Wit in the Dungeon: The Life of Leigh Hunt* (London: Little, Brown, 2005)
Horn, Pamela, *The Rise and Fall of the Victorian Servant* (London: Macmillan, 1986)
Howe, P. P., *The Life of William Hazlitt* (Harmondsworth: Penguin, 1949)
Hyde, Ralph, *Panoramania* (London: Barbican Art Gallery, 1988)
Innes, Joanna, 'The King's Bench in the Later Eighteenth Century: Law, Authority and Order in a London Debtors' Prison', in *An Ungovernable People*, ed. by J. Brewer and J. Styles (London: Hutchinson, 1980)
Jackson, Peter, *George Scharf's London: Sketches and Watercolours of a Changing City 1820–1850* (London: John Murray, 1987)
James, Louis, 'Cruikshank and Early Victorian Caricature', *History Workshop Journal*, 6 (Autumn 1978), 107–20
Fiction for the Working Man 1830–50 (Oxford University Press, 1963)
Johnstone, Christopher, *John Martin* (London: Academy Editions, 1974)
Jones, Elizabeth, 'Keats in the Suburbs', *Keats–Shelley Journal*, 45 (1996), 23–43
'Suburb Sinners: Sex and Disease in the Cockney School', in *Leigh Hunt: Life, Poetics, Politics* (London: Routledge, 2003)
'Writing for the Market: Keats's Odes as Commodities', *Studies in Romanticism*, 34 (1995), 343–64
Jones, Stanley, *Hazlitt: A Life* (Oxford University Press, 1989)
King, Ross, 'Wordsworth, Panoramas, and the Prospect of London', *Studies in Romanticism*, 32, 1 (1993), 57–73

Klancher, Jon, *The Making of English Reading Audiences 1789–1832* (Madison: Wisconsin University Press, 1987)

Klingender, Francis, *Art and the Industrial Revolution* (London: Routledge, 1968)

Kucich, Greg, 'Cockney Chivalry: Hunt, Keats and the Aesthetics of Excess', in *Leigh Hunt: Life, Poetics, Politics*, ed. by Nicholas Roe (London: Routledge, 2003)

Laqueur, Thomas, 'The Queen Caroline Affair: Politics as Art in the Reign of George IV', *Journal of Modern History*, 54 (1982), 417–66

Lefebvre, Henri, *Critique of Everyday Life*, 3 vols. (London: Verso, 2008)

Writings on Cities, ed. by Eleonore Kofman and Elizabeth Lebas (Oxford: Blackwell, 1996)

Lukacher, Brian, *Joseph Gandy: An Architectural Visionary in Georgian England* (London: Thames and Hudson, 2006)

'Joseph Gandy and the Mythography of Architecture', *Journal of the Society of Architectural Historians*, 53 (1994), 280–99

Levinson, Marjorie, *Keats's Life of Allegory* (Oxford University Press, 1988)

Lodge, Sara, *Thomas Hood and Nineteenth Century Poetry* (Manchester University Press, 2007)

Lucas, E. V., *The Life of Charles Lamb*, 2 vols. (New York: Puttnam, 1905)

McCalman, Iain, *Radical Underworld: Prophets, Revolutionaries and Pornographers in London 1795–1840* (Cambridge University Press, 1988)

Matthews, William, *Cockney Past and Present: A Short History of the Dialect of London* (London: George Routledge and Sons, 1938)

Mayer, Arno J., 'The Lower Middle Class as Historical Problem', *Journal of Modern History*, 47, 3 (1975), 409–36

Meisel, Martin, *Images of Romanticism: Verbal and Visual Affinities* (New Haven, CT: Yale University Press, 1978)

Miller, J. Hillis, 'The Fiction of Realism: *Sketches by Boz, Oliver Twist* and Cruikshank's Illustrations', in *Charles Dickens and George Cruikshank*, ed. by Ada B. Nisbet (Los Angeles, 1971)

Moers, Ellen, *The Dandy: Brummell to Beerbohm* (London: Viking, 1969)

Monckton, Norah, 'The Architectural Backgrounds in the Pictures of John Martin', *Architectural Review*, 104, 620 (1948)

Monsman, Gerald, *Charles Lamb as the London Magazine's 'Elia'* (Lewiston, NY and Lampeter: Mellen Press, 2003)

Moretti, Franco, *Atlas of the European Novel 1800–1900* (London and New York: Verso, 1998)

Morris, Pam, *Dickens's Class Consciousness: A Marginal View* (Basingstoke: Macmillan, 1991)

Motion, Andrew, *John Keats* (London: Faber & Faber, 1998)

Mumford, Lewis, *The City in History: Its Origins, Its Transformations, and Its Prospects* (New York: Harcourt Brace, 1961)

The Culture of Cities (London: Routledge, 1938)

Nadel, I. B. and F. S. Schwarzbach, eds., *Victorian Artists and the City* (London and New York: Pergamon Press, 1980)

Natarajan, Uttara, *Hazlitt and the Reach of Sense* (Oxford University Press, 1998)

Neale, R. S., 'Class and Class Consciousness in Early Nineteenth Century England: Three Classes or Five', in *History and Class: Essential Readings in Theory and Interpretation* (Oxford: Basil Blackwell, 1983)

Newlyn, Lucy, '"In City Pent": Echo and Allusion in Wordsworth, Coleridge and Lamb, 1797–1801', *The Review of English Studies*, 32, 128 (November 1981), 408–28

'Lamb, Lloyd, London: A Perspective on Book Seven of "The Prelude"', *Charles Lamb Bulletin*, 47–8 (1984), 169–87

Nord, Deborah Epstein, 'The City as Theater: From Georgian to Early Victorian London', *Victorian Studies*, 31, 2 (Winter 1988), 159–88

Walking the Victorian Streets: Women, Representation and the City (Ithaca, NY and London: Cornell University Press, 1995)

O'Keefe, Paul, *A Genius for Failure: The Life of Benjamin Robert Haydon* (London: Bodley Head, 2009)

O'Leary, Patrick, *Regency Editor: The Life of John Scott* (Aberdeen University Press, 1983)

Oliphant, Margaret, *Annals of a Publishing House: William Blackwood and His Sons*, 3 vols. (Edinburgh: William Blackwood, 1899)

Olsen, Donald, *The Growth of Victorian London* (London: Batsford, 1976)

Paley, Morton D., *The Apocalyptic Sublime* (New Haven, CT: Yale University Press, 1986)

Palmeri, Frank, 'Cruikshank, Thackeray and the Victorian Eclipse of Satire', *Studies in English Literature 1500–1900*, 44, 4 (2004), 754–77

Parissien, Stephen, *Regency Style* (London: Phaidon, 1992)

Parker, Mark, 'Ideology and Editing: The Political Context of the Elia Essays', *Studies in Romanticism*, 30 (1991), 473–94

Literary Magazines and British Romanticism (Cambridge University Press, 2000)

Paulin, Tom, *The Day Star of Liberty: William Hazlitt's Radical Style* (London: Faber & Faber, 1998)

Payne, David, 'The Cockney and the Prostitute: Dickens and the Literary Market 1836–7', *Journal of Victorian Culture*, 4, 2 (Autumn 1999), 171–96

Pendered, Mary L., *John Martin, Painter, His Life and Times* (London: Hurst and Blackett, 1923)

Perkin, H. J., 'Middle-Class Education and Employment in the Nineteenth Century', *Economic History Review*, 14, 124 (1961)

Ready, Robert, 'The Logic of Passion: Hazlitt's *Liber Amoris*', *Studies in Romanticism*, 14 (1975), 41–57

Reid, J. C., *Bucks and Bruisers: Pierce Egan and Regency England* (London: Routledge, 1971)

Thomas Hood (London: Routledge & Kegan Paul, 1963)

Rendell, Jane, *The Pursuit of Pleasure: Gender, Space and Architecture in Regency London* (London and New Brunswick NJ: Rutgers University Press, 2002)

Ricks, Christopher, *Keats and Embarrassment* (Oxford University Press, 1974)

Riehl, Joseph E., *That Dangerous Figure: Charles Lamb and the Critics* (Columbia, SC: Camden House, 1998)

Robbins, Bruce, *The Servant's Hand: English Fiction from Below* (New York: Columbia, 1986)

Roberts, M. J. D., *Making English Morals: Voluntary Association and Moral Reform in England 1767–1886* (Cambridge University Press, 2004)

'Reshaping the Gift Relationship: The London Mendicity Society and the Suppression of Begging in England 1818–1869', *International Review of Social History*, 36 (1991), 201–31

Robinson, Alan, *Imagining London 1770–1900* (Basingstoke: Macmillan, 2004)

Roe, Nicholas, *Fiery Heart: The First Life of Leigh Hunt* (London: Pimlico, 2005)

John Keats and the Culture of Dissent (Oxford University Press, 1997)

Keats and History (Cambridge University Press, 1995)

'Keats's Lisping Sedition', *Essays in Criticism*, 42, 1 (January 1992), 36–55

Roe, Nicholas, ed., *Leigh Hunt: Life, Poetics, Politics* (London: Routledge, 2003)

Rose, Jonathan, *The Intellectual Life of the British Working Classes* (New Haven, CT and London: Yale University Press, 2001)

Sales, Roger, 'Pierce Egan and the Representation of London', in *Reviewing Romanticism*, ed. by Philip W. Martin and Robin Jarvis (Basingstoke: Macmillan, 1992)

Schoenfeld, Mark, 'Voices Together: Lamb, Hazlitt and the *London*', *Studies in Romanticism*, 29 (1990), 257–72

Schwarz, L. D., *London in the Age of Industrialisation* (Cambridge University Press, 1992)

'Social Class and Social Geography: The Middle Classes in London at the End of the Eighteenth Century', *Social History*, 7 (1982), 167–85

Scott, W. S., *Bygone Pleasures of London* (London: Marsland, 1948)

Seed, David, 'The Shifting Subjects of Dickens's London Sketches', *Yearbook of English Studies*, 34, 'Nineteenth-Century Travel Writing' (2004), 155–70

Shattock, Joanne, ed., *The Victorian Periodical Press: Samplings and Soundings* (Leicester University Press, 1982)

Sheppard, Francis, *London 1808–1870: The Infernal Wen* (London: Secker and Warburg, 1971)

Sheringham, Michael, *Everyday Life: Theories and Practices from Surrealism to the Present* (Oxford University Press, 2006)

Simmel, Georg, 'The Metropolis and Mental Life', in *On Individuality and Social Forms*, ed. by Donald N. Levine (Chicago University Press, 1971)

Simmel on Culture, ed. by David Frisby and Mike Featherstone (London: Sage Publications, 1997)

Stanton, Phoebe, 'The Sources of Pugin's Contrasts', in *Concerning Architecture*, ed. by John Summerson (London: Penguin, 1968), pp. 120–39

Stedman Jones, Gareth, 'The "Cockney" and the Nation 1780–1988', in *Metropolis London: Histories and Representations since 1800*, ed. by David Feldman and Gareth Stedman Jones (London and New York: Routledge, 1989)

The Languages of Class (Cambridge University Press, 1984)

Outcast London: A Study of the Relationship Between the Classes in Victorian Society (Oxford University Press, 1971)

Steedman, Carolyn, 'Servants and Their Relationship to the Unconscious', *Journal of British Studies*, 42, 3 (July 2003), 316–50

Stewart, David, 'T. G. Wainewright's Art Criticism and Metropolitan Magazine Style', *Romantic Textualities: Literature and Print Culture, 1780–1840*, 17 (Summer 2007). Online: www.cf.ac.uk/encap/romtext/issues/rt17.pdf

Stone, Lawrence, *The Family, Sex and Marriage in England 1500–1800* (London: Weidenfeld & Nicholson, 1977)

Stones, Graham and John Strachan, eds., *Parodies of the Romantic Age*, 5 vols. (London: Pickering & Chatto, 1999)

Summerson, John *Georgian London* (London: Pimlico, 1988)

The Life and Work of John Nash, Architect (London: HarperCollins, 1980)

'The Vision of J. M. Gandy', in *Heavenly Mansions, and Other Essays on Architecture* (London: Cresset Press, 1949)

Terdiman, Richard, *Present Past: Modernity and the Memory Crisis* (Ithaca, NY: Cornell University Press, 1993)

Thompson, E. P., *The Making of the English Working Class* (London: Gollancz, 1963)

Thompson, F. M. L., *Hampstead: Building a Borough* (London: Routledge & Kegan Paul, 1974)

The Rise of Respectable Society: A Social History of Victorian Britain 1830–1900 (London: Fontana, 1988)

The Rise of Suburbia (Leicester University Press, 1982)

Trott, Nicola, '"The Old Margate Hoy" and Other Depths of Elian Credulity', *Charles Lamb Bulletin*, 82 (1993)

Trotter, David, 'The Invention of Agoraphobia', *Victorian Literature and Culture*, 32 (2004), 463–74

Paranoid Modernism (Oxford University Press, 2001)

Wahrman, Dror, *Imagining the Middle Class: The Political Representation of Class in Britain c.1780–1840* (Cambridge University Press, 1995)

Watkin, David, 'Freemasonry and Sir John Soane', *Journal of the Society of Architectural Historians*, 54, 4 (1995), 402–17

Weber, Max, *Essays in Sociology*, ed. by H. H. Gerth and C. Wright Mills (London: Routledge, 1993)

Whale, John, 'Hazlitt on Burke', *Studies in Romanticism*, 25 (1986), 465–81

Imagination under Pressure 1789–1832: Aesthetics, Politics and Utility (Cambridge University Press, 2005)

Wheatley, Kim, 'The *Blackwood's* Attacks on Leigh Hunt', *Nineteenth-Century Literature*, 47 (1992), 1–31

ed., *Special Issue on Romantic Periodicals and Print Culture*, *Prose Studies*, 25, 1 (April 2002)

White, Jerry, *London in the Nineteenth Century* (London: Vintage, 2008)

Wiener, Jonathan M., 'Note: Marxism and the Lower Middle Class: A Response to Arno Mayer', *Journal of Modern History*, 48 (1976), 666–71

Wild, Jonathan, *The Rise of the Office Clerk in Literary Culture, 1880–1939* (Basingstoke: Palgrave Macmillan, 2006)

Williams, Raymond, *The Country and the City* (London: Hogarth Press, 1985)

Wirth, Louis, 'Urbanism as a Way of Life', *American Journal of Sociology*, 44 (1938), 1–24

Wood, Christopher, *Victorian Panorama: Paintings of Victorian Life* (London: Faber & Faber, 1976)

Wroth, Warwick, *The London Pleasure Gardens of the Eighteenth Century* (London: Macmillan, 1896)

Wu, Duncan, *William Hazlitt: The First Modern Man* (Oxford University Press, 2008)

Wunder, Jennifer, *Keats, Hermeticism and the Secret Societies* (London and Burlington: Ashgate, 2008)

Young, Arlene, *Culture, Class and Gender in the Victorian Novel* (Basingstoke: Macmillan, 1999)

'Virtue Domesticated: Dickens and the Lower Middle Class', *Victorian Studies*, 39, 4 (Summer 1996), 483–511

Index

CAMBRIDGE STUDIES IN ROMANTICISM

General Editor
JAMES CHANDLER, University of Chicago

1. Romantic Correspondence: Women, Politics and the Fiction of Letters
   MARY A. FAVRET
2. British Romantic Writers and the East: Anxieties of Empire
   NIGEL LEASK
3. Poetry as an Occupation and an Art in Britain, 1760–1830
   PETER MURPHY
4. Edmund Burke's Aesthetic Ideology: Language, Gender and Political Economy in Revolution
   TOM FURNISS
5. In the Theatre of Romanticism: Coleridge, Nationalism, Women
   JULIE A. CARLSON
6. Keats, Narrative and Audience
   ANDREW BENNETT
7. Romance and Revolution: Shelley and the Politics of a Genre
   DAVID DUFF
8. Literature, Education, and Romanticism: Reading as Social Practice, 1780–1832
   ALAN RICHARDSON
9. Women Writing about Money: Women's Fiction in England, 1790–1820
   EDWARD COPELAND
10. Shelley and the Revolution in Taste: The Body and the Natural World
    TIMOTHY MORTON
11. William Cobbett: The Politics of Style
    LEONORA NATTRASS
12. The Rise of Supernatural Fiction, 1762–1800
    E. J. CLERY
13. Women Travel Writers and the Language of Aesthetics, 1716–1818
    ELIZABETH A. BOHLS
14. Napoleon and English Romanticism
    SIMON BAINBRIDGE
15. Romantic Vagrancy: Wordsworth and the Simulation of Freedom
    CELESTE LANGAN

16. Wordsworth and the Geologists
JOHN WYATT

17. Wordsworth's Pope: A Study in Literary Historiography
ROBERT J. GRIFFIN

18. The Politics of Sensibility: Race, Gender and Commerce in the Sentimental Novel
MARKMAN ELLIS

19. Reading Daughters' Fictions, 1709–1834: Novels and Society from Manley to Edgeworth
CAROLINE GONDA

20. Romantic Identities: Varieties of Subjectivity, 1774–1830
ANDREA K. HENDERSON

21. Print Politics: The Press and Radical Opposition in Early Nineteenth-Century England
KEVIN GILMARTIN

22. Reinventing Allegory
THERESA M. KELLEY

23. British Satire and the Politics of Style, 1789–1832
GARY DYER

24. The Romantic Reformation: Religious Politics in English Literature, 1789–1824
ROBERT M. RYAN

25. De Quincey's Romanticism: Canonical Minority and the Forms of Transmission
MARGARET RUSSETT

26. Coleridge on Dreaming: Romanticism, Dreams and the Medical Imagination
JENNIFER FORD

27. Romantic Imperialism: Universal Empire and the Culture of Modernity
SAREE MAKDISI

28. Ideology and Utopia in the Poetry of William Blake
NICHOLAS M. WILLIAMS

29. Sexual Politics and the Romantic Author
SONIA HOFKOSH

30. Lyric and Labour in the Romantic Tradition
ANNE JANOWITZ

31. Poetry and Politics in the Cockney School: Keats, Shelley, Hunt and their Circle
JEFFREY N. COX

32. Rousseau, Robespierre and English Romanticism
GREGORY DART

33. Contesting the Gothic: Fiction, Genre and Cultural Conflict, 1764–1832
JAMES WATT

34. Romanticism, Aesthetics, and Nationalism
DAVID ARAM KAISER

35. Romantic Poets and the Culture of Posterity
ANDREW BENNETT

36. The Crisis of Literature in the 1790s: Print Culture and the Public Sphere
PAUL KEEN

37. Romantic Atheism: Poetry and Freethought, 1780–1830
MARTIN PRIESTMAN

38. Romanticism and Slave Narratives: Transatlantic Testimonies
HELEN THOMAS

39. Imagination under Pressure, 1789–1832: Aesthetics, Politics, and Utility
JOHN WHALE

40. Romanticism and the Gothic: Genre, Reception, and Canon Formation, 1790–1820
MICHAEL GAMER

41. Romanticism and the Human Sciences: Poetry, Population, and the Discourse of the Species
MAUREEN N. MCLANE

42. The Poetics of Spice: Romantic Consumerism and the Exotic
TIMOTHY MORTON

43. British Fiction and the Production of Social Order, 1740–1830
MIRANDA J. BURGESS

44. Women Writers and the English Nation in the 1790s
ANGELA KEANE

45. Literary Magazines and British Romanticism
MARK PARKER

46. Women, Nationalism and the Romantic Stage: Theatre and Politics in Britain, 1780–1800
BETSY BOLTON

47. British Romanticism and the Science of the Mind
ALAN RICHARDSON

48. The Anti-Jacobin Novel: British Conservatism and the French Revolution
M. O. GRENBY

49. Romantic Austen: Sexual Politics and the Literary Canon
CLARA TUITE

50. Byron and Romanticism
JEROME MCGANN
JAMES SODERHOLM

51. The Romantic National Tale and the Question of Ireland
INA FERRIS

52. Byron, Poetics and History
JANE STABLER

53. Religion, Toleration, and British Writing, 1790–1830
MARK CANUEL

54. Fatal Women of Romanticism
ADRIANA CRACIUN

55. Knowledge and Indifference in English Romantic Prose
TIM MILNES

56. Mary Wollstonecraft and the Feminist Imagination
BARBARA TAYLOR

57. Romanticism, Maternity and the Body Politic
JULIE KIPP

58. Romanticism and Animal Rights
DAVID PERKINS

59. Georgic Modernity and British Romanticism: Poetry and the Mediation of History
KEVIS GOODMAN

60. Literature, Science and Exploration in the Romantic Era: Bodies of Knowledge
TIMOTHY FULFORD
DEBBIE LEE
PETER J. KITSON

61. Romantic Colonization and British Anti-Slavery
DEIRDRE COLEMAN

62. Anger, Revolution, and Romanticism
ANDREW M. STAUFFER

63. Shelley and the Revolutionary Sublime
CIAN DUFFY

64. Fictions and Fakes: Forging Romantic Authenticity, 1760–1845
MARGARET RUSSETT

65. Early Romanticism and Religious Dissent
DANIEL E. WHITE

66. The Invention of Evening: Perception and Time in Romantic Poetry
CHRISTOPHER R. MILLER

67. Wordsworth's Philosophic Song
SIMON JARVIS

68. Romanticism and the Rise of the Mass Public
ANDREW FRANTA

69. Writing against Revolution: Literary Conservatism in Britain, 1790–1832
KEVIN GILMARTIN

70. Women, Sociability and Theatre in Georgian London
GILLIAN RUSSELL

71. The Lake Poets and Professional Identity
BRIAN GOLDBERG

72. Wordsworth Writing
ANDREW BENNETT

73. Science and Sensation in Romantic Poetry
NOEL JACKSON

74. Advertising and Satirical Culture in the Romantic Period
JOHN STRACHAN

75. Romanticism and the Painful Pleasures of Modern Life
ANDREA K. HENDERSON

76. Balladeering, Minstrelsy, and the Making of British Romantic Poetry
MAUREEN N. MCLANE

77. Romanticism and Improvisation, 1750–1850
ANGELA ESTERHAMMER

78. Scotland and the Fictions of Geography: North Britain, 1760–1830
PENNY FIELDING

79. Wordsworth, Commodification and Social Concern: The Poetics of Modernity
DAVID SIMPSON

80. Sentimental Masculinity and the Rise of History, 1790–1890
MIKE GOODE

81. Fracture and Fragmentation in British Romanticism
ALEXANDER REGIER

82. Romanticism and Music Culture in Britain, 1770–1840: Virtue and Virtuosity
GILLEN D'ARCY WOOD

83. The Truth about Romanticism: Pragmatism and Idealism in Keats, Shelley, Coleridge
TIM MILNES

84. Blake's Gifts: Poetry and the Politics of Exchange
SARAH HAGGARTY

85. Real Money and Romanticism
MATTHEW ROWLINSON

86. Sentimental Literature and Anglo-Scottish Identity, 1745–1820
JULIET SHIELDS

87. Romantic Tragedies: The Dark Employments of Wordsworth, Coleridge, and Shelley
REEVE PARKER

88. Blake, Sexuality and Bourgeois Politeness
SUSAN MATTHEWS

89. Idleness, Contemplation and the Aesthetic
RICHARD ADELMAN

90. Shelley's Visual Imagination
NANCY MOORE GOSLEE

91. A Cultural History of the Irish Novel, 1790–1829
CLARE CONNOLLY

92. Literature, Commerce, and the Spectacle of Modernity, 1750–1800
PAUL KEEN

93. Romanticism and Childhood: The Infantilization of British Literary Culture
ANN WIERDA ROWLAND

94. Metropolitan Art and Literature, 1810–1840: Cockney Adventures
GREGORY DART

Lightning Source UK Ltd.
Milton Keynes UK
UKHW022144230922
409344UK00006B/404

9 781107 507746